THE CAMBRIDGE COMPANION TO WORLD-GOTHIC LITERATURE

Monsters have always swarmed around the frontiers of colonialism and capitalism, from Europe's invasion and occupation of the Americas to the planetary emergency of the present day. In this volume, we discover how the early British gothic – far from a progenitor – is in fact a belated cultural response to capitalist modernity, one anticipated by myriad spectres haunting the plantations of the 'New World'. Gothic did not begin in Britain and then become global over time. Rather, as the volume reveals, gothic has always been world-gothic: a way of dealing with the alienation and anxiety that erupt with capitalist modernisation, when- and wherever this is taking place. Essays in the volume chart the new links and comparisons enabled by this insight, renovating established gothic concepts and outlining groundbreaking new theoretical infrastructure. Together, the chapters provincialise the 'Western' gothic tradition, in order to open up new possibilities for world-gothic reading.

REBECCA DUNCAN is Associate Professor of Literature at Linnaeus University and Research Associate in English at the University of the Witwatersrand. Her recent publications include the edited volume *The Edinburgh Companion to Globalgothic* (2023), which won both the Justin D. Edwards prize and a Choice Outstanding Academic Title Award in 2024.

REBEKAH CUMPSTY is Associate Professor of Anglophone World Literature at Weber State University. She is the author of *Postsecular Poetics: Negotiating the Sacred and Secular in Contemporary African Fiction* (2022). Her recent publications have appeared in *Gothic Studies, The Edinburgh Companion to Globalgothic* (2023), and *Contemporary Literature and the Body* (2023).

A complete list of books in the series is at the back of the book.

THE CAMBRIDGE COMPANION TO WORLD-GOTHIC LITERATURE

EDITED BY

REBECCA DUNCAN

Linnaeus University

REBEKAH CUMPSTY

Weber State University

Shaftesbury Road, Cambridge CB2 8EA, United Kingdom

One Liberty Plaza, 20th Floor, New York, NY 10006, USA

477 Williamstown Road, Port Melbourne, VIC 3207, Australia

314–321, 3rd Floor, Plot 3, Splendor Forum, Jasola District Centre, New Delhi – 110025, India

103 Penang Road, #05–06/07, Visioncrest Commercial, Singapore 238467

Cambridge University Press is part of Cambridge University Press & Assessment, a department of the University of Cambridge.

We share the University's mission to contribute to society through the pursuit of education, learning and research at the highest international levels of excellence.

www.cambridge.org
Information on this title: www.cambridge.org/9781009382588

DOI: 10.1017/9781009382595

© Cambridge University Press & Assessment 2026

This publication is in copyright. Subject to statutory exception and to the provisions of relevant collective licensing agreements, no reproduction of any part may take place without the written permission of Cambridge University Press & Assessment.

When citing this work, please include a reference to the DOI 10.1017/9781009382595

First published 2026

Cover image: Engraved illustration of sugarcane. Photo: mikroman6 / Moment / Getty Images

A catalogue record for this publication is available from the British Library

A Cataloging-in-Publication data record for this book is available from the Library of Congress

ISBN 978-1-009-38258-8 Hardback
ISBN 978-1-009-38256-4 Paperback

Cambridge University Press & Assessment has no responsibility for the persistence or accuracy of URLs for external or third-party internet websites referred to in this publication and does not guarantee that any content on such websites is, or will remain, accurate or appropriate.

For EU product safety concerns, contact us at Calle de José Abascal, 56, 1º, 28003 Madrid, Spain, or email eugpsr@cambridge.org

Contents

List of Contributors	*page* vii
Acknowledgements	xi
Introduction: Five Hundred Years of World-Gothic *Rebecca Duncan and Rebekah Cumpsty*	1

PART I GOTHIC IN THE WORLD: (RE)CONCEPTUALISATIONS

1	The Undead's Capitalist World-System *Stephen Shapiro*	25
2	Whiteness and the 'Western' Gothic Tradition *Rebecca Duncan and Johan Höglund*	44
3	Gothic and Labour: Metabolic, Reproductive, International *Esthie Hugo*	61

PART II WORLD-MONSTERS: GLOBAL TRANSMISSIONS AND GENEALOGIES

4	Pre-colonial Gothic and the Windigo *Krista Collier-Jarvis*	81
5	Hauntings: African-Based Spirituality in World-Gothic Literature *James Mellis*	99
6	Vampiric Exhaustion and Extractive Form: The Mozambican Miner *Thomas Waller*	117

7 Subversive Sorcery and Reparative Witchcraft: *Huesera*'s
   Challenges to Coloniality   133
   Valeria Villegas Lindvall

PART III WORLDING GOTHIC THEORY

8 World-Gothic and the Sublime   151
   Jana M. Giles

9 A Planetary Grotesque   169
   Rune Graulund

10 Uncanny Animism: Reframing the World-Gothic
   with Amos Tutuola   186
   Ryan Topper

11 Abject/Abhuman/Human: Provincialising
   World-Gothic Monstrosity   205
   Rebekah Cumpsty

PART IV WORLD-GOTHIC: TRANSREGIONAL COMPARISONS

12 Gothic Inheritances in Oceania: Problems of Origins
   and Ownership   225
   Caitlin Vandertop

13 Tough Oil Gothic: Contemporary Petrofiction across
   the North–South Divide   242
   Karl Emil Rosenbæk Reetz

14 Scheherazade and Bluebeard: The World-Gothic
   and Bloody Chambers in Arab Women's Writing   259
   Roxanne Douglas

   Coda: Catachresis and the Politics of Gothic Naming   276
   Rebekah Cumpsty and Rebecca Duncan

Further Reading   284
Index   293

Contributors

KRISTA COLLIER-JARVIS, PhD, is a member of the Mi'kmaw First Nation and an assistant professor in the Department of English at Mount Saint Vincent University. Her research centres Indigenous voices and applies Indigenous ways of knowing and being to horror and the gothic. She has published on uncanny play in *Pet Sematary*, haunting back in *Blood Quantum*, and has forthcoming articles on the rise of the endemic zombie as well as climate entanglements in *The Last of Us*.

REBEKAH CUMPSTY is Associate Professor of Anglophone World Literature at Weber State University. She is the author of *Postsecular Poetics: Negotiating the Sacred and Secular in Contemporary African Fiction* (Routledge, 2022). Her research interests include religious studies, the postsecular, postcolonial, and world-literatures, with a focus on anglophone African fiction. Her recent publications have appeared in *Gothic Studies*, the *Edinburgh Companion to Globalgothic* (2023), and *Contemporary Literature and the Body* (2023).

ROXANNE DOUGLAS is the co-founder and leader of the Women in World-Literature project. She specialises in bringing together feminist theory and world-literature with genre. Her first book, *Feminist Gothic, Critical Irrealism and Arab Women's World-Literature: 'Living with Ghosts'* is out now with Palgrave Macmillan's 'New Comparisons in World Literature' series.

REBECCA DUNCAN is Associate Professor and Researcher in Literature at Linnaeus University (LNU) and Research Associate in the Department of English at the University of the Witwatersrand. At LNU, she sits on the steering committee of the Centre for Concurrences in Colonial and Postcolonial Studies, and is co-director of the research cluster for Ecology, Culture, and Coloniality. She has research interests in world-literature, political ecology, and speculative and gothic forms. Her recent substantial publications include *Decolonising Gothic* (2022) – a special issue of *Gothic Studies* – and *The Edinburgh Companion to Globalgothic* (2023), which won both the Justin D. Edwards Prize and a Choice Outstanding Academic Title Award in 2024. Currently, she is Principal Investigator of *Resources and Energy in South African Literature*, a three-year research project generously funded by The Swedish Research Council (2024–7).

JANA M. GILES is Professor of English at the University of Louisiana at Monroe. Her areas of research include British modernism, postcolonialism, and the aesthetics of the sublime, and her work has appeared in such journals as the *Cambridge Journal of Postcolonial Literary Inquiry*, *Conradiana*, *The Conradian*, *FICTIONS: Studi Sulla Narratività*, *Samuel Beckett Today/Aujourd'hui*, and *Ma'Comère*, as well as anthologised collections including *Reading Coetzee's Women*, *Joseph Conrad and Postcritique: Politics of Hope, Politics of Fear*, *The Sublime Today*, and *New Approaches to Dubliners*. Her essay on the postcolonial sublime is appearing in the forthcoming *Oxford Handbook of the Sublime*. She serves as the managing editor of *Conradiana* and is currently vice president of the Joseph Conrad Society of America.

RUNE GRAULUND is Associate Professor in American Literature at the Centre for American Studies at University of Southern Denmark. He has published widely in gothic studies, including the books *Grotesque* (New Critical Idiom, Routledge, 2013), co-authored with Justin D. Edwards, and *Dark Scenes from Damaged Earth: The Gothic Anthropocene* (University of Minnesota Press, 2022), co-edited with Justin D. Edwards and Johan Höglund. He is currently working on a second edition of *Grotesque*, which will include new chapters on planetary grotesque and political grotesque.

JOHAN HÖGLUND is Professor of English at Linnaeus University, a founding member of the Linnaeus University Centre for Concurrences in Colonial and Postcolonial Studies, and co-director of the research cluster Ecology, Culture, and Coloniality at Linnaeus University, Sweden. He has published extensively on the relationship between popular culture, colonialism, and extractive capitalism with particular attention to gothic and climate fiction. He is the author of *The American Climate Emergency Narrative* (Palgrave Macmillan, 2024) and *The American Imperial Gothic: Popular Culture, Empire, Violence*

(Routledge, 2016), and co-editor of *Dark Scenes from Damaged Earth: Gothic and the Anthropocene* (University of Minnesota Press, 2022), *Nordic Gothic* (Manchester University Press, 2020), *B-Movie Gothic: International Perspectives* (Edinburgh University Press, 2018), *Animal Horror Cinema* (Palgrave Macmillan, 2015), and *Transnational and Postcolonial Vampires* (Palgrave Macmillan, 2012).

ESTHIE HUGO is Lecturer in English literature at the University of the Witwatersrand in Johannesburg. Esthie has published on contemporary gothic fiction, Caribbean women's poetry, food, and feminism, as well as atmospheric terror and racial violence in postcolonial African writing. Esthie is currently working on her first academic monograph, provisionally entitled *Intimate Invasions: Literature, Ecology and the New Feminist Gothic*.

JAMES MELLIS is Associate Professor of English at Guttman Community College whose research is primarily concerned with African American literature and culture. He holds an MPhil in Anglo-Irish literature from Trinity College, Dublin, and a PhD from Tulane University. He is the editor of *Voodoo, Hoodoo and Conjure in African American Literature: Essays* (McFarland, 2019), has published on African-based diasporic spiritual practices in the works of Jesmyn Ward and Colson Whitehead, and John Coltrane as a muse for Black Arts Movement poets, and has essays on Sterling Brown and Colson Whitehead forthcoming. He is currently editing *Zora Neale Hurston in Context* for Cambridge University Press and is working on a literary history of African-based spiritual and religious practices in African American and Caribbean literature.

KARL EMIL ROSENBÆCK REETZ has a PhD in comparative literature from the University of Southern Denmark. He works on contemporary fiction and combines world-literature/world-ecology studies with petroculture studies and the broader aspects of energy humanities to answer questions about literary fiction's registration of the present oil impasse and the global albeit uneven planetary emergency this has brought on. Presently, he works as a postdoc at the University of Copenhagen on a project titled 'Reading the Nordic Seas: Oceanic Literacy in a Wetter World' generously funded by the Carlsberg Foundation (CF25-0498).

STEPHEN SHAPIRO teaches in the Department of English and Comparative Literary Studies at the University of Warwick. Recent publications include *Tracking Capital: World-Systems, World-Ecology, World-Culture* (with Sharae Deckard and Michael Niblett, SUNY Press, 2024) and *Pentecostal Modernism: Lovecraft, Los Angeles, and World-Systems Culture* (with Philip Barnard, Bloomsbury, 2017).

RYAN TOPPER is the author of *Animist Poetics: Ancestral Trauma and Regeneration in African Literature* (SUNY Press, 2025). He is Associate Professor of English at Western Oregon University and Research Fellow in the English Department at Stellenbosch University.

CAITLIN VANDERTOP is Associate Professor in the Department of English and Comparative Literary Studies at the University of Warwick. She previously taught at the University of the South Pacific's Laucala campus in Fiji. She is the author of *Modernism in the Metrocolony: Urban Cultures of Empire in Twentieth Century Literature* (Cambridge University Press, 2021) and co-editor (with Sudesh Mishra) of *Commodities and Literature* (Cambridge University Press, in press). She is currently working on a project about island literatures and resource regimes in the Pacific World.

VALERIA VILLEGAS LINDVALL, PhD, is an interdisciplinary film scholar and specialist in Latin American horror film with a feminist and decolonial focus. She is Reviews Editor for *MAI: Feminism and Visual Culture* and member of the advisory board of MAI Imprint at Punctum Books. She has collaborated in several publications, most prominently as former co-editor, writer, and translator at *Rolling Stone Mexico*. Her writing has been featured in publications like the award-winning *Women Make Horror* (2020), *The Body Onscreen in the Digital Age* (2021), *Folk Horror: New Global Pathways* (2023), and *The Oxford Handbook of Black Horror Film* (2024), among others. She is a video essayist and active collaborator for physical media with distributors such as Arrow, Vinegar Syndrome, and Powerhouse.

THOMAS WALLER, PhD, is a postdoctoral affiliate at University College Dublin. He is the author of *Genres of Transition: Literature and Economy in Portuguese-Speaking Southern Africa* (Liverpool University Press, 2024) and the editor of *Roberto Schwarz and World Literature* (Palgrave, 2024). He has published widely in journals such as *Modern Fiction Studies*, *Textual Practice*, *Qui Parle*, and *Rethinking Marxism*.

Acknowledgements

Rebecca Duncan's contributions to this volume were made possible by a Riksbankens Jubileumsfond project grant, which she acknowledges with much gratitude here. I – Rebecca – would also like to thank the members of the Research Cluster for Ecology, Culture and Coloniality (ECCo) at the Linnaeus University Centre for Concurrences in Colonial and Postcolonial Studies, for their invaluable feedback on draft versions of material featured here. Elliott Berggren, Mike Classon Frangos, Emily Hanscam, Lucia Hodgson, Johan Höglund, Lobke Minter, Beatriz Carlsson Pecharroman, Felicia Stenberg, and Martin van der Linden – I'm extremely grateful to be part of such a rigorous and collegial research community.

Thanks to Maisha Wester, and to Esthie Hugo and Simon van Schalkwyk, for their kind invitations to talk about world-gothic at the University of Sheffield and the University of the Witwatersrand respectively. Also much appreciated are the comments and reflections offered by the Gothic Reading Group at the University of Stellenbosch – my gratitude to Lobke Minter and Jeanne Ellis for organising the workshop that allowed me to discuss this project with an interested and engaging group of graduate students and early career scholars.

> Thanks to Rebekah: the best friend, colleague, and co-editor anyone could ask for.
> And thanks to Rune, for everything.

***

The idea at the heart of this book is the product of many conversations undertaken when Rebecca and I managed to be in the same place at the same time, notably at the International Gothic Association conferences in Dublin in 2022 and Halifax in 2024. I am immensely grateful to Rebecca for her intellectual generosity, commitment to collaboration, and, most importantly, for her friendship. Thank you to Liv Ozmun and Jazmyne

Olsen for their assistance with copy-editing. Their work on this project and my own was supported by a Faculty Vitality Grant from Weber State University's Research, Scholarship, and Professional Growth Committee. I acknowledge this here with gratitude.

As ever, I am grateful to my family: to my mother for her unwavering love and support, to Wilson for being an exceptional partner in all things, and to our children, Levi and Ariah, for always bringing the joy.

***

Thanks from both of us to the Linnaeus University Centre for Concurrences in Colonial and Postcolonial Studies, who generously provided a grant for the indexing of this volume. Thanks to Lobke Minter for her hard work completing the index, and thanks to the team at Cambridge University Press – and especially Bethany Thomas and George Laver – for all their support.

Finally, thanks to all the scholars who contributed chapters to this collection, for agreeing to think so carefully, consistently, and seriously about the possibilities and parameters of world-gothic fiction.

Introduction
Five Hundred Years of World-Gothic
Rebecca Duncan and Rebekah Cumpsty

Four decades ago, gothic literature was largely considered to be a weird footnote to the English literary canon. Today, gothic studies encompasses fiction from six continents, and, by virtue of this transregional scope, is a field increasingly engaged with urgent crises that define our turbulent global present. From the Leviathan of climate breakdown to the vital spectres of colonialism and enslavement: numerous critics have positioned the gothic as a form capable not only of figuring these and related monsters actually proliferating on a planetary scale, but also of interrogating them and even potentially subverting their power. This ascent and regional diversity of the gothic may strike some readers as surprising, not least because the symbology with which the mode is enduringly associated – crumbling castles, glowering aristocrats, damsels in distress – seems so thoroughly rooted in Europe, where traditional literary history teaches us that it first appears. According to this established origin story, gothic emerges in the late eighteenth century, just as bourgeois revolution and nascent industrialisation were sweeping away the last remnants of a feudal order. The form responds to these circumstances, and to the self-conscious culture of modernity by which they were accompanied, typically by looking back with ambivalence to the Europe of a darkly imagined medieval past: a haunted and often terrifying place of villainous overlords and oppressive traditions, rife with the superstition and magic of an ostensibly more primitive, and now bygone, age.

When scholars have relocated the gothic outside its European – and principally British – contexts of production, they have mainly done so by examining how these shadowy landscapes and characteristic monsters provide a malleable vocabulary that can be adapted to address the anxieties local to a different time and place. Hence, critics now routinely consider not only gothic, but a wide range of national and regional variations: Canadian Gothic, South African Gothic, Asian Gothic, and so on. The term 'globalgothic', coined by Glennis Byron in her 2013 collection of the same name, captures this general travelling tendency: in Byron's formulation, the concept identifies late-twentieth-century economic globalisation as the mechanism through which gothic forms have been disseminated around the world, where they come to be hybridised with other cultural traditions of the monstrous, producing a composite lexicon that can (supposedly) no longer be attached to any single point of origin.[1] Though not identical, both these transregional approaches rely on a similar strategy: taking the 'original' gothic as a yardstick, they track the modulations and dislocations that reconfigure this form – sometimes beyond recognition – for particular national, regional, or global settings. To speak of gothic in the international context is therefore almost always to speak of a mode invented under the socio-economic and political pressures of late-eighteenth-century Britain, and then exported elsewhere.

This collection offers a different perspective, which we will define as world-gothic across this introduction. World-gothic affirms the transregional scope of gothic production, but it does not understand this as primarily constituting a global distribution and adaptation of conventions and aesthetics. Instead of tracking the outward spread of gothic forms from their birthplace in Europe, world-gothic places a question mark over this widely accepted origin story, asking us to think critically about the world-historical picture it assumes. To do this, we situate the late-eighteenth-century literary form that has come over time to be identified as 'gothic fiction' in the context of what Immanuel Wallerstein called the capitalist world-system, a concept influentially reformulated by the environmental historian Jason W. Moore as the capitalist world-ecology, and which provides the basis for an approach to transregional cultural production named world-literature – or, more extensively, world-culture – by critics associated with the Warwick School.[2]

From this interdisciplinary field of scholarship, we draw an understanding of modernity – of the modern world in which we still live – which locates its origins in the 'long' sixteenth century. At this time, the powers of Europe invaded and colonised the Americas, and, overseeing a vast project of extermination, enslavement, and ecological theft, extracted the wealth that enabled their subsequent rise to global hegemony. In the crucible of the Atlantic world there thus emerged a transregional relationship of core to periphery – to use Wallerstein's terms – which binds the prosperity and influence of certain places to the plunder of others in a pattern that would structure the world-system for centuries to come, albeit in shifting ways. Because the central dynamic of capitalism is to exhaust its own socio-ecological conditions of possibility – to corrode the very sources of labour and energy on which it depends – the history of the world-system has unfolded in a recurring boom-and-bust rhythm of crisis and renewed expansion, with each new historical cycle of accumulation deepening and enlarging the extractive relations set in place by the last. Accounting for this history brings into focus the long roots of social and environmental catastrophe blooming unevenly across the globe today – and indeed, for Moore, climate breakdown, deepening inequality, and global economic turbulence suggest that we have entered the world-ecology's terminal phase. At the same time, a world-historical view of capitalism also shows us – crucially – that globalisation is by no means a twentieth-century phenomenon. Britain in the late 1700s was already global: the socio-economic revolution out of which gothic emerged is in fact the situated effect of a long-standing core-periphery relation. The capitalist modernisation that creates the local world to which gothic responds needs therefore to be understood as reliant on an aggressive regime of capitalist extraction and exploitation long active elsewhere.

Several interesting possibilities arise if we expand the established contextualising narrative of gothic's emergence to accommodate the trans-oceanic pre-history of European capitalist industrialisation. Most significantly, the move allows us to see that the conditions in which gothic appears in eighteenth-century Britain were already in place in the colonies, where the largescale incorporation of people into a transregional capitalist socio-ecology had begun in extremely violent forms two centuries earlier. This insight in turn destabilises conventional gothic aetiology, and raises important questions: If industrialisation produced narratives of haunting and terror in eighteenth-century Europe, then can these not be considered belated part-echoes of monstrous figures and tales that were at large much earlier, across the plantations of the New World? In a vital contribution to studies of gothic in the world-system, Stephen Shapiro provides good reasons to explore this possibility, proposing that gothic fiction cannot be fully disentangled from a wider body of 'folk' forms, which appear in Europe and its colonies to mediate the violent socio-cultural effects of a given region's induction into global networks of capitalism.[3] This volume takes cues from this and related arguments and builds out their possibilities, with major critical implications for gothic scholarship generally, and transregional studies of the mode in particular. As we will explain below, our contention is that prevailing understandings of the form called 'the gothic' may need to be strongly reconfigured – including disbanding the view in which this initially European invention now circulates rootlessly in flat globalised space.

Instead, we will propose that 'the gothic' can better be understood as one (albeit hegemonised) name for a particular form of world-culture – 'the manifold and many-sided culture of the capitalist world-system'[4] – which arises specifically to encode and negotiate the alienating local effects of incorporation, or reincorporation, into global capitalist modernity. World-gothic forms are thus plural, culturally specific and always highly situated, but they appear within the shared historical horizon of the uneven world-system. In this conception, gothic has in fact always been world-gothic: a vernacular iteration of the monstrous cultural forms that tend invariably to follow encounters with a new regime of capital, in whatever part of the world-system this is being is implemented. Without relying on the export or hybridisation of 'original' gothic conventions, world-gothic thus allows us to discern the linkages between these and a much wider array of located figures and tales of alienation and anxiety.

Over the rest of this introduction, we put some flesh on the bones of this as-yet abstract exposition by demonstrating how a world-gothic approach helps to reconstitute the familiar origin story of gothic literature. From here, we consider the critical affordances that emerge with this revised account, specifically in respect to questions of Eurocentrism and critical imperialism that are currently resurfacing, despite the ostensible development of a deterritorialised globalgothic mode. We conclude with a selection of snapshot analyses of contemporary transregional gothic production, showing that a world-gothic reading sheds light on the close association, mentioned above, between gothic forms and unfolding planetary crises. Finally, we provide an overview of the chapters to come, each of which engages with the opportunities to revisit and rethink gothic scholarship's parameters, theoretical infrastructure, and central figures of analysis that open up once gothic is acknowledged as world-gothic.

The Literature of Alienation

The relationship between gothic and industrialisation has recently been foregrounded by Brigit M. Marshall, who, in her monograph of the same name, provides an extensive analysis of 'industrial gothic': a central strand, she argues, of transatlantic cultural production across the nineteenth century. 'As communities and individuals' lives were transformed by the Industrial Revolution', writes Marshall, 'the Gothic provided an existing framework through which writers could explore and readers could comprehend the disruptions that industrialization was causing'.[5] This point resonates with, but also significantly differs from, earlier analyses of gothic and industrialisation, which – as we will see – are in fact more enabling in respect to a world-gothic perspective. Writing in the last decades of the last millennium, Franco Moretti and David Punter each situated the rise of gothic in Britain amid the largescale reorganisation of the pre-existing social order represented by the arrival in this region of capitalism in its industrial form. For Moretti, the gothic appears 'in the full spate of the industrial revolution' as a means of articulating novel structures of feeling generated by this development: in the figures of Frankenstein's monster and Dracula – emblems of 'the disfigured wretch and the ruthless proprietor' – he discerns the dual spectres of proletarian revolution and total, cold-blooded monopolisation that haunt bourgeois society from its inception. 'The literature of terror is born precisely *out of the terror of a split society*',[6] Moretti concludes, the point being that the fears encoded in gothic forms are fears particular to the capitalist mode of production, in which the prosperity of the capitalist is inversely correlated to that of the worker.

Punter reiterates and nuances this claim, proposing that gothic can be considered 'a literature of alienation': a form of narrative that arises to encode the specifically estranged experience of existence under capitalism.[7] To make this argument, Punter turns to *The Economic and Philosophic Manuscripts of 1844*, where the early Marx outlines the socio-ecological and psychic ruptures that open up as capitalism divorces people from their means of subsistence outside the market, and makes survival dependent on waged work and commodity consumption. According to Marx, there are four dimensions to the form of alienation that emerges under these conditions. First, workers are alienated from the products of their labour, which – though an incarnation of their own energy – come to be weirdly animated by the market and so seem to escape their creator's control. Second, the worker is alienated from the activity of labour itself, which appears to belong not to them, but to the owner of the means of production; third, the worker is alienated from their own body, now an instrument of production, and from the natural world, which disappears as a source of subsistence; and finally, the worker is alienated from their fellow human beings, who do not exist in community, but as individuals in competitive relation within the market.[8] Since the late eighteenth century, Punter proposes, gothic fiction has registered each of these processes of estrangement. The world of the gothic is, in this view, the alienated world of capital: a place inhabited by 'arrant individualists' and 'psychotic heroes and heroines', where human energies regularly bring forth 'monsters which destroy their creators', and the landscape 'vanishes from sight' behind terrifying 'expressionistic substitutes'.[9]

Moretti and Punter therefore offer a different – if not entirely incompatible – analysis of gothic and industrialisation to the one made by Marshall, who understands gothic as a set of pre-existing conventions, amenable to the representation of 'workers' struggles against the powerful forces of capitalism' across the nineteenth century.[10] What the earlier critical work makes clear, however, is that this pre-existing, eighteenth-century gothic is already intertwined with capitalism as a cultural form which registers the estranged reality it creates. The point is confirmed by Shapiro, who – drawing on the later Marx's account of the commodity fetish – emphasises the nightmarishness of the situation in which our own energy confronts us as a powerful and unpredictable force that seems to act on us from outside. Under such conditions, where human creativity is externalised and reanimated by the market, the commodity mysteriously hold its own producers in weird thrall, as if it were – in Shapiro's memorable phrasing – 'an awful, supernatural alien towering before its human meat puppets'. The encounter with capitalist modernity can thus be grasped with Shapiro as an 'intrinsically gothic experience', by which we should understand not only an experience worthy of premade gothic description, but rather one that produces the narratives of alienation and anxiety that have acquired the designator 'gothic' within the Western canon.[11]

World-Gothic Origins

Conceptualising gothic as a literature of alienation allows us to expand the regional and historical parameters of gothic's established European origin story, because, as we have begun to see in the above, the process of capitalist modernisation to which early British gothic responds does not take place in a global vacuum. Rather, the industrialisation of Britan is facilitated by two preceding centuries of brutal human exploitation and ecological extraction in the colonies of the so-called New World. Eric Williams documented this economic relation in *Capitalism and Slavery*, which outlines in detail the central 'role of . . . the slave trade in providing the capital which financed the Industrial Revolution in England'.[12] Britain entered into the transoceanic traffic in enslaved African people in the mid-sixteenth century, and was, by the time gothic emerged on the literary scene, the pre-eminent actor in this trade. It is no surprise, then, that the history of enslavement exerts a shaping force on gothic fiction. Gothic vocabularies of fear and monstrosity are, from their early British iterations, fundamentally informed by the narratives of race invented to serve the Caribbean plantation system, as well as by pro- and anti-abolitionist discourse. A recurring preoccupation in these texts, as Lizabeth Paravisini-Gebert observes, concerns the syncretic spiritual practices developed by enslaved people, such as Vodou, Obeah, and Myal. From the beginning of the nineteenth century, repeated gothic renditions of these rites translate them into a paranoiac colonial imaginary, presenting their practitioners as an 'obscene cannibalistic personification of evil ... thereby mirroring political and social anxieties close to home'.[13]

As it fabricates monsters from Caribbean spiritual practice in the way Paravisini-Gebert suggests, the colonial gothic strand of British gothic production can in part be understood in relation to the real connection between these rites and rebellion. As Simon Gikandi observes of early-nineteenth-century Jamaica, '[p]lanters and government officials alike seemed to believe that the African resistance to slavery ... [was] embedded in magic'[14] – and not without reason. In *The Black Jacobins*, C. L. R James accords a prominent place to Vodou in fomenting and facilitating the slave-led Haitian Revolution across the last decade of the eighteenth century, and Gikandi develops a related argument around the subversive function of the cult of Myal. What he calls the 'terror associated with magic in the official narrative of ... slavery'[15] thus helps to explain the colonial construction of slave rituals in gothic's terms of heightened dread, which would seem to grasp something of the actual threat represented by these practices – especially after the successful rebellions in Haiti – to the plantation order, on which slaveholding nations' prosperity significantly rested. At the same time, however, this interconnection between subversion and the Caribbean occult also points to another, partial and imperfect connection, which takes us from a colonial- to a world-gothic reading.

In *Black Metamorphosis*, Sylvia Wynter's unpublished treatise on historical Black experience in the Americas, the Jamaican author and theorist outlines her formative argument that the syncretic rites, tales, dances, and festivals forged by enslaved people – what she calls Caribbean 'folk culture'[16] – represent 'an indigenization process':[17] a practice she describes as 'the rerooting of the uprooted, the mutation of an ancient traditional culture into a new'.[18] Wynter understands the relationship between resistance and folk culture as inseparably entangled with the operation of indigenisation, and indeed her conception of the folk is informed by Mikhail Bakhtin's strategic use of the term to suggest an opposition to the official culture of the European bourgeoisie. In Wynter's argument, indigenisation is a cultural response to the 'near total alienation' of the plantation,[19] which subsumes and also violently surpasses the forms of alienation unleashed across Europe two hundred years after the initiation of slavery in the New World. This analysis rests on a critical revision of the view in which industrialisation appears for the first time in Britain after the middle of the eighteenth century. As Wynter puts it, 'the alienated waged worker of the Industrial Revolution was preceded by the black slave',[20] a claim drawn in part from James' famous observation that slaves in revolutionary Haiti should be understood as 'closer to a modern proletariat than any workers in existence at the time'.[21] Sidney Mintz develops the point in his now-classic study of sugar in the Atlantic world. While conventional European historiography teaches us that '[t]he seventeenth century was preindustrial', Mintz shows that the highly disciplined organisation of labour on plantations in the 1600s made these spaces 'a synthesis of field and factory', and so 'really quite unlike anything known in mainland Europe' at the time.[22]

Building on the same insight, Wynter explains plantation labour as representing, in the first place, 'the extreme case' of estrangement within the framework described by Marx. Enslaved people were forced, under conditions of lethal duress, 'to create a product ... alien to [their] own needs', and as they 'created this product, it produced more capital, whose power over [the slaves] was thus enforced'.[23] As Wynter emphasises, however, enslavement also profoundly exceeds the Marxist paradigm. It was predicated on the brutal physical and social rupture perpetrated by the Middle Passage, which expresses the concomitant transformation of the human body itself into capital. Writes Wynter of the enslaved person: '[h]e [sic] was not only alienated ... from his means of production, from the use of his own labour for the communal purpose defined by his culture'; additionally, enslavement entailed alienation from an entire lifeworld – from the 'social fabric' within which personhood had been constituted – and so also from 'former being ... humanity'.[24] It is in relation to this structural refusal of selfhood that Wynter understands indigenisation emerging as a process through which to generate modes of being that actively negate this imposed negation. The folk cultures within which indigenisation unfolds represent, she summarises, a 'cultural response to the dehumanizing alienation of the capitalist plantation system of the New World', one that allowed slaves to 'reroot' themselves, 'making use of the old cultural patterns ... in order to create a new vocabulary for the new existence'.[25]

This conception of the practices and tales enframed by syncretic Caribbean cosmologies brings into view a partial, imperfect resonance with the cultural form that will come to cohere under the sign of the gothic in Britain, and which itself develops from an encounter with the alienating effects of industrialisation once this permutation of the capitalist mode of production reaches Europea in the eighteenth century. Important groundwork for understanding this connection has been laid by Kerstin Oloff in her study of the Caribbean zombie, a figure she locates within the deep 'socio-ecological rifts' underpinning the plantations of the early capitalist world-system.[26] Zombie lore belongs to Haitian Vodou, though related monstrous figures are visible across Caribbean spiritual systems, in all cases synthesised from reconfigured African belief systems transplanted through the Middle Passage. Unlike the zombies of contemporary horror fiction (though also connectable with these, as Oloff shows across her analysis) this zombie is not itself predatory. Instead, it is a creature whose soul has been captured or extracted by a sorcerer for nefarious, gainful ends. In its embodied iteration, the zombie is a corpse resurrected with magic, and put to work on the plantation. Encoded in such beings, Oloff discerns the experience of 'a ruptured connection to the land ... to one's own body (and hence labour-force) and to knowledge production',[27] which bespeaks all the dimensions of alienation Wynter describes. As Oloff herself notes, the undead in African-derived Caribbean cosmologies foreshadow anxious images of fragmentary embodiment circulating in Romantic and gothic fiction – Coleridge's 'Rime of the Ancient Mariner', Shelley's *Frankenstein* – written amid the industrialisation of Britain, leading her to conclude that the 'zombie-esque figure' is 'a monster that registers the emergence of the capitalist world-ecology on both sides of the Atlantic'.[28]

To draw these transregional and historical linkages is not, importantly, to propose that the monsters of Caribbean folk cultures are gothic fiction. As we have seen with Wynter, the figures and practices synthesised by enslaved people gain their meaning in the specific and extreme context of the plantation, where – unlike in the later factories of industrial Europe – human beings were treated as both labour and capital: brutally exploited, and wrenched from the social worlds that provided co-ordinates for selfhood. These are the conditions under which practices, narratives, dances, and magical rites are developed as a process of indigenisation, resignifying the plantation in ways that run counter to its logic dehumanisation. Quite clearly, the gothic that appears in industrialising Britain does not possess the same social meaning; this form negotiates an individualised world in which work, ecology, and the body are subject to alienation, but is not compelled to address the systemic denial of selfhood. Taken together with Punter, Moretti, and Shapiro, Wynter and Oloff's analyses should prompt us to look anew at gothic form, however, both in its early British iterations, and more generally. Most significantly, these interventions help us to see the gothic as the product of a located and – crucially – belated encounter with global capitalist modernity, and so as an echo of situated cultural responses to the world-system already long underway elsewhere. As we will see in the following section, one key effect of this perspective is to provincialise European gothic production, which ceases to be an aesthetic yardstick against which other monstrous cultures are measured, and becomes instead just one regional iteration of a much wider, more varied, and plural mediation of alienation and anxiety. The Caribbean zombie is not gothic fiction, but it can productively be grasped within this broader field of world-gothic production, which includes, but is not organised around or originated by, a strange and gloomy corner of the eighteenth-century British literary canon.

Beyond Eurocentrism

Significant critical opportunities open up on taking a world-gothic perspective. Perhaps most importantly, it becomes possible to generatively complicate existing assumptions about transregional gothic reading that – though increasingly fraught with difficulties – remain central to much scholarship that addresses the fiction of fear. As we saw earlier on in this introduction, the concept of globalgothic postulates the emergence of a culturally hybrid gothic mode, which appears with the late-twentieth-century global expansion of the market, and is now so complex and composite that it cannot be pinned down to any regional, local, or national origin. This deterritorialised understanding of contemporary gothic aesthetics was developed in part to facilitate gothic analyses outside 'the West', so it is significant that questions relating to gothic studies' residual Eurocentrism have recently begun to resurface.[29] As a new wave of gothic scholarship moves decisively beyond Europe and the settler nations, critics are often finding that even globalgothic sits uneasily in the context of the fiction they address (a point made by several contributors to this volume). In the face of this challenge, two apparently inconsistent strategies for validating the use of gothic hermeneutics have emerged: The first entails pointing to conscious intertextual dialogues with 'original' gothic conventions, a tactic which hinges on the assumption that gothic is, in essence, a 'Western' cultural form, and can only legitimately be deployed as a category for reading 'non-Western' fiction if this fiction self-consciously relates to the gothic canon. The second strategy relies on the seemingly opposing premise that the West is not alone in having developed a gothic tradition; in his view, other regions and cultures have independently produced their own kinds of gothic, and have done so away from 'Western' influence.[30]

Though not without value, neither of these responses to the problem of critical imperialism in gothic reading can fully dispel the charge of Eurocentrism. The requirement that fiction perform a deliberate relationship to the Western gothic mode risks limiting 'non-Western' gothic writing to a kind of re-writing: an albeit-creative derivative of an originally 'Western' gothic script. Though it may accurately identify transcultural resemblances, the notion that all cultures have developed their own parallel gothic traditions is not more enabling, since it provides no rationale for connecting monstrous forms emergent outside the hegemonic cultures of Britain, Europe, and the settler nations with the gothic fictions that appear within these regions. In fact, in the picture of global culture that underpins this notion, it is difficult to see how the imposition of the term gothic beyond the so-called West could be anything other than a Eurocentric act. Notably, these views seem to take opposing perspectives, on one the hand affirming gothic as a deeply and exclusively 'Western' phenomenon, and on the other proposing that gothic-like traditions exist across a much wider spectrum of cultures and regions. That both are ultimately amenable to the logic of Eurocentrism attests, however, to shared assumptions about the modern world in which the gothic is implicitly being placed.

According to the decolonial philosopher Enrique Dussel, 'Eurocentrism' refers to the perspective that takes 'intra-European phenomena as the starting point for modernity',[31] failing to acknowledge that the prosperity and development of Europe is, from the end of the fifteenth century, predicated on relationships of genocide, enslavement, and extraction in the New World. By obscuring these transregional connections, it becomes possible to lift European culture out of the crucible of world-history in which it is shaped, treating it as an 'abstract universality', rather than imbricated in the dynamics of colonialism and capitalism.[32] The culture of 'Western' modernity thus comes to appear unique and self-constituting. It can be opposed to other, 'non-Western' cultures on the basis of this exceptionalism – a move that supports colonial projects across their history – while also entrenching a view in which all cultures are in some way essential (and essentially modern or non-modern), rather than formed across the board within pressures locally exerted by the same uneven, modern/colonial world-system. Though Dussel does not use the term, it is this more productive, latter view that is encapsulated by the concept of world-culture.

Traces of Dussel's account of Eurocentrism are visible both in the claim that gothic is an essentially 'Western' form, and in the view that multiple gothics have co-evolved along parallel cultural tracks. Overlooked by each of these analyses is the possibility that what undergirds the various cultural forms in question is the same modernity – the same uneven modern world-system – in relation to which each takes shape in irreducibly specific and located ways. Acknowledging this shared historical horizon provides the otherwise absent rationale for drawing imperfect but enabling linkages between the European gothic mode and monstrous figures developed in other cosmological formations, as we have suggested with Oloff in the preceding discussion of the zombie. Further, though, it helps to address problems that arise when the imperative to dialogue with canonical gothic conventions becomes the criterion for entry into the globalgothic mode. Though well-meaning, the concept of cultural hybridisation on which this condition hinges appears, paradoxically, to affirm an essential distinction between gothic, a product of 'Western' modernity, and other cultural discourses of the numinous and threatening, which are thus seemingly positioned as expressions of static, autochthonous tradition.

We have already seen this view strongly contested in Wynter's analysis of Caribbean folk culture, which tracks how pre-colonial cultural formations are synthesised into new figures and concepts to deal with the experience of a reality violently shaped by alienation in the early world-system. A substantial body of scholarship on manifestations of the occult in colonial and postcolonial societies further outlines and affirms the novelty – the modernity – of narratives and practices prosaically distinguished from European culture on the basis of their indigeneity or proximity to tradition. A selective sample of this work would include Luise White's meticulous oral history of vampire (*mumiani*) tales in recently colonised East and Central Africa, which reveals these to be new stories, invented around the unprecedented figure of the colonial vampire, that appear to give shape to unfamiliar and alienating regimes of labour and extraction from the end of the nineteenth century. Similarly, Aihwa Ong's extensive analysis of the phenomenon of spirit possession afflicting women industrial workers in Malaysia's Free Trade Zones after the 1970s emphasises that, though drawn from ancient cosmology, the *hantu* (spirits) stalking these highly-technologised factory floors are not archaic, but novel apparitions, which respond creatively to the newly exploitative organisation of labour in the neoliberal world order. A related point undergirds Michael Taussig's influential account of devil beliefs in late-twentieth-century Latin America, which emerge, he argues, to make located sense of the bewildering experience of subordination to commodity logic. Back on the African continent also at the end of the twentieth century, Peter Geschiere, Jean and John Comaroff, and David McNally (among others) all outline how a surge in occult ritual, vampire tales, and zombie-making accompany neoliberal programmes of economic structural adjustment, which intensify unemployment, deepen exploitation and entrench old inequalities, while conspicuously enriching a mysteriously chosen elite.[33]

To extract 'the gothic' – born amid the capitalist modernisation of Europe – from this (inexhaustive) catalogue of situated monstrous responses to capitalist modernity seems, at best, misguided, and at worst to represent a kind of dogged Eurocentrism, which insists on the exceptionalism of 'Western' culture. Aiming to subvert this misapprehension, world-gothic takes cues from the historian Dipesh Chakrabarty, who – broadly in line with Dussel – understands dismantling Eurocentrism as a matter not of de- but *re*territorialising Europe's intellectual and cultural bequests. What he calls 'provincialization' is a strategy for disrupting the pervasive narrative that makes 'modernity or capitalism' appear phenomena 'that became global *over time*, by originating in one place (Europe) and then spreading outside it', with the effect that all other places are consigned 'to the waiting rooms of history'.[34] The counter-perspective Chakrabarty offers dethrones 'Western' culture from its self-appointed position of abstraction, by asking 'how and in what sense European ideas that were universal were also, at one and the same time, drawn from very particular intellectual and historical traditions', thus underscoring 'how thought [i]s related to place'.[35] This volume follows the provincialising imperative in the field of gothic studies. World-gothic positions the 'Western' tradition of gothic fiction within a wider world-culture of alienation, of which it represents a single example, rooted – as in the case of all world-gothic apparitions – in the socio-ecological, epistemic, and historical conditions of a particular world-systemic position.

World-Gothic Now

While world-gothic reading does not consist in enumerating intertextual relations with 'Western' gothic conventions, it does help us to look afresh at the fiction in which such dialogues are taking place. The hybridisation of canonical gothic forms is – as globalgothic analyses rightly point out – a key feature of the contemporary gothic canon, central to the work of such writers as Jesmyn Ward, Silvia Moreno-Garcia, Stephen Graham Jones, Siphiwe Gloria Ndlovu, Mariana Enriquez, and Clare Kohda (among many others). From a world-gothic perspective, what is interesting about the aesthetics of this fiction has less to do with the interpenetration of cultural references than with the ways in which gothic is (re)activated, alongside differently located mediations of alienation, in order to address newly hostile and estranged realities erupting at our present moment of global socio-ecological turbulence. As we have seen with Jason W. Moore in the first section of this Introduction, this situation represents the likely terminal crisis of the capitalist world-ecology. It is characterised by the cumulative biospheric consequences of five centuries of ecological extraction, and by frenzied but increasingly short-lived efforts to reinstate profitability through neoliberalisation – asset stripping, aggressive cost-cutting, financial speculation, and intensifying human and environmental exploitation. Contemporary world-gothic production can be understood as providing situated responses to this latest phase of attempted frontier expansion, not primarily because it hybridises different traditions, but because the traditions that it does draw from and integrate together are themselves often the cultural markers of (previous) encounters with colonial capitalist modernity.

Here we might think of Mariana Enriquez's two celebrated collections, *Things we Lost in the Fire* (2017 (2016)) and *The Dangers of Smoking in Bed* (2021 (2009)), where references to Mary Shelley and Stephen King interweave with the folk saints and devils of an Argentina ravaged by economic crises and neoliberal structural adjustment – for example, San La Muerte, practitioners of *brujería*, and transmogrified images of the poor, the young, and the unhoused. Similarly illuminating is a text like Clare Kohda's *Woman, Eating* (2022), a vampire story of migration and manifold inequality – racialised, gendered, generational – in millennial London. Critically recalling *Dracula* (itself a xenophobic response to economic decline at the dusk of the British empire), the novel centres on the Malay figures of the *lansuyar* and the *pontianak*: both examples of the *hantu* that carry with them to the neoliberalising English capital a history of Malaysia's induction into the late-capitalist world-system. The work of Jesmyn Ward is perhaps more instructive still, for its combination a Faulknerian gothic tradition – forged during the early-twentieth-century modernisation of the American south – with Vodou cosmology developed in defiance of the plantations at the heart of an earlier phase in the world-history of capitalism. As demonstrated with particular clarity in *Sing, Unburied, Sing* (2017), Ward invokes these differently situated responses to alienation to envision a contemporary Mississippi shaped by active and catastrophic processes of racialised and ecocidal exploitation, emblematised in the novel by the industrialised prison on the one hand, and oil rig on the other.

Each of these writers demonstrates gothic's intimate relationship – noted at the beginning of this introduction – with crises of capital and ecology underway unevenly across the planet today. At the same time, each also reveals that what underpins this relationship is a much more structural connection than is allowed by readings that identify the monsters of the gothic canon as a deterritorialised and hybridisable vocabulary, which can be reshaped to capture a wide range of anxieties. Instead, it is precisely the rootedness of gothic, both in its European and wider variations, that ties this form to present socio-ecological shifts. What makes the gothic appropriate to address situations as diverse as those explored by Enriquez, Kohda, and Ward is, in other words, its historical function as a located cultural encoding of encounters with capitalist modernity, which, over and over again, creates worlds distorted by strange, bewildering, and deeply threatening forces. World-gothic names the full scope of these always-situated and diversely mediated encounters, making visible partial connections between Africa-derived folk cultures on the industrialised plantation of the New World and the literary forms that, over a century later, register the anxieties of industrialising Britain, often in highly racialised scenarios that precisely demonise their Caribbean precursors. Following the frontiers of capitalist extraction and exploitation, world-gothic allows us to track these resonances all the way into our contemporary moment, when the much-remarked explosion of gothic across the globe attests less to a severing of regional ties, than it does to the scale and intensity of the present world-systemic, or world-ecological, crisis, which provokes renewed efforts to extract value from any and all remaining territories of relatively uncapitalised life. In this view, gothic is not a marginal niche in the Anglophone literary canon, but neither is it a generalised aesthetics of global anxiety. Rather, world-gothic offers a cultural history of the catastrophic world-systemic present.

As we noted at the outset, taking the perspective we have outlined in this Introduction has significant implications not only for the transregional study of gothic forms but also for gothic criticism generally. Proceeding from the premise that gothic is initiated with bourgeois and industrial revolutions in Europe, this field has developed a critical vocabulary, and defined a set of parameters, that are chiefly informed by a particular, regional variation of what is in fact a much broader, more variegated and historically extensive cultural form. In this collection, we redress this situation. The chapters assembled here examine the implications of a world-gothic approach for established understandings of the contexts in which gothic emerges, and the issues to which it responds, as well as for the theoretical frameworks through which gothic is now routinely considered – the vast majority of them rooted in, or reactive to, intellectual traditions inaugurated by Europe's Enlightenment. Contributors further reassess gothic literature's familiar cast of monstrous characters, considering how tropes of haunting, vampirism, undeath, and witchcraft are not forged in Europe and carted out to the rest of the world, but emerge in complex historical and geographic patterns that contour the empty time and space of Eurocentrism and globalisation. A final part of the volume takes up the comparative possibilities of world-gothic reading, exploring connections and regional permutations that affirm the provincial nature of European gothic production, while also augmenting the possibilities of gothic analysis on a transregional scale.

Outline of Chapters

The chapters in the volume's first part – 'Gothic in the World' – reconceptualise the gothic by offering alternative accounts of transnational relationships to those provided by the concept of globalisation. Instead, contributors foreground how European hegemony emerges through the exploitation of gendered and racialised labour in the colonies, and through biophysical extraction in these same regions. These chapters thus provide a theoretical vocabulary for addressing gothic engagements with urgent global issues, such as uneven climate emergency, and racialised and gendered inequality. Stephen Shapiro opens with 'The Undead's Capitalist World-System'. This chapter locates the undead within contemporary world-culture, identifying gothic as a form closely linked to crises of liberalism, as the political position which attempts to mediate between conservativism and radicalism. In 'Whiteness and the "Western" Gothic Tradition', Rebecca Duncan and Johan Höglund then turn to the eighteenth and nineteenth centuries, demonstrating how the cultural forms now habitually understood to inaugurate gothic as a 'Western' literary tradition are shaped by and reproduce historically specific and mutating categories of whiteness, which emerge to manage the located effects of capitalist modernisation, from the era of enslavement, through to the aftermath of abolition, and the new age of imperialism that emerges in the fin-de-siècle period. Esthie Hugo's chapter re-theorises the domestic gothic from a world-gothic perspective, drawing on social reproduction theory to suggest that gothic forms encode the interlocking violence of gendered exploitation and ecological extraction in two contemporary texts: the HBO television series *Sharp Objects* (2018) and the film *Mlungu Wam* (2022).

The second part – 'World-Monsters' – examines recognisable figures in gothic literary production, with the understanding that zombies, vampires, ghosts, and witches ought not to be reduced to a European origin, but instead have longer and more plural genealogies. The chapters address the question: How might canonical gothic creatures be meaningfully compared to other traditions of the supernatural, in ways that expose their resonance and analogous cultural functions, without occluding their difference? Krista Collier-Jarvis responds first with a discussion of the possibility of 'pre-colonial gothic', which centres on the Windigo/Wendigo/Windego. Collier-Jarvis details ongoing debates about how 'stories by and about Indigenous peoples and cultures fit' within the gothic, emphasising the need for local, culturally specific scholarship which equally acknowledges the wider horizon of coloniality. James Mellis echoes this point with a focus on haunting. In an analysis of African, Caribbean, and African American literature, Mellis finds that hauntings, both ancestral and otherwise, assume the reality of African indigenous and diasporic epistemes. Thomas Waller then develops a world-gothic account of bloodsuckers by framing Orlando Mendes's novel *Portagem* through Marx's famous vampiric characterisation of capital. With colonial coal mining in Mozambique as its setting, Waller's chapter demonstrates how mining capital survives by degrading and feeding off of lives of local workers, and how fiction in the region mediates these processes in spectral and monstrous forms. The final chapter in this part by Valeria Villegas Lindvall reconsiders the witch from a world-gothic perspective, arguing that the Mexican-Peruvian film *Huesera* (*The Bone Woman*, 2022) depicts *brujería* as an antidote to heteronormative constructions of motherhood and the feminine. The chapter situates the figure of the witch within the history of enclosure and the depoliticisation of women's labour, before illustrating the ways that the film 'remixes' the trope of the witch to critique the coloniality of gender/sexuality/knowledge.

The contributions in the third part – 'Worlding Gothic Theory' – address key theoretical concepts in gothic criticism, with the intention first of locating them in the intellectual and geopolitical heritage out of which they emerge, and second of revising them for application in a world-cultural context. These chapters thus examine the limitations and possibilities of gothic studies' established critical vocabulary. Beginning with the sublime, Jana Maria Giles traces a genealogy from its earliest Greek formulations to a revised account based on Jean-François Lyotard's concept of the differend. In the process, Giles exposes both the colonising and the decolonising possibilities of the sublime, providing a framework that can be taken up for world-gothic reading. Taking a similar approach to the grotesque, Rune Graulund locates this concept within a dialectic between the culture of modernity, and the transgressive ways of being that modernity attempts to regulate. From here, Graulund's chapter tracks manifestations of this grotesque dynamic across a transregional corpus, asserting in conclusion the ecological possibilities of such an analysis in the age of planetary emergency. Ryan Topper then addresses the uncanny – a cornerstone of gothic analysis – from a world-gothic vantage, illustrating his argument with reference to the work of Amos Tutuola. As Topper shows, Tutuola shifts the coordinates of the real beyond the European rationalism on which the uncanny rests, to include Yoruba conceptions of the real where physical and spiritual spheres are mutually constitutive. The final chapter in this part revises the interrelated concepts of the abject and abhuman. In her contribution, Rebekah Cumpsty critiques the primitivist underpinnings of European constructions of the category 'human' upon which both the abject and abhuman rest. Cumpsty then demonstrates the world-gothic potential of other-than-human modes of being through readings of African and African diasporic fiction.

Key to the concept of world-gothic theorised across this collection is the insight that analogous experiences of alienation within the world-system provide a basis for comparisons between fictions produced in different cultural contexts and/or different historical moments. The chapters in the volume's fourth part – 'World-Gothic: Transregional Comparisons' – demonstrate this possibility. Rather than examining how pre-existing gothic conventions are locally adapted for a particular national context, these contributions consider how traditions of the monstrous and the supernatural emerge across different regions to mediate, critique and/or obscure the repatterning of an established local socio-ecological order. In 'Gothic Inheritances in Oceania' Caitlin Vandertop examines Albert Wendt's 'Inside us the Dead' and Robert Barclay's *Melal* as examples of world-gothic, identifying a preoccupation across the two texts with genealogical disruptions perpetrated by colonial extractivism and toxification. Karl Emil Rosenbæk Reetz then uses gothic forms as a comparative frame for oil encounters in the Niger Delta and the Nordic region, identifying a visceral vocabulary in Niger Delta writing, and an uncanny vocabulary in the Nordics. Rosenbæk Reetz shows that imminent and abstracted aesthetics register the regionally differentiated experiences of oil across the two areas, with the Niger Delta forging a path the Nordics are likely to follow. Finally, Roxanne Douglas looks back to eighteenth-century chapbook publishing, which used virtually identical illustrations for 'Bluebeard' and *The Thousand and One Arabian Nights*. These stories, Douglas argues, demonstrate the transregional origins of certain female gothic tropes that are taken up in contemporary Arab women's writing back to the 'bloody chamber'.

The collection closes with a Coda that returns to the imperfect nature of the resonances between differently located world-gothic manifestations, which – as this introduction has emphasised – share a relationship to the alienating effects of capitalist modernity, but in each instance possess irreducible social meanings, cosmological inheritances, and regional significance. The Coda reflects on the notion of catachresis as a valuable concept for clarifying these tensions between relationality and specificity, developing key interventions around the term made previously by world-literary and postcolonial thinkers. World-gothic, we propose, offers one catachrestic – imperfect, non-exhaustive, extemporaneous – term that inadequately but generatively addresses the heterogeneity of monstrous production, as this unfolds within the common cultural horizon of the world-system.

Notes

1. Cynthia Sugars, *Canadian Gothic: Literature, History, and the Spectre of Self-Invention*, Cardiff, University of Wales Press, 2014; Katarzyna Ancuta, 'Asian Gothic', in D. Punter (ed.), *A New Companion to the Gothic*, Chichester, Wiley Blackwell, 2012; Rebecca Duncan, *South African Gothic: Anxiety and Creative Dissent in Postapartheid Literature and Beyond*, Cardiff, University of Wales Press, 2018; Glennis Byron, 'Introduction', in G. Byron (ed.), *Globalgothic*, Manchester, Manchester University Press, 2013, 6.
2. Immanuel Wallerstein, *World-Systems Analysis: An Introduction*, Durham, NC, Duke University Press, 2004; Jason W. Moore, *Capitalism in the Web of Life: Ecology and the Accumulation of Capital*, London, Verso, 2015; Sharae Deckard et al. [Warwick Research Collective], *Combined and Uneven Development: Towards a New Theory of World Literature*, Liverpool, Liverpool University Press, 2015; Sharae Deckard, Michael Niblett, and Stephen Shapiro, *Tracking Capital: World-Systems, World-Ecology, World-Culture*, New York, SUNY Press, 2024.
3. Stephen Shapiro, 'Transvaal, Transylvania: *Dracula's* World-System and Gothic Periodicity', *Gothic Studies*, 10:1 (2008), 30–47.
4. Sharae Deckard and Kate Houlden, 'Social Reproduction Feminism and World-Culture', *Feminist Theory*, 25:2 (2024), 137.

5. Bridget M. Marshall, *Industrial Gothic: Workers, Exploitation and Urbanization in Transatlantic Nineteenth-Century Literature*, Cardiff, University of Wales Press, 2021, 8.
6. Franco Moretti, *Signs Taken for Wonders: Essays on the Sociology of Literary Form*, trans. S. Fischer, D. Forgacs, and D. Miller, London, Verso, 1983, 83.
7. David Punter, *The Literature of Terror: The Modern Gothic*, London: Longman, 2013[1996], 197.
8. Karl Marx, *Economic and Philosophic Manuscripts of 1844*, Moscow, Progress Publishers, 1977 [1959], 68–74; Karl Marx, *Capital, Volume 1*, Harmondsworth, Penguin, 1982, 163.
9. Punter, *The Literature of Terror*, 197.
10. Marshall, *Industrial Gothic*, 5.
11. Shapiro, 'Transvaal', 30.
12. Eric Williams, *Capitalism and Slavery*, Richmond, NC, University of North Carolina Press, 1944, vii.
13. Lizabeth Paravisini-Gebert, 'Colonial and Postcolonial Gothic: The Caribbean', in Jerrold E. Hogle (ed.), *The Cambridge Companion to Gothic Fiction*, Cambridge, Cambridge University Press, 2002, 231.
14. Simon Gikandi, *Slavery and the Culture of Taste*, New Jersey, Princeton University Press, 2011, 260.
15. C. L. R. James, *The Black Jacobins: Toussaint L'Ouverture and the San Domingo Revolution*, New York, Vintage, 1989[1938], 86; Gikandi, *Slavery*, 260.
16. Sylvia Wynter, *Black Metamorphosis: New Natives in a New World*, unpublished manuscript (1970s) housed at the Schomburg Centre for Research in Black Culture, New York, 63.
17. Wynter, *Black Metamorphosis*, 71.
18. Wynter, *Black Metamorphosis*, 54.
19. Wynter, *Black Metamorphosis*, 17.
20. Wynter, *Black Metamorphosis*, 114.
21. James, *Black Jacobins*, 86.
22. Sidney Mintz, *Sweetness and Power: The Place of Sugar in Modern History*, New York, Penguin, 1985, 47–8.
23. Wynter, *Black Metamorphosis*, 52.
24. Wynter, *Black Metamorphosis*, 44.
25. Wynter, *Black Metamorphosis*, 18.
26. Kerstin Oloff, *Ecology of the Zombie: World-Culture and the Monstrous*, Liverpool, Liverpool University Press, 2023, 2.
27. Oloff, *Ecology of the Zombie*, 8.
28. Oloff, *Ecology of the Zombie*, 7.
29. Rebecca Duncan (ed.), *The Edinburgh Companion to Globalgothic*, Edinburgh, Edinburgh University Press, 2023.
30. Ian Conrich, 'Maori Tales of the Unexpected: The New Zealand Television Series Mataku as Indigenous Gothic', in G. Byron (ed.), *Globalgothic*, Manchester, Manchester University Press, 2013, 41; Ruth Heholt, 'Global

Gothic: Decentering the Urban Gothic', in H.-G. Millette and R. Heholt (eds.), *The New Urban Gothic: Global Gothic in the Age of the Anthropocene*, London, Palgrave Macmillan, 2020, 169.
31. Enrique Dussel, 'Europe, Modernity and Eurocentrism', *Nepantla: Views from the South*, 1:3 (2000), 465–78, 469.
32. Dussel, 'Eurocentrism', 471.
33. Luise White, *Speaking with Vampires: Rumor and History in Colonial Africa*, Berkeley, CA, University of California Press, 2000; Aihwa Ong, *Spirits of Resistance and Capitalist Discipline: Factory Women in Malaysia*, New York, SUNY Press, 2010 [1987]; Michael T. Taussig, *The Devil and Commodity Fetishism in South America*, Chapel Hill, NC, University of North Carolina Press, 2010 [1980]; Jean Comaroff and John L. Comaroff, 'Occult economies and the Violence of Abstraction: Notes from the South African Postcolony', *American Ethnologist* 26:2 (1999), 279–303; Peter Geschiere, *The Modernity of Witchcraft: Politics and the Occult in Postcolonial Africa*, Charlottesville, VA: University of Virginia Press, 1997; David McNally, *Monsters of the Market: Zombies, Vampires and Global Capitalism*, Leiden, Brill, 2011; Duncan, 'Colonialism'.
34. Dipesh Chakrabarty, *Provincializing Europe: Postcolonial Thought and Historical Difference*, Princeton, NJ, Princeton University Press, 2000, 8.
35. Chakrabarty, *Provincializing Europe*, xiii.

PART I

Gothic in the World: (Re)conceptualisations

CHAPTER 1

The Undead's Capitalist World-System

Stephen Shapiro

Benjamin Franklin famously wrote, in the context of his doubts about the durability of the new American constitution, that only two things were certain – death and taxes. Gothic, Horror, and the Weird's (GoHoW) use of the undead would disagree about the inevitability of both.[1] But while tales and images of the undead convey the possibility of evading mortality's limits and the state's policing, they do have a history and terrain defined by the geography and chaotic rhythms of the capitalist world-system. A world-cultural approach argues that a system seeking the endless accumulation of profit began to coalesce as a self-defining arena in Mediterranean Europe by the fifteenth century.[2] While this set of new social relations was initially limited to a small fraction of the world, today it encompasses nearly the globe; and even if there exist a few remaining pockets beyond its influence, its effects damage the entire planet. The study of the capitalist world-system's search for profit by extending its interests far beyond its historical origin and delving deeper into more crevices of everyday life has plenty of explanatory value to offer world-gothic studies and its registrations of the undead.

World-gothic as a project (where the hyphen indicates a world-systems relational perspective) is not meant to simply expand our horizon, by studying gothic that arises beyond the culture industries of the United States and Europe; it looks to redraw the terms and frames of reference used. A world-gothic approach does not simply seek to highlight non-American-European productions within already existing Eurocentric literary categories, lineages of influence, and definition by generic traits. World-gothic looks instead to change our perspective of how we understand gothic, even for those works already long studied and taught.

The undead is a category that includes, but is not limited to, reanimated flesh (like Frankenstein's creature, zombies, and mummies), and subjects transformed through bodily alteration (like vampires or spirits inhabiting human bodies through telepathic domination, temporal transubstantiation, or extraterrestrial alien management). The undead indicates the presence of *abformation*, a deviation from the expected transition from life to death, a blockage of the expected metamorphosis from an organic state to its mortal end. In this sense, the undead often paradoxically convey the possible liberation from physical and mental decay, even while removing death's promise to finally release us from human pain. The contradictory feelings of repulsion and attraction to the undead convey similar ones about existing within a capitalist system that we may despise, but at whose possible removal we also quiver, since we have, nonetheless, become accustomed to the knowability of its procedures.

Here, Robin Wood's influential claim that horror is fear of the Other seems applicable, especially when Otherness is not entirely external, but also comes with a warped mirror that our own bodies could have an entirely different appearance than expected.[3] While Wood's definition seems commonsensical, it remains too general to explain why the undead appear in tales and imagery more in certain times and places than others. Here, a world-systems approach may better explain the undead's appearance, since figurations of the undead tend to mainly emerge at times and spaces of crisis for centrist liberalism, its promises of equality and faith in upwards, linear development, and in spaces that are charged by the tension between elites and the groups exploited or dominated within capitalism.

World-systems perspectives are chiefly associated with work by Immanuel Wallerstein, who argues that the main framework for social and cultural studies should not be the self-contained nation-state (an idea used in titles like *English* Gothic, *American* Gothic, etc.) or even area studies (such as *African* Gothic), but a world-system created by a capitalist geography formed by a core region, a zemiperiphery (conventionally called semiperiphery, but spelled this way for reasons explained in what follows), and peripheries. The core is not a single nation-state, but a group of states that respects each other's sovereignty over a territory and population, even as they compete against one another for advantage as producers of finished goods and managers of complex commodity chains. The peripheries are regions with weak or corrupt states that are forced to sell the labour of their peoples or their natural resources cheaply to the core, often to the nation that had previously colonised them. The zemiperipheries are the buffering regions 'in-between' the core and the peripheries that contain aspects of both and can potentially move 'upwards' or 'downwards' in the core-periphery hierarchy. This brief and traditional definition has been recently revised to claim that the zemiperipheries not only act as the realm of vertical communication (from core to periphery), but also horizontally, linking zemiperipheries to each other (and to capture this transversality, the semiperiphery is now called zemiperiphery). As the zemiperipheries form their own channel, it is possible for one zemiperiphery to dilute pressures between one core-nation and the peripheries, by circulating these tensions through the network of other zemiperipheries.[4] A world-systems argument about the transmission of social tensions through the zemiperipheries thus sees world-gothic as mainly appearing from the zemiperipheries, which include both extramural territories and interior zemiperipheral zones within core states, since these are the zones where social confrontation is often, but not solely, seen, experienced, and, in turn, circulated. Gothic tensions often seem inexplicable only because their origins extend beyond the familiar recognition of some readers, who only look at culture from within an official national framework and thus ignore the zemiperipheries and their links to the peripheries.

World-gothic has an international appeal for audiences who would not otherwise watch or read texts in translation because it arises at moments when the shape of global power relations is changing in ways that force the zemiperipheries to carry extra burdens in maintaining the overall existence of the capitalist world-system. The current flow of global rearrangements offers one explanation for why we are now speaking about world-gothic. In one sense, the digitisation of culture, including the ease of file-sharing and machine translation of text and subtitles, has made access to internationally produced gothic far easier than it would have been just a short time ago. Yet technological facilitation of cultural transfers does not automatically create consumer interest. The relatively new and increasingly wider audience for world-gothic comes about because the contemporary moment is experiencing large-scale changes in the global order (including climate catastrophe). Put less generously, our initial interest in world-gothic comes less from curiosity about other cultures, and more as a means of understanding how the world we live in is now undergoing unexpected changes.

In this way, world-gothic not only has a place – the zemiperiphery – it also has a time when heightened tensions make the undead arise. The social geographies of capitalist exploitation and extractive coercion construct time frames of longer and shorter rhythms and trends: the two most pertinent are the 'long spirals' (secular trends, long durations) of 150–250 years, and the Kondratieff waves (K-waves) of between forty and sixty years (named after their proponent, the Soviet economist Nikolai Kondratieff).[5] To properly understand why world-gothic becomes more pronounced at certain times, the distinction between periodisation and periodicity matters. Periodisation is the commonly known idea that time can be separated into relatively distinctive, named phases, such as Romanticism, the nineteenth century, and so on. The concept of periodisation relies on notions of homogeneity so that each phase is considered as clearly dominated by a set of attitudinal elements, cultural forms, or technical-industrial processes. Additionally, the idea of periodisation relies on a belief in major social replacement, as it suggests that one phase can largely differ from another through totalising breaks from the past. Versions of periodisation helped support the idea that leading culture and society emerge from the 'West', or core nation-states, to then be copied elsewhere by the non-European zemiperipheries and peripheries. As a category, periodisation usually has conservative and Eurocentric tendencies, but even otherwise oppositional figures, like Marx, used periodisation schemes to characterise the emergence and territorial expansion of capitalism.

On the other hand, Marx also argued that capitalism's drive for endless accumulation created recurring cycles of investment and reinvestment, what he called the reproduction of capital. The presence of these cycles thus suggests that time is also repetitive in ways that allows for a similarity of operations or events to recur, a process he called periodicity. In this sense, the end of one noteworthy place generates something more akin to repetition, rather than replacement. Periodicity is drawn less as an upwards or downwards line than as a spiral.[6] The two perspectives of periodisation and periodicity are not exclusive, since they can be combined to produce a historical narrative that acknowledges large-scale change, while also recognising patterns that endure even after periodising crises. Long spirals can help to show how they work together, in a way that is particularly useful for the study of world-gothic: secular trends contain multiple, nested K-waves of boom-and-bust phases that seek to resolve tensions so that capital processes can be renewed and continue over time. But over several K-waves, these attempted fixes no longer work well and their failure leads to an overall end of a long spiral. In this way, recurring K-waves create both periodised changes as well as periodic regenerations.[7]

The Capitalist World-System's Emergence Sets the Stage for Gothic

This somewhat abstract description is better understood with a historical example. Immanuel Wallerstein argued that there have been two secular trends (long spirals) within historical capitalism.[8] The first began loosely around the end of the fifteenth century as modern-looking capitalism began to appear, first in the Italian city-states, like Venice and Genoa (or places linked to them like Istanbul/Constantinople), and then with the rise of the Spanish (and to a lesser degree, the Portuguese) empires. European land-owning aristocrats faced a series of interlocking crises around the mid fourteenth century as epidemiological and social crises intersected with one another to end the forms of social organisation that arose after the collapse and break-up of the Roman empire, a phase sometimes called feudalism.[9] In a signal event, the onset of the Black Death, which eventually reduced Europe's population by about a third, sped social unravelling. The countryside population ('peasants') saw that their reduced numbers gave them greater leverage against nobles, who needed their labour, and allowed them to demand that less of their work and produce be forcibly redistributed upwards to the local lord. With their ability to garner wealth at risk, the aristocrats began to look for a replacement source of income through a series of civil wars against one another. With the nobility busy fighting over land and wealth, they, in turn, sent less money upwards to their weak monarchs and the Roman Catholic Church, which also fell into crises. Due to the increase in peasant rebellion and inter-aristocratic conflicts, a group of landed elites began to compromise and seek alliance with some of their antagonists, such as urban merchants, and from this coalition came a new social order, one based less on domestic land control and more on labour exploitation. Today, we often see these complex processes – nowhere simple or without resistance – as initiating the rise of capitalism as a post-feudal system.

Emergent capitalism in Europe depended on overseas imperialism to finance sovereign coffers. Conquistador capitalism saw the emergence of the first racialising codifications of civilised/barbarism that differed from pre-capitalist forms of xenophobia as racialising difference became the means to legitimise profiteering exploitation with the blessing of religious authorities. By the last quarter of the eighteenth century, the internal pressures of social contradictions built up over several K-waves had grown too great, and a periodising rupture occurred with the revolutions in France, America, and Haiti, rebellions in Egypt and Ireland, and uprisings by Indigenous peoples in South America.[10] Wallerstein argues that two larger social truths came to be acknowledged because of these changes. The first was that social transformation would from now on be a constant, a realisation that finally put an end to the contradictory dreams of restoring a pre-capitalist Holy Roman Empire alongside new capitalist practices. The second realisation was that power would continually ebb from the shock and awe of the monarch and (Catholic) Church to forms of popular sovereignty and democracy.

Three overall political 'metastrategies' developed in response to these new truths.[11] The first to emerge in the 1790s was conservatism. Conservatives sought to prevent democratic-driven change as much as possible, often by enlisting state police and legislation. Their vision of society was one organised by small groups of elites, through a language of ethno-racialised, organic (unchanging) community and deference to the received opinions of already established elites and religion. One response was radicalism (socialism/Marxism), which emerged through the 1840s. Radicals embraced the two social truths and sought to accelerate their expansion through events of abrupt and total change (revolution). Their preferred unit of society was not the small group, but the mass collective, and rather than rely on state legislation, they sought to organise activist resistance.

In between conservatives and radicals, both in terms of historical emergence and position, were centrist liberals. Liberals acknowledged the inevitability of the two truths, but sought to moderate their tempo, lest it erupt into the explosive transformations that radicals sought. Liberals regulated the pace of change through a gradual enlargement of the right to vote, as an act of self-representation, and adoption of some of the language of the other approaches, like supporting an idealised national identity and creating forms of limited social welfare redistribution. This included state-sponsored education, housing, health care, and support for the elderly and very young. Rather than the small group or mass collective, liberals saw the individual as the main unit of society. Unlike conservative use of legislation or radicals' creation of activist organisations, liberals governed through 'theory'. They reconfigured the university away from the early modern model that only had the four faculties (Law, Medicine, Theology, and the Arts) into one divided by disciplines (economics, political science, etc.) that would be used to credentialise meritocratic individuals who would be authorised to make decisions about social organisation. Liberalism reshaped the kinds of knowledge that were produced in universities as a means of justifying their own right to rule instead of the 'uneducated' nobility or popular masses. These disciplines often relied on constructing binarised identities (like white/Black, male/female, culture/nature, normal/abnormal, and so on) used to legitimise social science-type laws of civilisational development, market competition, and state domestic and international policing.

Of these three ideologies, liberalism became the most successful and dominant, especially as its claims for developmental progress rhymed with a long phase of technological and medical advances. One of liberalism's most successful cultural technologies in maintaining the constructed borderlines between the subjectivity of active citizenship and the social death of those who were treated as exchangeable objects (of study, rule, and exploitation) was the transformation of long-form fiction into the category of the novel.

The rise of the category of 'the novel' as the default term for long-form literary prose suited liberalism as it helped manage one key binary division between the public and private spheres. On the one hand, Benedict Anderson showed that the novel helped consolidate the national imaginary by training readers into the belief that reading novels constituted participation in a linguistic and territorial nation. In this way, novels came to be categorised primarily as documents of national identity, even more than language.[12] Even today, we tend to overwhelmingly approach novels through signatures of national identity. On the other hand, as Lukács argued, the novel helped define privateness and interiority, and illustrated to its readers how they should feel and interact with other (liberal) subjects, as well as how to develop slowly into a flourished state of active citizenship, rather than its reverse of social death, through claims of a florid emotional life.[13] The novel's yoking together of these dual purposes meant that at times of capitalist crisis, the novel could be relied on to help maintain systemic continuity. Even ostensibly radical authors could be enrolled in the preservation of capitalism when they accepted the structural implications and limits inherent in the category of the novel.

The rise of the liberal novel in the second long spiral, beginning in the late eighteenth century, is necessary as a first step to understanding the undead. For the novel's abjected Other were all those fictions that did not function formally like novels, partly because they devoted themselves less to individual, rather than collective, concern, and did not seek to maintain an expert separation and upholding of the binary oppositions. These non-novelistic texts were consigned to low status as sub-literary. This was, in short, all 'genre' fiction, like gothic, horror, science fiction, detective fiction, romance, and so on. Yet these genres reveal a sort of truth about the cultural organisation of the world-system's second long spiral. For example, Jeffrey Andrew Weinstock has argued that the three main forms of sensational fiction are spectrality, monstrosity, and apocalypse.[14] This trinity can be used as a way of distinguishing between gothic, horror, and weird fiction, as seen in Table 1.1.

Table 1.1 *Cultural scheme of the second long spiral*

Conservatism	Liberalism	Radicalism
Small group	Individual	Mass collective
Nostalgia	Rationality	Fraternity, liberty, equality
State legislation	Binary theories and academic disciplines	Revolution
Gothic	Horror	Weird
Spectrality	Monstrosity	Apocalypse
Thematic	Theoretical	Transformative

Hence, the object of 'gothic' is primarily the theme of conservatism's resistance to modernity, and spectrality's ghostliness or haunting often explores not simply justice frustrated, but justice blocked by the continuing undertow of conservative forces and aristocratic/Church residues. This is not to say that gothic's cultural politics are always or simply conservative or reactionary (though they often might be), but that the motivating project of their narratives is directed to conservatism's legacy. In this scheme, the object of 'the weird' is radicalism's notion of large-scale, immediate change at the level of the social collective.

The object of horror is centrist liberalism's reliance on the individual and its paradoxical relationship to simultaneously promulgating 'human rights' as grounded in the corporeal (rather than 'natural rights' that were increasingly conceptualised as a conservative ideal associated with landed elites), while also advancing the idea that disembodied rationality was the hallmark of liberalism's disinterest and move away from blood lineage. Liberalism's tension between human rights and disembodied reason created its reverse: the bleeding and traumatised body and the monster whose bodily excesses staged their exclusions from society. In this way, objects of social death (women, non-whites, proletarians) are marked as grotesque specifically because of their embodied features. The 'monster', be it of teratological shape or mentality (and these tales often conflate the two), usually appears when liberalism's boundary lines begin to be challenged, especially in the chaotic crossover between K-waves. Horror, thus, appears more in those moments and spaces where liberalism's regulation of society is under threat.

This scheme is a constellation, not a structure. Its use lies best as a touchstone or perspective, rather than as a set of rigid, impermeable categories. Instead of binary (or tertiary) differences, it is better to consider the scheme as one of binomial (or trinomial) distributions, where elements of one column can often contain aspects of the others. Yet the scheme described alone does allow for a greater historical and regional particularity than has often been the case in GoHoW studies. A truism from gothic studies is that gothic emerges as the dark twin of the Enlightenment. This claim is descriptively apt, but it misses the social context, where it is less an abstract category – 'the Enlightenment' – that is an actor, and more 'the Enlightenment' as a category, deployed to advance the social strategies of a class (the insurgent bourgeoisie) that deployed the rhetoric of rationality as a means of legitimising their own replacement of the spectacular displays of courtly and (Catholic) cathedral property. Catholic rituals are often invoked in gothic tales because of sectarian, Protestant resistance to the spectral remnants of the pre-bourgeois social order of things.

Reading World-Gothic

Horror can therefore be read as a key index to the time and place where the matrix of liberal centrism is under duress. The form of horror differs depending on where the challenge comes from (i.e., women's rights in one time and place, non-white concerns in another), even while it is difficult to neatly separate the cause of the pressure as all social elements are entangled in the world-system. If horror tends to appear in the zemiperipheral places and periodic/periodising crossovers, then the undead, as one of the main figures of horror's abformation, stands as a register of liberalism's broken promises.

The model proposed thus far helps provide a set of tools to consider world-gothic, even when it becomes more complex as we move beyond the European core to those regions formerly colonised by European imperial powers, where the ghosts of the past are not only the European aristocracy, but also the liberal managers of civilisational imperialism. To help approach world-gothic then, two other features are worth mentioning in preparing an approach to the undead's world-system. The first is the trinity of the thematic, theoretical (or analytical), and the transformative.[15] Works can be described as thematic when they often register a social concern without any direction or intent. This functions *symptomatically* by acknowledging that there are current issues of concern and attention. Often these themes appear early in a work's expository phase before the 'portal' moment, when the narrative or characters move from one space to another in ways that indicate the transfer from the mundane to the supernatural.

At other times, a work may function more theoretically or critically to *diagnose* the cause or context for issues of thematic concern. Frequently, these diagnostic elements can be in the middle of a text and are organised around a *pivot*: a scene that has actions or events that break prior expectations to force new reflections or realisations. Finally, there is the *transformative*, which seeks to change the alliances or affiliations of the audience, after they have consumed the cultural object through reading, viewing, listening, and so on. The transformative generates fan worlds of cosplay, fan fiction, and re-enactments. Often these emerge in the spaces of fragile endings, the 'double-tap' moments when resolution seems to have been achieved, but is then seen as still provisional or temporary.

This scheme should not be seen as exclusive or hierarchical. No work is simply or homogenously thematic, theoretical, or transformative. Rather, every cultural object combines aspects of all three, so that it is the relative ratios that may characterise its overall shape. Often theoretical material is thwarted from continuing due to assumed audience hostility to its message. An important feature, however, is that as liberal centrism created the university as its material apparatus, this too resulted in valorising 'the critical' or 'theoretical' as the ideal. Furthermore, literary, graphic, and televisual studies have developed complex vocabularies of formal characteristics that can facilitate the study and celebration of works deemed to be critical. Works that are felt to be uncritical have been traditionally consigned as 'generic' and lacking individuality. Yet to be 'un-critical' does not mean a work is unworthy of study or lacking in social purpose. Indeed, *generic* works often combine and convey themselves as thematic/transformational, in order to evade the category of the liberal individual and direct themselves to a more collectivised audience. The challenge for GoHoW beyond Eurocentrism is to forge a language for discussions of the thematic/transformative in post-liberal ways.

All of these variations help to give a sense of how we might approach the undead and the problem of speech. If Abrahamic religions tell the origin of humanity as the divine's breath into matter, then the undead often are represented as the breathless copies of the human. Yet breathlessness can be configured in different ways, ranging from the mainly thematic to the critical (where it might recite Black Lives Matter's use of 'I can't breathe' to critique the police) to the transformative. A second aspect which may help us to craft a language for the thematic/transformative lies with the possibility of dissolving the boundary line between the genres and seeing them as functioning in complementary ways. Considering science fiction, Steven Shaviro writes that 'sometimes sf *extrapolates*; it pushes existing conditions to their logical extremes. Sometimes sf *speculates*: it uncovers incipient or hidden potentials ... and imagines the differences their unfolding might make for the ways we live our lives. Still other times, it *fabulates*: it imagines new sorts of stories, ones that do not merely replicate tired, overfamiliar narratives, or fit into our customary patterns'.[16] Shaviro's comments on science fiction also pertain to gothic, horror, and the undead, as they variously register the world-systemic times and places these forms inhabit. GoHoW need not only respond to trauma; it can also function in a more utopian fashion.

Examples of World-Gothic

With all of the preceding in mind, let us consider some works of world-gothic in the Caribbean, Africa, and the Americas, even as we are mindful of the limits to these groupings from area studies. It is common to say that the zombie is the first non-European monster (unlike the vampire or werewolf) to become a global figure. In some ways this is true, but less so than initially considered, as the zombie combines a zemiperipheral refiguring of peripheral African notions of a spirit from the body, and the wageless conditions of Caribbean slavery as continually shaped by the European core.

In this light, Sylvia Wynter argues that traditional Marxist analyses that focus on the exploited wage labourer poorly recognise the conditions of the enslaved, as well as the interconnection between European industrialism and plantation monocrop extraction.[17] Marx's contribution to the understanding of the profitable commodity was the insight that it is formed by the combination of waged labour and unpaid labour-time. A slave's labour is difficult to integrate within this model, given that slaves are purchased as a whole, rather than given wages for time segments of work. Wynter suggests that if Marx described capital as the metamorphosis of money into commodities meant to generate money, and a slave's non-waged labour is difficult to discern in the commodity, then slavery within the capitalist world-system is best approached from another vantage point – as aspects of the *money-form*, where currency is used as a numerical marker to help the exchange of commodities. For this reason, Wynter argues that the concept of alienation is poorly suited to those who could not be estranged from their subjectivity, since the conditions of racial slavery did not grant them any subjectivity at all. Instead, they stand as figures of *financial metamorphosis*: the transfer of money for commodities. When the flow of the metamorphosis of commodities and money, and back again, is blocked, it creates a crisis of abformation within the capitalist world-system. This tension becomes materialised when liberalism's promise of enfranchisement is likewise broken in ways that may explain the figures of zombies arising.

Wynter continues to explain that the enslaved on the Caribbean plantation lost more than mere physical contact with their African homelands, as a result of hunger for coerced labour for the capitalist monocrop farming of sugar cane; they often lost the medium for their spiritual connections as well. A plantation owner sees land only for what it might generate in profitable commodities (cotton, sugar, etc.). Land functions in a radically different way in African cosmography. Within the belief systems of the captured Africans, a grave is not considered as the barrier between living individuality and dead matter but is rather a medium for the deceased to become a spirit among one's ancestors, who have themselves turned into divine spirits after death. African funeral practices confirm a process of entering into one's ancestral community, not, as they do in Europe, a ritual marking the end of membership in the community. The figure of the zombie thus emerges from the plantation's commodification of earth, which denies its communal function and its disruption of death's connections.

However, rather than the zombie being an immediate response to slavery, it seems to consolidate as a figure of frustration in Haiti at the failure of liberal emancipation to endure past the American military occupation of 1915–34. After the Haitian Revolution in the 1790s, the island eventually abandoned sugar cane production in large-scale plantations for small farm subsistence agriculture. When the sugar industry returned in the late nineteenth century, often backed by capitalist imperialist companies, tales of zombie creation re-emerged. In this sense, the zombie responds less to the legacy of Atlantic slavery than moments of the returned implementation of the capitalist world-system's dictates.[18]

One complaint about the proliferation of the zombie beyond the Caribbean, whether it is through Hollywood or East Asian films, is that non-Caribbean zombies stand as acts of cultural appropriation. Yet the zombie can function as a viable language throughout the zemiperipheral network whenever and wherever the liberal promise of citizen enfranchisement remains blocked. It was in this sense that decolonial critic Albert Memmi called the Algerian youth in Paris 'zombies', as they were displaced from both their ethnic homelands and the imperial centre in ways that made them spiritually and socially listless and wandering through that zemiperipheral space, the ghetto.[19]

A similar disquiet about failed liberalism as driving the zombie is captured in *Zombi Child* (2019). This film intersperses the depiction of Clairvius Narcisse, who claims to have escaped from being zombified and made to work in the sugarcane fields in the 1960s, with a contemporary narrative about a character meant to be his granddaughter, a young Black Haitian woman in an elite French private school for the female children of those who have meritoriously served the Republic. Depicting a woman caught between the French Republic's mythology of disembodied citizenship, which does not officially recognise the presence of racial difference, and her felt continuing connection to Haiti's history of Black revolution, the film abjures the paraphernalia of jump scares and gore to display a seemingly quiet school without the generic bullying by mean girls. Yet the placid air of amnesia surrounding meritocracy based on past imperialism cannot contain frustration about the lack of ostensible equality amidst structural racism and the continuation of white privilege that still assumes the peoples of France's former colonies are expendable in order to satisfy the core's consumer pleasures.

The theme of enfranchisement denied is also presented in *Talk to Me* (2022).[20] The film depicts a teenage woman of Australian aboriginal background who is functionally adopted within the embrace of a white family. Yet after communication with the dead goes wrong and the white biological son becomes possessed by demons, the young aboriginal woman is cut off from the family's circle. In the end, order is restored only as she allows herself to be sacrificed as a victim. Here the film conveys a sense of decolonial frustration that the promises of contemporary equality remain unfulfilled and the settler colonial erasure of Indigenous communities continues apace, even in the contemporary moment.

Some African horror acknowledges the legacy of slavery and imperialism, but it also sees horror as providing an alternative to this past. *Atlantique* (*Atlantics*) (2019) is a tale of spirit possession set in contemporary Dakar.[21] The film can be read as testing the conservative–liberal–radical spectrum outside of Europe in a continent currently experiencing rapid demographic growth.[22] The movie is organised around a pentangle of social forces: the household of patriarchal Islam; a neoliberal building site of labour exploitation; a nightclub run by women; the state apparatus of an investigative police unit; and the sea that swallows up young men seeking to travel without papers to Spain. The film begins with construction workers demanding owed wages at a building site. Unsuccessful in this struggle, the men gather at a club where women, like Ada, meet their beloved, in her case, Souleiman. Yet the men, upon realising they will never receive their back wages, unexpectedly decide to hazard a boat crossing to Spain, a journey that ends in their being drowned. While the undertow of the sea is the refugee crisis, the wake of Atlantic slavery also lurks in the background. The film then follows Ada's attempt to break free from the male control of her Islamic father and an arranged marriage that only cushions traditional male control over women with gifts of the West's new technology. After a mysterious fire in the intended husband's bed, a young, promising detective, as representative of the liberal, modern state, begins to investigate. The film's resolution occurs as the dead men's spirits inhabit the bodies of the club's women, who successfully demand that the construction site's owner pay the back wages and provide a burial for the men. Souleiman, however, inhabits the police detective's body for a night so that Ada can consummate the relationship.

Here horror provides a mechanism for radical emancipation as it resists both conservatism's attempt to preserve the past, since the past is corrupted, while also rejecting liberalism's celebration of the meritocratic expertise of the state-credentialised individual, since the policeman is shown to be incapable of analytically controlling events. Folklore is deployed not in a backwards-looking search for authenticity, but as a means of imagining the living conditions of a new Africa that may eventually be able to exist without the deadly pull of Europe and without denying women (collective) agency.

Saloum (2021), like *Atlantique*, displays no significant white characters.[23] The film involves a revenge horror tale of a group of mercenaries, experienced in multiple African civil wars, who are paid to rescue a Mexican drug lord from a coup d'état in Guinea-Bissau. A petrol leak in their escape airplane forces the band to land unexpectedly in Senegal where one member of the group leads them to a village near the Saloum delta. The damage to the plane and the retreat to the village is later revealed as sabotage, a decoy for the leader to take revenge on the man who had forcibly conscripted him as a child soldier. Yet justice backfires, as the warlord has been holding back supernatural swarms associated with the curse of an ancient king. While some of the group eventually escape, the former child soldier does not. Since the escape occurs by covering the ears, *Saloum* suggests that the screams of past African trauma need to be given less airtime and the solution to the legacy of civil war and traumatic conflict among Africans is to break the cycle of revenge. The dead are undead only because there has not been a desire to move forward beyond the internecine conflicts that are a result of incomplete decolonisation. In both films, horror's purpose is to highlight trauma so that it can be openly stored away for the living to go forward.

Anglophone horror is, likewise, increasingly focussed on reckoning with the violence of slavery and imperialism, but often in ways that emphasise inter-ethnic coalition-building. Televisual horror like *The Terror* (2018–), *Lovecraft Country* (2020), *True Detective: Night Country* (2024), and *Penny Dreadful: City of Angels* (2020) all depict the confrontation with white imperialism that becomes resolved by differently racialised groups coming together to invoke and then contain demons. The overall theme of these television shows is that a binary understanding of race is part of the problem, and a new multicultural society needs to be established.

In this way, the new horror seems to reject the individualism of the 'Last Girl' slasher films of the 1980s and 90s. Carol Clover's *Men, Women, and Chainsaws* (1992) gave a name to the figure of the female character who survives bodily trauma and murderous pursuit to take revenge on their assailant: the 'Final Girl.' Films like *Halloween* (1978) can be seen as a feminised version of the Western genre, entries of which often tell the pursuit of revenge through a racialised landscape of Native American encounters. The Final Girl films lack the Western's confidence in American manifest destiny and telegraph the rise of conservative, white anxieties about the onset of a majority non-white United States through their narratives about the need to protect the white suburban home from murderous pursuit by a figure that seems like the undead, as impossible to kill, and whose motives often seem inexplicable. Slasher films thus convey fears of racial desegregation, which is not explicitly mentioned, but only because white privilege is taken for granted. The slasher films are both conservative and liberal in that they seem to both thematise the rise of feminist demands for equality, even if they also seem to encourage audiences to take perverse pleasure in women's humiliation, and suggest that a community based on whiteness can now be safeguarded only by ultimately allowing women access to vigilantism previously felt to be a prerogative of the cowboy male police and military.

Contemporary American horror thus often responds to the past's racisms by arguing in favour of ethnic empowerment. Today we see the Latinxification of American GoHoW as familiar tales are reset with Mexican elements. The Netflix series *Wednesday* turns the previously archetypal New England Addams family (the name echoing the Massachusetts family that provided two presidents) into a largely Latinx one, with a cast led by Puerto Rican Jenna Ortega. *What We Do in the Shadows* similarly presents the Dutch Van Helsing's line as now carried by a Mexican family, with the vampire killer Guillermo de la Cruz (Javier Guillén) caught between a family mission to slay vampires and a desire to serve as one's familiar. The FX series' comedy rests on the tensions of an American ethnic identity torn between desires for inclusion in a time of renewed hostility to ethnic immigrants, and desire to be acknowledged as actually the better and more skilled member of the United States. Similarly, the *Scream* franchise, which rose through its postmodern explicit naming of the structural rules of a slasher film, was saved from boredom by handing its reins over to Ortega and Melissa Barrera.

The horror of the USA functions as a way for Americans to see their future as part of the Americas, rather than as exceptional or distinct from other nations on the continents. This question of incorporation within the core is carried with a slightly different emphasis in recent Central and South American GoHoW, which, like African GoHoW, combines a respect for the past (Indigenous) folklore, but also sees it as a tool to be renovated for the future. Yet because the Americas have a legacy of revolutionary upheaval and repression longer even than Africa's, and greater proximity to 'El Norte' (the USA), Central and South American contemporary tales of the undead also respond to their own prior cultural efforts.

Silvia Moreno-Garcia's *Mexican Gothic* (2020) ultimately asks the question of whether Anglo-European gothic can survive only by allowing for a more diverse array of producers and consumers.[24] The novel is the story of a Mexican comprador bourgeois woman, Noemí Taboiada, who wants to resist the gendered expectations of marriage, and is thus offered a deal by her father: if she goes to a remote mining region to investigate some worrying mail sent from her cousin, she will be granted the right to go to university. Travelling to a remote mansion run by the English mining quasi-aristocrat, Howard Doyle, to make contact with her cousin, Noemí falls into a trap as Howard, empowered by sentient fungi, feels that the family line needs reinvigorating with non-European blood and wants to shift into her body. Through help from a loose network of an Indigenous woman and the spirit of a previously killed woman, Noemi escapes with her cousin and the sole decent male member of the Doyles, implying her future marriage. On the one hand, *Mexican Gothic* is self-consciously invested within the lineage of prior Eurocentric work, as the book knowingly recalls Charlotte Brontë's *Jane Eyre*, Charlotte Perkins Gilman's *The Yellow Wallpaper*, and Shirley Jackson's *The Haunting of Hill House*. On the other hand, the villain's name – Howard – as well as the topoi of intelligent fungi and weird transubstantiation, indicate the contemporary influence of the racist author Howard Philips (H.P.) Lovecraft as a force to be overcome.

Mexican Gothic is set in the silver-mining region of Mexico, but it appears to argue that the violent legacy of extraction and conquistador capitalism can be countered by mining the narrative resources of the core for the benefit of those in the zemiperiphery. But doing so seems to be a mechanism for female-authored Mexican and South American horror, like that by Moreno-Garcia and Mariana Enriquez, to critique the male-defined South American magical realism, exemplified by Gabriel García Márquez's *One Hundred Years of Solitude* (1967). The horror by women suggests that the male writers of the magical realism boom were too invested in the pursuit of liberal acclaim, especially by encoding depictions of core capitalist violence (like the United Fruit massacre that lies at the heart of Márquez's novel) within wondrously wrought prose and surrealist fantasy description, in order to gain access to the North American canon. A truer form for the content of imperial violence is *horror*, a medium that does not submerge violence within the marvellous and fantasy, but treats violence as violence, amplifying it only to ensure some clear recognition of historical trauma.

The future of the undead and world-gothic rests with the realisation that the long spiral of liberal centrism's dominance seems to have come to a juddering end, and with it, the regularities emerging out of conservatism's ghosts, liberalism's monsters, and radicalism's apocalypse. Chief among the moves of this still-new and emerging moment is the rejection of liberalism's claims to be objective and neutral, and a willingness to disallow liberalism the right to define others as monstrous. Increasingly, it is liberalism itself that is seen as monstrous, while the monster seems utopian. Consider the zombie: today the zombie seems a desirable identity, since zombies are free from bullying over body shape or clothing style, free from the humiliations placed on the less-abled or aged, and free from neoliberal precarity as liberated from the anxiety over wages. Zombies also have time to simply hang out in non-purposeful ways with each other, in the kind of non-hierarchal practice for which hippies used to be mocked. World-gothic will follow this lead less by being anti-Eurocentric, than by rejecting the categories that capitalist nations used to self-create themselves. Even in the West, Generation Alpha's fascination with horror registers their lack of confidence in the false dreams of liberal progress. World-gothic means not only gothic from around the world, but, mainly, gothic that moves beyond the capitalist world-system.

Notes

1. Stephen Shapiro, 'The World-System of Global Gothic, Horror, and the Weird', in R. Duncan (ed.), *The Edinburgh Companion to Globalgothic*, Edinburgh, Edinburgh University Press, 2023, 38–52.
2. Immanuel Wallerstein, *Historical Capitalism: With Capitalist Civilization*, London, Verso, 1983; Immanuel Wallerstein, *World-Systems Analysis: An Introduction*, Durham, Duke University Press, 2004.
3. Robin Wood, *Robin Wood on the Horror Film: Collected Essays and Reviews*, ed. B. Grant, Detroit, Wayne State University Press, 2018.
4. Stephen Shapiro, 'Zemiperiphery Matters: Immigration, Culture, and the Capitalist World-System', in F. Jacob (ed.), *Wallerstein 2.0: Thinking and Applying World-Systems Theory in the 21st Century*, Bielefeld, Transcript Press, 2023, 49–71.
5. Stephen Shapiro, 'The Weird's World-System: The Long Spiral and Literary-Cultural Studies', *Paradoxa*, 28 (2016), 256–77.
6. Karl Marx, *Capital: Volume 1*, trans. B. Fowkes, London, Penguin, 1976, 786, 198.
7. Immanuel Wallerstein, 'Long Waves as Capitalist Process', *Review (Fernand Braudel Center)*, 7 (1984), 559–75.
8. Immanuel Wallerstein, *The Modern World-System IV: Centrist Liberalism Triumphant, 1789–1914*, Berkeley, University of California Press, 2011.
9. Immanuel Wallerstein, 'The West, Capitalism, and the Modern World-System', in G. Blue and T. Brooks (eds.), *China and Historical Capitalism: Genealogies of Sinological Knowledge*, Cambridge, Cambridge University Press, 1999, 10–56.
10. Immanuel Wallerstein. 'The End of What Modernity', in *After Liberalism*, New York, The New Press, 1995, 126–44.
11. Wallerstein, 'The End of What Modernity', 126–44.
12. Benedict Anderson, *Imagined Communities: Reflections on the Origin and Spread of Nationalism*, London, Verso, 1983.
13. Georg Lukács, *The Theory of the Novel: A Historico-Philosophical Essay on the Forms of Great Epic Literature*, trans. A. Bostock, Cambridge, The MIT Press, 1971, 89.
14. Jeffrey A. Weinstock, 'The Anthropocene', in J. D. Edwards, R. Graulund, and J. Höglund (eds.), *Dark Scenes from Damaged Earth: The Gothic Anthropocene*, Minneapolis, University of Minnesota Press, 2022, 7–25.
15. Stephen Shapiro, 'The Cultural Fix: Capital, Genre, and the Times of American Studies', in V. Dussol and J.-H. Coste (eds.), *The Fictions of American Capitalism: Working Fictions and the Economic Novel*, London, Palgrave, 2020, 89–108.
16. Steven Shaviro, 'Introduction', in *This Is Not a Science Fiction Textbook*, M. Bould and S. Shaviro (eds.), London, Goldsmiths Press, 2024, 8–9.
17. Sylvia Wynter, 'Black Metamorphosis: New Natives in a New World', unpublished manuscript (1970s) housed at the Schomburg Centre for Research in Black Culture, New York.

18. Kerstin Oloff, *Ecology of the Zombie: World-Culture and the Monstrous*, Liverpool, Liverpool University Press, 2023.
19. Albert Memmi, *Decolonization and the Decolonized*, trans. R. Bononno, Minneapolis, University of Minnesota Press, 2006, 119–20.
20. *Talk to Me*, dirs. D. Philippou and M. Philippou, Manhattan, A24, 2022.
21. *Atlantique (Atlantics)*, dir. Mati Diop, Los Gatos, Netflix, 2019.
22. Declan Walsh, 'The World Is Becoming More African', *The New York Times*, 28 October 2023, www.nytimes.com/interactive/2023/10/28/world/africa/africa-youth-population.html.
23. *Saloum*, dir. J. L. Herbulot. New York, IFC Films, 2021.
24. Silvia Moreno-García, *Mexican Gothic*, New York, Del Ray, 2021.

CHAPTER 2

Whiteness and the 'Western' Gothic Tradition
Rebecca Duncan and Johan Höglund

The introduction to this book notes how studies of the gothic over the past two decades have increasingly recognised gothic traditions outside of the canonical British strain, while at the same time tending to understand these as (sometimes very complex) reconfigurations of an initially European, and specifically British, form. The now fairly commonplace practice of referring to the gothic as a 'Western' literary tradition demonstrates this approach, often functioning as shorthand for a history in which gothic conventions are developed in Britain and Europe, and subsequently taken up and modulated across the settler nations (chiefly the United States, but also Canada, Australia, South Africa, and others). In this view, the 'Western gothic' is fundamentally linked to the publication of *The Castle of Otranto* in 1764, and to the ensuing emergence in Britain of a literary mode – represented by, for example, Matthew Lewis, Ann Radcliffe, William Beckford, and Mary Shelley – that would over time come to be identified as the gothic novel. At times, and especially when justifying gothic analysis beyond the so-called West, critics have officially recognised this body of texts as inaugurating the cultural form they study. Even when this connection is unspoken, however, gothic produced outside of the British context is typically perceived as a more or less provincial adaptation of originally British gothic tropes and conventions. In other words, the British type of gothic has remained a kind of invisible yet ubiquitous standard: the original dark sun around which all the other gothic satellites must inevitably orbit.

The concept of world-gothic outlined across this collection aims to provide a different perspective on the relationship between 'original' (British) gothic and the wider transregional body of monstrous narratives that are often understood primarily as hybridisations, interrogations, or derivatives of it. As the editors of the volume explain in the introduction, world-gothic can account for these invocations and adaptations of canonical gothic conventions; however, world-gothic also asks us to see the early

British gothic not chiefly as the wellspring of an aesthetic that would eventually become transnational, but rather as, from the outset, just one, local instance of a much wider and culturally more varied response to encounters with global capitalist modernity. This view challenges the assumption that industrialising Britain produced the first gothic forms, since situated cultural narratives of the monstrous have tended to proliferate on the regionally differentiated frontiers of capitalism over the last five centuries. This point is made formatively by Stephen Shapiro, who proposes that catachrestic responses to the enclosures in fifteenth-century England can be considered proto-gothic narratives.[1] Building on this and connected arguments, Duncan and Cumpsty's introduction to this collection illustrates world-gothic's capacity for decentring the established gothic origin story by linking monsters haunting the New World's industrial plantations to those appearing amid the later industrialisation of Britain – a process of capitalist modernisation that was itself significantly funded by enslavement in the Atlantic world. Many of the contributors to this collection examine the new connections and resonances that emerge with these insights, considering how the reconceptualisation of gothic as world-gothic accommodates a transregional range of narratives and texts, without demanding that these directly dialogue with, or even consciously depart from, 'original' gothic conventions. Complementing these interventions, the present chapter takes a world-gothic approach to this 'original' gothic of eighteenth- and nineteenth-century Britain, with a view to complicate its status as the invisible yardstick against which other instances of gothic are routinely, if tacitly, assessed.

Across the ensuing discussion, we suggest that one way to restore the British gothic tradition to its actual position of provinciality is to foreground its involvement in the production of historically specific racial identities, and categories of whiteness in particular. As we have begun to outline in the preceding discussion, a world-gothic perspective on the early British gothic underscores how this fiction appears in response to the local effects of a transoceanic capitalist relationship, emerging under conditions of capitalist modernisation financed by slavery across the preceding centuries. Taking up this insight, we emphasise that the world-systemic context in which British gothic manifests also provides the historical conditions under which modern categories of racial difference were being incubated and instrumentalised. As Simon Gikandi notes, 'the beginnings of modernity in the sixteenth century' are marked by a shift in the mode of conceptualising

Europe's relationship to peoples of disparate regional and cultural heritage:

> people considered to be other had been central to the emergence and consolidation of European identity since the Middle Ages, but in the modern period, alterity had become more than a simple inscription of the differences of other peoples, other cultures, other histories; it had now assumed a structural function: the designator of what enabled Europe ... to assume a position of cultural superiority and supremacy.[2]

From the vantage of decolonial and world-systems thinkers – as for Gikandi – this transformation develops with the rise of transregional capitalism. As Aníbal Quijano writes, 'the idea of race in its modern meaning does not have a known history before the colonization of America' which inaugurates the world-system. In this context, race was constructed 'to refer to the supposed differential biological structures' between European colonisers, Indigenous people, and – subsequently – enslaved Africans, in order to justify the stealing of land, genocide, and extreme exploitation.[3] Building on this and related arguments, this chapter examines how eighteenth- and nineteenth-century British gothic forms encode the weird and alienating effects of a local world repeatedly transformed by capitalist modernisation, while at the same time bearing witness to the processes of race-making through which the wider system of capitalism operates.

A number of scholars have observed that early British gothic invokes colonial discourses of race to produce its figures of threat.[4] Yet to be fully examined, however, is the possibility that, in harnessing the racial infrastructure of a capitalist world-system centred on Europe, these gothic fictions also make visible the shifting discursive technologies through which forms of European – and specifically British – identity become inseparable from whiteness: a modern racial category that emerges in counterpoint to the identification of various 'others', who – also understood through the prism of race – are positioned as not only different, but structurally subordinate, and thus as exploitable or disposable. Writing of the eighteenth century, Gikandi names this process 'white self-fashioning',[5] and, as we will demonstrate, gothic is a form to which it bears an intimate relation: if modern conceptions of race help to produce the monsters of the British gothic imaginary, then these colonial images of otherness also describe the negative space within which the protean and lethal racial category of whiteness appears.

Taking this perspective on the early British gothic is generative because, as Richard Dyer argues in his germinal *White* (1997), whiteness tends to be characterised by its 'invisibility ... as a racial position in white (which is to

2 Whiteness and the 'Western' Gothic Tradition

say dominant) discourse'. Like all 'prevailing norms', Manuela Boatcă affirms, whiteness often operates through 'unmarked categories':[6] central to its power is precisely its capacity for self-erasure, its location as the unspoken standard against which other identities are calibrated. Positioning the canonical British gothic in its world-historical contexts helps to *re*-mark the categories of whiteness that this form is instrumental in constructing. At the same time, this critical move re-territorialises – provincialises – British gothic conventions, by embedding them within the located, socio-economic, and cultural conditions to which they respond. Accordingly, we begin the following analyses in the late eighteenth century, with the inception of the gothic in a Britain awash with commodities and cash – the spoils of enslavement in the Atlantic world. After examining Walpole's *Otranto* and William Beckford's *Vathek* (1786) in this context, we turn to the early nineteenth century, and Mary Shelley's *Frankenstein* (1818): a novel that appears in the wake of slave-led revolution and fraught debates over abolition on the one hand, and amid accelerating industrialisation in Britain and concomitant industrial action on the other. In a final section, we consider the marked return of the gothic in the fin-de-siècle period, which corresponds to the decline of Britain's industrial boom; deepening inequality and social unrest; and the rise of a new wave of imperial expansion. Positioning a cluster of imperial gothic fictions in this context – *She* (1886), *Dracula* (1897), and *Prester John* (1910) – we consider how, like their precursors, these narratives respond to mutating constructions of racial identity, which develop with the transforming requirements of transregional capitalism.

Our readings therefore address signal moments in British gothic history, examining exemplars of the form that provide foundations on which the wider notion of the Western gothic tradition is built. Taking a world-gothic approach to these keystone texts, we emphasise how, in all instances, they appear to negotiate local socio-economic turbulence unfolding from shifts in the configuration of capitalist relations. We focus in particular on the forms of racialised identity that emerge within, and organise, these periods of upheaval, tracking how gothic fiction repeatedly participates in establishing categories of whiteness that serve the changing demands of capitalist production. In this way, we show not only how plastic conceptions of whiteness have informed British gothic fictions across salient phases in the history of Western gothic, but also how a world-gothic reading of the British gothic strain helps to foreground whiteness as a deeply contingent category. Far from representing an unchanging characteristic of skin morphology, whiteness emerges across our analyses as a flexible technology of power. Its various formulations respond with a degree of extemporaneity to the socio-economic pressures of the historical moments in which they arise. As we will see, whiteness has been constantly made and remade, meaning that it can be unmade in turn.

Whiteness, Consumption, and the Culture of Taste: Eighteenth-Century Gothic Excess

In *Slavery and the Culture of Taste*, Gikandi provides an entry point into questions of whiteness in the eighteenth-century gothic, by demonstrating that the hegemonic aesthetic values to which gothic is a formal reaction are not only responsive to socio-economic shifts unfolding in Britain, but also deeply – if covertly – racialised. That gothic literature inverts dominant principles of order, reason, and virtue – the cornerstones of what Gikandi refers to as the 'culture of taste' – is by now a critical truism in gothic studies. In Fred Botting's highly influential formulation, gothic is 'a writing of excess' that 'appears in the awful obscurity that haunted eighteenth-century rationality and morality'.[7] Where the mores of the age valorised restraint and balance, gothic revels in the irrational and the improbable, accentuating urge, impulse, and a range of emotions and figures at odds with normative codes of detachment and control. As Botting himself notes, these characteristics of the gothic text need to be understood in the context of a Britain transforming with the gathering momentum of capitalism: with 'the shift from feudal to commercial practices in which notions of property, government, and society were undergoing massive transformation'.[8] In this context, the gothic novel itself circulates as a commodity within a new bourgeois reading economy, but its formal excesses also make manifest the 'unbridled, appetitive consumption' that this economy conjures up.[9] In the language of Marx, these fictions imagine a world shaped increasingly by the alienating effects of the commodity fetish: they register the fearful and mesmerising power of proliferating consumer objects which – enlivened by the market economy – are in reality not potent in themselves, but the product of mystified social relations of exploitation and extraction.[10]

For Gikandi, eighteenth-century principles of taste, which stress order, reason, and virtue, are precisely a mechanism for purifying the domain of culture of this system of commerce with which it was increasingly imbricated: taste was a response to the 'suspicion that commerce, lacking an inherent moral value in itself, needed a set of principles to ameliorate its roughness'. It did this through a process of what Gikandi thinks of as 'quarantine', which isolated 'the tasteful the beautiful and the civil' from

2 Whiteness and the 'Western' Gothic Tradition 49

the experience of commercial life that otherwise constituted the middle-class British everyday.[11] If taste functioned in this way as a strategy for constructing a cultural world in opposition to the material world of domestic capitalism, then – as Gikandi argues – is it is equally and profoundly implicated in the making of new racialised identities, since the engine driving socio-economic transformation in Britain was enslavement in the Atlantic world. As he puts it, 'millions of African slaves ... were a key ingredient in the production of the wealth that made the culture of consumption possible'.[12] By extricating the domain of art and aesthetics from consumerism, taste therefore not only defines culture in opposition to capitalism, but more fully describes a world that takes shape against the unspoken negative image of one occupied by the African slave. In this way, '[t]he world of ... the slave, considered far removed from the drawing rooms of the cultured, would become a ... point of reference, in absentia, for the rules that governed high culture'.[13] Taste is, in other words, a mechanism for 'white self-fashioning': a process that makes slavery, in Gikandi's phrasing, 'the great unconscious in the infrastructure of modern identity' itself.[14]

This analysis opens up questions relating to the gothic's function within the forging of racial identities, since, as we have seen with Botting, gothic form precisely witnesses those aspects of socio-economic life which the culture of taste sought to regulate into invisibility. How, we might therefore ask, does gothic register the historical production of whiteness through taste? If the tasteless and commercial form of gothic fiction provides more space than its high-cultural contemporaries for the effects of capitalist restructuring, then might it be that such narratives also bear the marks of the race-making project, which operates through the denial of those very effects? In the light of this possibility, it becomes newly interesting, for example, that Walpole's *Castle of Otranto* – though it unfolds in an imagined medieval Italy – is identified, in the mock preface to the first edition, as having been penned sometime 'between 1095, the era of the first Crusade, and 1243, the date of the last'.[15] As Helen Young observes, by the time Walpole's novel had been published, the crusades had begun to be understood via modern categories of racialised difference:[16] those which, as we have seen with Quijano and Gikandi, cast Europeanness as not only distinct, but as an essentially superior category that gains meaning in opposition to its supposed racial subordinates.

The implications of this insight become visible if we look closely at the complex project of history-making undertaken in Walpole's text. The novel demonstrates the dual gesture of temporal dislocation and reconnection that Botting sees as characteristic of the gothic more widely: *Otranto* transposes contemporary apprehensions of excess into a highly synthetic and supposedly surmounted European past, thus fostering a sense of the eighteenth century as civilised, ordered, and historically discontinuous. In the same moment, however, the novel's historical vision also allows the imagined past to be rejoined to the present, in a narrative that posits the evolution of a more primitive social organisation into the civilised condition of modernity. As Botting summarises, gothic 'preserves an imagined and ideal continuity with the past, but it also serves as an inverted reflection marking a distinct break with history'.[17] Walpole's reference to the Crusades unveils the racialising principle that underpins this reconstruction of modernity's history, because it demonstrates that not only did the eighteenth century need to be understood within a progress narrative tracking the emergence of distinct modern society from a supposedly darker and more savage age, but this story needed at the same time to be one of European triumph over its – in this case – Orientalised 'others'. What we see in *Otranto* is therefore a projection into history of the category of whiteness that Gikandi identifies taking shape in the Britain in which the novel was written. As it implicitly affirms contemporary principles of order, reason, and virtue by relocating the excess and alienation of capitalist modernity into the medieval past, *Otranto* equally shores up the project of white self-fashioning inherent in the culture of taste, by positioning its central values as the achievement of a social organisation conceptualised not only as belonging to Europe, but to a Europe understood in racial terms.

If *Otranto*'s participation in eighteenth-century white self-fashioning requires some analytical excavation, other gothic novels of the moment wear their relationship to this project much more squarely on their sleeves. For example, William Beckford's *Vathek* imagines excess in vivid and explicitly racialised terms. Inspired by *One Thousand and One Nights* (first translated from the French in 1706 as *Arabian Nights Entertainments*) the novel describes the destinies and travails of the ninth caliph of the Abbasid Empire. Vathek is governed by his desires and abandons Islam to satiate his appetites for wealth and sexual conquests, traversing a world ruled by gods and demons before ultimately arriving in Eblis, or hell. Hinging on visions of extreme consumption – of food, goods, and bodies – Beckford's novel clearly exemplifies gothic's relationship to the rise of the consumer economy, the effects of which hegemonic principles of aesthetic order and virtue sought to manage. As Samuel Rowe asserts, *Vathek* precisely registers an eighteenth-century moment in which 'Britons experienced an explosion in the affordability, variety and transitivity of consumer goods'.[18] At the same time, the novel recasts the impulse to consume in highly racialised terms, drawing – as Rowe demonstrates – on the exoticised and atavistic political figure of the oriental despot in order to articulate economic shifts unfolding much closer to home. In this way, *Vathek* engages quite explicitly in the project of race-making that is central to the culture of taste. The novel aligns the potential for excess inherent in eighteenth-century consumerism with an Orientalised economy, thus simultaneously projecting and affirming a counter-vision, in which restraint, balance, and order themselves become the properties of a racial category: whiteness.

That *Vathek* should so clearly illuminate the culture of taste's racial scaffolding is in fact unsurprising, since not only was Beckford himself an infamously prolific consumer of cultural commodities, but also the heir to his family's vast plantations in Jamaica. As Gikandi argues, the source of Beckford's sizable wealth cultivated in the writer an unusually sharp appreciation for the connection between taste and race. Though his fortune provided him with the means to participate in and patronise the upper echelons of high culture, Beckford's acceptance as a 'man of taste' was always conditional, and – according to Gikandi – largely withheld by the British establishment. His status as a so-called white Creole – his Jamaican heritage – meant that the purity of his white identity was a matter of public speculation; at the same time, the fact of his slaveholdings jammed the mechanism of taste, which could not regulate away the obvious role played by the plantation in enabling his entry into high cultural life.[19] As someone rendered marginal to the domain of taste precisely by its affinity with whiteness, Beckford could therefore grasp how culture was organised by and organising racial categories. As Gikandi suggests, *Vathek* attests to the author's 'deep anxieties about his identity, his genealogy and his relation to public culture';[20] in the novel's vivid racialisation of consumerist excess, we might thus discern one aspect of Beckford's efforts to affirm, in the same gesture, his own whiteness and proximity to taste.

Bourgeois Whiteness: Gothic and Industrialisation

Thus far, we have considered how gothic forms participate in the fabrication of whiteness under conditions where it was at least theoretically possible to occlude the central role played by slavery in Britain's material and cultural life. Towards the end of the eighteenth century, however, successive uprisings in the Caribbean – and not least the successful Haitian

Revolution across the 1790s – increasingly brought the relationship to the Atlantic world into domestic view. Concerns around the morality of enslavement, and anxieties about the possible effects of dismantling the institution, were ventilated in public discourse up to and beyond abolition in 1807. In the early nineteenth century, concepts of race thus held a key place in Britain's social imaginary, meaning that, as H. L. Malchow observes, racial discourse increasingly provided 'allusive and metaphorical ammunition' for a range of causes, some directly concerned with colonialism and slavery, and some oriented towards developments in Britain itself.[21]

Key among these latter were the social effects of accelerating industrialisation, encapsulating the mechanisation of production, the incorporation of agricultural workers into the factory system, deepening poverty, and – concomitantly – intensifying divisions between the rising bourgeoisie and the working class. Across the early nineteenth century, these inequalities came to be framed in the discourses of the British establishment via racial taxonomies, which rendered the poor and the proletariat marginal to the developing category of whiteness. In the late 1700s, Malchow observes, 'a specifically bourgeois humanity' had begun to define itself against an '"inhumanity"' ostensibly shared by the 'foreign and pauper native';[22] by the middle of the following century, Alastair Bonnet argues, 'allusions to, as well as metaphors and literal depictions of, racial ... difference had become integrated into the way working class distinctiveness was understood by the middle and upper classes'.[23]

Gothic fiction registers this project of race-making, as is made evident by Mary Shelley's *Frankenstein*: a novel long understood to be shaped by rising industrialisation on the one hand, and the aftermath of abolition on the other. Indeed, *Frankenstein* offers a particularly vivid example of gothic as the 'literature of alienation', a concept developed in the introduction to this volume with the assistance of David Punter, who in turn draws from Marx. As Punter notes, Frankenstein's fabrication of the monster stages a scenario in which 'the techniques of creativity escape from control', thus apprehending the sensorium of life under capitalism – a system in which humans apparently conjure forces they cannot command.[24] Also invoking Marx, Franco Moretti similarly situates *Frankenstein* in a world distorting under pressure from potent and suppressed social energies. In a now-classic analysis, he reads the relationship between Frankenstein and his creation as encoding the bourgeois nightmare of proletarian revolution: '*the moment the monster opens its eyes*, its creator draws back in horror ... he is immediately afraid of it and wants to kill it, because he realises he has given life to a creature stronger than himself and of which he henceforth cannot be free'.[25] That *Frankenstein* so clearly registers the anxious phenomenology of industrial capitalism can in fact be understood as an effect of social developments in the historical context in which it was written. As Edith Gardner notes, for example, the novel follows in the wake of bourgeois panic around Luddite uprisings in Nottinghamshire, Leicestershire, and Derbyshire: instances of intensive industrial action through property destruction and violence, which were crushed by a militarised government response. The Luddites materialised the already palpable threat of revolution breeding in a deeply unequal early-nineteenth-century Britain; in *Frankenstein*, Gardner proposes, this fear is allegorised and realised.[26]

Also noting the conditions of class tension under which Shelley's novel in written, Malchow complicates analyses that make recourse to anxieties about proletarian revolution alone by underscoring how intertwining contemporary discourses of class *and* race inform the construction of the monster. Malchow's extensive reading reveals the debt owed by Shelley's vision of the monster to racist contemporary discourses around the supposedly characteristic features of African peoples, including skin tone, strength, size, and virility. Imagined precisely as a dark-skinned figure of great stature, capable of enduring very harsh conditions of existence, the monster appears, as Malchow observes, quite unlike the popular 'image of the wan and bowed pauper or the proletarian labourer'. '[A]t the level of physiognomy at least', he concludes, Shelley's creation bears a much closer resemblance to the profoundly racist portrayals drawn in colonial travelogues by so-called explorers such as Mungo Park.[27] Malchow goes on to detail linkages between *Frankenstein* and a range of differently politicised images of slavery proliferating around the turn of the nineteenth century, including those in which the white planter class is overwhelmed by violent slave rebellion, and those which frame the enslaved African person as an object of pity, waiting for the freedom and guidance of a moral colonial order. Summarising these influences, Marie Mulvey-Roberts conceptualises the novel as a 'textual patchwork of abolitionist writing and pro-slavery propaganda, inscribed upon the body of the monster'.[28]

'The Monster as industrial worker does not have to be a literal image', Malchow notes, acknowledging *Frankenstein*'s clear relationship to class anxieties unleashed in Britain through capitalist modernisation. However, as we have seen, the terms in which these fears are imagined in the novel rely 'on the coded language of racial prejudice, as well as on a deeply embedded cultural tradition of xenophobia'.[29] Together, these insights help to bring into view the intersecting conceptions of race and class that both inform the novel, and which the novel participates in reproducing. *Frankenstein* may register the threat of proletarian revolution born of industrialisation; however, the conceptualisation of this threat tells us something not only about bourgeois identity, but also the category of whiteness from which this identity was inseparable at the moment of the novel's production.

Fin-de-Siècle Gothic and the Expansion of Whiteness

The end of the nineteenth century witnessed a resurgence of gothic writing in Britain, which corresponds to the decline of the boom period inaugurated by industrialisation, and the rise of a new wave of imperial expansion. As we will see with Hannah Arendt, this latter sought to stave off dawning economic crisis, by finding new outlets for the excess money piling up in British coffers with nowhere profitable to go at home. Out of these conditions, there emerges a strand of late-Victorian writing that Patrick Brantlinger influentially dubbed the 'imperial gothic': a category of fiction often (though not always) set in the outposts of empire, and which typically stages, in intensely racist terms, encounters between intrepid colonial Brits and Indigenous peoples, whose (regularly fabricated) cultural practices are offered as evidence of their strangeness and primitivism. The Britain in which these fictions appeared continues to be shaped by the bourgeois whiteness underpinning *Frankenstein*: As treatises on domestic poverty such as William Booth's *In Darkest England* (1890) vividly demonstrate, the poor and the working class remained codified in significant ways through the prism of racialised difference. Imperial gothic witnesses the enduring grip of this existing formation of race and class; however, as we will show, it also begins to demonstrate a shift in the parameters of white identity, and its changing function within the transforming system of transregional capitalism.

Bonnet identifies the reconfiguration of whiteness with the crisis of the system of laissez-faire industrialisation operational across the nineteenth century: since this mode of capitalism 'largely did without ... welfare', it required (and fostered in turn) 'the formation of ideologies that naturalised and reified social difference' – and specifically ideologies which conceptualised class in racial terms.[30] The rise of imperialism brought about a shift because it inaugurated an alliance between capitalist expansion and the British state, which, in Bonnet's view, ultimately expanded the parameters of whiteness from bourgeois to national proportions. By the middle of twentieth century, Bonnet writes, whiteness remained 'a supremacist identity', but it had also come to signal 'a lack of exceptionality, the homely virtues of quietness, tidiness, cleanness and decency'. Above all, this – still salient – formulation of whiteness designated 'the identity of the ordinary' – of the British majority, the working class.[31] It is the first shudders of this transformation to which fin-de-siècle imperial gothic, and specifically the signal trope of reverse colonisation, bears witness.

As Brantlinger notes, reverse colonisation narratives characteristically invert 'the outward movement of the imperialist adventure',[32] staging scenarios in which the British metropole is rendered vulnerable to invasion and domination from a would-be imperial power. Often, this colonising force is identified among the peoples of Britain's own colonial territories, who – according to the violent ideological schema of colonialism – are supposed to belong to essentially subordinate races. Reverse colonisation therefore discloses, in Brantlinger's words, 'anxieties about the ease with which civilisation can revert to barbarism or savagery', and articulates these fears in visions of 'British progress transformed into British backsliding'.[33] Bram Stoker's *Dracula* is probably the most famous example in this respect, centring on the colonising intentions of the Eastern European vampiric count, and raising the possibility that he will make of England an empire of the undead. The adventure fiction of colonial administrator H. Rider Haggard offers further examples, and in particular his novel *She*, in which the seemingly omnipotent (white) African enchantress Ayesha horrifies colonial protagonists Holly and Vincey with her plans to displace Queen Victoria. A related narrative arc structures John Buchan's *Prester John*, which tracks the sensible young David Crawfurd's confrontation with a mutinous colonial workforce in British Southern Africa, led by the charismatic and terrifying Reverend Laputa – ostensibly heir to the mythical (also white) African king of the novel's title. Like Dracula and Ayesha before him, Laputa has imperialist designs.

A late-nineteenth-century crisis in the bourgeois conception of whiteness shapes these and related narratives of reverse colonisation. It is significant in this respect that imperial gothic visions of Britain in the grip of racial decline are indebted to narratives actually circulating in public discourse, and pre-eminently to those promoted by advocates of the new Victorian racial pseudoscience. As Sally Ledger demonstrates, the racial anxieties espoused by eugenicists such as Francis Galton cannot be understood outside of the contemporary socio-economic and political shifts unfolding from the end of the industrial boom. This was a moment of intense inequality, Ledger notes, as well as one of newly prominent labour struggles and the rise of socialist politics. Since bourgeois identity had been racialised across the preceding century, the threat of revolution represented by these developments was equally understood in racial terms: as Ledger puts it, 'fear for the future of the British "race"' actually expresses a 'fear of the British working class'.[34] When imperial gothic fiction – including narratives of reverse colonisation – imagine the fin-de-siècle as a moment of racial corruption and decline, they are thus reacting (as was racial pseudoscience generally) to a crisis in the specific formation of nineteenth-century white identity, which erupts from the wider crisis of capitalism within which bourgeois whiteness had been incubated and operationalised.

As imperial gothic responds to pressures on established bourgeois whiteness in this way, it also registers, and participates in producing, the expanded category of whiteness that Bonnet identifies becoming dominant across the early twentieth century. The point begins to shift into focus with Shapiro's observation that none of Britain's colonies ever represented an actual threat to Britain itself (though, of course, colonial resistance frequently destabilised colonial administrations on the ground). The racialised vocabulary in which fears about reverse colonisation are articulated therefore needs to be understood as part of a discursive strategy, which – in Shapiro's argument – actually functions symbolically to neutralise real competition to the ailing British economy represented by other industrialised players in the fin-de-siècle world-system, such as Germany and the United States.[35] Race is thus leveraged in these imperial gothic texts as a mechanism through which to assert British supremacy over other sovereign nations, and this insight in turn makes visible a slippage, perpetrated by the scenario of reverse colonisation, between the historical construct of bourgeois whiteness and Britain as such. Racially coded imperialist monsters such as Dracula, Ayesha, and Laputa may incarnate fears deriving from a particular class position hegemonically racialised as white during the nineteenth century; in the narratives in which these figures operate, however, they level threats at the British nation as a whole.

To grasp what is at stake in this sleight of hand for the conception of whiteness, Arendt's analysis of what she calls racial 'chauvinism' is instructive. Arendt argues that imperialism was instrumental in defusing threats to the bourgeois order brewing in nineteenth-century Britain, because – as well as providing an outlet for stagnating capital – it also offered an opportunity to export the 'human debris' of the economic downturn, that is, the poor and the working class.[36] 'The new fact of the imperialist era', Arendt writes, 'is that . . . the owners of superfluous capital and the owners of superfluous working power . . . left the country together'.³⁷ Stabilising the socio-political establishment in this way, colonial expansion also served the ideological function of obscuring the inequalities that generated social unrest in the first place: imperial chauvinism – the racial principle that 'makes the members of one people superhuman, and the members of all others sub-human'³⁸ – conjured an illusion of ethnic unity, bringing together the fractious strata of British society into one racialised nation, the counterpoint to which were colonised people. Summoning monstrous and racialised threats to Britain's national sovereignty, imperial gothic narratives of reverse colonisation participate in the production of this revanchist conception of expanded whiteness. By augmenting the monsters haunting nineteenth-century bourgeois white identity to spectres of national proportion, these narratives sever the old bonds between race and class which held industrialising British society and economy in place, retying them in a new configuration to serve a rising regime of capitalism.

Having established this newly capacious conception of whiteness, imperial gothic reverse colonisation narratives then go on to essentialise it in a de-historicising manoeuvre that resembles the strategy we have seen at work in Walpole's *Otranto*. It is not insignificant that Ayesha and Laputa are explicitly placed within a mythical lineage of white African royalty, nor that Dracula's physical whiteness is stressed by Stoker, along with his ancient Transylvanian heritage. The 'whitening' of these otherwise racially othered figures serves a dual ideological purpose. In the first place, it reinforces the oppositional mechanics through which racial identities are forged by the narratives, suggesting that what allows agents of reverse colonisation to launch meaningful challenges to the British nation is their own proximity to whiteness. Buchan's narrator crystallises the point when, on witnessing the ritual that unites African workers in revolutionary protest, he opines that this could not possibly be of African invention: 'It must have come straight from Prester John, or Sheba's queen, or whoever ruled in Africa when time was young'.³⁹ In the second place – and especially in the cases of *She* and *Prester John* – the location of proximally white figures of threat within a fabricated ancient history of whiteness lifts the category of white identity out of the socio-economic conditions to which it is actually a response, and instead synthesises a trajectory of white development that – as in Walpole's text – makes an evolutionary pinnacle out of the contemporary moment. Thus, the white-but-racially-othered villains in the scenario of reverse colonisation on the one hand affirm whiteness as an essential quality of superiority, which is proper to some humans and can be tracked back through history; on the other, they enable a projection of the British nation, newly reconceptualised in ethnically homogenous terms, as embodying these superior characteristics in supreme form.

Conclusion

Across this chapter we have outlined how, at key moments in its eighteenth- and nineteenth-century history, gothic fiction in Britain participates in the production of categories of whiteness, which organise and naturalise relationships of exploitation, while also facilitating revanchist efforts to stabilise the social order in moments when capital is challenged. We have thus attempted to make visible, or *re*-mark, the often-unmarked white identities that inform the development of British gothic – the cornerstone of the wider 'Western' gothic tradition. At the same time, we have demonstrated how a world-gothic approach to this canon helps to expose the situatedness, contingency, and changeableness of whiteness as a racialised social category. In view of this latter point, our analysis opens up space for further investigation across the 'Western' gothic tradition and beyond. From Charles Brockden Brown to Edgar Allan Poe and H. P. Lovecraft, the American gothic provides fertile ground for examining how forms of whiteness develop to scaffold exploitation and regulate socio-economic turbulence. Similar possibilities exist across the settler colonial nations of Canada, Australia, South Africa, and New Zealand, as well as throughout South and Central America, and across the European continent. How are gothic forms in the literatures of these regions implicated in specific formations of whiteness, constructed to address particular historical constellations of economy, society and culture? A world-gothic response to this provocation might assist in de-reifying and re-historicising whiteness, foregrounding its function as a mutating technology of power, which – prone to crisis and fracturing, and having been repeatedly reinvented – might also be unmade.

Notes

1. Stephen Shapiro, 'Transvaal, Transylvania: *Dracula's* World-System and Gothic Periodicity', *Gothic Studies*, 10:1 (2009), 30–47, 31.
2. Simon Gikandi, *Slavery and the Culture of Taste*, New Jersey, Princeton University Press, 2011, 8.
3. Aníbal Quijano, 'Coloniality of Power, Eurocentrism, and Latin America', *Nepantla: Views from the South* 1:3 (2000), 533–80, 534.

4. Corinna Lenhart, *Savage Horrors: The Intrinsic Raciality of the American Gothic*, New York, Columbia University Press, 2020; Ruth Bienstock Anolik and Douglas L. Howard (eds.), *The Gothic Other: Racial and Social Constructions in the Literary Imagination*, Jefferson, McFarland, 2004; Lizabeth Paravisini-Gebert, 'Colonial and Postcolonial Gothic: The Caribbean', in J. E. Hogle (ed.), *The Cambridge Companion to Gothic Fiction*, Cambridge, Cambridge University Press, 2002, 229–258; H. L. Malchow, *Gothic Images of Race in Nineteenth-Century England*, Stanford, Stanford University Press, 1996.
5. Gikandi, *Slavery*, 97.
6. Richard Dyer, *White*, London, Routledge, 1997, 3; Manuela Boatcă, 'The Centrality of Race to Inequality Across the World-System', *Journal of World-Systems Research*, 23:2 (2017), 465–73, 471.
7. Fred Botting, *Gothic*, London, Routledge, 2013, 1.
8. Fred Botting, 'In Gothic Darkly: Heterotopia, History, Culture', in D. Punter (ed.), *A New Companion to the Gothic*, Chichester, Wiley Blackwell, 2012, 13.
9. Botting, 'In Gothic Darkly', 19.
10. Shapiro, 'Transvaal', 30.
11. Gikandi, *Slavery*, 6.
12. Gikandi, *Slavery*, 63.
13. Gikandi, *Slavery*, 103.
14. Gikandi, *Slavery*, 97, 109.
15. Horace Walpole, *The Castle of Otranto*, Oxford, Oxford University Press, 2014, 5.
16. Helen Young, 'Race, Medievalism and the Eighteenth-Century Gothic Turn', *Postmedieval*, 11:4 (2020), 468–75, 471–3, https://doi.org/10.1057/s41280-020-00203-7.
17. Botting, 'In Gothic Darkly', 18.
18. Samuel Rowe, 'Beckford's Insatiable Caliph: Oriental Despotism and Consumer Society', *Eighteenth-Century Studies* 52:2 (Winter 2019), 183–99, 185, https://doi.org/10.1353/ecs.2019.0006.
19. Gikandi, *Slavery*, 125, 136–7.
20. Gikandi, *Slavery*, 131.
21. Malchow, *Gothic Images*, 13.
22. Malchow, *Gothic Images*, 12.
23. Alastair Bonnet, 'How the British Working Class Became White: The Symbolic (Re)formation of Racialized Capitalism', *Journal of Historical Sociology* 11:3 (1998), 316–40, 320.
24. David Punter, *The Literature of Terror: The Modern Gothic*, London, Longman, 2013 (1996), 197.
25. Franco Moretti, *Signs Taken for Wonders: Essays on the Sociology of Literary Form*, trans. S. Fischer, D. Forgacs, and D. Miller, London, Verso, 1983, 85, emphasis in original.
26. Edith Gardner, 'Revolutionary Readings: Mary Shelley's *Frankenstein* and the Luddite Uprisings', *Iowa Journal of Cultural Studies* 13: 1 (1994), 70–91, 72–3.

27. Malchow, *Gothic Images*, 19.
28. Marie Mulvey-Roberts, *Dangerous Bodies: Historicizing the Gothic Corporeal*, Manchester, Manchester University Press, 2015, 53.
29. Malchow, *Gothic Images*, 19, 38.
30. Bonnet, 'Working Class', 320.
31. Bonnet, 'Working Class', 330.
32. Patrick Brantlinger, *Rule of Darkness: British Literature and Imperialism, 1830–1914*, Ithaca, NY: Cornell University Press, 1988, 233.
33. Brantlinger, *Rule of Darkness*, 230.
34. Sally Ledger, 'In Darkest England: The Terror of Degeneration in Fin-de-Siecle Britain, in P. Childs (ed.), *Post-Colonial Theory and English Literature: A Reader*, Edinburgh: Edinburgh University Press, 1999, 219.
35. Shapiro, 'Transvaal', 36–7.
36. Hannah Arendt, 'Imperialism, Nationalism, Chauvinism', *The Review of Politics* 7:4 (1945), 441–63, 452, www.jstor.org/stable/1404068.
37. Arendt, 'Imperialism', 452–3.
38. Arendt, 'Imperialism', 458.
39. John Buchan, *Prester John*, London: Thomas Nelson and Sons, 1910, 182.

CHAPTER 3

Gothic and Labour
Metabolic, Reproductive, International

Esthie Hugo

Introduction: Home Is Where the Horror Is

'Throughout its tradition', observes Andrew Hock Soon Ng, 'the Gothic has consistently recognised a quality invested in domestic space that has the power to unnerve, fragment, and even destroy its inhabitants'.[1] Examples of gothic novels that deploy the home and household as settings 'for the unspeakable' are numerous;[2] from Ann Radcliffe's *The Mysteries of Udolpho* (1794), Charlotte Perkins Gilman's *The Yellow Wallpaper* (1892), and Toni Morrison's *Beloved* (1988), through to more recent novels like Helen Oyeyemi's *White Is for Witching* (2009) and Sarah Gailey's *Just Like Home* (2022), the domestic sphere has long provided fertile terrain for engendering terror and unease in the reader. To narratives such as these, which employ gothic tropes like haunting and the uncanny to 'challenge . . . beliefs in domestic bliss', critics have given the name 'domestic gothic' – a categorisation meant to underline how gothic narratives specifically portray the domestic realm as a place of imprisonment and danger.[3] For Gina Wisker, the defining feature of the domestic gothic is 'its location, the home, which seems safe but in fact imprisons physically and psychologically, and undermines from within its walls the certainties of identity, family, nurturing and security'.[4]

Women have long recognised the artifice of patriarchal ideologies that construct the home as 'the most sacrosanct of domestic spaces'.[5] Despite the progress that has been made in women's rights over the last three decades, domestic and gender-based violence remain 'devastatingly pervasive',[6] with the highest ever annual number of international killings of women and girls recorded very recently, in 2022.[7] Current estimates show that almost one third of women globally have 'experienced some form of physical and/or sexual violence by their intimate partner' (UN Women). Domestic gothic holds the potential, then, to serve as a poignant outlet for women's lived experiences by giving expression to what Meg Vann terms 'the menace of intimacy',[8] and the chilling axiom, common to media reports on femicide, that 'the person most likely to kill you is the one who shares your bed' (UN Women). Indeed, as Wisker argues, domestic gothic casts a 'disquieting peek' behind the (false) promises of domestic tranquillity and, in so doing, questions long-held associations of the home with 'the everyday, the familiar, and the complacently secure'.[9]

Fruitful as these readings have been in claiming the suitability of the domestic gothic for feminist expression, they have tended to dematerialise the systemic oppressions that have given rise to the household's historical construction as a private sanctuary, and therefore as a site apart from the external forces of the marketplace. Scores of scholars working in the field of social reproduction feminism have illustrated the falsehood of the separation of the private and the public by emphasising how the association of the home with seclusion from the outside world is a product and function of historical capitalism, which inaugurated the divide between productive (waged) labour and reproductive (under- or devalued) labour. In contrast to waged productive labour, reproductive labour constitutes forms of work that take place 'outside the market, in households, neighbourhoods and a host of public institutions [such as] schools and childcare centres', and includes 'the forms of provisioning, caregiving and interaction that produce and maintain social bonds'.[10] While there is nothing innately 'gendered' about social reproduction itself, it is upon the shoulders of women (and feminised bodies) that the burden of reproductive labour predominately falls given their supposed '"biologic proclivities" towards kinship creation, motherhood, and so forth'.[11] As Nancy Fraser explains, the naturalisation of 'women's work' is what led to the ideological split between 'productive' waged work and unwaged 'reproductive' labour, a historical form of separation that has underpinned women's subordination since the early capitalist period.[12] One of (patriarchal) capitalism's defining features is therefore also what Maria Mies famously terms 'the gendered division of labour' and the relegation of social reproduction to the 'private' domestic domain, where the value of women's work can be naturalised into nonexistence and obscured from view, all the better for it to be freely appropriated and put to the work of profit production.[13]

If social reproduction feminism has been foundational to illustrating the dependence of capitalism on the exploitation of the world's households, then it has been equally significant to more recent scholarship that emphasises the world-system's reliance on the metabolic energies of extra-human nature. In her study on capitalism's 'hidden abodes' or 'background conditions', Fraser makes a parallel case about women's labour exploitation and ecological appropriation by arguing that capitalism 'free-rides' as much on devalued women's work as it does on natural resources. 'Like women's labour', she writes, 'nature is made into a free resource for capital, one whose value is both presupposed and disavowed. [Nature] is expropriated without compensation or replenishment and implicitly assumed to be infinite'.[14] To the 'hidden abode' of social reproduction we must thus add another dimension – that of nature's metabolic energies – because the capacity of the environment to support life and renew itself constitutes another background condition for commodity production and value accrual.

To make visible these 'hidden abodes' is therefore to argue for the household's centrality to capitalism despite its conceptual relegation to outside of the market's terrain. But doing so also attends to the oversights in traditional understandings of the domestic gothic, and gothic studies more generally, which fail to adequately account for the genre's mediation of the structural violences that shape and sustain capitalist globalisation. Rebecca Duncan, in her gloss on Glynnis Byron's 2013 edited collection *Globalgothic*, describes how the field of gothic studies responded to globalisation through an emphasis on its registration of twentieth-century discourses around cosmopolitanism, cultural hybridity, and global citizenry. Shaped by 'issues such as the transnational mobility of people and commodities', globalgothic 'came to be understood as the product of a novel and multipolar political landscape, reflecting new pluralities and intersections of cultural voices, and at the same time articulating anxieties that emerged from the disturbance of established identities and traditions'.[15] Thus, the use of the descriptor 'global' in *Globalgothic* refers less to 'predatory transnational vectors of exploitation and domination' and more to transnational mobility and flows – 'of people, money, goods and cultures' – with gothic being one exemplar of a new landscape of cultural instability and exchange opened by twentieth-century global market conditions like deregulation and free trade.[16] Such analyses curb gothic's potential to address world-systemic shifts in favour of capturing global capitalism as 'a sophisticated marketplace, its sprawling circuits and channels cutting across national boundaries to deposit in any given location (cultural) commodities and images from different parts of the world'.[17]

Since the publication of Byron's collection, several Marxist literary scholars have renewed materialist approaches to gothic by reading the form as a key vocabulary for capitalist crisis and transformation. In place of *Globalgothic*'s dematerialised conception of globalisation, these scholars draw on the theoretical insights of world-literature – understood as the literature of the capitalist world-system – to offer instead the term *world-gothic*, a definition which sees the form as a cultural response that emerges in a given region or community's (re)incorporation into capitalist modernity. World-gothic provincialises the Anglo-American gothic canon as one example of a much wider cultural phenomenon, while also productively opening the door for comparisons between gothic cultures from different regional locations in the same world-system. I build on these materialist and comparative possibilities in this chapter, specifically by bringing a world-gothic perspective to bear on the category of the domestic gothic, and by drawing on the conceptual insights of social reproduction feminism and world-literary criticism.

My aim here is, then, to join with an existing lineage of materialist interpretations that advance gothic as giving expression to the estranging effects generated by the capitalist separation of the labourer from their means of production. As Stephen Shapiro has shown, 'Gothic effects occur as capitalism separates laborers from any means of production ... that might sustain them outside of or in tension with a system that produces commodities only for their profit-generating potential'.[18] For Shapiro, no site more poignantly captures the 'grotesque anamorphosis' that capitalist commodification brings into being than 'the sphere of capitalist (factory) production, a veritable "House of Terror," and no poltergeist is more effective than the workplace thumping that is often literalized with disfiguring industrial accidents'.[19]

As Shapiro's example makes clear, materialist approaches to gothic often coalesce around the genre's capacity to capture both the real-life horrors involved in the factory unit and the struggles of a waged, predominately male, proletariat. Yet, gothic might go further than merely encoding the oppressions involved in the labour exploitations that typically take place in the public sphere of the factory. This has been the argument of a range of feminist world-literary scholars who embrace a world-ecological methodology spearheaded by Jason W. Moore.[20] By drawing on Moore's theorisation of capitalism as emerging through both social relations and ecological regimes, critics like Kerstin Oloff have offered world-gothic as a key genre that 'registers the violence against women and the violence of an increasingly unequal capitalist world-system that develops through the downgrading and exploitation of natural resources'.[21] As Oloff and others have shown, world-gothic can inscribe both the exploitation of paid work *and* the appropriation of unpaid work that underpins capitalist value accumulation, illustrating the importance of interpreting the development of the world-system in terms that go *beyond* 'a theory of value in relation to the exploitation of surplus value through economic waged labour'.[22]

Such analyses have productively attended to the gaps that prevail not only in gothic studies, but also in world-literature, which is yet to fully incorporate the role of women's work and the domestic realm in its critique of culture's response to global capitalism. As Sharae Deckard and Kate Houlden have recently observed, 'Using a social reproduction lens ... provides an opportunity for scholars who approach world-culture as that of the capitalist world-system – or indeed capitalist world-ecology – to integrate a deeper analysis of gender, patriarchy and heterosexism into their critique of cultural mediations of capitalist power and accumulation'.[23] Responding to Deckard and Houlden's invitation, this chapter seeks to showcase how *Sharp Objects* (2018) and *Mlungu Wam* (2022) portray the home in ways that demand to be understood from a world-gothic perspective that foregrounds 'the ecological regime of capitalist patriarchy and the manifold forms of exploitation and appropriation it engenders'.[24] As I will show, it is through their use of gothic that these works deny the relegation of the home to its historic position as capitalism's 'hidden abode'. In so doing, both *Sharp Objects* and *Mlungu Wam* pull from the darkness into the light the intersecting violences that sustain the world-system and thus force us to attend to the systemic horrors that have, thus far, remained obscured in studies on the domestic gothic.

Mothers and Daughters, Farms and Factories

A woman kneels before a child's dollhouse, her hand reaching into its ornate interior. From the dollhouse she pulls a single human tooth; it is one of many. The maker of the dollhouse – the younger sister of the kneeling woman – enters to find her secret exposed: these are the souvenirs from the three girls that the young woman has killed; she has been using their teeth to make up the intricate tiles of her dollhouse's main bedroom floor. Terrified, the young woman implores her sister, 'Don't tell Mama'. So concludes the final scene of HBO's *Sharp Objects*,[25] a 2018 TV adaptation of Gillian Flynn's 2014 debut novel by the same name. *Sharp Objects* tells the story of Camille Preaker, an investigative journalist living in St Louis but who originally hails from Wind Gap, a fictional town located in the midwestern border state of Missouri. After an extended period of absence, Camille returns to Wind Gap when her editor sends her there to investigate the recent murder of a young local girl and the disappearance of another. Despite Camille's reluctance to cover the case, her editor insists that her personal history with Wind Gap will add an unusual dimension to the investigation. Her editor is correct: Camille's own mother, Adora Crellin (née Preaker), is eventually found guilty and jailed for the murder of the girls. But Adora is not the true killer; as Camille's gruesome discovery reveals, the person responsible for the killings is her thirteen-year-old half-sister, Amma.

The conclusion of *Sharp Objects* puts an unusual spin on the assumption that serial killers are, at least statistically, most often men. Working against these notions, *Sharp Objects* locates some of its most vicious cruelties in Amma, a young teenage girl. This is a deliberately subversive tactic of Flynn's, who has suggested that her portrayal of violent women (and girl) protagonists works to challenge patriarchal ideals of what constitutes the 'proper' feminine role.[26] Flynn's commitment to undoing patriarchal equations of womanhood with feminine virtuousness manifests in both her portrayal of Amma and Adora. As we later come to learn, Camille's other younger sister, Marian, died in childhood after a protracted series of unexplained illnesses that were all of Adora's making. Marian's death was the result of a homemade poison that Adora – a sufferer of fictitious disorder imposed on another (FDIA), otherwise known as Munchausen's by proxy – had been feeding her over many years.

Camille's mother is the incarnation, then, of what Barbara Creed, in her study on women in horror film, famously terms 'the monstrous-feminine'.[27] Of the many forms that the monstrous-feminine takes, the most prolific is that of the monstrous 'archaic' mother, which Creed, borrowing from Julia Kristeva, reads as frightening because she 'threatens to incorporate what [she] once gave birth to'.[28] For critics who favour such interpretations, Adora functions as the embodiment of the 'monstrous mother' through her enactment of what Michael Eigen calls 'toxic nourishment'[29] and thereby draws into focus the intimate, and sometimes deadly, workings of hereditary hierarchies, particularly those between mothers and daughters.

The idea that Adora's daughters – including Camille, who is a self-harmer – are genetically programmed towards violence is continually accentuated in the series by the dollhouse that Amma obsessively builds and maintains. Amma's dollshouse is a replica of the luxurious Preaker mansion that was originally built in the nineteenth century and which Adora inherited from her great-great-great-grandmother. The dollhouse bedroom in which Amma hides her victim's teeth is an imitation of one of the household's most elaborate sleeping quarters. But the room is not merely a copy of the most ornate chamber in the Preaker home; it is also

Amma's *mother's* bedroom and thus the focal site wherein the hidden dynamics of the mother–daughter relationship are brought to the surface. None of Adora's daughters are allowed into her room for fear that they will damage its delicate ivory floor, one of the mansion's original features. That her mother's bedroom serves as the storehouse for Amma's victims' teeth is, therefore, apt. In hiding these enamel souvenirs in her mother's bedchamber, Amma undoes the association of women's bedrooms with seclusion and refinement, while also highlighting a familial tendency to hoard precious objects. As the veneer of feminine delicacy deteriorates into the revelation of murder, we are forced to engage with the underlying horrors of the Preaker family order and the repressed traumas that Adora has passed on to her daughters. In Amma's vicious killings we thus recognise her desire to recreate herself in her mother's 'monstrous' image; Amma – whose name is a pointed anagram for Mama – is her mother in miniature.

To read the mother–daughter relationship in this way emphasises the psychogeography of the home; 'what the room immediately signifies', observes Mattias Pirhol, 'is the unbridgeable distance between mother and daughter and the transgenerational female trauma inherited from mother to daughter'.[30] Yet, these interpretations remain grounded in prevailing conceptions of the domestic gothic to which I have already referred, for they understand the sinister domesticity of the Preaker household as both the reservoir of, and breeding ground for, the family's collective trauma and psychic disintegration. In so doing, they overlook several key aspects raised in *Sharp Objects*'s disturbing conclusion. Particularly telling in this regard is that Amma's dollhouse makes continual reference to the commodities and forms of trade that underpin the family's functioning, or indeed, its *dysfunctioning*.

The first insight we are given into the Preaker household's various 'background conditions' – what Marx would term the home's 'substructure' – concerns the provenance of the family's wealth, which is made from pig farming. Adora is the owner of several large pork factory farms that run on the labour of short-term workers, mostly illegal Mexican immigrants. These workers provide the basis for the Preaker family's fortune by undertaking the undesirable work of hog-slaughtering, thereby referencing the reliance of the contemporary American pork industry on cheap, often undocumented, immigrant labour, itself a product of the trade liberalisation policies of the North American Free Trade Agreement (NAFTA) that took effect in 1993 and which ensured that America overhauled 'one-third of Mexican pork production while developing Mexico into a leading importer of U.S. pork'.[31] By exploiting Mexico's newly relaxed land ownership regulations and minimised restrictions on foreign investments, American multinationals oversaw the transformation of the United States into the world's third largest producer of pigmeat, a position that it presently still holds. While Americans account for a large proportion of the international consumer market, the majority of US hog products are exported to China, which consumes half of the world's pork.[32]

Most of America's industrial pig farms are concentrated in the midwest (where Wind Gap is located) and are known for having some of the world's most hazardous working conditions: alongside exposure to the pollutants and pathogens produced by the breeding of pigs for large-scale consumption, Hispanic workers – who account for the majority of the pork trade's labour force – are subjected to hugely exploitative work contracts that take advantage of their position as undocumented, first-generation immigrants.[33] The labour vulnerabilities of the real-life pork industry, which treats its workers as disposable and sacrificial humans,[34] likewise befall the fictional workers in Adora's slaughterhouses, for they are quickly rendered expendable when news of the Wind Gap murders spreads. Despite the outside detective's insistence that the girls were killed 'by someone they knew', the local chief of police pins the murders on one of Adora's workers when the bicycle of Amma's latest victim is found in the factory's overflowing lagoon of pig manure, one of the pork industry's leading causes of pollution.

The series thus gestures to the contaminating effects of the production processes that provide for the Preaker family's wealth, while also capturing the pervasive anti-Mexican, anti-immigrant stance in Wind Gap, and contemporary America more broadly, despite the essential role played by immigrant labour in providing 'food for the family'. The series offers an insight, in this way, into industrial pig farming's concealing blindfolds – what food critics term the 'cognitive gap between what people eat and how it is made'[35] – by showcasing the violent processes of production that undergird the Preaker family's 'innocent' acts of domestic consumption, of which the teeth that Amma hoards are particularly suggestive.

If *Sharp Objects* casts an uneasy light upon the Preaker household's dependence on the exploitative operations of the US hog industry, then it likewise draws into focus how the factory shapes the familial relations that take place within the home. Like all factory farms, industrial pork production in present-day America is structured by the characteristics of confined animal feeding operations (CAFOs), which operate on a system of mass confinement, and which tie the reproductive capacities of the sow to the making of commodities in service of the marketplace. In this system of large-scale incarceration and commodity production, sows are the most brutally treated: after being artificially inseminated, they are confined in two-foot-wide gestation crates; once their piglets are born, sows are moved to equally small farrowing pens that serve the sole purpose of fattening their piglets for slaughter – a process referred to by the industry as 'farrow-to-finishing'. *Sharp Objects* takes us into precisely one such pen, where Camille spies Amma cooing over several squealing piglets suckling from the bleeding teats of an incapacitated sow. While Camille is clearly disgusted at what she sees, Amma's reaction is to take delight in the scene: she watches the farrowing with a disquieting sense of fascination and eventually has one of Adora's workers remove a suckling piglet so she can use it in one of Wind Gap's traditions, a perverse game of 'here piggy-piggy'.

In this sequence, it becomes clear that Amma cannot place the act of nurturing outside of the processes of domination that the farm – in operating like a factory – requires for its success. This implies in turn that Amma's murders are a differently inflected iteration of the farm's system of absolute brutality. The same can be said of Adora's 'monstrous' approach to motherhood: Adora's breeding pens foretell how her own acts of mothering can only culminate in incarceration and eventual death. Like the industrial slaughterhouse, which intertwines breeding with inevitable butchery, an impending death is what awaits each of Adora's daughters. This indeed comes to pass in *Sharp Objects*'s climax. After years of being denied access, Camille is finally allowed into her mother's bedroom only for Adora to subject her to another of factory farming's practices – force-feeding – when she makes Camille drink the same homemade poison that she used to kill her sister. Thus, the violence of the Preaker family and the Preaker farm emerge in tandem, as the external operations of the factory find a gothic echo in the brutal behaviour of those who occupy the interior of the mansion's four walls.

In its prioritisation of capital accumulation for the family, the Preaker factory distorts not merely the relations of animals to other animals through its fracturing of the relation between sow and piglet, but also the relations of humans to animals, and even humans to other humans, for which Adora's murderous relationship with her daughters stands as a particularly horrifying totem. This is reinforced in the series' final dinner scene, where the Preaker family are shown gorging themselves on a roast ham while discussing the death sentence that awaits Jon Keene, the man falsely accused of being the Wind Gap Killer. Camille, by now sure that her mother is to blame, is pictured fixing Adora with an accusing stare, but she quickly drops her gaze to the carving knife next to the ham and stares at it while Amma relays a local folktale about 'little girls being yanked from the woods by the Woman in White'. Here, then, the shot of the ham, carved to pieces, along with Amma's warning, encapsulates the connection between the violence of the farm and the violence which pervades the family home, while also foreshadowing Camille's subjection to her mother's poison bottle, itself a murderous inversion of the act of nursing, as alluded to by the title of the final episode: 'milk'.

Yet, the family's factory farm is but a contemporary manifestation of older forms of horror to which *Sharp Objects* continually refers. Adora's slaughterhouse is something of a vector for showcasing the longstanding practices of domination that the Preaker family have inherited and reproduce in turn. The ivory tiles that make up the floor of Adora's bedroom are particularly telling here since ivory was synonymous with colonial slavery in Africa. The late 1800s saw an unprecedented rise in demand for elephant tusks due to the dwindling numbers of elephant populations in Central Africa. As a result, the East African coast became the focus of intensified European – and soon American – demand, which grew to such proportions that the East African elephant population was virtually eliminated by the end of the nineteenth century. Enslaved Africans provided the labour needed for the transportation of elephant tusks out of East Africa and across the world; that slaves could be used to move ivory to the coast and thereafter sold at the same ports only increased the profit of the trading venture.[36]

Much like the floor that lies in the feminine heart of the Preaker mansion, which was tellingly constructed during the heyday of the global ivory trade, the homes of upper-class American citizens became key components in the functioning of the ivory commodity chain. Elephant tusks provided the material for the manufacturing of household items like combs, cutlery handles, billiard balls, and piano keys – the symbolic instruments of colonial wealth and opulence, which glorified the domination of science over 'nature' (of the gun over the elephant), as well as the domination of America over the African continent (of 'civilisation' over 'barbarity'). Adora's bedroom floor thus calls to mind the intersecting horrors behind America's historical appetite for ivory: the colonisation of Africa, the mass killing of elephants, and the thousands – perhaps millions – of African captives whose embondaged labour provided for the trade's global expansion.[37]

These, then, are some of the conditions that produce the wider social, ecological, and economic forces at play in the (dis)functioning of the Preaker home. Because ivory serves as the literal floor upon which Adora stands, it signifies how the family repeats the violent cycles set in motion during the colonial period, which Adora describes as something of a golden era – 'before anybody knew what endangered was'. Indeed, Adora's obsessive commitment to preserving the ivory floor in its original state speaks powerfully to the sequences of repetition to which the family remain wedded: 'this floor', Adora proudly remarks, 'was supposed to last forever. And it has, just'. In focusing on the Preaker home, the series thus audits the detrimental effects of systems of exploitation and appropriation at various scales and across a range of historical periods, from the violence of the colonial slave trade and the cruelty of the contemporary pork trade through to the intimate workings of the American family and domestic unit.

'This House Doesn't Like Mama'

Sharp Objects invites us to examine the horrors that constitute the very basis of American wealth through its focus on the workings of the Preaker mansion; *Mlungu Wam*[38] asks us, relatedly, to pay attention to the women who labour in the upkeep of the white, middle-class South African home. The film's English title is *Good Madam*, a reference to the historical Zulu name ('my white') given by Black servants to their white employers. *Mlungu Wam* chronicles the relationship between a Black domestic worker, Mavis, and her white employer, a rich 'madam' named Diane who lives in a mansion in Constantia, one of Cape Town's oldest, and most luxurious, neighbourhoods. Mavis's relationship to Diane is modelled upon the exploitation of Black domestic work that has been the mainstay of white South African life for centuries. While post-apartheid South Africa underwent radical political transformation when the African National Congress (ANC) came to power in 1994, similar changes failed to take place in private domestic arrangements despite the implementation of the 1997 Domestic Worker's Act, which contains specific laws pertaining to the rights of domestic workers. In fact, many white South Africans deliberately exploit the ideological construction of the household as 'private' to facilitate their noncompliance with these laws. As Ena Jansen argues, 'many domestic workers are still treated in accordance with centuries-old behaviour patterns which the vast majority of white South Africans internalise from childhood'.[39]

Interrogating the contemporary endurance of this 'centuries-old' system lies at the heart of *Mlungu Wam*. Director and co-writer Jenna Bass describes how the film grew out of a need to capture 'the national malaise typified by the maid-madam dynamic', because, for Bass, 'the domestic worker is the symbol of everything that remains wrong with the end of apartheid'.[40] In the film, the dependence of white South Africa on Black women's work is presented in Pavlovian terms: while Diane never leaves her upstairs bedroom, her presence is manifested by the bell that she routinely rings and to which Mavis is conditioned to respond without question or hesitation.

Like *Sharp Objects*, *Mlungu Wam* interrogates the mother–daughter relationship. The film's action is set in motion when Mavis's daughter Tsidi arrives seeking shelter for herself and her daughter, Winnie, after having been forcefully evicted by relatives from their home – previously Tsidi's grandmother's – for not following proper inheritance protocol. Tsidi clearly feels a deep resentment towards her mother's loyalty to Diane, for whom Mavis has worked for more than thirty years. In that time, Mavis raised Diane's two sons (who now live in Australia) while Tsidi was brought up by her grandmother. As a result, Tsidi refuses to call Mavis by the traditional title of 'Mama', opting instead for the term 'Sisi', a Black African title typically used when addressing a younger woman or sister. The troubled relationship between Tsidi and Mavis is compounded by Tsidi's brother, who was raised as one of Diane's adoptive sons. Recalling the colonial-era practice of Black South Africans adopting two names, their birth name and 'colonial name', Tsidi's brother now goes by Stuart, the name allocated to him by Diane, in place of Gcinumzi, the name given to him by Mavis. So inculcated is Stuart into white society that he no longer speaks to his family in their native isiXhosa. Despite this, Mavis takes great pride in Stuart's achievements, which, while estranging him from his traditional familial and cultural roots, she views as signalling his upward mobility thanks to the supposed 'goodness' of Diane, whose generosity has enabled Stuart to break free from the family's cycle of poverty.

Mavis's complicated relationship with her children is the first of many gestures the film makes to the disintegration of the Black family that was the historical product of colonial and apartheid-era South Africa's dependence on racial capitalism, the most powerful symbol of which was the migrant labour system, which forced Black men to abandon their families in order to labour in the mines, factories, and farms that provided for South Africa's industrialisation and economic development. While Black men are often presented as the predominant victims of the migrant labour system, its flipside was the creation of what Mies would term the 'housewifization' of Black women, whose presiding means of earning a wage was to work as domestic servants for white families in urban areas, often located far from their rural homes. The effects of this system, built on the patriarchal capitalist assumption that 'a woman with children has to accept any wage if she want[s] to survive',[41] are still apparent in South Africa today. So formative has Black women's work been to South African society that it pervades nearly all spheres of South African life: 'the lives of practically all South Africans', writes Jansen, 'have been touched by the institution of paid domestic work: either because of the *presence* of an often motherly carer and cleaner, or by the *absence* of a mother who does paid housework for others'.[42] It is this historic economic relation, then, which lies behind Mavis's vexed maternal relations and her inability to develop a bond with her daughter: 'I have no birth mother', Tsidi furiously remarks to Mavis one day, 'My birth mother raises white kids in the suburbs!'.

In the film, suburban South African society's reliance on racialised reproductive labour is portrayed as having emerged through an enchantment or curse that literalises the wholesale integration of gendered racial capitalism into the functioning of white South African life. As we come to learn, Mavis's mysterious attachment to Diane is not, in fact, of her own making, but the result of a sinister enchantment cast upon her by Diane to ensure Mavis's unconditional – and everlasting – servitude. Mavis, however, is aging and unable to work as productively as before. Diane, too, is old and likely to die soon. It is here that Diane's supposed 'goodness' gives way to her true malevolence: her plan is to replace Mavis with the younger and stronger Tsidi, whose labour will sustain Diane not only until she dies, but even afterwards, in the afterlife. With the help of Stuart, Diane hopes to achieve this with a supernatural family ritual modelled upon the ancient Egyptian tradition of the Shabti doll, whose purpose was to provide the labour required to sustain their master in the necropolis.

Like the Shabti tradition, which dates back to 1570–1069 BCE, Diane's plan is part of a much longer family tradition begun centuries before, during South Africa's colonial era, and perhaps even earlier, as suggested by the location of Diane's home – Constantia – an area celebrated for pioneering South Africa's famous wine economy, a direct product of the Cape Colony's reliance on slave labour for more than a hundred years. Diane's familial connection to this history is revealed when Tsidi stumbles upon the graves of Diane's predecessors. Each of their gravestones is accompanied by the headstones of their respective servant, whose date of death corresponds to the death of their employer. While Diane's family members are honoured with elaborate messages of commemoration, their servant's lives are memorialised in terms that merely underscore their labour power. Under the name 'Ma Maria' lies neither a description of her history nor her last name, but simply the phrase 'our Second Mother. For Eternity'. Thus, *Mlungu Wam*'s commentary on Black women's exploitation makes clear the continuity between colonial, apartheid, and post-apartheid South Africa. Black domestic servitude, the film suggests, is the spectre that contemporary white South African society cannot – indeed, *will not* – exorcise.

The film fits within the tradition of the domestic gothic in various ways. Not only does it make use of gothic images like graveyards and curses to comment on the endurance of Black domestic exploitation in South Africa, but Tsidi feels a deep sense of unease whenever she enters Diane's house. When Winnie asks her mother, 'Why don't you like this house?', Tsidi responds, 'It's not that Mama doesn't like this house. But it seems that this house doesn't like Mama'. While Tsidi's answer describes her experience of being unwelcome in a white suburb as a young Black girl – 'Mama grew up coming here ... So when I'm here I get many memories. Bad memories' – it is also a more literal turn of phrase. Each time Tsidi criticises Mavis's loyalty to Diane, the house strikes as if to mould Tsidi in the image of a domestic worker: one moment she is locked in Mavis's servant's quarters, the next assaulted by various domestic objects. The home even attempts to take wholesale possession of Tsidi's body. Winnie finds her mother one night frantically scrubbing the bathroom floor in a scene reminiscent of earlier images of Mavis compulsively cleaning the house's floorboards. So obsessively do the women clean that they are left with bloodied, torn hands. The film draws, then, on the tropes of the domestic gothic to express the household as a site of terror for its Black inhabitants but does so by placing the horrors of the home within a specific South African context and history. In particular, the film borrows from the domestic gothic to subvert racist South African anxieties around 'home invasions', and attacks by Black others, showing instead how the house's horror derives not from the outside but from its internal occupants.

Crucial, therefore, to *Mlungu Wam*'s particular brand of domestic gothic is its play on a white South African imaginary built upon the contradiction of intimacy, on the one hand, and anonymity, on the other. Despite the intimate nature of domestic work, very few South African employers take an interest in the lives of their 'helpers'; few know where their domestic workers come from, where they live, or even what their real names are. Many critics have observed how the 'madam-maid' relation often pivots on notions of domestic workers being 'part of the family', yet their lived experience remains grounded in a process of profound anonymisation and estrangement.[43] It is the latter part of this contradictory relation that *Mlungu Wam* harnesses and takes to a gothic extreme. Diane assumes that Mavis's devotion to her is so ingrained that she will accept the ritualistic sacrifice of her daughter. The same applies to

Stuart, who Diane has tasked with the killing of Tsidi. But Diane is mistaken; she doesn't know Mavis – or indeed, Stuart – at all. The film's climax takes place when Mavis interrupts the ritual, Stuart sacrifices himself in place of Tsidi, and Diane is left in a catatonic state from which she cannot awaken. Thereafter, the film traces Diane's subjection to the process of domestic imprisonment to which Mavis has for so long been enslaved: Tsidi and Mavis move Diane's body from her lush upstairs bedroom to Mavis's crumbling servant's quarters in the basement. Together, the two women take ownership of Diane's home by making a series of household changes that had previously been forbidden: replacing the furniture, redecorating, and eating from Diane's silverware. The film comments, in this way, as much on the post-apartheid endurance of domestic labour exploitation as it does on the urgent question of Black land repossession and redistribution, which, thirty years into South Africa's democratic era, still remains largely unresolved.

Yet, even as *Mlungu Wam* makes use of the domestic gothic to highlight the present-day effects of the South African institution of racialised reproductive labour and its concomitant horrors, it ends on a more international note. Echoing *Sharp Objects*'s reflection on cycles of intergenerational violence, *Mlungu Wam* concludes not with a triumphant final image of Mavis and Tsidi's newfound freedom from the familial inheritance of domestic servitude, but with the relocation of that servitude elsewhere. This the film achieves by moving in its concluding scene from South Africa to Australia, where Diane's two sons now live. Diane's eldest son, Grant, is on the phone to Mavis, who reassures him that his mother is well taken care of and not imprisoned downstairs while she and Tsidi enjoy the full occupation of her home. With a false sense of security that 'Mavis has it all under control', Grant hangs up the phone and leaves the table where he has been sitting having an elaborate family meal. The film's final shot is of a young Aboriginal woman, clearly the family's housekeeper, arriving to clear the dirty plates. The film insists, then, on an interpretation of domestic labour exploitation as not merely a 'South African' problem; but rather that, without the wholesale transformation of the transregional system of capitalism itself, the violent condition of women's work will simply be relocated elsewhere and the relationship between economic exploitation and racialised gendered oppression will remain intact.

This chapter has furnished a novel materialist approach to the category of the domestic gothic that combines social reproduction feminism with world-literary criticism. I have compared how *Sharp Objects* and *Mlungu Wam* imagine the terrain of the household in ways that foreground the dependence of the world-system on the unpaid work of nature's metabolic energies and women's social reproduction. By focusing on how these works portray the domestic sphere, I have illustrated the role played by gothic in illuminating the manifold ways in which capitalism exploits the household. In so doing, I have argued for, and demonstrated, the comparative possibilities of the world-gothic method. This method not only productively opens the door for comparisons between gothic 'texts' from different regional locations in the same world-system, but also casts a searchlight on a series of intersecting exploitations that are both hidden from view and typically thought of in isolation. If *Sharp Objects* and *Mlungu Wam* refuse the home's relegation to capitalism's 'hidden abode', then this refusal is explicitly a product of their deployment of *gothic*, a form that is capable of continually and urgently exposing to critical scrutiny the wider social, economic, and ecological forces that sustain this system in the first place.

Notes

1. Andrew Hock Soon Ng, *Women and Domestic Space in Contemporary Gothic Narratives: The House as Subject*, New York, Palgrave Macmillan, 2015, 1.
2. Hock Soon Ng, *Women and Domestic Space*, 1.
3. Gina Wisker, 'Houses of Death: Ruth Rendell's Domestic Gothic and the Emptying Out of Romance', *Contemporary Women's Writing*, 1 (2017), 66–84, 68.
4. Wisker, 'Houses of Death', 73.
5. Shelly Ingram and Willow G. Mullins, '"[T]he People That Should Have Lived Here": Haunting, the Economy, and Home in Tana French's *Broken Harbour*', in Laura Joyce and Henry Sutton (eds.), *Domestic Noir: The New Face of 21st Century Crime Fiction*, London, Palgrave Macmillan, 2018, 161–79, 162.
6. World Health Organisation, 'Devastatingly Pervasive: 1 in 3 Women Globally Experience Violence', 9 March 2021, www.who.int/news/item/09-03-2021-devastatingly-pervasive-1-in-3-women-globally-experience-violence.
7. UN Women, 'Five Essential Facts to Know about Femicide', 20 November 2022, www.unwomen.org/en/news-stories/feature-story/2022/11/five-essential-facts-to-know-about-femicide.
8. Meg Vann, 'The Menace of Intimacy: Domestic Noir, Feminist Criminology, and Emily Maguire's An Isolated Incident', *Australian Literary Studies*, 33 (2018), 1–18.
9. Wisker, 'Houses of Death', 68.
10. Nancy Fraser, 'Behind Marx's Hidden Abode: For an Expanded Conception of Capitalism', *New Left Review*, 86 (2014), 55–72, 63.
11. Maria Mies, *Patriarchy and Accumulation on a World Scale: Women in the International Division of Labour*, London: Zed Books, 1986, 45.

12. Fraser, 'Behind Marx's Hidden Abode', 63.
13. Mies, *Patriarchy and Accumulation on a World Scale*, 48.
14. Fraser, 'Behind Marx's Hidden Abode', 66.
15. Rebecca Duncan, 'Introduction: Globalgothic beyond Globalisation', in Rebecca Duncan (ed.), *The Edinburgh Companion to Globalgothic*, Edinburgh, Edinburgh University Press, 2023, 1–20, 1.
16. Duncan, 'Introduction', 1.
17. Duncan, 'Introduction', 8.
18. Stephen Shapiro, 'Transvaal, Transylvania: Dracula's World-system and Gothic Periodicity', *Gothic Studies*, 10 (2008), 29–47, 30.
19. Shapiro, 'Transvaal, Transylvania', 30.
20. Jason W. Moore, *Capitalism in the Web of Life: Ecology and the Accumulation of Capital*, London, Verso, 2015.
21. Kerstin Oloff, 'Marie Vieux Chauvet's World-Gothic: Commodity Frontiers, 'Cheap Natures' and the Monstrous-Feminine', in S. Casanova-Vizcaíno and I. Ordiz (eds.), *Latin American Gothic in Literature and Culture*, New York, Routledge, 2018, 122–36, 135.
22. Kate Houlden and Sharae Deckard, 'Social Reproduction Feminism and World-Culture: Introduction', *Feminist Theory*, 25 (2024), 131–48, 138.
23. Kate Houlden and Sharae Deckard, 'Social Reproduction Feminism and World-Culture', 139.
24. Sharae Deckard, 'Social Reproduction, Struggle and the Ecology of "Women's Work" in World-Literature', *Feminist Theory*, 5 (2024), 222–41, 238.
25. *Sharp Objects*, dir. Jean-Marc Vallée, New York, HBO, 2018.
26. Oliver Burkeman, 'Gillian Flynn on her Bestseller *Gone Girl* and Accusations of Misogyny', *The Guardian*, 1 May 2013, www.theguardian.com/books/2013/may/01/gillian-flynn-bestseller-gone-girl-misogyny.
27. Barbara Creed, 'Horror and the Monstrous-Feminine: An Imaginary Abjection', *Screen*, 27 (1986): 44–71.
28. Creed, 'Horror and the Monstrous-Feminine', 64.
29. Michael Eigen, *Toxic Nourishment*, London, Karnac, 1999.
30. Mattias Pirholt, '"Southern Living from a Bygone Time": Gothic Spatialization of History in Gillian Flynn's Sharp Objects', *Mississippi Quarterly*, 75 (2022), 381–403, 390.
31. Pamela A. Vesilind, 'NAFTA's Trojan Horse & the Demise of the Mexican Hog Industry', *The University of Miami Inter-American Law Review*, 43 (2011), 143–63, 151.
32. Daisuke Wakabayashi and Claire Fu. 'China's Bid to Improve Food Production? Giant Towers of Pigs', *The New Times*, 8 February 2023, www.nytimes.com/2023/02/08/business/china-pork-farms.html?searchResultPosition=1.
33. Nicole Greenfield, 'COVID-19 Has Exposed the Gross Exploitation of Meatpacking Workers', *Natural Resources Defence Council*, 30 October 2020, www.nrdc.org/stories/covid-19-has-exposed-gross-exploitation-meatpacking-workers.

34. Valerie Baron, 'Pandemic Endangers Slaughterhouse Workers and Supply Chains', *Natural Resources Defence Council*, 16 April 2020, www.nrdc.org/bio/valerie-baron/pandemic-endangers-slaughterhouse-workers-and-supply-chains.
35. Ivy Ken and Kenneth Sebastian León, 'Regulatory Theater in the Pork Industry: How the Capitalist State Harms Workers, Farmers, and Unions', *Crime, Law and Social Change*, 78 (2022), 599–619, 601.
36. John Frederick Walker, *Ivory's Ghosts: The White Gold of History and the Fate of Elephants*, New York, Atlantic Monthly Press, 2009, 117.
37. Walker, *Ivory's Ghosts*, 117.
38. Mlungu Wam, dir. Jenna Bass, New York, Visit Films, 2022.
39. Ena Jansen, *Like Family: Domestic Workers in South African History and Culture*, Johannesburg, Wits University Press, 2019, 218–19.
40. Lumumba Mthembu, '*Mlungu Wam*: The International Success Story that Returns to South Africa', *Mail and Guardian*, 10 October 2022, https://mg.co.za/friday/2022-10-10-mlungu-wam-the-international-success-story-that-returns-to-south-africa/.
41. Mies, *Patriarchy and Accumulation on a World Scale*, 43.
42. Jansen, *Like Family*, 2.
43. Shireen Ally, *From Servants to Workers: South African Domestic Workers and the Democratic State*, Ithaca, Cornell University Press, 2009.

PART II

World-Monsters: Global Transmissions and Genealogies

CHAPTER 4

Pre-colonial Gothic and the Windigo

Krista Collier-Jarvis

Introduction: Halfway-Human-and-Mean-as-Starving-Eyes

The world is overrun by flesh-eating creatures. They arise when man greedily extracts the earth's resources and now they wander the land with 'halfway-human-and-mean-as-starving-eyes', insatiably consuming everything they encounter.[1] No, this is not the ghoul of George A. Romero's 1968 *Night of the Living Dead*, nor is it the rage-based monster that populates Danny Boyle's *28 Days Later* series, although they share much in common with both. This tale is about the Windigo/Wendigo/Windego (Anishnabe, Chippewa, Odawa, Potawatomi), Wîhtikow (Rocky Cree, Atikamekw, Métis), Wheetago (Dene), and relatedly, Giwakwa (Abenaki), Stone Coat (Huron-Wendat), and Chenoo (Mi'kmaq), just to name a few. Spellings of these figures vary by nation, tribe, or community and can change over time as Indigenous languages are used to reclaim names and stories. The Chenoo, from my own Mi'kmaw culture, is described by settlers as 'a zombie-like creature . . . supernatural beings, often considered mischievous and dangerous, that were said to inhabit the dense forests'. The Chenoo has 'the power to shape-shift and could cause harm to those who ventured too deep into the woods'.[2] Indigenous tribes and nations across Turtle Island (North America) share many similar stories and customs,[3] and while there are variations of the Windigo tale, most tend to focus on a former human who has transgressed, through acts such as cannibalism or resource extraction, and who, consumed by their own greed, turn into an insatiably hungry creature of hulking stature.

   The version of the story that opens this chapter is Richard Van Camp's (Dene) 'On the Wings of This Prayer', which takes place across multiple temporalities. It details one of two possible stories for our world with the use of second-person pronouns positioning the reader as an agent in determining how the second, unwritten story might go. In the story, the Wheetago, sometimes referred to as 'zombies', 'Hair Eaters', 'Shark

Throats', and 'boiled faces', have emerged from the Alberta tar sands. They are unsated in their hunger. For example, as the first woman bitten begins to transform, her pleas for death give way to hunger: 'Kill me please. Your meat is magnificent and what roars in your veins is calling me. It's calling me to drink you open and warm me so sweetly'.[4] This example embodies a common element in Windigo stories, that is, engaging the freezing wintery conditions that come with living in the North, and for the Wheetago in Van Camp's version, feeding the hunger keeps the cold at bay, warming them so sweetly. Unlike their zombie counterparts, the Wheetago tend to require more than mere violence to be defeated. The 'old ways',[5] such as singing and chanting 'in the first tongue' can slow them down, as can tattooing syllabics on the body.[6] Ultimately, this is because the Wheetago are born from the same land as that of the Dogrib and their language, and because their manifestation is described as a 'return' rather than something new, they are not a uniquely contemporary creature despite the circumstances that give rise to them.[7] Just like the Dogrib, the Wheetago have always been on this land, and while this particular version of the story is relatively new, stories of the Wheetago more broadly were around long before settler colonisation on Turtle Island, or what is commonly called North America. They are signifiers of a gothic aesthetic that has existed as long as Indigenous peoples have been telling stories.

Much of this chapter details the ongoing debates regarding how stories by and about Indigenous peoples and cultures fit within conversations of the gothic, arguing for a recognition of a kind of pre-colonial gothic aesthetic. Pre-colonial does not designate the sense of a separate subgenre within the gothic itself, but rather functions as part of a 'world-gothic: that is gothic as a cultural index for local experiences of relations that constitute the modern world' put forth by Rebecca Duncan and Rebekah Cumpsty in the Introduction to this collection. In the case of Van Camp's Wheetago, the creature is not necessarily created by the Alberta tar sands but has been awakened by it as the modern world signified by the oil industry has reached a critical crisis point in the ways it damages the environment and threatens the health and well-being of local Indigenous peoples. This local experience manifests as gothic, but more than this, points to a gothic that has always been. And so, a pre-colonial gothic engages a temporality and the ways in which stories and traditional Indigenous figures that were born prior to colonisation have survived, albeit transformed by and through their need to respond to colonisation. The purpose of exploring questions about a pre-colonial gothic is to demonstrate how the elements that come together to produce a gothic aesthetic have existed for hundreds of years and were not new or unique to Europe in the late eighteenth century. I am not the first to make this argument, of course. In 'Is There an Indigenous Gothic?' Michelle Burnham proposes a similar line of inquiry: 'that indigenous cultures and histories of storytelling in the Americas were *already* populated by gothic elements, representing a literary and cultural history that not only predates the importation of the European gothic into the Americas, but predates the arrival of Europeans in the Americas altogether'.[8] The emergence of a globalgothic, as coined by Glennis Byron, demonstrates how the gothic is not 'fixed in terms of any one geographically circumscribed mode'.[9] While the globalgothic displaces the locality of a gothic origin and addresses the ways in which 'national and regional myths and folklore are increasingly appropriated, recycled and commodified for a global audience',[10] it still sees the gothic in terms of a colonial temporal approach. And while Burnham notes how the presumed birth of the gothic within eighteenth-century Britain as 'a geographical location and historical moment ... are equally distant from Native American and indigenous traditions of storytelling', she goes on to highlight how these distances are 'seem[ing]' and that the gothic's 'form and meaning can change'.[11] Emma McEvoy similarly argues that the gothic 'endlessly reinvents itself',[12] and so, if the gothic can consistently transform moving forward, why not also backward? As such, if we view elements of the gothic as existing prior to colonisation, Britain's claim to the gothic can be seen as part of the longer history of ongoing colonisation as well as the appropriation of various elements of Indigenous culture. In other words, Indigenous gothic today is a reclamation not merely of our stories, but also of the longer history of a gothic predicated on misrepresenting and appropriating Indigenous peoples and cultures. This dialectic, at least in the manner in which it unfolds here, is limited in scope, focusing strictly on a small selection of works about the Windigo written by Indigenous storytellers from Turtle Island. Similar trends in the gothic have been taken up by Indigenous peoples from other regions around the globe, and these too have garnered scholarly debate in recent years; other Indigenous gothics have and should also be given their due, but I will leave that to the Indigenous scholars from those regions, tribes, and nations.

Background: Claims to the Gothic

The origin of a literary gothic tradition is often associated with the publication of Horace Walpole's 1764 novel *The Castle of Otranto*, with its dark aesthetics, meandering passageways, and animated dead. Importantly, the first edition of *The Castle of Otranto* did not lay claim to the 'gothic', although the second edition adopts 'A Gothic Story' as its subtitle. Rather, the novel was largely inspired by the history and culture of the Goths, and later, many of the elements it takes up become repeated within literature and culture that would become classified as gothic, reproducing tropes made popular by Walpole's novel. Nick Groom claims that *The Castle of Otranto* 'is best understood not as the first rudimentary attempt in a new genre or as the genesis of the Gothic literary tradition in English, but rather as the climax of eighteenth-century discussion and debate about the Goths and "Gothick"'.[13] As such, the novel did not inaugurate something new so much as it embodied and gave literary space to ideas and tensions already existing. Leading up to *The Castle of Otranto*, literature that looked to the Goths often represented them as the inverse of classical Rome, and thus they were considered 'crude, ignorant, vulgar, brutish ... barbarous and rude' who 'laid waste' in their 'uncivilized' and 'primitive' ways.[14] The colonial representations of the Goths are not so different from the ways in which Indigenous peoples of Turtle Island have been represented. The Goths therefore demonstrate not only how the qualities that manifest as tropes in gothic literature existed hundreds of years prior to their inspiration in *The Castle of Otranto* but also how these qualities are interwoven with coloniality.

Britain's claim to gothic's origins with the publication of Walpole's novel is therefore part of Britain's coloniality, that is, a 'sort of permanent dissociation'. For Aníbal Quijano, who proposed such a 'coloniality of power', dissociation occurs 'between the Eurocentrist perspective of knowledge and the specific history of Latin America', but it becomes applicable for all 'conquered populations'.[15] Quijano demonstrates how 'along with America there was produced a mental category to codify the relations between conquering and conquered populations' that ultimately resulted in 'the associated cultural differences [becoming] codified as well, respectively, as superior and inferior'.[16] Britain's claim to the gothic tradition therefore establishes a superiority counter not just to the inferiority of the culture of the Goths as well as the oral stories of Indigenous peoples, but to all cultures they deem 'conquered'. For instance, in *The Castle of Otranto*, Manfred considers the former inhabitants of the Castle to be conquered, but his power is questioned when the descendants of those with legitimate claim return to assert said claim with the help of, presumably, supernatural aid. It is an early example of 'land back', 'the demand for the return of lands and waters, [that] is central to the struggles of Indigenous peoples against

4 Pre-colonial Gothic and the Windigo

the forces of settler colonialism and neoliberal capitalism'.[17] The novel as well as the gothic thus bespeaks the big IBG (Indian burial ground) trope where any present and future inhabitants of the land are doomed to be haunted by its former residents. Works such as Tobe Hooper's *Poltergeist* (1982), Stephen King's *Pet Sematary* (1983), and Stanley Kubrick's cinematic adaptation of *The Shining* (1980) each embody the big IBG as the finality of the vanishing Indian trope and demonstrate how the former Indigenous population remains silent. Amy Elizabeth Gore would refer to this as the 'Indigenous unspeakable', and while silencing is problematic, it can also 'productively redirect' attention away from 'a text's *manifest* content' or the Indigenous 'monster' 'to a text's *latent* content of historical trauma, instigated by experiences of genocide and colonization'.[18] The Windigo does not necessarily become a metonymic vehicle for the larger issues of trauma and genocide so much as the Indigenous Gothic works to unveil how the manifestation of the Windigo in contemporary culture is the result of such latent issues.

Gore, while exploring the etymology of the term 'gothic', asserts that it was 'only a matter of time before Indigenous writers and critics would reclaim the Gothic genre' as the literary aesthetic is defined as '[b]arbarous, rude, uncouth, unpolished, in bad taste. Of temper: Savage. It does not take a postcolonial critic to recognise the metanarrative of colonialism in this definition or the parallels to common derogatory terminology such as 'savage' hurled at Indigenous people.'[19] However, classicists of the Goths are interrogating the ways in which their culture has been represented, and instead, assert the obverse interpretation: 'while the Goths can certainly still be seen as a horde of destructive thugs who had razed classical civilization, they could also be understood as presenting an alternative to the imperial hegemony of ancient Rome – an alternative that resisted and rebelled against tyranny'.[20] In and of itself then, the gothic is not solely a mode of storytelling that creates monsters, but a method for resisting coloniality, which is what Indigenous storytellers who take up the aesthetic are doing.

When Drew Hayden Taylor published his vampire novel, *The Night Wanderer*, in 2007, he subtitled it 'A Native Gothic Novel' in what can be seen as a parallel to Otranto's novel. In doing so, Taylor's subtitle is less about asserting its claim to the gothic more broadly and more about entering into a dialogue about its origins. Whether this is what Burnham calls 'Indigenous Gothic' or Velie calls 'tribal gothic' or 'Indian gothic' or a kind of 'ethno-gothic',[21] in the hands of Indigenous writers, such as Taylor, these works 'represent an effort to 'write back' to a colonialist tradition in which the Indian represented the repressed unconscious of the nation's (and the continent's) own violent history'.[22] On the ethno-gothic, which is not exclusive to Indigenous storytellers, Arthur Redding claims that 'contemporary ethnic writers strive to undo prevailing racist and racially inflected stereotypes',[23] such as the uncivilised savage, as discussed earlier in this chapter, the vanishing Indian, and pan-Indianism. Yet, in many ways an ethno-gothic (and Indigenous Gothic) shares much in common with the gothic deployed by colonialists as both are haunted by the same history – however, one seeks to continue to repress their haunting while the other seeks to liberate it. World-gothic becomes particularly salient here, as, proposed by Duncan and Cumpsty in this volume, 'it is not a matter of subdividing the gothic into yet another subspecies, but rather a place in which to collect gothic production from the full scope of regions and perspectives (including the 'original' British version), by proposing that gothic forms in all their diversity appear in response to local realities shaped by the same world-system'. A pre-colonial gothic aesthetic is world-gothic, and what it does is to engage both the Eurocentrist attempt to maintain repression as well as the Indigenous attempt to liberate it – they are both located responses to coloniality.

Indigenous peoples, as world-gothic demonstrates, are also not necessarily the first to harness the potential of the gothic, so it seems rather telling of coloniality to single out Indigenous groups in particular. Redding argues that '[c]ontemporary ethno-gothic nurtures the hybrid potentials of the genre itself',[24] highlighting how the genre has never been exclusive to one group. So, to argue for the inclusion of Indigenous storytellers within contemporary gothic conversations is to participate in a longer history of celebrating the genre's hybrid potential. To accomplish this, I look to stories of the Windigo for various reasons: (1) these stories have captured the attention of non-Indigenous writers and filmmakers; (2) these stories predate colonialism and yet contemporary Indigenous storytellers continue to engage and adapt them; and (3) ultimately, the Windigo calls for an exploration of a kind of pre-colonial gothic, one that demonstrates the existence of a gothic aesthetic within Indigenous cultures that prefigures and predates *The Castle of Otranto*.

Ultimately, what the gothic in the hands of Indigenous storytellers reveals is that Indigenous traditions were never conquered, and within pre-colonial stories reside methods for understanding both pre-colonial as well as contemporary concerns facing Indigenous peoples. The failure to include Indigenous works within conversations of the gothic is a further act perpetuating coloniality and Indigenous erasure. As Byron argues, on the globalgothic, 'one of the effects of the increasing mobility and fluidity of people and products in the globalised world has been a growing awareness that the tropes and strategies Western critics have associated with the gothic, such as the ghost, the vampire and the zombie, have their counterparts in other cultures, however differently these may be inflected by specific histories and belief systems'.[25] The globalgothic, Byron claims, is 'about a need to decentre the West'.[26] But again, the globalgothic takes spatiality as its reference point and does not question the gothic's beginnings. Because the slippages between the Windigo and the zombie, for instance, demonstrate a shared gothic aesthetic with both temporal and geographical implications, world-gothic provides an important and rich space of exploration. Productively, this chapter asks several fecund questions in this dialectic. In what ways does reading the Windigo through a Western gothic sensibility destabilise the genre/mode? What might we learn about pre-colonial Indigenous culture from reading the Windigo in this manner? And, in so doing, can we consider the possibilities of a pre-colonial gothic as a method for critiquing and dismantling the 'coloniality of power'?

Do Not Consume Yourself: 'Wendigo Story'

The events detailed in Isaac Murdoch's (Anishnaabe) oral 'Wendigo Story' take place 'a long time ago', perhaps even before colonisation.[27] The story follows an uncle and his nephew on a hunting trip when they suddenly realise that they want to eat each other but they do not seem to understand why. In response, they make traditional offerings and ask the spirits to help them. Suddenly, they are accosted by a smell of death drifting into their cabin, so they vacate it, but as they travel towards the lake with their dogs, they encounter a Wendigo. He looks like a man, but he is a 'monster' that is much larger, and he has a heart of ice and no lips because he has chewed them off. He speaks 'Indian', telling the two men that he must eat.[28] Despite the uncle shooting him, the Wendigo proceeds to eat the nephew. The uncle is a strong medicine man and eventually he manages to overcome the Wendigo and cut out its icy heart. Similar to 'On the Wings of This Prayer', the body of Murdoch's Wendigo is plagued by a coldness that transforms the body itself. The uncle cuts the Wendigo into pieces, but the creature is still overcome by its own insatiable hunger, and so it eats the pieces of its own body. This Wendigo is too far gone. The boy, however, is just turning Wendigo, and so his uncle can use ceremony to cure him. While the remaining bits of the Wendigo are buried within a circle of stones, the story warns the listener that if those stones are ever disturbed, he may return. Similar to Van Camp's story, Murdoch's 'Wendigo Story' acts as a warning against extracting from the earth, as doing so really just demonstrates that one is consuming oneself.

As an oral story that can be accessed online, Murdoch's tale is a living document that bridges traditional forms of oral storytelling with contemporary modes of story production and dissemination. As such, it is of the past, present, and future, existing simultaneously within multiple temporalities in much the same way that Van Camp's story does. Because Murdoch does not position the story within a particular time, and the characters and events are not indicative of any specific moment within history, the story simultaneously marks a pre-coloniality even as it critiques issues that plague contemporary Indigenous peoples. As such, 'Wendigo Story' can be read as an example of a pre-colonial gothic aesthetic that resists as much as it embodies coloniality.

Appropriating the Windigo

In 1910, Algernon Blackwood, one of the most prolific writers of the gothic, took up the Wendigo in his short story of the same name. Blackwood's story is one of many in the trend by non-Indigenous authors in addressing, but ultimately misrepresenting and misappropriating, Indigenous figures that lend themselves to a gothic aesthetic. For non-Indigenous gothic writers, Indigenous peoples and cultures primarily function as 'a source of horror, guilt, and trauma'.[29] Whereas 'On the Wings of This Prayer' represents a strong Dogrib approach to the Wheetago. Blackwood's story, like many settler stories that appropriate Indigenous culture, empties the figure of any distinct tribal or national characteristics.

Similarly, Jim Makichuk's 1981 film, *Ghostkeeper*, takes a pan-Indianist approach to the Windigo. The film introduces us to its central topic with an intertitle: 'In the Indian Legends of North America, there exists a creature called Windigo ... a ghost who lives on human flesh.'[30] With over 600 federally recognised First Nations communities representing fifty different Nations in Canada alone, each having a distinct language and culture, and many of which having their own version of the Windigo story, Makichuk's intertitle is rather vague and misrepresentative of the diversity of Indigenous communities. The film follows three friends exploring along the side of a mountain when they are forced to take refuge inside a lodge. When Jenny admits that she believes someone else might be wandering around the lodge, Chrissy jokingly says, 'What, like a vampire?' It is not, of course, a vampire, but a mother, her son, and a Windigo that they keep locked away behind a wall of ice. Chrissy's response therefore collapses any significant distinctions between monsters and Indigenous creatures that lend themselves to a monstrous sensibility. In the film, the Windigo is represented as a pale man with dark liquid running down his face, and he seems largely incapable of leaving his icy refuge/prison. Chrissy first falls victim not necessarily to the Windigo, so much as to the creepy, isolated family who feed the Windigo, and shortly thereafter, Walter becomes infected with the Windigo psychosis, evidenced by the appearance of dark liquid running down his face and his ramblings as he runs off into the woods. While it seems as if Jenny becomes a kind of final girl at the end of film, killing both the mother and son, she vows to care for the Windigo, and the final scene slowly zooms in on her sitting contentedly in a chair inside the lodge while the mother's voice over tells Jenny she will be alright.

While Jenny presents no external markers of the Windigo psychosis, she does embody 'the particular madness represented by the windigo ... of possessive individualism in which the isolated self chooses to preserve itself quite literally at the expense of others; windigo describes a person or condition characterized by the destructive consumption and unhuman humanity of hyperindividualism'.[31] In Jenny's case, this is due in part to circumstance, having to survive the mother and son, but also due to her boyfriend's lack of hunger for her. During the first half of the film, her boyfriend pines for the affections of Chrissy, and when he goes off seeking an unsuccessfully fulfilled sexual encounter with her, both he and Jenny succumb to the Windigo psychosis – him as infected and she as hyperindividualised.

Much of these works have been criticised for appropriating and misrepresenting Indigenous culture, yet – at the same time – gothic scholarship seems to insist on keeping Indigenous-made works entirely separate from the gothic. This presents us with a kind of non-choice where Indigenous storytellers cannot contribute to the gothic, and yet those gothic writers and filmmakers who engage Indigenous culture in their works are potentially doing so problematically. In many ways, this bespeaks a 'coloniality of power'. Gore argues, '[a]lthough Native literature for cultural epistemology is essential, the Indigenous, Tribalistic Gothic literature remains still underutilised'.[32] As such, the solution to both of these problems is to acknowledge Indigenous contributions to the gothic. When discussing Charles Brockden Brown's gothic novel, *Edgar Huntley*, for instance, Christine Yao argues that the novel 'suggests that when it comes to monstrous tropes in the American gothic, Native Americans may seem to be absent but their presences and history will eventually be revealed, demonstrating their continual survival and resistance.'[33] While Yao might have envisioned said revelation to take the form of monsters and ghosts, the sudden (re)turn of Indigenous storytellers taking up the gothic better encapsulates this continued survival and resistance.

We might consider the more recent parallels drawn between the Windigo and the zombie as an assertion of not just survival and resistance but also contemporary sovereignty on the part of Indigenous storytellers. Indigenous Gothic demonstrates not a colonisation of Indigenous culture in the manner that Blackwood and Makichuk approach it, but more accurately a resistance to being subsumed under contemporary Western media. As I noted at the beginning of this chapter, many contemporary Indigenous Gothic works use the term 'zombie' in stories of the Windigo or as a contemporary reworking of what the Windigo represents, but they also play with the zombie subgenre more broadly to make claims of Indigenous sovereignty. This may seem as if Indigenous storytellers are being subsumed under contemporary Western media, but in actuality, they are morphing the contemporary gothic to better embody Indigenous lived experience. I would now like to turn to two tales that deal exclusively with the zombie: *Zombies and Indians* and *Blood Quantum*. This is not to assert that the zombie, which is born from transatlantic slavery and the plantations in Haiti, is synonymous with the Windigo, although more research on this comparison may reveal a shocking list of similarities; rather, this is to demonstrate how the similarities in the two ensure that the Windigo is always already primed for the gothic.

Let Him In: *Zombies and Indians*

When the seeming Other is banging on the door, threatening to let the monsters in, Indigenous stories tell us that we need to constantly reassess not so much who the monsters are but rather why the monsters have come. American gothic has always been concerned with questions of the Other threatening to get inside, only to reveal that the Other, in many cases, was already there. Eric Savoy addresses this, claiming that the 'entire tradition of American gothic can be conceptualized as the attempt to invoke "the face of the tenant" – the spectre of Otherness that haunts the house of national narrative'.[34] Burnham, responding directly to Savoy, points out how the 'house', or rather the continent, 'belongs to its indigenous peoples ... invert[ing] the traditional racial dynamics of American Gothic. In this view, it is the settler colonist whose face has taken up an unwelcome tenancy in the Native American home, and whose threatening presence haunts American Indian narrative'.[35] Building on this dialectic, I wish to posit that Indigenous peoples, far more than settler colonists on Turtle Island, are deserving of inheriting the power to wield the gothic trope of the unwelcome tenant, and we would be remiss to assume that the Indigenous stories that came before Brown or Edgar Allan Poe did not fully explore its power.

While Keith Lawrence's 2019 short film *Zombies and Indians* takes a futuristic zombie apocalypse as its topic, the zombie here can be seen to embody the trope of the unwelcome, monstrous settler. In fact, the characters in the film refer to them as 'Other'. The film follows Kirt and Will, two Indigenous survivors standing atop a gate, guarding the entrance to the Rez. An Elder, dressed in traditional clothing and pulling a covered cart, stumbles up to the gate, but he only speaks in traditional Indigenous language. Kirt and Will are unable to understand him and so Kirt demands that he 'speak English'. While Will seems to still value tradition, Kirt wrestles with whether it has a place in this world: 'this isn't about tradition; this is about life and death', Kirt asserts, while Will counters, 'What's the difference?' Kirt's view suggests that tradition should be abandoned when faced with monsters whereas Will demonstrates that the two are always already interconnected. However, both of the survivors panic when the Elder starts banging on the gate to get inside, attracting every zombie in the area.

The mise en scène in this moment is a high-angle shot typically designed to displace the viewer from the characters and actions depicted onscreen – separating us, like Kirt, from the Elder and everything he signifies. The Elder is centred at the metal gate, which is covered in bloody handprints, and as the Elder bangs, placing his hands again and again in the spaces between the bloody handprints, the fragmentation between tradition and survival suggests a loss of the Elder and their signification, such as stories, traditional language, and cultural knowledge. Will does not take action here, but pleads with Kirt to 'let him in'. Kirt refuses, and as he does so, the zombies move ever closer, but also, in this moment the non-diegetic soundtrack morphs into drumming, suggesting that tradition is exactly what is required in this situation. As Kirt wrestles with whether he should let him in, flashes of a traditional Indigenous dancer in front of a bullet-riddled metal wall break through, and just as the zombies encroach on the Elder, Kirt opens the gates. When the Elder and his cart are finally inside, Kirt throws back the blankets, and while the contents of the cart are never revealed on-screen, whatever is inside is bright and lights up Kirt's face while he laughs, and then suddenly, he awakens. Kirt and Will still stand atop the gate amidst a zombie apocalypse, but everything else seems to have been a dream. Kirt smiles, claiming he 'just had a visit with his grandfather, a damn good visit'. The dream of Kirt's grandfather demonstrates how the monsters at the door are not the real threat; rather, in battling monsters, Indigenous characters risk losing their culture and languages and traditions. While *Zombies and Indians* does not use the name Windigo when referring to its monsters, Kathleen Brogan's take on the Windigo might be applicable here. Burnham, quoting Brogan, claims that 'the fear of cannibalism is associated with the fear of "the eating away of tribal culture by an invasive new culture"'.[36] However, it is not in the power of the monster to take these things in *Zombies and Indians*; the Indigenous survivor here has the agency as to whether they continue to let those stories in.

Colonial Whiplash: *Blood Quantum*

Jeff Barnaby's 2019 zombie film *Blood Quantum* asks similar questions about Indigeneity – is it in the blood? And, if we lose the Elders who carry our stories and language, how do we continue? Gore asserts that times of transition often engender the gothic,[37] and the burgeoning of Indigenous Gothic, such as *Zombies and Indians* and *Blood Quantum*, represents Bruno Starrs's 'literary retaliation' whereby previously silenced Indigenous peoples, or rather the Indigenous unspeakable, have 'wrestl[ed] the keyboard away' and are finally 'writing back'.[38] And, nowhere is this more apparent than in *Blood Quantum*, which references the ongoing coloniality marked by Canadian/Indigenous conflicts and the transference of the Elder into story.

Blood Quantum is set in 1981 – the same year that the Quebec Provincial Police raided the Listuguj community, violating their Treaty Rights. The film follows a group of Indigenous survivors on the fictional Red Crow Indian Reservation during a zombie apocalypse. Both Indigenous and settler survivors inhabit Red Crow, although the inclusion of the latter is a point of contention for some characters. Like many zombie narratives, the pathogen eventually makes its way into the safe zone, leading to the downfall of the reservation. The film ultimately ends with three Indigenous survivors floating away on a fishing boat in what is a kind of reclamation of the Treaty Rights taken during the 1981 raids – it is land back. What sets the film apart from other zombie stories, however, is that Indigenous survivors, and only Indigenous survivors, are immune to the zombie virus, and so the film constantly asks its characters, and the

4 Pre-colonial Gothic and the Windigo 93

audience, to question how much Indigenous blood is enough to establish immunity, hence the title *Blood Quantum*.

Whether the immunity of the Indigenous characters arises in tandem with the zombie infestation or has always been a part of Indigenous being is unclear. One theory presented in the film is that the land brought forth this virus to eliminate the invasive species – which we could otherwise call settlers – and establish a kind of land back, suggesting the virus and thus immunity come from the land itself, similar to the Wheetago in Van Camp's story. Scientifically, this makes sense, for when humans travel into areas that they have not previously explored, they make contact with new microbes.[39] Therefore, if the zombie virus in *Blood Quantum* is native (so to speak) to Turtle Island, then contact with the virus becomes deadly for those who are newer to the area. Regardless, the zombie infestation allows for a restructuring of dominant groups in times of transition, that is, when Indigenous rights are most at risk, such as the salmon fishing raids in 1981.

In an interview with *The Globe and Mail*, Barnaby reveals that one of his earliest memories of contact with people from off Listuguj was a rifle butt to the head during the 1981 raids.[40] Therefore, Restigouche marks Barnaby's 'first contact' – literally – and was clearly a colonial encounter that inspired much of his film. In a way, Barnaby's experience suggests that the pre-colonial has no end as contact and the 'coloniality of power' are constantly reified through settler/Indigenous encounters. For instance, the actual fish used in the opening scene of *Blood Quantum* are salmon, and because they are inedible, Elder Gisigu is barred from being able to engage with his Treaty Rights in a reference to the 1981 raids. By turning the salmon into zombies, not only is Barnaby drawing attention to how the salmon were historically taken from the Mi'kmaq during the raids, but he also makes them inedible for settler peoples in a kind of haunting back against the raids and restrictions and warning against the dangers of overconsumption, similar to tales of the Windigo. As a result, neither the settlers nor the Mi'kmaq survivors can consume the zombie fish and thus, the overfishing of the species effectively comes to a halt.

Consumption is therefore a prominent concept throughout *Blood Quantum*, beginning with the two 'Ancient Settler Proverbs' that open the film. One of them states, 'Take heed to thyself, that thou make no treaty with the inhabitants of the land whither thou goest lest it be the cause of ruin among you. . . . when they whore themselves to their demons and sacrifice to them, you will eat their sacrifices. And when you choose some of their daughters for your sons, they will lead your sons to do the same.' This 'Ancient Settler Proverb' comes from Exodus 34: 12–17, which deals with the issue of whether it is still idolatry to eat the meat sacrificed to idols if one does not partake in the sacrifice itself. The eating of sacrifices in this passage becomes intertwined with interracial coupling, and whether the offspring of said coupling should be sacrificed, which returns us to the title of the film. Disturbingly, such a consumption literally occurs in an early uncanny scene in which a white, zombified mother is depicted devouring her biracial baby. This scene is one of many in *Blood Quantum* that reinforce the constant anxiety about whether the offspring of interracial coupling will result in there being *enough* Indigenous blood to ensure immunity: will these babies be consumers like the settler zombies or consumables like the immune Indigenous survivors? Essentially, will they let their Elders in? Immunity therefore places Indigenous bodies (and so, their culture) at risk of erasure via consumption (and coloniality), but it also invests them with the opportunity to resist, the opportunity, like the survivors in *Zombies and Indians*, to continue to let one's ancestors in.

The film's conclusion best embodies this idea in an animated scene depicting Elder Gisigu's 'last' stand. In the live action scene, it appears as if Gisigu perishes as he goes down fighting a horde of zombies at the edge of Red Crow. However, when the scene changes from live action to animation, Gisigu emerges from beneath the mass of zombie bodies. He holds up the head of one zombie and, in the Mi'kmaw language, he declares, 'none of you are getting past this line'. Because this statement is in Mi'kmaw, it is not necessarily meant for the settlers, which means *Blood Quantum* hails the Indigenous viewer and critiques the dearth of Indigenous representation in gothic media more broadly. The tension between the live action and animated parts of Elder Gisigu's 'last stand' forces us to question his fate – does he survive, or has he perished? Our privileging of live action (or history) over animation (or story) might entice us to give in to the idea that Elder Gisigu has fallen. However, I argue that both are true – to disrupt the binary of life and death as well as past and present, the seemingly random animated scenes in the film are story, and while Elder Gisigu may indeed perish beneath the zombies in live action, he lives on in the animated scene as story. Elder Gisigu's fate in *Blood Quantum* is part of the film's resistance to the binary because it 'imagine[s] other space-times',[41] as Billy-Ray Belcourt calls it, as well as life and death occurring simultaneously, similar to the manner in which a haunting occurs. Belcourt believes that part of the process of decolonisation comes from theorising temporality through 'Indian time' or 'the regularity with which Indigenous peoples arrive late or are behind schedule'.[42] Belcourt does not propose this in the literal sense of being late to work, for instance, but in bringing the past into the present as well as future imaginings,[43] similar to Van Camp. In many ways, world-gothic is about including 'other space-times'. Both the Windigo and zombie stories discussed throughout this chapter demonstrate such a collapse of temporality, for instance. Specifically, Belcourt argues that Indian time 'nullifies the normative temporality of settler colonialism in which death is the telos of the human and being-in-death is an ontological fallacy'.[44] While Belcourt is using the figure of the poltergeist to remodel understandings of queer Indigeneities, his focus on figures of haunting to resist the telos of death is applicable to Elder Gisigu and *Blood Quantum* as well as Windigo and Indigenous Elders more broadly. Elder Gisigu's animated scene resists death and repositions his character in a synchronous lifeline. Moreover, the figure of the zombie is literally an embodiment of death in life. Belcourt suggests that to decolonise is to 'imagine other time-spaces' and 'we must become feral' in order to fully accomplish such an imagining.[45] Ferality to Belcourt comes in the form of the poltergeist, but for Barnaby and *Blood Quantum*, it is the zombie, and for Van Camp and Murdoch, it is the Wheetago/Windigo.

Conclusion

While Burnham never quite settles on whether an Indigenous Gothic indeed does exist, I find myself more concerned with the potential of the question she puts forward in regard to a kind of pre-colonial gothic: 'If we extend our search to other places, times, and traditions – such as the figures and stories of windigo, witches, and ghosts in the precontact Americas – how might those discoveries change, complicate, and enrich our understanding of the Gothic and its history?'.[46] Whereas, as Burnham notes, stories of the Windigo both by Indigenous and non-Indigenous peoples depict the figure as terrifying, the big difference is that Indigenous traditions see such a figure as also valuable, carrying the potential for 'wholeness and healing'.[47] First and foremost, to quote Burnham, these stories 'represent Native American contributions to – but also Native American interventions in – American Gothic' where Indigenous characters are not the source of the fear and danger but rather can finally experience the fear and danger they have been repressing since colonisation.[48] In so doing, gothic in the hands of Indigenous peoples allows for 'overturning the kinds of possessive acts (possession by ghostly spirits, but also possession of material land) established by America's Gothic tradition'.[49]

In terms of the gothic's pre-colonial potential, 'The indigenous prehistory of the gothic, and its continued place in contemporary fiction by both Native and non-Native writers, suggests that the gothic may not have been invented in eighteenth century Britain so much as it was expressed there in a particularly powerful and resonant form. That site has since become crystallized as the point of origin for a form whose history may be much longer, more global, and less linear than we have supposed'.[50] Globalgothic scholarship expanded the gothic's geographical confines, and now it is time for a world-gothic to emerge to shatter the spatial and temporal parameters by looking to the ways in which Indigenous storytellers have and will continue to take up the genre. Likely, we can expect many more gothic-esque works coming from the mouths and the pens of Indigenous peoples as, to quote Velie, after being the monster in the gothic for too many years, we are 'anxious to even the balance'.[51]

Notes

1. Richard Van Camp, 'On the Wings of This prayer', in S. Moreno-Garcia (ed.), *Dead North: Canadian Zombie Fiction*, Toronto, Exile Editions, 2014, 167.
2. Obscure Life-Forms, 'Creatures', Obscure Life-Forms, n.d., https://obscure.gamepuppet.com/data/jenu.htm.
3. Alan R. Velie, 'Vizenor's Indian Gothic', *MELUS*, 17:1 (1991–2), 75–85, 78.
4. Van Camp, 'On the Wings of This prayer', 164.
5. Van Camp, 'On the Wings of This prayer', 166.
6. Van Camp, 'On the Wings of This prayer', 170.
7. Van Camp, 'On the Wings of This prayer', 168.
8. Michelle Burnham, 'Is There an Indigenous Gothic?' in C. L. Crow (ed.), *A Companion to the Gothic: American Gothic and Race*, North Carolina, John Wiley & Sons, 2014, 226.
9. Glennis Byron, 'Introduction', in G. Byron (ed.), *Globalgothic*, Manchester, Manchester University Press, 2016, 1.
10. Byron, 'Introduction', 6.
11. Burnham, 'Is There an Indigenous Gothic?' 225–6.
12. McEvoy, Emma. 'Gothic Traditions', in C. S. and E. McEvoy (eds.), *The Routledge Companion to Gothic*, London, Routledge, 2007, 7.
13. Nick Groom, 'Introduction', in N. Groom (ed.), *The Castle of Otranto*, Oxford, Oxford University Press, 2014, ix.
14. Groom, 'Introduction', xi.
15. Aníbal Quijano, 'Coloniality of Power and Eurocentrism in Latin America', *International Sociology*, 15:2 (2000), 215–32, 215.
16. Aníbal Quijano, 'Coloniality of Power and Eurocentrism in Latin America', 216.

17. Julia Tomiak, 'Land Back/Cities Back', *Urban Geography*, 44:2 (2023), 292–4, 292.
18. Amy Gore, 'Gothic Silence: S. Alice Callahan's *Wynema*, the Battle of the Little Bighorn, and the Indigenous Unspeakable', *Studies in American Indian Literatures*, 30:1 (2018), 25.
19. Amy Gore, 'Intersections of Indigenous and Tribalistic Gothic', Atmostfear Entertainment, n.d., www.atmostfear-entertainment.com/culture/traditions/intersections-indigenous-tribalistic-gothic/. All further references made in text to this version.
20. Groom, 'Introduction', xii.
21. Arthur Redding, 'Ethno-Gothic: Repurposing Genre in Contemporary American Literature', in J. Faflak and J. Haslam (eds.), *American Gothic Culture: An Edinburgh Companion*, Edinburgh, Edinburgh University Press, 2016, 60.
22. Burnham, 'Is There an Indigenous Gothic?' 226.
23. Redding, 'Ethno-Gothic', 61.
24. Redding, 'Ethno-Gothic', 74.
25. Byron, 'Introduction', 3.
26. Byron, 'Introduction', 4.
27. Isaac Murdoch, 'Isaac Murdoch's Wendigo Story', CBC, n.d., www.cbc.ca/player/play/audio/1.6633650.
28. Murdoch, 'Isaac Murdoch's Wendigo Story'.
29. Burnham, 'Is There an Indigenous Gothic?' 226.
30. *Ghostkeeper*, dir. Jim Makichuk, Alberta, CA, Badland Pictures, 1981.
31. Burnham, 'Is There an Indigenous Gothic?' 231.
32. Gore, 'Intersections of Indigenous and Tribalistic Gothic'.
33. Christine Yao, 'Gothic Monstrosity: Charles Brockden Brown's *Edgar Huntley* and the Trope of the Bestial Indian', in J. Faflak and J. Haslam (eds.), *American Gothic Culture: An Edinburgh Companion*, Edinburgh, Edinburgh University Press, 2016, 40.
34. Eric Savoy, 'A Theory of American Gothic', in R. K. Martin and E. Savoy (eds.), *American Gothic: New Interventions in a National Narrative*, Iowa City, University of Iowa Press, 1998, 13–14.
35. Burnham, 'Is There an Indigenous Gothic?' 227.
36. Burnham, 'Is There an Indigenous Gothic?' 232.
37. Gore, 'Intersections of Indigenous and Tribalistic Gothic'.
38. Bruno Starrs, 'Writing Indigenous Vampires: Aboriginal Gothic or Aboriginal Fantastic?', *M/C: A Journal of Media and Culture*, 17:4 (2014).
39. Priscilla Wald, 'Preface', in S. Becker, M. de Bruin-Molé, and S. Polak (eds.), *Embodying Contagion: The Viropolitics of Horror and Desire in Contemporary Discourse*, Cardiff: University of Wales Press, 2021, xiv.
40. Sarah-Tai Black, 'Blood Quantum's Jeff Barnaby on the History and Horror of His Indigenous Zombie Movie: "I feel like I barely got out of this one alive"', *The Globe and Mail*, last modified 27 April 2020, www.theglobeandmail.com/arts/film/article-blood-quantums-jeff-barnaby-on-the-history-and-horror-of-his/.

41. Billy-Ray Belcourt, 'A Poltergeist Manifesto', *Feral Feminisms Feral Theory*, 6 (2016), 22–32, 28.
42. Belcourt, 'A Poltergeist Manifesto', 28.
43. Belcourt, 'A Poltergeist Manifesto', 28.
44. Belcourt, 'A Poltergeist Manifesto', 28.
45. Belcourt, 'A Poltergeist Manifesto', 28.
46. Burnham, 'Is There an Indigenous Gothic?' 226.
47. Burnham, 'Is There an Indigenous Gothic?' 233–4.
48. Burnham, 'Is There an Indigenous Gothic?' 228.
49. Burnham, 'Is There an Indigenous Gothic?' 228.
50. Burnham, 'Is There an Indigenous Gothic?' 234.
51. Velie, 'Vizenor's Indian Gothic', 78.

CHAPTER 5

Hauntings
African-Based Spirituality in World-Gothic Literature
James Mellis

As a vehicle for uncovering buried secrets or revealing historical transgressions, haunting in gothic literature typically assumes that the ghost is an extraordinary and disruptive figure. The inheritance of this view lies in Western Judeo-Christian traditions, according to which spirit visitations are rare and troubling occurrences, and the world of the living is clearly delineated from that of the dead. 'As a cloud vanishes and is gone,' reads an exemplary line from Job 7:9–10, 'so one who goes down to the grave does not return'. This association between gothic and a Euro-Christian conception of the ghost can be tracked back to the early British gothic novels of the eighteenth and nineteenth centuries, where images of spirits and the spectral are shaped by the religious, cultural, and intellectual bequests of the Enlightenment, and appear in response to local shifts in the nature of commerce, finance, and commodity circulation. Though the characteristic features of this corpus have long been considered to provide the model for later gothic fiction, contributors to this collection propose that it may be more generative to view the 'original' British gothic as just one among many regionally and culturally situated mediations of encounters with global capitalist modernity. Bringing this world-gothic perspective to bear on haunting therefore opens up the possibility that this trope may be more variegated in its forms and functions than has generally been assumed within gothic theory. World-gothic ghosts might encompass a range of spiritual traditions, including those in which spirit presences among the living are not unnatural expressions of unresolved conflicts or historical violence, but rather a more ordinary feature of the world as it usually is. In the light of this more plural view of haunting, it becomes necessary to provincialise the Eurocentric notion of spirit visitation that has so far predominated in gothic criticism.

This chapter contributes to this project of provincialisation by examining tropes and figures of haunting in a selection of narratives from the African continent and African diaspora. Spirit encounters in these texts are deployed to negotiate experiences and legacies of enslavement and colonisation: the systems of intense racialised oppression and exploitation which underpin the capitalist world-system across different phases of its history. Legible as examples of world-gothic in this way, the ghosts in this corpus are rooted in a range of African and African-derived traditions. If they invoke canonical gothic hauntings, they do so – as Sheri-Marie Harrison and Maisha Wester have respectively observed – in order to decentre this model of the ghost, by placing it alongside a different view that takes the existence of spirits in people's daily lives as given.

Within many Indigenous African religious traditions and their diasporic iterations, the spheres of the living and the dead remain connected. Traditional African religions are comprised of manifold differing belief systems that have changed and adapted through the diaspora and encounters with Europeans, including through slavery, evangelising, and conversion. Nevertheless, despite profound differences in their mythologies and cosmologies, both Western and African spiritual traditions share some fundamental commonalities. Yvonne Chireau notes when considering the supernatural that:

> Many Anglo-American Christians, for example, believed the celestial domain to be occupied by an almighty, benevolent deity *and* a host of spirits, including angels, archangels, and other malevolent entities, powers and principalities. Similarly, West and Central Africans would have viewed the cosmos as a heavily populated world in which a reciprocating traffic of invisible and visible beings moved, interacted and influenced each other.[1]

However, while in the Western episteme ghosts and spirits might occasionally and transgressively cross from one plane to the next, for the peoples of West Africa and some of their diasporic descendants, communion with the deceased is profoundly different. For example, in West African cosmology and its derivatives, there generally exists a Supreme Being, and a spiritual hierarchy consisting of: 'ancestral spirits, whom West Africans believed existed alongside their living descendants ... [and] a variety of lesser deities, who, unlike the supreme being, could be relied upon to take direct action in the lives of their followers'.[2] These deities, whether ancestral spirits or other supernatural beings (orishas, loas, jumbies, duppys, etc.), are believed to be perpetually present and regularly involved in African, African American, and Caribbean people's lives. 'Not only are the ancestors revered as past heroes, but they are felt to be still present, watching over the household. Directly concerned in all the affairs of the family and property, giving abundant harvests and fertility ... For many people, especially older ones who will soon join the ancestors, the invisible is almost as real as the visible.'[3] These Afro-centric spiritualisms, while nearly eradicated through the horrors of the Middle Passage and generations of slavery, nevertheless proved to be both malleable and durable, manifesting in the Americas and Caribbean as Vodou, Hoodoo, Conjure, Obeah, Santeria, Myal, Palo, and other syncretic spiritual traditions. In order to convey the durability of these traditions and their manifestation as world-gothic hauntings, this chapter compares representations of spirits in fiction from Nigeria and the Black diasporas of the United States and Caribbean.

Jesmyn Ward and Toni Morrison: A Black Atlantic of Seething Spirits

One recent example that centres Afro- and-Caribbean-centric renditions of hauntings is a scene from Jesmyn Ward's 2023 novel *Let Us Descend*. The scene can serve as a bridge both connecting and differentiating Eurocentric and Afrocentric conceptions of hauntings. *Let Us Descend* tells the story of Annis, an enslaved woman who, after being sold from the plantation of her birth, is forced to march from North Carolina to New Orleans as part of a coffle, a group of enslaved people chained together. During the journey, Annis is visited sporadically by Aza (the ancestral spirit of her grandmother) with whom Annis struggles as she remembers her family history, coming as she does from a line of women warriors in service to the Fon king. As she endeavours to survive the dangerous journey south, Annis remembers her mother's lessons regarding their spiritual legacy: '"They [white people] don't know", my mama said. "Them got to open a door, walk through a cave, go down into a valley or up a mountain to find spirit". My mama looked up to the wind tossing the trees. "This world is seething with it ... It's everywhere ... When you ask, spirit answer, Arese"', she said.[4] This exchange follows Annis' contemplation of Canto III of Dante's *Inferno* ('Through me you go to the grief wracked city / Through me you go to everlasting pain / ... Abandon all hope – Ye Who Enter Here') overheard being taught to her owner's children (and Annis' half-sisters). Ward's use of the descent into hell in Dante's *Inferno* suggests a metaphor for Annis' journey to New Orleans and serves to juxtapose Eurocentric and Afrocentric perspectives of human interaction with the supernatural. Like Esch, the teenaged protagonist of Ward's 2011 novel *Salvage the Bones*, who sees parallels between Medea's abandonment by Jason and her unrequited love for the teenage boy who impregnated her, Annis uses lessons from the Western cannon to frame and process her own horrific journey.

Through this framing, Ward contrasts Dante's need to physically journey to the netherworld to engage with spirits with the 'seething',[5] pervasive presence of spectres in Annis's family's episteme. For when Annis's mother remarks that 'They' (ostensibly white people who adhere to a Judeo-Christian Western tradition) must visit particular locales in order to commune with the spiritual realm, she clearly differentiates the ways that people of European descent and people of the African diaspora engage with and access the spiritual world. Whereas within the Eurocentric tradition of haunting spirits can enter the world through ritual, psychological disturbance, prayer, or journeying to a particular place, representing disruption or transgression, in African diasporic literature (though ritual is sometimes needed to gain access to the spiritual world), the barriers between the realms are more porous. The ancestral spirits and other ethereal beings are more readily available to be honoured, implored, wrestled with, or otherwise engaged. Ward contrasts Western myths and stories against an Afro/Caribbean supernatural spiritual tradition: a conceit that proves liberating for characters in *Let Us Descend* and in Ward's 2017's *Sing, Unburied, Sing*, which culminates in a Vodou ceremony as Mam, the matriarch of the family at the centre of the novel, dies and journeys to the afterlife aided by her living daughter Lonnie and the spirit of her pre-deceased son, Given. As Ward's novels demonstrate, the crosscurrents and cross-pollinations of African cosmological traditions into gothic cultural production significantly expands the rendering of hauntings.

However, before exploring ways that some literary works have addressed hauntings based on an Afro-centric cosmology, it is important to acknowledge that there are several Black authors (including Charles Chesnutt, Rudolph Fisher, Jean Toomer, Zora Neale Hurston, and Richard Wright, to name only a few), who have written within this 'traditional' western gothic. Like Ward, they have incorporated elements of the African diasporic experience into their work, crafting a genre of 'African-based spiritual fiction', which I've identified elsewhere as 'African-American realist fiction with African-based spiritual and religious elements (particularly Voodoo, hoodoo, conjure and rootwork) incorporated into the universe of the work'.[6] The merging of traditions in this body of work impeaches the notion of gothic literature as a primarily, or indeed a firstly European genre, necessitating a reconsideration of hauntings from a world-gothic perspective. In this conception, culturally specific monstrous forms of haunting or spirit presence tend to recur following encounters with colonial and capitalist regimes, of which slavery and its aftermath are prime examples.

Slavery, and its lasting effects, loom large in African and Black diasporic memory and consciousness. In 'The African American Slave Narrative and the Gothic', Teresa Goddu writes, 'Slavery – along with imperialism and revolution – served as a core cultural context for the Gothic'.[7] Indeed, slavery and its attendant construction of race helped to create and reinforce the tropes of 'Otherness' that inform gothic fictions. Imperial and pro-slavery gothic fictions cast African peoples as bestialised and racialised others. Black writers in the United States, like postcolonial writers of common cause, have appropriated the gothic mode to register the brutality of slavery and its violent afterlives through ghosts and hauntings. By writing from within an established Western literary tradition and incorporating non-Western spiritual elements into their work, these writers ask us to reconsider the long-standing Eurocentric perspective of gothic hauntings in lieu of varying localised folk and cultural responses to world-altering events, processes, and traumas. These responses, then, 'meet' the advance of encroaching capitalist and colonial projects in ways that decentre and destabilise Eurocentric conceptions of gothic literature. Toni Morrison's *Beloved* (1987) is one of the most significant tales of haunting in African American literature, but the spectre does not emerge from a purely Euro-Christian paradigm. To represent the generational trauma of the Middle Passage the novel adapts the traditional gothic ghost story by incorporating aspects of African cosmology. Based on the true story of Margaret Garner, who killed her two-year-old daughter rather than see her returned to slavery, Morrison's novel won the Pulitzer Prize and is widely recognised as one of the most important works of American fiction. In the novel, Sethe, her surviving daughter Denver, Paul D (whom she knew while they both were enslaved), and other members of their household are haunted by the ghost of Beloved, the child that the escaping Sethe killed when slavecatchers were closing in. In the novel, the ghost of Beloved develops relationships with Sethe, Denver, and Paul D, becoming increasingly demanding and powerful as the narrative progresses.

A world-gothic conception of haunting profoundly nuances Morrison's representation of spirits. Beloved monstrously embodies the trauma of slavery as a world-capitalist trade, but she is not merely a ghost in the Euro-Christian sense. Following West African religious traditions, she is the angered spirit of a child perceived, and eventually exorcised, by the community. Maisha Wester affirms this hybrid view of Beloved: 'a mysterious woman who is equally child, ancestral spirit, poltergeist, and succubus; and a community of tormented people plagued by infanticide, rape and madness'. Moreover, *Beloved* demonstrates 'the ways the Gothic may be deployed as a historical mode, using the disquieting and perplexing realities of African American existence' – and Afro-centric spiritualism – 'rather than imagined terrors, to sustain its aura of apprehension'.[8] Eventually, in stark contrast to Euro-Christian exorcisms which are typically performed by a sole white male, the novel ends somewhat optimistically with the women of the town communally exorcise Beloved from the home and Paul D tries to get Sethe to accept that she is her 'own best thing'.[9] Guilt, trauma, lost love, community, and the profound effects of slavery are pervasive themes in the novel, which has been read from a plethora of critical perspectives. Yet, 'at the most basic plot and setting, *Beloved* is a ghost story' that 'creates dissonance through increasingly intrusive manifestations of haunting'. As Carol Schudde further notes,

> Morrison's narrative treats the presence of the ghost with folkloric givenness; in contrast to most conventional ghost stories, suspense and terror are created not by the supernatural per se but by the effect on the main characters of confronting the undead past in the context of the present, and by the effect on the reader of confronting the historical past through the mythic past of fiction.[10]

Morrison leaves no doubt as to the historical and multigenerational trauma of the transatlantic slave trade undergirding Beloved, dedicating the novel to 'Sixty Million and more', a framing device which reaches back across the Atlantic to encompass the history of slavery, the idea of ancestral spirits ('folkloric givenness'), and the manifold ways that the structures of racialised capitalism continue to haunt the Americas and elsewhere. As seen in the novel, however, it is more than simply memory that haunts the characters in Beloved; it is the manifestation of traumatic history and cultural and spiritual syncretism fed by both sides of the Atlantic and infused with the 'seething' closeness of the living and dead. The communal exorcism of Beloved at the end of the novel is, then, more than 'folkloric givenness', it demonstrates the meeting of local, African-based spirituality with the world-systemic changes wrought by slavery and its echoes in Sethe and her extended community's lives.

It is important to delineate the work by Morrison, Ward, and others who are drawing explicitly from 'traditional' gothic aesthetics, from work by African, African American, and Caribbean authors who address the concept of haunting from a wholly different, more fully Afro-centric perspective. As Duncan and Cumpsty explain, world-gothic makes this distinction generative by allowing 'us to discern the linkages between' 'traditional', Euro-Christian forms of haunting and 'a much wider array of located figures and tales of alienation and anxiety'. Wester and Xavier Aldana Reyes note the expanding parameters of the gothic, writing, '[i]n the Anglo-American world, and, increasingly, the global sphere, the Gothic has become a wider term to designate non-realistic modes of writing and now encompasses horror, certain strands of science fiction and speculative fiction ... and all generic hybrids that contain elements traditionally associated with the Gothic'.[11] The 'non-realistic' modes of writing alluded to by Wester and Aldana Reyes echo similar conceptions of an expanded perspective of the gothic articulated by Sheri-Marie Harrison, who defines global horror as made up of characteristics including 'generic instability tentatively organised around the category of speculative fiction ... and reliance on a multi-generic, international, and transhistorical network of texts that links the local with the global, while bypassing the nation'. Additionally, Harrison notes speculative fiction's possibilities for accommodating a global perspective: 'terms like magical realism, the fantastic, hoodoo, and voodoo all reflect historically-and geographically-situated meanings, the reach for speculative forms in the present uproots and combines these previously located concepts in a manner that reflects the global circulation of texts and people'.[12] We should note that this 'global circulation' has existed since the long sixteenth century, straining the application of gothic forms and figures. Thus, we might consider that the very concept of 'haunting' in African diasporic literature is a misnomer, as the popular conception of the term stems from a Judeo-Christian, rather than Afro-centric perspective. At the very least, with merging supernaturalisms of Europe and the Black Atlantic resulting in unique heteroglossic texts and perspectives, the notion of "haunting" in diasporic literature must be reconceived. Viewing a selection of African and Black diasporic texts as culturally and geographically specific responses to world-historical events (such as the slave trade), and situating these narratives within their respective monotheistic, pantheistic, and/or animist belief systems, expands and nuances how we are able to read world-gothic haunting.

For the remainder of this chapter, I will examine three short stories that demonstrate the ways in which some African American, Caribbean, and African writers, respectively, have deployed hauntings in ways that reconceived supernaturalist traditions of haunting within the world-gothic. In these tales the presence of spirits, 'seething' in daily life, serves multiple functions. For some writers, these spirits are vengeful, meting out justice for wrongs perpetrated on African people and their descendants; for others, the spirits serve as a bulwark against modernity, or as a restorative reminder of originary defining beliefs that persist despite the imposition of a Western, technocratic world.

Henry Dumas' Revenge: An African American Example

On 23 May 1968, thirty-three-year-old African American writer Henry Dumas died young and violently. Shot and killed by a New York City transit policeman on a Harlem subway platform just after midnight, Dumas' life and career was abruptly ended, leaving behind a legacy of poems and stories that, with Toni Morrison and others' help, has been promoted, published, and kept in print. In the foreword to the 2003 edition of *Echo Tree: The Collected Short Fiction of Henry Dumas*, Eugene Redmond conceives of Dumas' early death: 'Thirty-five years ago, Henry Lee Dumas transitioned (from the *natural*) to the *spectacunatural* – thus entering the world that informs and configures so much of his writing and thought'.[13] Almost two decades later in the foreword to the 2021 edition of the same collection, Redmond quotes Chris King who writes, '"When you kill a man, you can never bring him back, but when you publish [him], even if the book goes out of print, you can bring it back into print. You can get it back. You can bring him back"'.[14] Dumas' tragic end and subsequent revival as a literary ancestor for voices advancing change and racial justice could be the plot of one of his own stories. Praise of Dumas from Morrison, and many others who have named Dumas as an influence, recognises his unique embrace and melding of religion, mythology and contemporary American issues, presaging the haunting presence of spirits that populate his work.

Dumas is probably best known for his magical-realism hoodoo short story, 'Ark of Bones', which, like Morrison's *Beloved* and Ward's *Let Us Descend*, makes use of bodies of water as both repositories for physical and spiritual being-ness and metaphorical connection between African and American culture. His short story 'Fon' also merits close attention, however, especially when considering ways that hauntings based on an African rather than Euro-American epistemology have been deployed. The story concerns a racist white man named Nillmon who, while driving near the Mississippi River (accompanied by a bottle of whisky, pistol, and stick of dynamite), has his windshield smashed by a rock seemingly hurled out of nowhere. Infuriated, Nillmon exits his car and, as night is falling, spies a young Black man sitting on a billboard. Nillmon orders him down and interrogates him at gunpoint. When asked, 'Who else is up there?' the young man responds, 'My brother',[15] though there is no one else that can be seen. As Nillmon continues to question the young man, his brutal bigotry is revealed and he is shown to be an exemplar of a prototypical racist Southern sheriff. He is as ready to kill as to arrest a perceived perpetrator in order to preserve the racist status quo of the Deep South, declaring: '"N*****, you in trouble ... Aside from getting your ass beat, and payin for that glass, you goin to jail"'.[16] When asked his name, the young man responds 'Fon', which he clarifies is short for Alfonso, and informs the white man that he has been teaching his unseen brother to shoot arrows, information that links the young man and the action to come with the martial and religio-magical traditions of the West African people who inhabited the Dahomey kingdom.

Nillmon proceeds to force Fon into his car while contemplating how to break the young man, deciding, 'This Fon n***** ain't scared. He knows now he has a n***** that needs a thorough job. Nillmon smiles and spits on the gravel in front of Fon. "Git in"'.[17] Fon escapes and Nillmon picks up two friends, forming an impromptu lynch mob intending to locate and kill Fon. As they drive towards where Fon was last seen in Canebreak, one of the white men advises, '"Them Canebreak shacks is haunted, I'm telling you. N****** ain't live in them since the flood back in ... you member, Gus? ... The time the n***** woman put hoodoo on Vacy's papa"'.[18] In this moment Dumas deploys a unique interplay between Euro-Christian notions of haunting and syncretic West African religions. The former is exemplified by the abandoned neighbourhood providing a typical gothic setting, infused with a merging of belief in ghosts (the unspecified flood which presumably led to many deaths), the latter exemplified by the white man's assumed belief in a hoodoo curse placed on someone for what we can assume is a racially motivated crime.

As the carload of white men fondly reminisce about past lynchings, they approach a crowd gathered in front of a small Black church, before locating Fon near one of the abandoned shacks. Fon identifies the crowd as 'my brothers' and as the white men force Fon into the car, 'a cheer leaps from them, such as the white men have never heard. A sound of distance and presence, a shaking in the air which comes from that invisible song,' that body of memory, ancient. A long-sustained roar from the bottom of the land, rising, rising'.[19] As the men prepare to lynch Fon, the spirits and ancestors seem to intervene: 'High in the heavens now, a star comes into view from the clouds. A thin glow from a hidden moon peeps ominously from the horizon of clouds. "My brother is in the trees somewhere, now."'[20] Suddenly, arrows fly out of the darkness, killing the white men. As he departs the scene, Fon thinks:

> *That was mighty close. But it is better this way. To have looked at them would have been too much. Four centuries of black eyes burning into four weak white men ... would've set the whole world on fire. Not yet*, he thinks, *not yet* ... He turns toward the levee where a light in the night reaches out to him and to the great distance between him and the far blinking of the stars. The light from the church reaches out almost to him. They are expecting him back ... When the tower is finished ... One more black stone.[21]

The repetition of 'not yet', with its implication of four centuries' worth of justifiably vengeful ancestors, expands the ways that hauntings have been deployed in gothic literature. Carter Mathes argues that what 'seems initially to be an all too recognizable tale of Jim Crow-era violence instead becomes a depiction of Black resistance in which white supremacy is first psychically displaced through Fon's mystical power, seemingly derived from ancient African connections, and then brutally vanquished by mysterious arrows that pierce the necks of the white men as they prepare to lynch Fon'.[22] But there is more to the 'mystical' elements of the story. For if, in the examples mentioned earlier, the presence of African ancestral and familiar spirits interacted with individuals and their specific circumstances (Beloved killed by Sethe, Annis remembering her family history), here, there are ostensibly millions of spirits preparing to avenge centuries of brutality, enslavement, and institutional racism in the United States. Encapsulating the revolutionary spirit of the Black Power movement, the hauntings in 'Fon' present a syncretic view of Black supernaturalism, where within a traditional gothic setting (dilapidated dwellings as night falls), aspects of Christian-influenced 'Invisible Churches', merge with hoodoo and arrow-shooting ancestral apparitions, who seemingly arrive from the heavens in a prelude of what is to come 'when the tower is finished'. Here, then, Dumas links Fon to the world-capitalist trade in enslaved Africans figured by a communal haunting over an entire land, where the spirits are already extant and present, waiting and practicing for the right time to descend on a racist planet and 'set the whole earth on fire'.

Chinua Achebe's Restorative Path: An African Example

The changes wrought by European colonialism in Africa are the predominant theme of much of Chinua Achebe's work. Born and raised in

5 Hauntings

British-colonised Nigeria, Achebe witnessed firsthand the effects of colonisation, one of them being the dissipation of traditional religious beliefs and practices as the influence of Western Christianity and its missionaries converted many, including Achebe's own family, to a Judeo-Christian belief system. The tension between the traditional ways and the new, often resulting in devastating consequences for the people who hold on to their traditional ways, is the thematic basis for his 'African Trilogy' and much of his other work.

In 'What Makes Someone Give Up Their Religion?', Achebe reflects on the duality of his spiritual upbringing, having been raised Christian while growing up in an Igbo culture. He shares that his sons were inducted into the Masquerade Society via a secret initiation called *ikpu-ani*. 'I hope that they, and the Ibos, make use of it to salvage a civilization that has been damaged', Achebe writes, going on to explain that, within the Masquerade Society, '[t]he Ibo people are told that the masks are our ancestors coming out of the ground, which is where they live. They exit through tiny holes made by ants'.[23] Later in the same interview, Achebe suggests that traditional Igbo culture had 'disintegrated' through colonialism to the point that his parents 'were no longer sure *what* their culture was' and were consequently susceptible to the efforts of Christian missionaries. Thus, caught between the two worlds, Achebe's renderings of hauntings reflect this movement between Western colonial advancement and resistance against it by practicing traditional beliefs. Uncomfortably existing within this tension are the spirits of the ancestors and the culture they represent.

Achebe's 'Dead Men's Path' is indicative of the way that traditional African religions can serve as a bulwark against modernity, offer new possibilities for cultural accommodation and expand how we think about spiritual visitations outside of the traditional Western conception of hauntings. The story tells of Michael Obi, the newly appointed headmaster of the mission Ndume Central School. Armed with 'wonderful ideas' and 'modern methods', Michael is determined to thoroughly transform the school: 'He had two aims. A high standard of teaching was insisted upon, and the school compound was to be turned into a place of beauty'.[24] The beautification is taken up by Michael's wife who, seeing herself 'as the admired wife of the young headmaster, the queen of the school',[25] curates the garden of her dreams within the school compound, in stark contrast to the 'rank neighbourhood bushes'.[26]

The couple's conversion of the school and its grounds is interrupted by the appearance of an elderly woman from the village traversing a faint footpath that runs through the garden. This path, the couple learns, is 'very important' to the villagers. 'Although it is hardly used, it connects the village shrine to their place of burial'.[27] Learning this, Michael decides to block the path with heavy sticks and barbed wire, lest a school room be used for a 'pagan' ritual during an upcoming inspection of the school. The closure of the path prompts a visit from the local Ani priest who emphatically explains: 'this path was here before you were born and before your father was born. The whole life of this village depends on it. Our dead relatives depart by it and our ancestors visit us by it. But most important, it is the path of children coming in to be born'.[28]

The priest's entreaty falls on deaf ears, as Michael smugly explains that '[t]he whole purpose of our school ... is to eradicate just such beliefs as that. Dead men do not require footpaths. The whole idea is just fantastic. Our duty is to teach children to laugh at such ideas'.[29] Soon afterward, a woman in the village dies in childbirth, and a local diviner holds the ancestral spirits of the village responsible, explaining that they are angry and insulted by the fenced-off path, and determines that sacrifices must be made to appease them. The following morning, Michael wakes to find his modern school and its compound destroyed, sacrificed to Ani by the villagers. The gardens and a school building are in shambles and a white Supervisor who has come to inspect the school writes a 'nasty' report about the condition of the school and the '"tribal-war situation developing between the school and the village, arising in part from the misguided zeal of the new headmaster"'.[30]

'Dead Men's Path' pits the colonial mindset of Michael against the traditional belief in Ani, the goddess of earth and fertility. As such, the story interrogates the effects of colonialism on some African colonial subjects who are willing to trade their cultural and religious heritage for a self-satisfied impulse towards so-called 'modernisation' and to gain the approval of the English colonial powers, here personified by the Government Education Officer. The officer ironically criticises Michael's 'zeal' and lack of respect for ancestor reverence, perhaps thinking that the European colonial project in Africa must progress gradually, and thus, 'The White superior has to restrain Obi before he wrecks [sic] further havoc on the plan to inculcate European culture and self-shame in African school children'.[31]

The Ani priest, representing the fertility and protection of the natural world, also represents potential accommodation between European and African cultural and spiritual traditions, stating to Michael: 'What I always say is: let the hawk perch and let the eagle perch'.[32] Margaret Bockting notes that Michael's refusal to compromise and allow the ancestral spirits to traverse the path, blocking the arrival of new spirits into earthly form, 'undermined an opportunity for peaceful interaction between different cultures. Perhaps he has even lost the chance to promote the endless traffic with others that produces great civilizations'.[33] Thus, this story is a critique not only of cultural imperialism, but also of the effects of *nso ala*, crimes against Ani's blessings and the earth. The story is realist, rather than evidently gothic, and assumes the vital influence of Ani, the spirits and ancestors as a matter of fact. And while it is never clearly stated whether the destruction of the school grounds is the work of the villagers or Ani's supernatural intervention, in the end, it hardly matters. It is rather the symbolic destruction of the colonial world's ideology and physical manifestations of that ideology that is paramount, as well as the insistence on remembering traditional ways of being close to the ancestors and allowing them to continue to be involved in the natural order of things.

Michael Obi's crime is his disdain for local traditions and beliefs, manifest in his manipulating the earth by blocking the path. In doing so, he is desecrating the land considered holy by followers of Ani. The living and the dead have heretofore existed in harmony, but now they face Michael's interference in their communion and thus have had their access to each other restricted. The destruction of the school and its gardens is done to satisfy vengeful spirits, and an attempt to resurrect and restore a spiritual equilibrium, one that will allow the living and dead and yet-to-be-born to continue living together as they have done for centuries with, or without, European bias against 'fantastic' ideas. The story ends with Michael chastened, and we therefore assume that the sacrifice has been accepted and the path reopened in perpetuity. The ancestral and soon-to-be manifest spirits are now unloosed from their colonial restraints and are free to continue their unencumbered, and joyful, haunting of the living.

Shani Mootoo's Warning: A Caribbean Example

The history of the Caribbean is shadowed by the legacy of slavery. These islands were the site of numberless plantations resulting in unfathomable exploitation and death. As Martin Munro writes, '[e]very island in the Caribbean is the site of a deep haunting'.[34] Munro names the decimated pre-Columbian Amerindian peoples, the Arawaks, Caribs, Tainos, and others, as the oldest ghosts in the Caribbean, adding that, for the Africans transported to these islands: '[t]o be a slave was to be a kind of ghost', and that the end of slavery did not 'erase the psychological, societal and economic effects of the institution'.[35] Additionally, Munro points to the compounding effects of environmental devastation and the import of Indian labourers enduring the *kala pani* to present the Caribbean as haunted by blood and despair. Noting that 'Caribbean folklore is itself extremely rich in its evocation of terrifying, ghostly figures',[36] Munro names duppies, duens, and other beings as evidence that within Caribbean literature, hauntings reflect world-historical events and movements that wreaked havoc on the people of those islands: 'ghosts are everywhere, be they of the Amerindians, the African ancestors, the slaves, the planters, the indentured workers, the victims of dictatorships, foreign invasions and natural disasters, or the modern exiles'.[37]

Many Caribbean writers have explored hauntings within the African diasporic, Indigenous Caribbean and European admixture of these islands, and, like Henry Dumas in 'Fon', and Chinua Achebe in 'Dead Men's Path', Indo-Caribbean author Shani Mootoo presents a distinctly Trinidadian and syncretic version of haunting that seeks redress for colonial, ecological, racial, and religious injustices in the short story, 'The Bonnaire Silk Cotton Tree'. This is at once a local ghost story and an index of Trinidad's place within the long history of world-capitalist expansion and extraction, depicted here as environmental devastation and urbanisation in service of the tourist economy.

The story begins with an epigraph that informs readers that every village on the island hosts a high silk cotton tree that houses, along with birds, bats, and snakes, 'restless duppies and the mischievous yet irascible jumbie'.[38] Both duppies and jumbies are spirits based in diasporic African and Caribbean spiritual belief systems, and in Mootoo's story their co-existence among the living is a given. The tale centres on Nandita Sharma, a non-practicing Hindu photographer who, disappointed in her faltering career and poor reviews of her exhibits, seeks out the help of the jumbie to improve her prospects. She does this despite warnings in the local paper penned by Father O'Leary, an Irish priest who inveighs against 'the dark arts of the Caribbean',[39] a preoccupation of the priest's that has the opposite of the intended effect and causes the 'church-, temple-, mosque-going people, and others with or without religious affiliations'[40] to seek out the jumbie for aid.

The contrasting and competing supernaturalisms are a primary theme in the story, as Father O'Leary argues that silk cotton trees should be cut down as they 'serve no purpose today, save as a lair of the unbaptised and their leader in the underworld, the jumbie'.[41] Interestingly, it seems that the priest himself subscribes to and legitimises the native beliefs inadvertently. While encouraging people to get baptised, he provides instructions to his readers who want to implore the jumbie for aid on how to locate the silk cotton tree that houses the spirit. The mix of religious traditions alluded to by Mootoo (Christian, Hindu, Muslim, Afro-Caribbean) speaks to the diversity of Trinidad, and Nandita's willingness to discount the priest's warnings, ignore her own religious upbringing, and seek out the jumbie demonstrates the enduring power of traditional belief systems (and human vanity).

As she journeys to Bonnaire to seek out the jumbie's aid in resuscitating her flagging career, Nandita reflects on the advancing modernisation of the island, noting lines of quarry trucks, the Hilton Hotel, and increasing crime. Locating the footpath that leads to the jumbie's silk cotton tree, Nandita finds the jumbie, who resembles an old man, arguing with a group of duppies inside the tree. He explains about O'Leary: 'He only singing out how jumbie and duppy bad-bad, but he self is the best advertising we ever had'.[42] While celebrating that the colonial-missionary project is failing in converting Trinidadians to Catholicism, the jumbie nevertheless laments the extraction of nature's resources:

> we living with the sound of quarrying all night long all along the Northern Range. Every day they come a little closer. Bulldozing all the trees and all the bush, all the flowers, all the nests, the homes of all the animals, and of all we. For hundreds of years people used to respect the silk cotton, but this generation think all the talk about the silk cotton, about jumbie and spirits is chupidness ... the forest is disappearing right before their eyes.[43]

This stark warning of impending environmental disaster, made more acute by Trinidad's historical respect for trees and the fruit they bear, is coupled with the jumbie's ominous warning: 'We will find somewhere else, that is certain, but town people might'n like where we choose to set up, you hear?'.[44]

Nandita tells the jumbie that she needs 'to be able to make great, important, worthwhile photographs',[45] and is offered a deal. Explaining that the silk cotton tree is filled with duppies, the ghosts of the unavenged dead of the island, who 'ent going to have no peace until their killers are caught and brought to justice', the jumbie offers Nandita the role of official photographer of the spirits when they make themselves visible the following week during *Dimanche Gras* and J'Ouvert, the beginning of Carnival.[46] Nandita agrees, and the jumbie identifies the innumerable spirits who will be made manifest and have their suffering acknowledged by the living:

> 'Every person who got killed on this island since the beginning of the first injustice all the way to the present-day wantonness – from the native people in the days of the early Spaniards, to the slaves of the British, to the present-day

victims of robberies and drug-related and poverty-related, greed-related and envy-, and jealousy-, and power-related crimes... All of us on whom justice turn its back'[47]

Here, the jumbie catalogues the destruction wrought on Trinidad and its people from the first colonial arrivals to the present day, while the litany of returning dead embodies the devastating continuation of capitalist and colonial extraction. The ruination of bodies through slavery, of indigenous customs and beliefs through cultural imperialism, of the environment through resource exploitation, and of community through drugs and poverty will all be represented and avenged by the rising dead. Like Dumas's horde of avenging ancestors, these ghosts illustrate a situated, culturally specific response to the ongoing entanglement of global colonial and capital regimes. '"We coming, thousand strong"', the jumbie warns Nandita, '"head bash in, eye poke out, neck break, vagina rip apart, heart blown up, brains hanging out, hand chop off, blood dripping, dripping fo so"'.[48] The jumbie insists that the litany of death be witnessed and acknowledged by the living, which, Mootoo seems to indicate, is a form of justice in and of itself. The jumbie adds that displaced animals will also join their procession and that only Nantia will be able to capture their images on film, resulting in success and fame.

This story catalogues the present-day challenges Trinidad faces as a result of its colonial past and marginalised position within the world-system. including religious and cultural imperialism, capitalism, environmental destruction, and advancing technology, resulting in diminishing cultural inheritance and fraying community ties. The jumbie and his army of duppies serve not only as protectors of the natural world, but also as a reminder that the past is always present, and that haunting can serve as a corrective: justice will not be denied even in the shadow of a new Hilton Hotel. As the story ends, Nandita, disoriented, is nevertheless preparing for the ancestral dead to leave the silk cotton tree and make themselves felt to the world of the living.

Conclusion

When we consider hauntings from culturally and religiously specific perspectives, specifically Afro-centric perspectives in this chapter, we allow for alternative and expansive possibilities of how spirits move in our world and literatures. A world-gothic frame then considers the ways that localised African and diasporic religious practices meet, merge, and confront capitalist modernity, cultural and environmental exploitation, and imperialism, moving beyond 'folkloric givenness' into a paradigm that allows for a decentred view of gothic literature. In this paradigm, these texts and the hauntings described within them are localised resistance serving as a bulwark against an increasingly technocratic and hyper-capitalist world. Conceptions of 'seething' Afro-centric ancestors who have active roles in the lives of the living invite a dynamic and vital consideration of the ways that haunting, or spirit persistence, can be conceived beyond Euro-Christian epistemes. The stories in this chapter prioritise Afro-centric ancestor work from three different cultures, demonstrating the resilience of African diasporic spiritual traditions as an example of how haunting can be reconceived from a world-gothic perspective.

Notes

1. Yvonne Chireau, *Black Magic*, Berkeley, The University of California Press, 2006, 45.
2. Jeffrey E. Anderson, *Conjure in African American Society*, Lafayette, University of Louisiana Press, 2005, 29.
3. Geoffrey Parrinder, *West African Religion*, Eugene, Wipf and Stock Publishers, 2014, 115.
4. Jesmyn Ward, *Let Us Descend*, New York, Scribner, 2023, 34.
5. Ward, *Let Us Descend*, 34.
6. James Mellis, 'Continuing Conjure: African-Based Spiritual Traditions in Colson Whitehead's *The Underground Railroad* and Jesmyn Ward's *Sing, Unburied, Sing*', *Religions*, 10:7 (2019), 403.
7. Teresa A. Goddu, 'The African American Slave Narrative and the Gothic', in C. L. Crow (ed.), *A Companion to American Gothic*, Chichester, John Wiley & Sons, 2014, 71.
8. Maisha Wester, 'Toni Morrison's Gothic: Headless Brides and Haunted Communities', in C. L. Crow (ed.), *A Companion to American Gothic*, Chichester, John Wiley and Sons, 2014, 378.
9. Toni Morrison, *Beloved*, New York, Alfred A. Knopf, 1987, 273.
10. Carol E. Schudde, 'The Haunting of 124', *African American Review*, 26:3 (1992), 409–16.
11. Maisha Wester and Xavier Aldana Reyes, 'Introduction: The Gothic in the Twenty-First Century', in M. Wester and X. A. Reyes (eds.), *Twenty-First Century Gothic: An Edinburgh Companion*, Edinburgh, Edinburgh University Press, 2019, 1–2.
12. Sheri-Marie Harrison, 'Global Horror: An Introduction', *Post45*, 4 April 2019, https://post45.org/2019/04/global-horror-an-introduction.
13. Henry Dumas, 'Fon', in E. B. Redmond (ed.), *Echo Tree: The Collected Short Fiction of Henry Dumas*, Minneapolis, Coffee House Press, 2021, xxiii.

14. Dumas, 'Fon', xxiii.
15. Dumas, 'Fon', 118.
16. Dumas, 'Fon', 118.
17. Dumas, 'Fon', 119.
18. Dumas, 'Fon', 122.
19. Dumas, 'Fon', 125.
20. Dumas, 'Fon', 126.
21. Dumas, 'Fon', 125–6.
22. Carter Mathes, 'The Second Sight of Henry Dumas: Envisioning Black (Im)possibility in the U.S. South', *Oxford American*, 114 (2021).
23. Arthur J. Magida, *Opening the Doors of Wonder: Reflections on Religious Rites of Passage*, Oakland, University of California Press, 2006, 58.
24. Chinua Achebe, 'Dead Man's Path', in *Girls at War and Other Stories*, New York, Penguin Books, 1991, 72.
25. Achebe, 'Dead Man's Path', 71.
26. Achebe, 'Dead Man's Path', 72.
27. Achebe, 'Dead Man's Path', 72.
28. Achebe, 'Dead Man's Path', 73.
29. Achebe, 'Dead Man's Path', 73.
30. Achebe, 'Dead Man's Path', 74.
31. Vimbai G. Chivaura, 'European Culture in Africa as Business: Its Implications on the Development of the Human Factor', *Journal of Black Studies*, 29:2 (1998), 189–208, 201.
32. Achebe, 'Dead Man's Path', 74.
33. Margaret Bockting, 'Traffic with Others', *CLA Journal*, 46:3 (2003), 337–48, 346.
34. Martin Munro, 'Introduction', in M. Munro (ed.), *The Haunted Tropics: Caribbean Ghost Stories*, Kingston, The University of the West Indies Press, 2015, vii.
35. Munro, 'Introduction', vii.
36. Munro, 'Introduction', ix.
37. Munro, 'Introduction', x.
38. Shani Mootoo, 'The Bonnaire Silk Cotton Tree', in M. Munro (ed.), *The Haunted Tropics: Caribbean Ghost Stories*, Kingston, The University of the West Indies Press, 2015, 102.
39. Mootoo, 'The Bonnaire Silk Cotton Tree', 102.
40. Mootoo, 'The Bonnaire Silk Cotton Tree', 103.
41. Mootoo, 'The Bonnaire Silk Cotton Tree', 105.
42. Mootoo, 'The Bonnaire Silk Cotton Tree', 108.
43. Mootoo, 'The Bonnaire Silk Cotton Tree', 109.
44. Mootoo, 'The Bonnaire Silk Cotton Tree', 110.
45. Mootoo, 'The Bonnaire Silk Cotton Tree', 110.
46. Mootoo, 'The Bonnaire Silk Cotton Tree', 112.
47. Mootoo, 'The Bonnaire Silk Cotton Tree', 113.
48. Mootoo, 'The Bonnaire Silk Cotton Tree', 113.

CHAPTER 6

Vampiric Exhaustion and Extractive Form
The Mozambican Miner

Thomas Waller

In a world-systemic approach to the history of southern Africa, Immanuel Wallerstein and Sérgio Vieira note that, as a result of the post-1945 upturn in the global economy, the state of South Africa 'was in a good position to try to create the "region" of southern Africa with itself as a now clearly semi-peripheral power, one that would dominate the region economically, and even politically and militarily'.[1] One of the strategies through which South Africa consolidated its status as regional hegemon was the establishment of a system of migrant labour that recruited workers from neighbouring countries for the development of coal and gold mining operations in places such as Witwatersrand and the Transvaal. This economic system took possession of the region as a spectral presence, haunting the landscape as a disembodied logic of accumulation that ensured the enrichment of the White settler class while perpetuating the immiseration of the colonised population. In his efforts to imaginatively capture the debilitating effects of capitalist production upon individual workers, Marx made frequent recourse to metaphors of vampirism and lycanthropy, writing that capital is 'dead labour which, vampire-like, lives only by sucking living labour', and alluding to the 'werewolf-like hunger' with which capital devours its undifferentiated human prey.[2] As this chapter will demonstrate, images of capital's bloodsucking thirst, as well the depleted appearance of labouring subjects, reappear in works of Mozambican literature as an aesthetic resource for registering the destructive impact of the colonial mining industry upon the life and land of southern Africa.

To do this, the chapter draws from what Christine Okoth has called 'extractive form', which names a process of mediation between the ecological and racial modalities of capital accumulation. By paying close attention to the figural strategies through which this back-and-forth movement is staged internally as a moment of textual form, such an approach gauges how literature speaks effectively to 'the unfolding relationship between historical and ongoing modes of racial subjection and the logics produced by regimes of extraction'.³ Often deploying gothic tropes and spectral motifs as a means of coming to terms with colonial mining's racialised division of labour, the extractive form of Mozambican literature limns a powerful critique of the world-systemic context within which this ecological regime took shape. In this way, these Mozambican texts broach a world-gothic sensibility, a term which, in Sharae Deckard's words, signifies 'a systemic consciousness' both of the world-scale of capitalist imperialism and of 'the accelerating planetary impacts of energy and resource extraction'.⁴ The world-gothic registrations of capitalist extractivism that feature in this chapter accordingly display a critical sensitivity to processes of semi-proletarianisation in Mozambique, to the construction of South Africa as a semi-peripheral power, and to the insertion of the southern African region into the global circuits of (post-)colonial capitalism. Before turning to the texts themselves, however, it is first necessary to briefly sketch the history of cross-border migrant labour in Mozambique.

Underdevelopment and Migrant Labour

In the classic study *O mineiro moçambicano: Um estudo sobre a exportação de mão de obra em Inhambane* (*The Mozambican Miner: A Study of the Export of Labour in Inhamabane*), co-ordinated by Marxist intellectual and anti-apartheid activist Ruth First for the Centro de Estudos Africanos (CEA) at the Universidade Eduardo Mondlane in Maputo in 1977, the authors detail the extent to which the historical legacy of migrant labour in Mozambique contributed to the country's state of economic underdevelopment and obstructed attempts to transition to socialism in the post-independence period of the late 1970s. This system of migrant labour was implemented under colonial occupation as a result of Portugal's semi-peripheral position in the capitalist world-system, which subordinated the interests of the Portuguese colonisers to stronger regional forms of industrial capital in neighbouring South Africa. In this way, the Mozambican economy in the late colonial era was structured by a double dependency: on the one hand, its productive forces were appropriated and administered by Portuguese settlers through colonial technologies of control; on the other, it was subjected to the imperatives of capital accumulation in the context of a regional southern African economy in which Portugal played only a minor role.⁵ With the victory of the anti-colonial movement in 1974–5, the nationalist party Frelimo inherited a local economy which had

6 Vampiric Exhaustion and Extractive Form 119

not only been plundered by centuries of European colonisation, but which had also been systematically exploited by capitalists outside its national borders. Upon independence, the Mozambican government was tasked with redressing the social consequences of this situation of colonial underdevelopment, which included illiteracy rates of around ninety per cent.[6] As Mozambique's first president Samora Machel put it in one speech: 'Some feel proud for having been colonised by the English, because the English are civilised and built a great empire. Others feel proud for having been colonised by the French, thinking that intellectually they are more developed, more civilised, more advanced. I was colonised by Portugal, the most underdeveloped country in Europe.'[7]

The development of coal and gold mining operations in South Africa's north-eastern municipalities towards the end of the nineteenth century created an expansive regional labour market which enlisted the Portuguese regime in the role of rentier state. In order to maximise the extraction of surplus value, South African capitalists displaced the costs of the migrant's reproduction onto subsistence agriculture in their country of origin, thereby exerting downward pressure on the price of labour power. This process – what Wallerstein influentially called 'semi-proletarianisation' – lowers the minimum acceptable wage threshold and neutralises collective bargaining power by spreading household reproduction over a mixed pool of income-generating activities.[8] As First wrote in her editorial to the inaugural issue of the journal *Estudos Moçambicanos* in 1980, which was dedicated to the topic of 'Underdevelopment and Migrant Labour': 'Capital has used this system of migrant labour to place part of the burden of the reproduction of the worker and his family on domestic production. Capital has thus paid the worker below the cost of reproduction, leaving it to the family plot to maintain the worker between spells of employment, in times of sickness and in old age, and to support the family as a whole'.[9] By the early twentieth century, almost half of the male population of southern Mozambique were employed in the mines of Johannesburg, leaving many women to take on the domestic tasks usually performed by their absent male partners.[10] The formation of an industrial reserve army in colonial Mozambique, one which could be intermittently recruited for periods of contract work across the border in the South African mines, was in this way achieved through a sexual division of labour that consigned women to socially reproductive activities and men to a life of nomadism.

Paired with the agricultural crisis generated by the colonial state's insistence on cash-crop cultivation of cotton (for export) and rice (for domestic consumption), which had detrimental effects on soil fertility and which jeopardised subsistence farming practices, the system of migrant labour in Mozambique presented a major barrier to post-independence attempts at establishing a Marxist-Leninist planned economy. In her introduction to the English edition of *O mineiro moçambicano* – written shortly before her assassination by apartheid agents at the CEA in 1982 – First spelled out the extent of these obstacles while upbraiding the Frelimo regime for misprising just how intertwined Mozambique's productive forces had become with the interests of South African mining capital. The country's subordination to South Africa, she argues, 'cannot be combated on an ideological level alone, by an appeal to the political commitment of the migrant', for this would be 'to miss the essence of a deep-seated economic system that has promoted the political economy of the countryside of Mozambique'.[11] Although this system was reproduced in part through the circulation of oral testimonies that portrayed South Africa as a space for adventure and conquest, its reproduction was not achieved primarily through acts of will on the part of individual workers. On the contrary, in First's words, '[e]ight decades of the system of migrant labour made it a structural necessity for rural producers living under colonialism'.[12]

Given its determining presence in the social and economic life of Mozambique, not to mention its centrality to the country's underdevelopment, it is unsurprising that the histories of mining and migrant labour have continued to haunt modern Mozambican literary production. However, due to its segregated location across the border, South African mining capital has at the same time been depicted as something of a ghostly presence, 'distant, unknown and virtually invisible'.[13] This contradiction between material and immaterial regimes of production – 'spilled blood and evanescent credit', to borrow a phrase from the Warwick Research Collective (WReC)[14] – poses a representational problem for the writer, who is tasked with figuring a structuring force that is both omnipresent and empirically unverifiable. This figurative dilemma is closely related to the vampiric character with which capital takes hold of the physical environment, which also turns on questions of visibility and invisibility. As David McNally writes, '[l]ike vampires, which are creatures of darkness and night, capital's bloodsucking is unseen', discernible only through the exhaustive effects it inflicts upon its victims.[15] This chapter will argue that forms such as vampirism and spectrality are uniquely the social contradictions of capitalist phenomenology, for they blur the opposition

6 Vampiric Exhaustion and Extractive Form   121

between presence and absence in a way that registers the ongoing historicity of colonial extractivism.

Spectral Objectivity

Paralleling the entrenchment of cross-border migrant labour in the political economy of colonial Mozambique, the image of the *magaíça* – a Mozambican word for migrant labourer that specifically refers to those seeking work in the mines of Johannesburg – emerges as a central trope in Mozambican poetry. As Stefan Helgesson has argued, by indexing the country's integration within global and regional circuits of industrial capitalism, the *magaíça* 'became an Everyman, an allegorical figure for the Mozambican experience of modernity'.[16] Exemplary in this respect is one of Noémia de Sousa's best-known poems, named simply 'Magaíça' (1950). The eponymous subject of Sousa's poem cuts an anxious and uncertain figure, presenting the system of migrant labour in terms not only of that 'draining' of skills to which First alluded in the preceding section, but also of a vampiric absorption of energy, dignity, and health. After leaving for Witwatersrand with wide-eyed misgiving, the *magaíça* finally returns from his period of contract work with an uprooted and disillusioned appearance, and is now described by the speaker as 'a dislocated being / shrouded in ridicule'.[17] The souvenirs with which the *magaíça* returns from his period of contract work are, however, repeatedly inscribed as symbols of falsity. While he is said to have buried his 'lost illusions' in the shafts of the mining complex, he returns with 'suitcases full of the false brilliance / of the scraps of the false civilisation of the Rand compound'.[18] In this way, 'Magaíça' presupposes a zone of authenticity that lends the poetic voice a paternalistic and at times demeaning quality, condescending the lowly worker with adjectives such as *mamparra* (meaning childlike or ingenuous) and verbs like *entontecer* (with its connotations of silliness and stupidity). The privileged position of the speaker in Sousa's poem reveals a degree of enunciative distance from the realities of migrant labour that indexes a material separation between literary production and the interests of the class struggle. As Mário Pinto de Andrade notes in a periodisation of Portuguese-language African poetry, this separation would only be overcome during the 1960s when writers moved beyond the limits of *négritudiste* consciousness-raising and into a more direct participation in the movement for national liberation.[19]

At the same time, the poem articulates a critique of colonial society that identifies the cause of the *magaíça*'s dejection as the extraction and commodification of gold at the Rand. As Marx argued in *Capital*, volume 1, the generalisation of commodity exchange under capitalism brings about a practical reduction of the various concrete activities expended during the production process to the one quality that all commodities hold in common: 'human labour in the abstract'.[20] Insofar as it determines the value of the product but cannot be apprehended directly by the senses, this social substance haunts capitalism as a 'gespenstische Gegenständlichkeit' or 'spectral objectivity'.[21] Sucked up into the vortex of capital's inexorable drive to accumulate, material wealth exists as a mere *Träger* or bearer for the process of valorisation, which is indifferent to the concrete attributes of its objects. In this sense, as Christopher J. Arthur writes, capital 'inhabits such material as a secret subject, animating it, and, vampire-like, communicating spectrality to all with which it has intercourse'.[22] The flipside to this system of abstract domination is the increasing immiseration of the worker. In an attempt to satiate what Marx describes as its 'werewolf-like hunger', capital continually spawns 'generations of stunted, short-lived and rapidly replaced human beings'.[23] This contradictory pairing of an immaterial logic of valorisation with the destructive effects of (semi-)proletarianisation – 'spilled blood and evanescent credit' – is registered in Sousa's poem through the juxtaposition of the *magaiça*'s disenchantment with the opulent status of the product of his labour. The final lines of the text read as follows: 'His youth and health, / the lost illusions / that will shine like stars on the neck of some lady / in the dazzling nights of some City'.[24] The value of luxury items and the prestige of colonial nightlife are in this way traced back to the exploitation and destitution of migrant workers in the South African mines. The extractive mode of production through which human labour yields gold for exchange is portrayed as a process of physical and mental debasement through which the *magaiça* is vampirically devoured by the automatic subject of capital. However, the source of his debilitation must remain ghostly, for the substance of value – abstract human labour – cannot be verified empirically. As Marx quips, '[s]o far no chemist has ever discovered exchange-value either in a pearl or a diamond'.[25] In its efforts to aesthetically figure the value-producing regime of colonial extractivism, the poem is thus pulled towards a spectral and vampiric register.

Representations of mining in Mozambican literature are too numerous to name, but one recent instance is noteworthy for its illustration of the continuing legacy of colonial extractivism within the national imaginary. In Jorge de Oliveira's novel *Pneu em Chamas* ('Flaming Tire') (2015),[26] mines function as an overbearing presence that consumes the lives of the text's miners and deprives them of any sense of individuality or agency. When the novel's protagonist – referred to throughout simply as 'the miner' – arrives at the mining complex for the first time and begins a period of contract work with a group of other men, he is immediately plunged into 'a veil of dust that covered their thick rubber boots, whitened their jeans, darkened their persons and clouded their minds'.[27] Later on, when an accident occurs which results in the miner becoming trapped alone in his tunnel, the mine is pervaded by a 'mysterious air' that disorients and suffocates him, distorting his sense of time and self.[28] The novel then closes with a set of reflections on the life of the Mozambican miner that explicitly aligns the experiences of exploitation and precarity with the redemptive or rejuvenating power of local beliefs in spirituality:

> Every miner, they say, was an artist in the extraction of riches and in moments of affliction the best thing to do was to dream, dreams were the messages of the spirits. We know the art of handling the subsoil. We survive because the dead remain with us. We are closer to them than those above us. The Black people keep the spirits down below, the White people send them up above. For this reason, we work in the mines and they go to the moon. Everyone stays close to where they deposit their own.[29]

The subterranean passageways of the mines are conceived as an oneiric space that absorbs the spirits of deceased workers in a way that sustains those who have managed to escape death, just as the vitality and aspirations of the *magaíça* were said to be consumed by his period of contract work in Sousa's poem. However, rather than critically equate the squandering of human life with the bloodsucking thirst of capital, the appeal to spirituality transhistoricises the perils of extractivist wage labour, as if they were self-evident facts of life rather than contingent results of the accumulation process that might ultimately be abolished. This faltering mediation between the ecological and racial modalities of (post-)colonial society brings extractive form to a standstill, immortalising capitalism's racialised division of labour. Yet, through this reification, the passage aesthetically formalises the petrifying world of capitalist biopower, which, in the words of Achille Mbembe, 'function[s] by dividing those who must live and those who must die'.[30]

Commodity Phantasmagoria

The literary figuration of mining's racialised division of labour is also at the heart of Orlando Mendes's 1965 novel *Portagem* ('Toll'),[31] which Peter J. Maurits has identified as the first Mozambican ghost story.[32]

Combining influences from Portuguese neo-realism with gothic motifs of haunting, Mendes's novel elaborated a critique of colonial society from the perspective of the *mestiço* or bi-racial subject, who is described as 'an illegal man, rejected by White people and Black people'.³³ The protagonist of the text is João Xilim, the offspring of an extra-marital affair between a colonial coal mine owner named Campos and a woman named Kati. Structurally excluded from the privileges conferred upon the White colonial elite, Xilim is equally rejected by the indigenous Mozambican population to which his mother belongs. The text unfolds as a bildungsroman that leads the reader through the ostracisation and socio-economic hardships to which João Xilim is subjected from childhood through to young adulthood. However, while *Portagem* in this way launches an explicit indictment of the caste system in colonial Mozambique, the Black semi-proletariat still features as a class with collective interests that fail to match up with the protagonist's own, evoking the enunciative distance and paternalistic sympathy with which the *magaiça* had been depicted in Sousa's poem. As David Brookshaw has speculated, this ambivalent relationship to organised forms of anti-colonial resistance was likely how *Portagem* was able to appease the colonial censors and get published in the first place.³⁴ As will be seen, a more uncompromising critique is developed in the passages that deal with the extractive regime of colonial mining, which bring about a shift in the narrative register from a neo-realist portrait of social classes to a gothic irrealism that aesthetically registers the spectral objectivity of capitalist commodity production.

In one of the novel's key scenes, Campos refuses to pay for the necessary safety measures that will ensure the upkeep of the mining complex. When the coal firm ruthlessly decides to ramp up production, the shafts predictably collapse, killing twenty-three miners. After years of travelling and trying to come to terms with his role in the incident, Campos finally returns to the city where the mine had collapsed. Finding himself overcome with emotion one night, he pays a visit to the site of the disaster and is horrified when he peers into the old mine and sees the twenty-three miners still there rotting beneath the rubble: 'He approaches the shaft and looks down below. Everything was just as it was after the disaster. There at the bottom are the bodies of the twenty-three miners buried and sleeping their final sleep, rotting in a strange tomb. He rubs his inflamed eyes with the backs of his hands and abandons that grim locale.'³⁵ As Campos attempts to flee the site of the mining disaster, the surrounding mountains now appear to him as 'a monster of earth and stone, born from the womb of the night'.³⁶ Hounded by the image of the putrefying remains of the workers, Campos stumbles confusedly across this gothicised landscape and subsequently falls off the edge of a cliff to his death – a ghostly retribution on the part of the dead miners and their families.

This gothic register is then extended when Campos's corpse is put on display at his house and appears to be breathing or sobbing to the surrounding onlookers. One of these observers is his son João Xilim, who gets the impression that Campos might spring back to life at any moment and complete the cycle of haunting:

> Then, he seemed to see the chest of the boss Campos rise up in the outline of a breath or a whimper. Would he wake up and get up from the bed and recognise him as his son? ³⁷

The eerie atmosphere derives its force from a personal desire for filial recognition that is disabled in advance by the contradictory interpellations of race, for the rift between father and son has occurred due to João Xilim's *mestiço* heritage, and is thus objectively grounded in the caste structure of colonial society. The situation recalls the ghost story in *Hamlet*. As Freud argued in *The Interpretation of Dreams*, although Hamlet is asked by his father's ghost to kill the current king Claudius, he is at the same time rendered helpless by the very thought of doing so, seeing as to commit this act of revenge would mean killing the man who has taken his father's place next to his mother, and thus, in the logic of the Oedipus complex, to commit revenge upon himself.³⁸ This contradictory demand – be like your father, but you have no right to be like your father – turns Hamlet's hatred into a form of self-reproach similar to that which takes hold of João Xilim at the sight of his father's corpse. In *Portagem*, however, it is the social hierarchy of race that has established the impossibility of the paternal relationship. With Campos deceased, João Xilim is tasked with taking the place of his father, but is prevented from doing so by his *mestiço* heritage, which disqualifies him from the legal and material privileges afforded to the colonial elite, while also barring any possible union with his mother Kati. The contradictory and unrealisable demands of João Xilim's position plunge him into a frantic state of internal conflict that culminates with him vomiting by the side of a tree outside his father's house, 'sicklied o'er', like Hamlet himself, 'with the pale cast of thought' (*Hamlet*, 3.1.85).

The socio-economic backdrop for this patrilineal drama is the uneven development of large-scale mining projects in colonial Mozambique, which subjected a class of Black labourers to dangerously unsafe working conditions for the enrichment of the capitalists. By mediating between the racial structure of colonial society and its ecological regime of accumulation, spectrality in *Portagem* is elevated to the level of 'extractive form', imbuing the text with a systemic consciousness of Mozambique's integration into the global circuits of capital. Set in a fictionalised town named Marandal, the text makes several references to the colonial coal mining industry in central Mozambique, with its fictional coal firm Santos & Alves which is concerned, above all, with 'the necessity to increase, at all costs, the daily yield of the exploitation of the mines'.[39] Coal itself occupies a key position in the novel, haunting the dreams and imaginations of its characters in a way that indexes the hyper-commodity fetishism of colonial capitalism. In one dream sequence, João Xilim finds himself stranded in his father's mineshafts, pursued by a large, animated block of coal that hunts him down in a way that portends the deaths of the twenty-three miners later on in the narrative. After an oneiric succession of bizarre images including flying goats and shapeshifting children, João Xilim is struck by a deafening noise emanating from the mine:

> Then he heard a boom from inside the mine as if an enormous block of coal had dislodged itself from the wall and had begun to roll. João Xilim took a fright and fell down the shaft. He ran in circles but the block of coal was always rolling after him. Exhausted, he stopped and shut his eyes and waited for the collision. The noise suddenly stopped and he was alive.[40]

Coal is here figured as an enigmatic presence that is endowed with a menacing intentionality of its own. This telluric phantasmagoria arises from what Marx called the 'mystical' or 'mysterious' character of the commodity form taken by the product of labour in capitalist society. Insofar as they represent the social characteristics of labour as if they were objective properties of the products themselves, commodities are 'sensuous things which are at the same time supra-sensible or social'.[41] The magical agency of coal in João Xilim's dream, through which the commodity dislodges itself from the wall of the mine and hunts him down of its own volition, is an imaginative recoding of this strange situation, in which material objects appear as if they were the masters of their producers rather than the other way around. As a consequence of this perceptual inversion, the commodity acquires a set of fantastic characteristics: 'It not only stands with its feet on the ground, but, in relation to all other commodities, it stands on its head, and evolves out of its wooden brain grotesque ideas, far more wonderful than if it were to begin dancing of its own free will.'[42]

6 Vampiric Exhaustion and Extractive Form

Reading representations of oil and sugar in other (post-)colonial contexts, Michael Niblett has noted that the phantasmagoric commodity character of resource extractivism 'tends to push cultural expression toward a gothic register', as otherwise immobile physical objects are ascribed a set of 'monstrous associations'.[43] The supernatural apparition of coal in *Portagem* is, likewise, directly connected to its function as bearer of a whole system of relations that is not immediately discernible in the empirical attributes of the object itself. To this extent, gothic motifs like haunting and spectrality in Mendes's novel are extractive forms that transpose the racial and environmental modalities of colonial capitalism into the level of the narrative. This mutability between gothic imagery, ecology, and the life of the colonised is poignantly evoked by Frantz Fanon in one passage from *The Wretched of the Earth*: 'In this becalmed zone the sea has a smooth surface, the palm-tree stirs gently in the breeze, the waves lap against the pebbles and raw materials are ceaselessly transported, justifying the presence of the settler: and all the while the native, bent double, more dead than alive, exists interminably in an unchanging dream.'[44] Just as Fanon's rhetorical juxtaposition of the exoticising colonial imaginary with the local hierarchies of extraction is here mediated by an appeal to the spectral, irreal ontology of the colonised, so are the class- and race-based contradictions of colonial coal mining in Mendes's novel symbolically resolved by the trope of the haunting oppressed and the fantastic appearances of commodity production. The dream-like landscape conjured up by Fanon finds a fictional analogue in one scene in *Portagem* where João Xilim, effectively excluded from the community by his *mestiço* status, is described as watching the life of the people of Marandal from afar, as if he were indeed 'a sleepwalker'.[45]

Although *Portagem* is principally preoccupied with Portuguese mining operations in central Mozambique, it also includes a series of references to the regional system of migrant labour through which Portugal's economic interests were subordinated to the imperatives of capital accumulation in neighbouring South Africa. The narrative arc of Mendes's novel follows João Xilim's failed attempts to pursue social mobility within the rigid racial hierarchies of the colonial administration, and ends finishes with his despair at ending up a poor wage labourer who is unable to protect his family from racist and class-based abuse. During his formative adolescent years, however, João Xilim decides to abandon Marandal and travel around 'the lands of the White people' (a reference to South Africa) in search of adventure. When he returns to his hometown, he does so with a fresh perspective on the exploitations of colonial society and with exciting stories with which he happily regales the Marandal locals. But when a foreign gangmaster turns up trying to recruit people for work in South Africa, Xilim attempts with difficulty to use his newfound perspective to alert the would-be miners of Marandal to the unfairness and dangers of this opportunity for labour migration:

> João Xilim revolts against this new attempt at exploiting the Black people of his land. Those that leave for the mines across the border leave behind women and children and, due to the fact they are illegal, often don't send back any money whatsoever. Some stay there forever and others return consumptive or crippled. João Xilim explains all this to the miners of Marandal. But the majority don't give up their hopes of entering into negotiations with the mestiço gangmaster. And they don't know how to say that this anxiety to emigrate arose within them as a result of the stories told by João Xilim.[46]

The system of migrant labour in Mozambique is thus cast as precisely that – a system – one that is reproduced not only on the economic level through modes of economic compulsion and expropriation, but also through the transmission of oral testimonies and the ideology of self-betterment. Paradoxically, it is João Xilim's own awareness of the system's inequalities and false promises that facilitates its perpetuation, for the stories with which he has returned from his cross-border migration have inspired the miners to follow in his footsteps, even though his intention was to provide a cautionary tale that would dissuade them from doing so. João Xilim is thus again presented as a liminal and contradictory character, declaiming the system of migrant labour but ultimately contributing to its consolidation, removed from the Black working class by his *mestiço* status and yet excluded by the colonisers for the same reason.

Even João Xilim's name bears the mark of his relative peripherality, as is explained when its origins are revealed early on in the narrative: 'When he was four years old, a relative who had returned from the mines in Kaniamato gave him a shiny coin. João never let go of this coin, even when he was sleeping, and he would constantly say: "I have a *xilim*, I have a *xilim*".'[47] Derived from the Portuguese corruption of the English word 'shilling', the name of *Portagem*'s protagonist serves as a reminder of the extent to which the Mozambican economy had become integrated within a regional system of migrant labour spearheaded by South African mining capital. The fact that Mozambican miners were paid their wages in British currency further indexes the rentier role that Portugal played within this extractive regime. Although the money economy had become an integral part of peasant life in Mozambique by the mid-twentieth century, the imposition of capitalist wage-labour processes was achieved through a structural reliance on pre-capitalist modes of work. For this reason, money only partially mediated the lives of Mozambican workers during the late colonial period, and given Xilim's status as an outsider to the local community of the text, it is then fitting that he should be named after the currency of a foreign imperial power. The reference to money also returns to the theme of spectrality, for in its role as a medium that facilitates the process of exchange by continually changing hands, money 'haunts the sphere of circulation'.[48] In a similar way, João Xilim is a spectral figure that is neither fully integrated into the indigenous population nor wholly excluded from it.

The world-gothic form of *Portagem* is an aesthetic registration of the bloodsucking thirst of colonial extractivism. As if possessed by a vampiric force, the life and land of southern Africa were integrated into a regional system of migrant labour that ensured wealth for the White settlers, while tying a racialised class of semi-proletarian subjects to a life of precarity and itinerance. As in Sousa's poem 'Magaíça', mining capital is figured in Mendes's novel as an exhaustive power occupying a space between visibility and invisibility: silently steering the colonised population towards waged employment in the mines across the border; erupting in the dreams of the protagonist as a phantasmatic ventriloquism; haunting the conscience of the capitalist through illusory images of rotting corpses. In the Mozambican literature of the 1980s, the themes of migrant labour, the money economy, and the spectrality of the mines would reappear throughout a number of texts that take up the gothic sensibility established by Mendes's earlier novel, such as Suleiman Cassamo's *O regresso do morto* ('The Return of the Dead Man') (1989), Heliodoro Baptista's *Por cima de toda a folha* ('Over All the Leaves') (1987), Aldino Muianga's *Xitala Mati* (1987), and Aníbal Aleluia's *Contos do fantástico* ('Stories of the Fantastic') (1988). However, whereas *Portagem*'s subject had been the colonial outsider, a *mestiço* son of a mine owner who tries with difficulty to communicate with the working-class miners, in the 1980s spectrality would be broadened to register the experiences of precisely those figures that were reduced to the level of local material in Mendes's text. For, although *Portagem* is eloquent in denouncing the racial injustices of Portuguese colonialism, it remains pessimistic with regard to the chances of actually overthrowing it, as the narrative closes with a forlorn João Xilim reconciling himself to a life of wage labour and racist abuse. With the success of the liberation wars and the commencement of the Marxist-Leninist nation-building project, this ambivalence was replaced by a new form of class consciousness, one which was duly registered by the country's literary production. While the haunting episode in *Portagem* is focalised through the perspective of the capitalist miner, the aesthetics of spectrality in texts from the 1980s are rather grounded in the standpoint of the newly independent subject, thus mirroring the decolonisation process. If this change in perspective restores a sense of dignity and empowerment to those who had suffered from the hardships of colonial exploitation, it also points to the fractures within the post-independence project itself. In *Portagem*, the motif of haunting is set up as a majority threatening a minority, with the twenty-three black miners taking ghostly revenge upon the mine owner Campos, whose avarice and negligence are responsible for their deaths. In the 1980s, this binary is reversed so that the individual now becomes the haunting presence, and the trope of ghostliness is domesticated and associated with the oppressed minority, as for example in Mia Couto's short story 'A história dos aparecidos' ('The Story of the Apparitions') (1986). By blurring the line between life and death, writers of the 1980s were thus able to critically register the dissolution of the Marxist-Leninist project and the start of Mozambique's reintegration into a now neoliberalised capitalist world-system.

Notes

1. Immanuel Wallerstein and Sérgio Vieira, 'Historical Development of the Region in the Context of the Evolving World-System', in S. Vieira, W. G. Martin, and I. Wallerstein (eds.), *How Fast the Wind? Southern Africa 1975–2000*, Trenton, Africa World Press, 1992, 3–15.
2. Karl Marx, *Capital: A Critique of Political Economy*, vol. 1, trans. B. Fowkes, London, Penguin, 1990, 342, 353.
3. Christine Okoth, 'The Extractive Form of Contemporary Black Writing: Dionne Brand and Yaa Gyasi', *Textual Practice*, 35 (2021), 379–94, 380.
4. Sharae Deckard, 'Extractive Gothic', in R. Duncan (ed.), *The Edinburgh Companion to Globalgothic*, Edinburgh, Edinburgh University Press, 2023, 132.
5. Ruth First et al., *O mineiro moçambicano: Um estudo sobre a exportação de mão de obra em Inhambane*, Recife, Editora UFPE, 2015 (1977), 44–5.
6. Margaret Hall and Tom Young, *Confronting Leviathan: Mozambique Since Independence*, Athens, University of Ohio Press, 1997, 56.
7. Quoted in João Maria Gusmão and Pedro Paiva, 'The Third Man Argument', *Buala*, 24 April 2013, https://www.buala.org/en/to-read/the-third-man-argument.
8. Immanuel Wallerstein, *Historical Capitalism*, London: Verso, 1983, 27–8.
9. Ruth First, 'Subdesenvolvimento e Trabalho Migratório', *Estudos Moçambicanos*, 1 (1980), 2–8, 6. All translations in this chapter are my own.

6 Vampiric Exhaustion and Extractive Form 131

10. Kathleen Sheldon, *Pounders of Grain: A History of Women, Work, and Politics in Mozambique*, Portsmouth, Heinemann, 2002, 53–8.
11. Ruth First, *Black Gold: The Mozambican Miner, Proletarian and Peasant*, Brighton, Harvester Press, 1983, 3–4.
12. First, *Black Gold*, 4.
13. Richard Bartlett, 'Beneficial Parasite to Heroic Executioner: South Africa in the Literature of Mozambique', *Alternation*, 3.:1 (1996), 94–108, 95.
14. Warwick Research Collective (WReC), *Combined and Uneven Development: Towards a New Theory of World-Literature*, Liverpool, Liverpool University Press, 2015, 70.
15. David McNally, *Monsters of the Market: Zombies, Vampires and Global Capitalism*, Leiden, Brill, 2011, 140.
16. Stefan Helgesson, 'Johannesburg, Metropolis of Mozambique', in S. Nuttall and A. Mbembe (eds.), *Johannesburg: The Elusive Metropolis*, Durham, Duke University Press, 2008, 260–1.
17. Noémia de Sousa, *Sangue Negro*, Maputo, Associação de Escritores Moçambicanos, 2001, 84.
18. Sousa, *Sangue Negro*, 84.
19. Mário Pinto de Andrade, 'Prefácio', in M. P. de Andrade (ed.), *Antologia temática de poesia Africana*, vol. 1, Praia, Instituto Caboverdiano do Livro, 1980 (1976), 9.
20. Marx, *Capital: A Critique of Political Economy*, 128.
21. Marx, *Capital: A Critique of Political Economy*, 128.
22. Christopher J. Arthur, 'The Spectral Ontology of Value', *Radical Philosophy*, 107 (2001), 32–42.
23. Marx, *Capital: A Critique of Political Economy*, 353, 380.
24. Sousa, *Sangue Negro*, 85.
25. Marx, *Capital: A Critique of Political Economy*, 177.
26. Jorge de Oliveira, *Pneu em Chamas*, Maputo, Associação dos Escritores Moçambicanos, 2015.
27. Oliveira, *Pneu em Chamas*, 61.
28. Oliveira, *Pneu em Chamas*, 73.
29. Oliveira, *Pneu em Chamas*, 165.
30. Achille Mbembe, *Necropolitics*, trans. S. Corcoran, Johannesburg, Wits University Press, 2019 (2016), 71.
31. Orlando Mendes, *Portagem*, Maputo, Instituto Nacional do Livro e do Disco, 1981 (1965).
32. Peter J. Maurits, *The Mozambican Modern Ghost Story (1866–2006): The Genealogy of a Genre*, Oxford, Peter Lang, 2022, Chapter 3.
33. Mendes, *Portagem*, 169–70.
34. David Brookshaw, 'Four Mozambican Writers', *Wasafiri* 5:10 (1989), 2–4.
35. Mendes, *Portagem*, 37.
36. Mendes, *Portagem*, 37.
37. Mendes, *Portagem*, 39.

38. Sigmund Freud, *The Standard Edition of the Complete Psychological Works of Sigmund Freud, Volume IV (1900): The Interpretation of Dreams (First Part)*, trans. J. Strachey, London, Hogarth Press, 1964, 265.
39. Mendes, *Portagem*, 35.
40. Mendes, *Portagem*, 22.
41. Marx, *Capital: A Critique of Political Economy*, 164–5.
42. Marx, *Capital: A Critique of Political Economy*, 163–4.
43. Michael Niblett, 'Oil on Sugar: Commodity Frontiers and Peripheral Aesthetics', in E. DeLoughrey, J. Didur, and A. Carrigan (eds.), *Global Ecologies and the Environmental Humanities: Postcolonial Approaches*, London, Routledge, 2015, 273.
44. Frantz Fanon, *The Wretched of the Earth*, trans. C. Farrington, London, Penguin, 1990 (1961), 39.
45. Mendes, *Portagem*, 31.
46. Mendes, *Portagem*, 32.
47. Mendes, *Portagem*, 16.
48. Marx, *Capital: A Critique of Political Economy*, 213.

CHAPTER 7

Subversive Sorcery and Reparative Witchcraft
Huesera's Challenges to Coloniality
Valeria Villegas Lindvall

Huesera (*The Bone Woman*, 2022),[1] co-written by Michelle Garza Cervera and Abia Castillo, follows the story of Valeria (Natalia Solián), a young pregnant woman in a loving relationship with her husband, Raúl (Alfonso Dosal). However, her pregnancy turns horrific with the assailment of a spectral presence, only made intelligible as the *Huesera*. Importantly, the appearance of this entity seems to be prompted by Valeria's re-encounter with her former teenage punk lover, Octavia. This instance triggers the continuous struggle between Valeria's punk past and her present of upward social mobility and reputability. Terrified by the apparition, the character turns to her aunt Isabel (Mercedes Hernández), who seeks the counsel of her queer-coded, middle-aged friends to perform a witchcraft ritual in order to banish the apparition. Valeria's struggle between her domestic stability with Raúl and her punk freedom with Octavia leads her to leave her family, a decision that entails her renouncing normativity.

I argue that Garza Cervera's *Huesera* provides a fruitful case study through which to explore this collection's understanding of world-gothic. The film exemplifies the generous flexibility of this conceptual tool to highlight culturally situated forms of resistance to capitalist modernity and coloniality. I approach this text as a case that remixes the gothic mode by reformulating the tropes of the witch and witchcraft, turning them into distinct avatars: the *bruja* and *brujería*, respectively, delineated by *but* critical of coloniality. I posit that *brujería* is portrayed in a reparative register that allows for the critique of the coloniality of gender and knowledge by prompting the main character to renounce the heterosexist arrangements of marriage and normative motherhood.

To establish this discussion, the chapter first navigates the pertinence of the tropical gothic to then engage with Latin American philosophy through concepts such as *codigofagia* – an aesthetic strategy of resistance that entails the remix of dominant discourses and codes – proposed by Bolívar Echeverría, which I employ as a comely expansion to the framework of the world-gothic. I then provide an overview of the *bruja* (witch) and its role in the colonial arbitering of gender and knowledge, relating it to the figure in Mexican visual culture from the second half of the twentieth century. Lastly, I provide an analysis on the ways in which *Huesera* demonstrates a subversive reformulation of the figures of witchcraft and witches as updated and valuable tropes in the interrogation of colonial constraints on gender and knowledge.

From the Tropics to the Cannibals: Tropical Gothic and *Codigofagia*

While I do not consider *Huesera* a strictly gothic film, it is possible to see the influence of the mode and its tropes in the delineation of the witch as a productive figure for critique, which in this case can exemplify world-gothic's versatility. The usefulness of the gothic as a mode has been fruitfully explored in the study of Latin American cultural production. Writing about the subject, Gabriel Eljaiek-Rodríguez affirms that the tropicalisation of the gothic can be widely understood as a transformation, translation, and an unsettling of nineteenth-century European and US American motifs for their integration to the cultural imagination in postcolonial settings.[2] In addition to Eljaiek-Rodríguez, authors like Gustavo Subero, Rosana Díaz-Zambrana, and Patricia Tomé have also explored how tropicalisation plays a fundamental role in the development of both horror and the gothic as modes that seek to make sense of crisis and cultural anxiety resulting from colonial exploitation of the Americas.[3] These considerations resonate with Esthie Hugo's writing, which introduces a distinction between the gothic mode and gothic effects. Recuperating Kerstin Oloff's and Rebecca Duncan's work, the author highlights the global possibilities of the gothic as an aesthetic response to capitalist exploitation and disaster. As Hugo notes, the tropics' colonial exploitation of land and labour has been associated in literary tradition with physical and mental degeneration, leveraging White subjectivity and mental stability as a measuring stick.[4] This cultural inscription on the tropics, Eljaiek-Rodríguez argues, is also based on the notion of these territories as an 'antipode': an opposite to Enlightenment, rationality, and order.[5] This has been reinforced in cultural production, Hugo notes, by the construction of the tropics as sites where Whiteness meets its peril, threatened by the gothically figured immoderation and excess.

The critique of the constitution of the tropics as an extreme Other holds kinship with, and can find support in, Latin American decolonial thought. By way of illustration, Enrique Dussel posits that the invention of Europe as the beacon of rationality was a by-product of the invasion of the Americas. The philosopher argues that Europe's predominance entailed the violent occlusion of the Americas and invented it as the proverbial Other, furthering the authority exercised by what he terms the *ego conquiro*. For Dussel, colonial and patriarchal law are one and the same. This is to say, the championing of Whiteness as a point of reference is accompanied by the language of patriarchy under coloniality.[6] To better understand coloniality, we can turn to Aníbal Quijano. Following thinkers like Dussel and Frantz Fanon, among many others, Quijano articulates a matrix of power prompted by two distinct, co-related historical processes derived from the invasion of the Americas: the invention of the category of race and the exploitation of labour. He offers that coloniality has outlived colonialism as a global system of power, shoring up its stronghold in four interrelated spheres of influence: labour, authority, gender/sexuality, and knowledge/intersubjectivity. The author asserts that its survival is ensured by the establishment of interdependent institutions and practices: capitalism to arbitrate labour; the bourgeois family to administer gender and sexuality; the nation-state to assert control over authority, and lastly, Eurocentrism as a means to police intersubjectivity and knowledge.[7]

Later, thinkers like María Lugones would come to complicate this model by arguing that sex and gender under coloniality are also traversed by compulsory heterosexuality, derived in what she terms the *modern/colonial gender system*. As she reevaluates Quijano, Lugones proposes that both race and gender are powerful fictions that inform social, cultural, political, and economic life. Crucially, Lugones underlines that the foundational opposition at the core of coloniality is, in fact, the distinction between human and animal. Therefore, racialisation came to configure the bodies of gendered peoples as closer to animality, delineating White, male subjectivity as the measure of Humanity.[8] Furthermore, the very conceptualisation of animality also illustrates the prevalence of colonial violence. As Aph Ko summarises with sharpness, 'animal is part of the vocabulary of white supremacist violence' and as such promoted the discursive constitution of inferior subjects – animals, feminised, and racialised bodies – for their use, abuse, consumption, and exploitation. Following Lugones and taking her statements further, Ko ascertains that colonial, 'racial terrorism' is inextricable from the coinage of 'animal' as conceptual colonial violence, as categories such as animality, race, and gender are discursively entangled.[9]

With these foundational, co-constitutive distinctions, the bodies and lands of the so-called tropics were made expendable and exploitable by the colonial enterprise, justifying their annihilation, enslavement, and marginalisation, and, in the process, allowing for the disavowal of their knowledges and beliefs in favour of White supremacy, patriarchy, and capitalism. The hierarchical play between Europe and 'the rest' in the crafting of a dominant Eurocentric horizon of meaning would also shape the constitution of the Americas as a place of abundant natural wonders and monsters. Drawing on Immanuel Wallerstein, Hugo notes that with this manoeuvre of exploitation and accumulation of wealth, the tropics would come to be understood as a commodified periphery prompting industrialisation and, in the end, providing the raw materials for colonial modernity.[10] These dynamics of oppression and power, as well as their subversions and negotiations, do certainly transpire in cultural production.

Informed by these processes, the gothic becomes a site where coloniality can be negotiated. To borrow from Carlos Jáuregui, cultural meaning-making in the Americas can also be understood as a cannibalistic enterprise where the desiring gaze cast upon racialised, gendered bodies and land is digested, transformed, and violently resisted.[11] The Americas were deemed an eternal in-between, a feared and desired *Canibalia*, Jáuregui posits. It is tropical commodified excess which stands at the core of an uneven, colonial modernity that seeps into Latin American cultural production, Bolívar Echeverría tells us in his conceptualisation of the *ethos barroco* (baroque ethos).[12] Underpinned by colonial modernity, Echeverría writes, Eurocentred aesthetic canons are naturalised as a way to police and adjudicate cultural production. Echeverría coins the term *ethos barroco* to refer to the aesthetic resistance to Eurocentrism's and capitalism's grasp over meaning-making: it is an alternative that embraces the contradiction and excess by which the tropics came to be conceptualised via their commodification. As capitalist destruction continues to encroach across the Global South, Echeverría posits that the *ethos barroco*'s imaginative, 'excessive', 'artificial', and 'esoteric' nature attributed to this aesthetic response revitalises and reformulates the cultural codes that have long characterised the Americas as the ultimate Other to Europe. This author's theory illuminates the role that the telluric effects of capitalism have in fashioning world systems that breed their own aesthetic frameworks – in this case, in a reformulation of the gothic witch that proves its global reach and transposition of tropes.

7 Subversive Sorcery and Reparative Witchcraft

Importantly, Echeverría's writing has been fruitfully taken up and applied by Ítala Schmelz to approach horror and science fiction visual culture in Mexico. The author underlines that the patterns of Global Northern cultural production, pushing towards the exoticisation of the Global South, have been successfully sabotaged and subverted as a response to colonial modernity in filmmaking. She recovers Echeverría's conceptualisation of *codigofagia* – in short, a discursive operation whereby dominant tropes, codes, and understandings (in this case, those proper to the gothic as a mode) can be digested, as the *ethos barroco* 'accepts the globalizing impositions of the realist ethos but, at the same time, does not assimilate them'.[13] Schmelz's writing illuminates the usefulness of Latin American, decolonial aesthetic critique to think through *Huesera*'s iteration of the gothic as a cannibalistic, digestive enterprise that can enable critical readings. In this case, it provides a steady foundation for the vindication and showcasing of *brujería* (witchcraft) as a form of communal knowledge rather than as a destructive force, underlining the ways in which *Huesera* can be read as an enterprise of *codigofagia*.

Ay, qué bonito es volar a las tres de la mañana: Witches in the Mexican Cultural Imagination

But how did the *bruja* charm the Mexican cultural imagination? The first line of the traditional Veracruzano *son* 'La Bruja' – referenced in this section's title – places the figure of the witch at the centre of sleepless nights: 'how nice it is to fly at three in the wee hours of the night', calls this musical lynchpin of the Mexican southwest. Song has been an instrumental form of oral dissemination in the propagation of pre-invasion and modern tales, myths, and legends. In several of these cultural manifestations, the witch is articulated as an alluring dual figure. Songs like 'La Bruja' and 'El Toro Zacamandú' are a testament to the crosspollination of musical tradition (it is suggested that 'La Bruja' is in fact originally from the Oaxacan Isthmus) that has, by and large, shaped the imagination of the Mexican witch off screen. Importantly, music often portrays the witch not as a perverse figure but rather as a liminal entity that plays the role of supernatural protector.[14] Furthermore, anthropological accounts suggest that in folk belief, the *bruja* is often conflated with her dual nature as a *nahual*.

A testament to pre-invasion belief, interethnic conceptions of the *nahual* remain enmeshed with that of the witch. A *nahual* can be largely defined, as Damián González Pérez writes, as a protective figure whose main attribute is turning into fearsome animals, or even into phenomena like lightning or comets. *Nahuales* had been previously conceptualised in Mexica belief in connection to magic and wizardry, preceding European conceptions of the witch. However, Isabel Jáidar and Verónica Alvarado situate the conception of the witch in the context of Mexico as a postcolonial nation-state that has been heavily influenced by both European and pre-invasion notions of magic and knowledge.[15] In other words, the conception of the witch is to be understood as a European label. Therefore, this chapter discusses this permutation with the terms *bruja* and *brujería* (witch and witchcraft in Spanish translation) to establish a clear differentiation and underline the conception's arbitrariness. By the time she arrived in the Americas, the witch had adopted a European form. The witch craze had gained momentum and the urtext of its machinations, the *Malleus Maleficarum* by Kramer and Sprenger, was published in 1486, just a few years shy of Columbus's genocidal invasion to the Americas. Consequently, the conception of the witch made native knowledges comprehensible in Christian terms and enabled their disavowal and condemnation as a tool of oppression. It is worth noting, however, that chroniclers of the invasion did give a sense of similar figures as part of the Mexica empire's oral tradition and popular culture: the *tlahuipuchme*. These women were described by Fray Juan Baptista in 1600: 'They wander at night, spit fire through their mouths and haunt those that wrong them so they become ill or due: they wander by the mountains, at night, and they carry a flame as a burning axe, and they can hide it if they want to.'[16]

Although similar figures were present in pre-invasion belief, several processes that surrounded the strategic reorganisation of the Church in Europe were concurrent with the invasion of the Americas, and consequently, religious authority became instrumental to delineate the basis of coloniality, pertaining to the policing of subjectivity and knowledge. This meant that former belief, as chronicled by Baptista, warranted overwriting by categories such as *witch*. The positioning of the Church as a device of control of belief had a significant influence in the legal, practical, and political dismissal of racialised and feminised subjects, advancing what Nelson Maldonado-Torres conceptualises as the coloniality of being.[17] Inspired by Fanon's formulations on the *damné*, Maldonado-Torres meditates on the ways in which the racialised body is allocated to the bottom rung of subjectivity within colonial logic, a matter that extends to racialised, feminised knowledges such as *brujería*.

Concurrently with the establishment of the hegemonic influence of the Church came the fencing off of communal property in Europe. This process, Silvia Federici and Maria Mies write, consistently sidelined women. Mies convincingly claims that the division of labour and land, as well as their exploitation, were conterminous with witch-hunts for a reason: the jettisoning of women from the accumulation of wealth and the depoliticisation of their labour and knowledge were fundamental to the development of capitalism as a system. This system is contested in cultural production, nowhere more so than in gothic and horror imaginaries.[18] Taking after Mies, Federici writes about the importance of witch-hunts for the hierarchisation and gendering of knowledge as a form of colonial control. This favoured the exploitation of land and bodies: the public and political were allotted to men, while the domestic and depoliticised became the province of women.[19] These processes profoundly impacted the organisation of life and labour in colonised countries, securing the stranglehold of coloniality as a world system.

The enclosure of land and the exclusion of women from its ownership not only severed communal relations between land and folk but also established the female body as an extension of conquered land, legitimising the violence of empire exercised on it, as Rita Segato avers.[20] A key facet of this violence was the dismissal of feminised knowledge, often associated with the domestic sphere. Eventually, postcolonial identities and the normative discourses that accompany them were constructed upon a naturalised set of aligned binaries to hierarchise knowledge: man/woman, public/domestic, political/depoliticised, religion/superstition. Following Mies, Federici, and Segato, the depoliticisation of feminised knowledge and its conception as witchcraft can therefore be read as a manifestation of the policing of knowledge, gender, and labour. Constantly labelled as foreign or alien to modernity and its national identities, spiritual practices outside of Christianity effectively became racialised, feminised, and depoliticised, proving fundamental in the construction of the nation-state as a place organised around a specific, 'reputable' belief system. In other words, the establishment of a postcolonial, Mexican national identity underpinned by coloniality of gender, labour, being, and knowledge passed through the disavowal of the witch.

Mexican *Brujas* on Screen

Mexican cinema's fascination with the gothic addresses gender roles and their potential to subvert and undo normative expectations on women as apolitical, domestic, and passive presences. Revealingly, since its earlier days, the gothic on the Mexican screen often adopted narratives that had colonial relations as a backdrop. The first horror feature with synchronised sound in the country exemplifies this: *La Llorona* (Ramón Peón, 1933) adopts the foundational, colonial tale of La Llorona ('The Weeping Woman') and brings it back to Mexican modernity, appealing to the inescapable contradiction in the co-existence of pre-invasion belief and colonial modern rationality. *La Llorona* kickstarted the first gothic cycle in the country alongside Juan Bustillo Oro's *Dos monjes* (1934) and Fernando de Fuentes's *El fantasma del convento* (1934). These films set the coordinates for the gothic to be embraced in Mexican genre cinema. As the 1930s ushered in an era of splendour in Mexican film production – labelled The Golden Age, roughly between 1936 and 1957 – the interest in drama features did not escape the veiled threat of the witch, nor the normative gender expectations that she challenges. The threat of the witch turned into the threat of the independent woman, best exemplified in features like *Doña Bárbara* (Fernando de Fuentes and Miguel Delgado, 1943). The film, which can be retroactively read as an early and subdued form of rape-revenge, stars the renowned María Félix, whose character is surrounded by accusations of witchcraft that characterise her ambition as down-right supernatural. The period would stay away from genre filmmaking, and yet found in Félix the embodiment of what I call the 'witch-bitch' of the 1940s. Portrayed as a woman without a soul (*La mujer sin alma*, Fernando de Fuentes, 1944); a man eater (*La devoradora*, Fernando de Fuentes, 1946) and a perfidious she-devil (*Doña Diabla*, Tito Davidson, 1949) Félix encapsulated the threat of the witch as a domestic fiend. In her, the model of a motherly, apolitical, and suffering woman found its opposite, though she is inevitably ostracised as punishment for her ambition.

As the second half of the twentieth century rolled in, the allure of the gothic witch came to occupy a privileged place. The 1950s and 1960s saw a decisive surge of the trope. With the release of features like *La bruja* (Chano Urueta, 1954), *Misterios de la magia negra* (Miguel M. Delgado, 1958), *Muñecos infernales* (Benito Alazraki, 1960), *El espejo de la bruja* (Chano Urueta, 1960), *El Barón del terror* (Chano Urueta, 1961 – which features a male witch), and *Espiritismo* (Benito Alazraki, 1962), the figure of the gothic witch was effectively delineated. During the 1960s, the witch would even intermingle with *luchador* (wrestler) films, in features like *Las mujeres panteras* (René Cardona, 1967) and *Santo en atacan las brujas* (José Díaz Morales, 1968). The *brujas* in these narratives always meet their destruction, or at the very least, are banished and exiled as punishment for their ambition. In addition, films like *La bruja* and *Misterios de la magia negra* underline the provenance of the witch as unequivocally foreign, suggesting that their knowledges and practices – coded feminine – are arcane and noxious formulations that stand outside of the proper exercise of Mexican identity, further marginalising feminised and racialised knowledges. It is in this way that the gothic *bruja* became a figure that mediated national expectations of gendered labour and knowledge.

Mexican audiovisual culture continued to flirt with the witch during the decades that followed, now focussed on imagery of possession and gothic environs in full colour, which enlisted titillating subject matter in films like *Satánico Pandemonio* (Gilberto Martínez Solares, 1975) and the cult classic *Alucarda* (Juan López Moctezuma, 1978). Portraying the witch as the violator of Christian imagery and as a much more explicitly blasphemous figure, the 1970s were briefly enamoured with her transgressions. At the margins, the gothic witch was even the subject of Carlos Enrique Taboada's unofficial trilogy of female debacle and identity, which spanned three decades: *Hasta el viento tiene miedo* (1968), *Más negro que la noche* (1974), and *Veneno para las hadas* (1984) kept establishing the witch as an embodiment of subverted gender expectations. Later, the *bruja* and *brujería* at large gained a foothold in television with *telenovelas* (soap operas) such as *El maleficio* (1983) and *El extraño retorno de Diana Salazar* (1988). The trope came back in a few salient features such as *La Tía Alejandra* (Arturo Ripstein, 1978) – which features *El espejo de la bruja*'s Isabela Corona, in a clever throwback – and *Sobrenatural* (Daniel Gruener, 1996). The films in this short survey demonstrate that the witch stokes capitalist fears about knowledge as power in the hands of the disenfranchised (as intergenerational epistemic legacy); female community as a threat to national social order; the establishment of the nuclear family as the foundation to the nation-state and the challenging of mandates on binary gender for the furthering of coloniality.

Rebellion Is Not Dead, It Lives in *las brujas*: *Huesera*'s Reformulation of the Witch

Brujería plays a vital role in *Huesera*. Nevertheless, its depiction departs starkly from the insistent characterisation of this practice as a foreign, sinister occurrence: rather, it is firmly associated with everyday environments and experiences. *Huesera*'s treatment of witchcraft as a pivotal and powerful intermediary between Valeria's unfolding and her suggested liberation from compulsory heterosexuality and normative motherhood underlines its possibilities as a baroque text. This is to say, in accordance with Echeverría and Schmelz, it provides a site of negotiation where the coloniality of gender and sexuality are disputed. The film aptly illustrates the recuperation and reformulation of the witch in the figure of Isabel, Valeria's *tía* (portrayed as a queer spinster auntie), and her friends (lovingly alluded to by Garza Cervera and Castillo as '*las brujas*').[21] Isabel is introduced as the main character's figure of support: before the disbelief that her mother expresses about Valeria's capabilities to be a good mother by relentlessly scolding and mocking her, Isabel offers solace and refuge. After facing a horrific encounter with the *Huesera* in her apartment, Valeria turns to Isabel. They meet in a *mercado* (market). The scene displays Valeria waiting in a nail salon that acts as a point of reunion for multiple middle-aged women drinking beer, as Isabel takes Valeria's hand in confidence, asking her not to tell her mother she's taken her to see a *bruja*. The setting, I would argue, directly challenges the preceding notions of the witch as a dangerous and alien presence. The significance of the *mercado* as a space of daily interaction marks a backdrop where *brujería* is not a foreign or extraordinary matter: it is interwoven in the fabric of day-to-day domestic life and labour. It is intimately related to everyday existence.

This is the film's first explicit acknowledgement of *brujería* as an affair in female conviviality, adding a queer register: Isabel encounters '*las comadres*' (loosely translated, her girlfriends), who affectionately greet each other. As she waits for her turn for a *limpia* (cleansing ritual) Valeria observes Isabel greet one of the women, as both exchange a brief, intimate touch holding each other by the waist and then by the hand. Medium shots of Valeria's satisfied smile waiting for her turn alternate with shots of the *comadres*'s joy, alluding to their interconnectedness as part of the same community. I would suggest that the inclusion of this scene also fulfils the function of uplifting queer community as a space where *brujería* acts as a uniting knowledge rather than a pernicious practice. Further, it offers a glimpse of queer ancestry as the guarantor of said knowledges: Valeria has rediscovered her queer past in her encounter with Octavia, and now she is given a queer elder in Isabel. Behind a plastic curtain at the back of the nail salon, Valeria is greeted by a young woman in boxer braids. The scene of the *limpia* prefigures the importance of witchcraft in the film. Enfolded in green hues, the camera captures the woman and Valeria in profile. The space surrounding them appears abundant in votive candles, plants, and images on the wall. The tightness of the shot and its shallow depth of field centres both actresses, stressing the intimacy that *brujería* can entail. The young woman blesses Valeria's belly with an egg, reciting a prayer that intends to banish all damage directed at her. The brief passage illustrates

7 Subversive Sorcery and Reparative Witchcraft 143

the potentiality of *brujería* as a practice of reparation and comfort. The egg, suspended in a glass of water, reveals that Valeria is trapped in a home that resembles a prison: it is female knowledge, displayed as *brujería*, which unveils the bare structure of the nuclear family as a trap. The oppression woven around Valeria, compared to a spiderweb in this scene, becomes an apt metaphor to highlight the ways in which the expectations of motherhood, domesticity, and femininity – understood in relation to binary gender – are firmly affixed in coloniality as a set of enmeshed oppressions.

Read against Valeria's narrative as one of struggle between her queer punk self and her normative facet as a mother, the introduction of *brujería* appears as a vital site where this dilemma is painfully put front and centre. Which role is she called to inhabit in the grander narrative of contemporary Mexico? This question is not resolved in full; instead, it is presented as a challenge to the constraints of gendered expectations on labour and knowledge under coloniality, and it is posited by the vindication of *brujería* as a catalyst to Valeria's personal journey by the end of the film. This update on the allegedly depoliticised and innocuous nature of domestic, collective, and female knowledge can therefore be read as a testament to the baroque 'impurity' of Latin American modernity, as Schmelz labels it.[22] In other words, the film offers a reformulation of collective *brujería* as a practice that puts the coloniality of gender and knowledge forward, allowing the questioning of normative models of family and motherhood disputed in Valeria's body and relations within and outside of her marriage.

The last ritual portrayed in the film, which intends to banish the *Huesera* once and for all, places the focus on the collective of *brujas* as holders of intergenerational, communal female knowledge. After several perilous encounters with the *Huesera* and the resulting, progressive fracture of her relationship with her husband and family, Valeria turns to Isabel once more. The scene is punctuated by a tight shot of both women forehead to forehead, Isabel's hands holding Valeria's tearful face, suggesting their intimate bond in knowledge, intimacy, and care. As the queer figure of the auntie becomes a referent for intergenerational care, her community also comes to Valeria's aid despite Isabel's hesitance to get involved in 'harsher' forms of *brujería*. The ritual, decisively ominous and allegedly dangerous, is offered as the film's most comprehensive portrayal of *brujería*. As Valeria arrives to a dilapidated house, the camera offers an almost *codigofágico* visual subversion of Shakespeare's Weird Sisters in *Macbeth*, as if offering a playful wink to the undoing of the transmogrification of women in Western imagination. Against a sullied, peeling mint green wall, we see three middle-aged women facing Valeria. They direct inquisitive looks at her, as one of them – on the right end of a couch that serves as a throne – smokes a cigar. Valeria's stepping into this community of shared knowledge is suggested by her reflection on the dirty, oval-shaped mirror that hangs on the wall. She is a stranger looking in, initiated in the ways of arcane, yet very much alive, spiritual practice. This visual juxtaposition also suggests the connection in knowledge that the characters are insinuated to hold. In practice, three generations of female-coded knowledge are joined during this ritual: Valeria, her baby daughter, *las brujas*.

This scene in the film suggests *brujería* as intergenerational bonding rather than as a curse, even reprising gestures of domestic care and tenderness amidst the horror: *las brujas* tuck Valeria's baby in, wrapping the cooing infant with red ribbon as they whisper. Christian Giraud's sound design plays with the blending of their prayers and the syncopated rattling of twigs and shells to build upon the esoteric ambiance that surrounds the women. Significantly, Valeria stays silent throughout the scene, as the emphasis shifts to the *brujas*'s voices, chants, and rattling of staffs and shells to show that their presence is not ancillary, but germane to the narrative and to the character's individuation from family and marriage, which also entails individuation from her child. The camera smoothly transitions from one *bruja* to the other, in different stages of trance, but always rendered in full, whispering, contorting, encircling Valeria. It is one of these women who leads Valeria to a cement vat full of water, holding her head into its depths. Valeria is submerged in a horrific, Dantesque hallucination where she is buried under a mountain of contorting bodies that crack, limbs in impossible positions. The frame is reminiscent of Lars Von Trier's sexualised take on the witch and female grief in *Antichrist* (2009). Performing yet another operation of *codigofagia*, *Huesera* offers the remix of this passage as a repurposing of witchcraft that, rather than reprising Von Trier's patriarchal dismissal of female grief and embodied knowledge under the accusation of hysteria, showcases pain and horror to convey an excruciating rift with gendered expectations on labour, sexuality, and knowledge to access a different future.

The passage suggests that, where Christian belief infers the doomed nature of the feminine, *brujería* can constitute an epistemology of feminised redemption and mending. As the traumatic moment ends, Valeria and her baby are portrayed surrounded by the care of Isabel and her friends, sighing with relief, embracing each other as part of a community bonded by *brujería*. The scene is bookended by the view of Isabel handing the baby to Valeria. Three generations in the same frame, straying from the

7 Subversive Sorcery and Reparative Witchcraft

naturalised notion of the nuclear family as the main model of relationality. The placement of this scene is key, as it precedes the ending of the film, where Valeria walks out on a sullen Raúl who holds the baby in his arms. The very last shot of the film is the door of the couple's apartment as it closes and Valeria walks out of frame. The direct renouncement to compulsory heterosexuality, as well as of the character's normative role as a mother, is prompted by the intervention of *brujería*. The practice issues a challenge to the roles allotted to the feminised body under coloniality which, to great distress, are negated as Valeria walks away into a different – yet uncertain – future. A baroque *codigofágico* future where the 'excessive' nature of Latin American creativity – as borne from the continuous rupture, cannibalisation, and digestion of the trope of the witch – enables a critique of the mandates of domesticity and heterosexual conviviality as the ultimate fulfilment of modernity.

The weight that the ritual carries in the narrative underscores the political potential of witchy intervention – and therefore, of female, collective knowledge – as a critique of the colonial and Mexican models constraining the protagonist's gendered identity. In other words, *Huesera*'s portrayal of the *brujas* and *brujería* winks at and updates the transgressive potential of their foremothers, the gothic *brujas* of the twentieth century on screen. *Huesera* can be said to offer an insurrectionary display of the world-gothic by embracing the potentialities of the gothic *brujas* that preceded it, introducing a *bruja* that is not a domestic fiend or an antithetical illustration of the (colonial) modern woman, but rather the holder of occluded epistemologies, embodied in middle-aged, queer-coded characters – which are articulated as the reversal of the fearsome, barren, and spiteful gothic crone. With the centring of these figures, the *bruja* is not the guardian of normativity but rather enables its undoing, even if only partially. To set the intercession of witchcraft as the catalyst for the character's becoming outside of the normative, heterosexist mandates of family and motherhood is to recognise the weight of cosmologies left behind by the project of colonial modernity.

These are no longer the fearsome *tlahuipuchmes* of indigenous belief either, but something else: a group of queer-coded women that hold powerful knowledge exercised at the margins of imposed Christianity. Their centring as guardians of intergenerational knowledge contributes to the assertion of their portrayal as figures of sedition. This discursive operation in horror visual culture emphasises the possibility of a baroque ethos, creative and resistant, that confronts and negates the mandates of coloniality – in this case, those confining older women, their knowledges and bodies, to the role of loathsome crones. Consequently, as Lugones writes,[23] colonial organisation of knowledge is shown to 'exclude indigenous women from the world, because to pursue what the White Man wants entails assimilating colonialism and Eurocentrism that requires the abandonment of practices, beliefs, languages, understandings of community and relations on which the cosmos is built'. With the overt rekindling of such practices and beliefs, the *brujas* usher in a different future for Valeria, allowing the character to escape the house turned a prison in colonial, heterosexual bondage. Therefore, the witch's reformulation into a community of *brujas* and the turning of their *brujería* into a solidary instance, allows *Huesera* to vindicate both tropes' subversive potential in a contemporary setting.

Conclusion

This chapter has discussed the cultural role that the witch – here, differentiated as the *bruja* – plays in Mexican visual culture as a site of negotiation, contestation, and subversion of colonial expectations on knowledge, gender, and labour. By engaging with Michelle Garza Cervera's *Huesera*, the chapter underscores the reformulation of the gothic witch as a productive occurrence that can be understood as a subversive enterprise when read through the lens of Latin American aesthetic theory. Understanding this portrayal of witchcraft as a consumption, digestion of, and mutiny against the witch as the limit of female obedience and compulsory heterosexuality, I explore the embrace of the *bruja* as a reparative presence.

As I demonstrate, *Huesera* skilfully reformulates the place that *brujería* holds as a communal practice of knowledge and invests it with renewed power by focusing on queer, middle-aged, women practitioners. In this narrative, witchcraft becomes a crucial element of the critique of staunch, colonial modern structures of heterosexist relationality crystallised in the middle-class nuclear family that the main character is suggested to inhabit by force and expectation. This reformulation of the witch, a trademark figure in gothic imagination, demonstrates both its potential to critique colonial constraints on gender, sexuality, and knowledge and its flexibility to reveal the overlooked power of intergenerational belief and female community as resistance.

Notes

1. *Huesera (The Bone Woman)*, dir. Michelle Garza Cervera, Mexico and Peru, Disruptiva Films, Machete Producciones & Maligno Gorehouse, 2022.

2. Gabriel Eljaiek-Rodriguez, *Selva de Fantasmas: Tropicalización de lo gótico en la literatura y el cine latinoamericanos*, PhD diss., ProQuest Dissertations Publishing, 2012.
3. Gustavo Subero, *Gender and Sexuality in Latin American Horror Cinema: Embodiments of Evil*, London: Palgrave Macmillan, 2016; HORROfílmico, *Aproximaciones al cine de terror en Latinoamérica y el Caribe*, San Juan, Editorial Isla Negra, 2012.
4. Esthie Hugo, 'Bodies Broken and Minds Lost: Tropical Gothic, Commodity Frontiers, and the Aesthetics of Excess', in R. Duncan (ed.), *The Edinburgh Companion to Globalgothic*, Edinburgh, University of Edinburgh Press, 2023, 395–410.
5. Gabriel Eljaiek-Rodriguez, *The Migration and Politics of Monsters in Latin America*, Cham, Palgrave Macmillan, 2018, 1.
6. Enrique Dussel, *1492. El encubrimiento del otro. Hacia el origen del mito de la Modernidad*, La Paz, Plural Editores, 1992, 40–53.
7. Aníbal Quijano, 'Coloniality of power, Eurocentrism and Latin America', *Nepantla: Views from South*, 1:3 (2000), 533–80, 545.
8. María Lugones, 'Heterosexualism and the Colonial/Modern Gender System', *Hypatia*, 22:1 (2007), 186–209; María Lugones, 'Subjetividad esclava, colonialidad de género, marginalidad y opresiones múltiples' in *Pensando los feminismos en Bolivia*, Serie Foros 2, La Paz, Conexión Fondo de Emancipación, 2012, 129–37.
9. Aph Ko, *Racism as Zoological Witchcraft: A guide to Getting Out*, New York, Lantern, 2019, 99; 53.
10. Hugo, 'Bodies Broken and Minds Lost', 398.
11. Carlos Jáuregui, *Canibalia: canibalismo, calibanismo, antropofagia cultural y consumo en América Latina*, Madrid, Iberoamericana/Vervuert, 2008.
12. Bolívar Echeverría, 'El ethos barroco', *Debate feminista*, 13 (1996), 67–87, 74–5.
13. Itala Schmelz, *Codigofagia. Cine mexicano y ciencia ficción*, Mexico City, Akal, 2022, 12. My translation.
14. María Arcelia Hernández Cázares, 'Mujeres divinas y profanas: La bruja, la llorona y la sirena en el imaginario social del movimiento jaranero contemporáneo', Veracruz: Maestría en Estudios de la Cultura y la Comunicación Universidad Veracruzana, 2016, 70–80.
15. Damián González Pérez, 'De naguales y culebras: Entidades sobrenaturales y "guardianes de los pueblos" en el sur de Oaxaca', *Anales de Antropología*, 47:1 (2013), 31–55; Isabel Jáidar Matalobos and Verónica Alvarado Tejeda, 'Brujas de dos mundos', *Anuario Universidad Autónoma Metropolitana*, X (2003), 11–19.
16. Marciano Netzahualcoyotzi Méndez, 'Mordida de bruja o enfermedad? Las muertes de niños en un pueblo tlaxcalteca, 1917-1922', *HiSTOReLo*, 7,:13 (2015), 112–45, 120. My translation.
17. Nelson Maldonado-Torres, 'On the Coloniality of Being: Contributions to the Development of a Concept', *Cultural Studies*, 21:2–3 (2007), 240–70.

18. Maria Mies, *Patriarchy and Accumulation on a World Scale: Women in the International Division of Labour*, London, Zed, 1986.
19. Silvia Federici, *Calibán y La Bruja: Mujeres, Cuerpo y Acumulación Originaria*, trans. V. Hendel and L. S. Touza, Madrid, Traficantes de Sueños, 2010, 287–317.
20. Rita Laura Segato, *La Guerra Contra las Mujeres*, Madrid, Traficantes de Sueños, 38.
21. Abia Castillo and Michelle Garza Cervera, 'Interview with Michelle Garza Cervera and Abia Castillo about *Huesera* (2022)', interview by Valeria Villegas Lindvall, 23 February 2023.
22. Schmelz, *Codigofagia. Cine mexicano y ciencia ficción*, 12.
23. Lugones, 'Subjetividad esclava, colonialidad de género, marginalidad y opresiones múltiples', 133.

PART III

Worlding Gothic Theory

CHAPTER 8

World-Gothic and the Sublime

Jana M. Giles

> But darkness was here yesterday... Land in a swamp, march through the woods, and in some inland post feel the savagery, the utter savagery, had closed round him... There's no initiation either into such mysteries. He has to live in the midst of the incomprehensible, which is also detestable. And it has a fascination, too, that goes to work upon him.[1]

These lines from Polish-British writer Joseph Conrad's 1899 novella, *Heart of Darkness*, present an unexpectedly gothic scene of a Roman legionnaire exploring an alien Britain around 63 CE. The gothic aesthetic exploded in Britain in the late eighteenth century to become one of the most popular modes and genres in art and culture. But while the gothic has long relied for its effects on the threat of the Other, Conrad, one of the most globalised of authors, plays a trick on his fin-de-siècle English reader by establishing *them*, the European Self, as the primitive Other. While *Heart of Darkness* and its author were criticised by Chinua Achebe as racist,[2] arguably Conrad's aim was far from such. By introducing in the novella's first pages a reversal of the racialised stereotypes of primitive and civilised, Conrad injects unreliability into his narrator Marlow's account of his journey into the Congo. As Marlow travels upriver, gothic images of the natural sublime predominate:

> Going up that river was like travelling back to the earliest beginnings of the world, when vegetation rioted on the earth and the big trees were kings. An empty stream, a great silence, an impenetrable forest... you lost your way on that river as you would in a desert, and butted all day long against shoals, trying to find the channel, till you thought yourself bewitched and cut off for ever from everything you had known once – somewhere – far away – in another existence perhaps. There were moments when one's past came back to one, as it will sometimes when you have not a moment to spare to yourself; but it came in the shape of an unrestful and noisy dream, remembered with wonder amongst the overwhelming realities of this strange world of plants, and water, and silence.[3]

The untamed forest terrifies the European sailor, but in terms of human culture what Marlow encounters are not the jungle's equivalents of menacing Black Africans or literal cannibals, or zombies, but starving workers in chains, European accountants dressed in pristine white suits, Christian pilgrims performing no charity, and finally Kurtz himself, the atavistic ivory dealer who has become a bloodthirsty warlord yet is the product of 'All Europe'.[4] Even if Marlow cannot fully calculate the meaning of his experience, Conrad suggests, his readers can.

Heart of Darkness begins with a gothic 'mournful gloom, brooding motionless over the biggest, and the greatest, town on earth',[5] London, seat of the world's largest empire. Yet after Marlow's account of his journey into sublime Africa, the novella ends with a parallel framing image: 'The offing was barred by a black bank of clouds, and the tranquil waterway leading to the uttermost ends of the earth flowed sombre under an overcast sky – seemed to lead into the heart of an immense darkness'.[6] Even these few pieces of textual evidence imply that the gothic 'heart of darkness' lies in the imperial metropole and not the so-called dark continent.

The gothic and the sublime, this chapter will argue, are not identical but sympathetic and have served similar social and political functions over their long careers. What is important to emphasise is their adaptability to rhetorical interests of those in power in a given place and time. Just as Conrad challenged rather than validated prevailing attitudes about race, Africa, and imperialism by deploying a gothic sublime that had previously been motivated by fear of the European Other, so it is that the very malleability of these aesthetics enable their utility for a world-gothic: a broader range of experiences than their historically Western cultural range. This chapter will discuss the sympathetic relationship between the gothic and sublimity, clarify their differences, and consider whether they have a more 'universal' application than is typically understood. It will do so by taking a broadly historical approach, reviewing the major theories of the sublime of Longinus, the circa first-century CE Greek author of the first extant text on the sublime, Edmund Burke, Arthur Schopenhauer, and Jean-François Lyotard in order to examine the xenophobic and gendered origins of the sublime, and the ideological change that comes with the latter two thinkers. The gothic, and the sublime as Lyotardian differend, alert us to imbalanced power relations and the demand for new idioms that give voice to the silenced.

Joseph Conrad features as the primary literary author as an especially productive example for thinking about the world-gothic sublime. As perhaps the first truly global author writing at the cusp of the decline of the British Empire, Conrad's oeuvre is saturated with the alienating local effects of incorporation, or reincorporation, into global capitalist modernity. Moreover, Conrad, born in Ukraine to Polish parents who died by the time he was eleven because of their nationalist activities, was himself a subaltern of the Russian Empire; Poland was not reconstituted as a nation-state until 1918, having been partitioned between Russia, Prussia, and Austria in the late eighteenth century. In 1874, at the age of sixteen, Conrad fled to France to join the merchant marine (having only read about the sea in books), and at age twenty joined the British merchant marine to avoid conscription into the Russian military. Over the next twenty years, he voyaged to Malaysia, Australia, the Caribbean, South America, and Africa. As this essay aims to show, Otherness is fluid and relative; while today Eastern Europe may be considered 'the West', for Bram Stoker's readers in 1895, Transylvania (today in Romania) was clearly despoiled for having been part of the Ottoman Empire. Conrad's example, along with others, is offered as a model for opening up possibilities for further, similar readings of the sublime and world-gothic.

Defining the Sublime

The sublime occurs when the magnitude or power of an object appears to exceed our ability to apprehend it imaginatively or seems to have the potential to overwhelm the subject. As Philip Shaw puts it, 'the sublime marks the limits of reason and expression together with a sense of what might lie beyond these limits; this may well explain its association with the transcendent'.[7] However, the sublime is differentiated from pure terror insofar as the subject must be at a safe distance, producing contradictory feelings of threat and elevation. For Longinus, Burke, and Immanuel Kant, the elevation of the sublime was the result of a connection to a metaphysical, transcendent realm associated either with the divine or humanistic pure reason. According to Vijay Mishra, however, in the gothic sublime, 'death is embraced and idealism is now tempered by pessimism and human insignificance'.[8] With this version of the sublime, 'there is no hope of self-transcendence available, as the subject simply dissolves into the pleasure principle and, finally, death'.[9] It is the very nature of the sublime to resist formal limits; taken to its extreme, this results in being faced with 'a radical incommensurability'.[10]

Gothic and postcolonial, or better, decolonial,[11] studies share an interest in interrogating Enlightenment assumptions about rationality. As Andrew Smith and William Hughes note, the gothic underscores challenges to rationality 'through its seeming celebration of the irrational, the outlawed and the socially and culturally dispossessed'.[12] Postcolonial critics have observed that Enlightenment humanism posited the white male European as the universal human subject, and the gothic sublime is moreover linked to 'histories of dispossession and colonization',[13] though this is complicated by Mishra's assertion that in the gothic there is only the triumph of the death instinct. The sublime as Thanatos may describe the gothic sublime, but we might wonder whether this is the most applicable, or only heuristic for a world-gothic.

As Glennis Byron writes in *Globalgothic*, one result of an increasingly globalised world has been 'a growing awareness that the tropes and strategies Western critics have associated with the gothic, such as the ghost, the vampire, and the zombie, have their counterparts in other cultures, however differently these may be inflected by specific histories and belief systems'.[14] The term 'globalgothic' was coined to 'decentre the West' and extricate the gothic from Enlightenment modernity,[15] but ultimately asks us to read 'non-Western' forms as derivative of the western gothic mode. To that end, it may be helpful to observe the similarities between the gothic and the sublime regarding social power differentials, though the sublime predates the gothic by at least two millennia and therefore is not a product of modernity, though it continues to take on new and particular significance in the context of modernity.

The Parallel Histories of the Gothic and the Sublime

If the political undertones of the gothic may have decolonial potential, the sublime was historically not regarded in the same light. Given its association with Orientalist imperial rhetoric, as Pramod K. Nayar details in *English Writing and India, 1600–1920: Colonizing Aesthetics*, it is understandable that decolonial critics have questioned whether the sublime can be extended to cultures beyond the West. The sublime produces gothic effects and vice versa, but they are not identical: 'The crucial activity of the gothic imagination was seen as inspiring terror and power, which was accomplished by creating sublime effects based on Burke's *Philosophical Enquiry* . . . and was best communicated by obscurity in various forms from meteorological, topographical, architectural, material, textual, spiritual, to psychological'.[16] But if the gothic is a cultural aesthetic emphasising decay, melancholy, and mortality, the sublime is not so limited. Indeed, the first extant treatise on the subject by Longinus, *On the Sublime*, aimed to position the sublime as the very opposite.

8 World-Gothic and the Sublime

The Greek title of the text, *Peri Hupsos*, more literally translated means 'On Height', height being associated with great writing that sweeps its audience off its feet based on its content – primarily cosmic subjects like divinity, storms, mountains, or astronomy – and its ability to stimulate violent emotion. 'Sublimity is a kind of eminence or excellence in discourse' that 'produces ecstasy rather than persuasion in the hearer; and the combination of wonder and astonishment always proves superior to the merely persuasive and pleasant'.[17] Sublimity should elevate and exalt the listener,[18] being the 'echo of a noble mind'.[19] Perhaps the link to the gothic is most evident in the discussion of *phantasia*, in which 'enthusiasm and emotion make the speaker *see* what he is saying and bring it *visually* before his audience'. While the aim of poetry is astonishment, that of sublime oratory is clarity, though both 'seek emotion and excitement'.[20] We might accordingly think of the gothic as further along the poetic scale of sublime writing.

Any subject that can excite an audience can be rendered in a sublime way. However, Longinus claims that only certain classical texts, as well as the right kind of person with the proper education and morals, can produce sublime writing. And it is here where we see the ethnocentrism of Longinus that contributed to the sublime's Western cultural allegiance. Assuming, as most scholars do now, that Longinus wrote in the first century CE, we can place him in the context of the 'decline of oratory' debate that began in the previous century, a context that offers insight into how the sublime came to be co-opted for later imperial discourse.

The theme of the decline of oratory as an indicator of a corrupted society subtends the early history of the sublime. After his defeat of Antony and Cleopatria in 31 BCE, Augustus aimed to consolidate power through military might bolstered by an ideology of a Rome founded in Europe. Invoking traditional masculinity by attributing Roman moral decline to an Asiatic, Hellenistic, feminised excess, embodied by the vanquished Egyptian queen, resulted in Roman male reputations relying on an Atticising, classicising, masculine restraint that looked to a past golden age illustrated by a canon of classical writers. Rather than an empirical distinction between rhetorical styles, however, what mattered was in-group identity, that is, whether the orator 'was an Atticist in his own eyes or in those of his contemporaries'.[21] The primary vehicle for cultural continuity thus became elite education that promoted classical texts and rejected Eastern influences. In the final chapter of *On the Sublime*, an unnamed philosopher blames the dearth of sublime writing on the lack of political freedom. Longinus counters with a moral argument blaming greed and luxuriance, locating the threat in the Other through figures of invasion and miscegenation. Political and literary qualities become interchangeable in order to instantiate Atticism: 'We are pure Greeks, with no barbarian blood'.[22] In Longinus we already see the rhetorical use of the Other to define the sublime. The same was true of the gothic.

Just as Cleopatra and Asia are constructed as the Other to distinguish sublime writing, so also the Goths and Gothicism came to constitute a kind of floating signifier for Otherness over the centuries. The Goths were considered 'barbarians' by the Romans, a term first applied to those who were neither Latin nor Greek, then to all those outside the Roman Empire, and finally all non-Christians.[23] Occupying a region north of the Black Sea before being driven west by the Huns, the Visigoths sacked Rome in 410 CE, and their Balkan presence can be detected in the Transylvanian origins of Bram Stoker's *Dracula*.

A new definition of the gothic emerged during the Renaissance, when, 'Much like the original classical historians before them, Renaissance scholars conflated the Gothic with the German tribes that had threatened and eventually overcome Imperial Rome'.[24] Just as Longinus judged Asiatic prose as florid and distasteful against Attic simplicity, so the Renaissance neo-classicists pronounced the embellished medieval cathedrals in bad taste, favouring instead symmetrical forms and restrained decoration. Moreover, the culture of death centred on the medieval church encouraged its association with the morbid.

This schism was further entrenched by the Protestant Reformation. In England, the monasteries were dissolved by 1539, leading to a redistribution of land ownership and gaps in the social fabric, and producing an aesthetic of ruin. The efforts of Henry VIII and his successors, however, only underscored the haunting presence of the past. Literature began to fill the communal void left by the Church and enormous upheaval. Popular ballads and revenge tragedies were the equally violent and irredeemable genres that carried most of the cultural freight. Shakespeare's *Hamlet* exemplifies revenge tragedy, with its gothic haunting of the betrayed father, mad dreams of the son, and bloody massacre that ends the family dynasty. At the same time, European colonialism was on the march, visible in works like *The Tempest*, with its colonial setting, supernatural characters, and raced 'savages'. Figures like Mephistopheles, in Christopher Marlowe's *The Tragical History of the Life and Death of Doctor Faustus*, and Satan, in John Milton's *Paradise Lost*, were precursors to the Romantic outlaw. Thus, bloody vengeance plots, supernatural beings, insanity, dreams, and annihilation of social fabric came to constitute the 'template' of gothic

8 World-Gothic and the Sublime

literature.[25] The sublimity of such gods and godlike heroes and antiheroes, powerful beyond the human, also set the precedent for today's cinematic superheroes and supervillains and their varied reception according to the cultural *Zeitgeist*. As film critic A. O. Scott recently noted, 'The supervillain is the hero now': 'world-dominatingly ambitious, wildly unpredictable, unbound by norms or rules', which fans of fictional characters like the Joker from *Batman* have promoted to 'main character status'.[26]

The most influential eighteenth-century English commentator on the gothic was Edmund Burke, whose *Philosophical Enquiry into the Origin of Our Ideas on the Sublime and the Beautiful* (1757) brought the sublime centre stage with a new focus on emotion rather than rhetoric. The key sublime emotion is terror, 'productive of the strongest emotion which the mind is capable of feeling' that overwhelms the rational mind.[27] Obscurity of any kind is productive of terror, and so the gothic mode, drawing on Burke's inspiration, relied heavily on mists, shrouds, foul weather, dark veils, moonlit skies, and all manner of night scenes.

The danger of power and terror, however, is that they may tip over into tyranny, horror rather than sublimity. To save sublimity from this peril, Burke casts the West's Others as limit cases.[28] Heathen religions worship in terrible (not sublime) darkness and Milton outdoes a barbarous poet by writing, if only negatively, about an unrepresentable God because language is closer to spirit than immanent ritual practices.[29] Only the European commander, the European poet, and the Christian god can produce the right proportion of pleasure and pain needed for the 'true' sublime. Burke's psychological account is rife with metaphysical subtexts and ethnocentric judgments that enable him to assert Western superiority during the accelerating expansion of the British Empire.

Yet Burke found himself modifying his approach some forty years later, during the French Revolution. As a conservative, Burke was alarmed at the threat the *sans-culottes* posed to traditional primogeniture and nobility, comparing the Revolution to parricide and rape, and troping it as a false sublime in his *Reflections on the Revolution in France*. Ronald Paulson claims that the popularity of gothic fiction 'was due in part to the widespread anxieties or fears in Europe aroused by the turmoil in France finding a kind of sublimation or catharsis in tales of darkness, confusion, blood, and horror'.[30] Together with the widescale social disruptions and urban poverty created by the Industrial Revolution,[31] and the metropolis's growing reliance on colonial chattel slavery for its wealth, a reliance that had to be disguised,[32] the democratic Revolution in France paved the way for the gothic mode to rule the Victorians, albeit from the shadows.

Mary Wollstonecraft fiercely defended the Revolution against Burke, but her more famous daughter, Mary Shelley, produced the ur-text of dystopian science fiction and body horror, *Frankenstein*, at the same meeting in Italy where John Polidori created 'The Vampyre', considered by many to be the progenitor of the English vampire genre of fantasy fiction, with Lord Byron as the model for the aristocratic blood-sucker. Vampire stories had previously appeared in Germany in the eighteenth century, influenced by conflicts between the Habsburgs and Turks in Central Europe,[33] again demonstrating the political subtext of the gothic. The abnormal strength of Frankenstein's monster recalls Satanic power, and his unnatural origins anticipate contemporary anxieties about cyborgs and artificial intelligence. In keeping with a gothic sublime, rather than a transcendent one, *Frankenstein* ends with the death of both the monster and his creator in the vast, inhospitable Arctic wastes.

In *Dracula*, sublimity appears in the supernatural immortality of the titular supervillain character whose seduction is nearly impossible to resist by men and women alike, and in the landscape. Arriving in the mountains of Romania, Jonathan Harker discovers what appears to be the transcendent Romantic sublime in the mountains: 'The grey of the morning has passed, and the sun is high over the distant horizon, which seems jagged, whether with trees or hills I know not, for it is so far off that big things and little are mixed'.[34] The landscape grows increasingly dramatic and mystical as he nears Dracula's castle, though what awaits him is not God's seat but the devil's: 'Right and left of us they towered, with the afternoon sun falling full upon them and bringing out ... an endless perspective of jagged rock and pointed crags, till these were themselves lost in the distance, where the snowy peaks rose grandly ... "Look! Isten szek!" – "God's seat!" – and he crossed himself reverently' (Stoker, 10–11).[35] The ambivalence of the sublime, like the gothic, can confuse the transcendent and the deathly, until the subject, like Harker, goes mad. The sublime storm that brings Dracula's ship to Whitby charges the price of all the human crew on board. Consistent with the association of both the gothic and the traditional sublime with xenophobia, Dracula's real threat is his invasion of England, where he intends to acquire property, wealth, and sanguinary victims, the former a threat to British global power, the latter to English male reproductive dominance: die he must.

Colonial settings played a critical role in European and specifically English gothic. As Lizabeth Paravisini-Gebert notes, many early gothic novels reflected fears of Britain's increasing exposure to 'colonial societies, non-white races, non-Christian belief systems, and the moral evils of slavery', as well as miscegenation.³⁶ For the colonisers, strange figures and practices like Vodou, zombies, and Obeah lent themselves to horror writing and ideological battle. Zombification, 'a Caribbean version of Frankenstein's monster',³⁷ 'conjures up the Haitian experience of slavery, of the disassociation of man from his will, his reduction to a beast of burden at the will of a master'.³⁸

Charlotte Brontë's *Jane Eyre* (and her sister Emily's novel *Wuthering Heights*) has had a profound influence on much Caribbean fiction in its portrayal of the zombified madwoman in the attic, Bertha Mason. Not exactly a supernatural ghost, Bertha's haunting turns out to be something even worse – a living death shut up in Thornfield Hall where Edward Rochester can control her yet never forget her. Being only human, though coded as rendering indeterminate the boundary between the human and the animal,³⁹ and thus perceived as a sublime hellion, Bertha lacks supernatural powers; her only real power lies in her ability to take her own life, leaving Edward and Jane free to marry. Discovering Edward is already married to Bertha, Jane retreats to the sublime, windswept Yorkshire moors, where she rediscovers her Englishness that will then facilitate Rochester's own patriotic recovery from Bertha's creole corruption.

Dominican writer Jean Rhys's 'prequel' to *Jane Eyre*, *Wide Sargasso Sea*, inverts the characters' subject positions; Jane is nearly absent from the text, while Bertha, originally named Antoinette, is the central figure with Edward, as the youngest son in search of a Caribbean sugar heiress, the antagonist. England is now peripheral and fantastical, while Jamaica and Dominica are an ambivalent home haunted by the legacy of slavery. Confronted by the 'green menace',⁴⁰ the 'extreme green'⁴¹ of the sublime tropical forest, Edward eventually adopts the persona of a deadly hurricane that will tear Antoinette from her home and carry her to an English prison:

> The hurricane months are not so far away, I thought, and saw that tree strike its roots deeper, making it ready to fight the wind. Useless. If and when it comes they'll all go ... The contemptuous wind passes, not caring for these abject things ... It's an English summer now, so cool, so grey. Yet I think of my revenge and hurricanes. Words rush through my head (deeds too).⁴²

In both novels, the natural sublime, the haunting supernatural (elven folklore in *Jane Eyre*, Obeah in *Wide Sargasso Sea*), and the law of the father come together to destroy the racially ambivalent, sexually deviant Antoinette/Bertha, who must be excised from the text to cleanse English identity. But Rhys's inversions and marginalising of English culture succeeds in producing not a collusion with imperial patriarchy but a critique.

If the applicability of the gothic to Caribbean and other postcolonial literatures is now clear, this has been less so regarding the sublime. Since Kant published the *Critique of Judgment* (1791), it has been customary to accept his version of the sublime as recuperating pure humanistic reason, a secular analogue to Longinus and Burke's appeals to the divine. This, however, has been anathema to postcolonial or decolonial scholars, who reject universal humanism but have erroneously assumed that to locate a postcolonial aesthetics would necessarily reinscribe Kant's 'pure', disinterested stance associated with the white male European subject;[43] however, the uncritical denunciation of the aesthetic overlooks its historical complexity.[44]

The Sublime Is Always Interested

The notion of a disinterested sublime comes under pressure with the investigation of the nature of the sublime object, the identity of the agent producing the object, and the ideology and culture of the audience encountering this object,[45] that is, when the aesthetic experience is placed in its historical context. While Kant's influence on Romanticism was pronounced, arguably it has been less significant with regard to the gothic, in which moral reason fails to take hold and instead 'the submission to the sublime is against our will, and transcendence is the bliss of pure negation'.[46] Therefore, this paper will not address Kant's theory but move on to post-Kantian Schopenhauer and postmodernist Lyotard, whose theories of the sublime better foment a 'universally subjective' sublime.

If their antecedents grounded the sublime in Orientalising and misogynist gestures, the potential for a liberatory and world-gothic sublime is evident in the works of Schopenhauer and Lyotard. Schopenhauer considers Kant's pure reason as theology in disguise,[47] but agrees with Kant that we can only perceive the world as phenomena (appearances), and never have access to the thing-in-itself. All phenomena are merely illusory manifestations of the blind force of nature he terms 'the Will'.[48] Absolute good and evil do not exist; instead, suffering is caused by the Will being in perpetual conflict with itself in the form of representation, a conflict that arises from the individual's inclination to see oneself as the knowing subject and all others as only representation.[49] Schopenhauer does believe it possible to have glimpses of the Will,[50] fleeting moments that provide temporary relief from suffering, revealing we are part of the whole: I am the Other.

8 World-Gothic and the Sublime

Along with Schiller and Hegel, Schopenhauer shifts the sublime away from Kant and towards the gothic.[51] When we lose ourselves in the contemplation of the vast infinitude of the universe, we feel ourselves reduced to 'transient phenomena of will, like drops in the ocean, dwindling and dissolving into nothing', and yet we also feel that the universe exists only in our minds, our representation. What arises is the feeling that 'we are one with the world, and are therefore not oppressed but exalted by its immensity'.[52] Mishra argues that the horror of this oceanic sublime is also the end of narrative and of history, the logic of which is found in the gothic.[53]

Yet Schopenhauer would reject the subsumption of his theory of the sublime into the gothic. The feeling of oneness with the universe provides relief, albeit temporary, from the endless suffering of existence. One important path to such insight is compassion, in which we recognise others as ends rather than means, and Schopenhauer insists that other cultures and religions are rational and moral, and that even animals are equally deserving of our compassion.[54] (Unfortunately, Schopenhauer's misogyny leads him to exclude women from reason and aesthetic sense, although by 1859 his views had moderated.[55]) Another path is the sublime, which enables oneness with the Will by temporarily dissolving the distinction between subject and object, producing a double vision of individuation and dissolution. However, a vision of dissolution may produce a humbling renunciation of the ego or a gothic horror at one's feebleness before the boundless universe; that is, the sublime is not wedded to a gothic outcome.

World-Gothic Sublimities

We can see the distinct possibilities of the sublime in a writer like Conrad. *Heart of Darkness* comes to a gothic end – Kurtz dies, Marlow lies to Kurtz's fiancée about how he died, and the torment in the Congo Free State goes on (though in 1904 the international Congo Reform Association began a global publicity campaign to raise awareness about the atrocities committed under King Leopold II of Belgium). Similarly, *The Secret Agent*, located in a dim and swampy gothic London that recalls Dickens as well as R. L. Stevenson's *Dr Jekyll and Mr Hyde*, ends in tragedy with the murder of Verloc by his wife Winnie, who later commits suicide. Echoes of Stoker's *Dracula*, at heart a critique of Victorian capitalism,[56] and Marx's claim that 'Capital is dead labour, that, vampire-like, only lives by sucking living labour, and lives the more, the more labour it sucks'[57] can be found in Yundt's exclamation, '"Do you know how I would call the nature of the present economic conditions? I would call it cannibalistic. That's what it is! They are nourishing their greed on the quivering flesh and the warm blood of the people – nothing else"'.[58] The novel ends with the anarchist Professor blending into the vast London crowd, 'unsuspected and deadly, like a pest in the street full of men'.[59]

To exclude all forms of reasoning from sublimity would support Mishra's argument that the gothic sublime is purely irrational but could also play into ideas of noble savagery and other pernicious stereotypes that would foreclose the path to a world-gothic sublime. This becomes more evident with the shift to the twentieth century, entailing rapid technological innovations and postcolonial movements following the Second World War. If colonial gothic literature in the early nineteenth century 'often turned the colonial subject into the obscene cannibalistic personification of evil, through whom authors could bring revulsion and horror into the text, thereby mirroring political and social anxieties close to home',[60] modernist and then postmodernist and postcolonial authors began to interrogate these racialised ideologies, as we see in *Heart of Darkness* when the alleged African cannibals refuse to eat Marlow despite their evident starvation.

The colonial space, Paravisini-Gebert notes, is 'a bifurcated, ambivalent space, where the familiar and unfamiliar mingle in an uneasy truce'.[61] Part of what makes the gothic gothic is this very obscurity between the known and the uncanny, high and low, revolutionary and conservative. The protagonists of gothic fictions traditionally dealt with the contradictions they encountered 'by throwing them off onto ghostly or monstrous counterparts that then seem "uncanny" in their unfamiliar familiarity while also conveying overtones of the archaic and the alien in their grotesque mixture of elements viewed as incompatible by established standards of normality'.[62] The normative 'dissociates from itself, and then fears, the extremes of what surrounds it'.[63]

Similarly, the sublime presents the subject with an ambivalent aesthetics of fear and desire. The sublime cannot be merely horrible: something must differentiate it from pure fear for it to be sublime, but what recuperates that fear has been subject to intense debate. In order to admit the Other into a world-gothic sublime, an Other that is no longer solely opposed to the European subject but relative to any given subject in any cultural and historical context, we must reconsider the nature of that recuperative element as well as the literary text in question. In some cases, a gothic sublime may only end in death, as in *The Secret Agent* and many horror stories; in others, the gothic element passes out of the text as the plot is resolved, as in *Dracula*. In Laguna Pueblo writer Leslie Marmon Silko's novel *Ceremony*,[64] the gothic element pertains to Tayo's Second World War post-traumatic stress disorder and self-medication with alcohol. But after encountering an animist native spirit woman, Ts'eh, and completion of a healing ceremony by recovering his uncle's cattle, he renounces his violent veteran drinking buddies as they fight near the Trinity nuclear test site and retires to a pastoral life. In setting the climactic scene in New Mexico, where the atomic bomb was first launched, Silko taps into one of the most sublime of modern fears: nuclear devastation. Haunted as the text is by the history of genocide in the Americas and Japan, Silko employs gothic elements yet recovers hope from a violent past.

For others, however, the technological revolutions of the twentieth century have changed the nature of gothic fictions. Mishra argues that the gothic sublime anticipates the postmodern in its 'disenchantment with scientific paradigms and theories of knowledge' and an 'abject failure to totalize'.[65] Fred Botting claims that postmodern technological innovation and consumption have rendered gothic images 'less able to restore boundaries by allowing the projection of a missing unifying (and paternal) figure'.[66] What Lyotard terms the loss of metanarratives in his influential *The Postmodern Condition* has produced an abyss of heterogeneous discourses. Vampires have become commodified, and inhuman economic interests increasingly disrupt communities, families, and bodies, as they did during the Industrial Revolution. Postmodern capitalism produces a sublime excess of consumer choice, while media overstimulation renders the consuming subject a kind of gibbering idiot.[67] These dark visions are especially visible in dystopian narratives, video games, and horror films like *Dawn of the Dead* (1978), in which people take refuge from flesh-eating zombies in a mega shopping mall. Postmodern capitalism, as Marx predicted, appears to have subsumed the entire globe, flattening cultural differences, reducing us all to algorithmic consumers of images that excite our neurons yet feel aesthetically identical.

Against a dystopian postmodernity, however, should be contrasted the reality that across the globe not everyone experiences this postmodernity in the same way or with identical historical pasts or generic traditions. As Paravisini-Gebert observes, some literary traditions may lack the gothic but authors can adapt it to particular cultural settings, such as the novel *Maldito Amor* (*Sweet Diamond Dust*) by Puerto Rican writer Rosario Ferré, which charts the 'decline of the planter class in the Caribbean and the exclusion of women from sources of power in patriarchal societies'.[68] If the gothic 'once provided the dark mirror in which modern culture recognized higher values and returned readers to normality',[69] this may be true again, against an ever-mutating, culturally specific normality.

It may therefore seem ironic to invoke Lyotard in the name of utopian possibilities. However, across his oeuvre, he offers an alternative theory of the sublime, the differend, that enables a universal yet subjective sublime that can promote a liberatory politics and aesthetics. Lyotard strips the sublime of metaphysics to understand it as the feeling of the differend, the incommensurability between experience and idea, imagination and reason,[70] an incommensurability that Mishra equates with the gothic sublime.[71] Extending this into the political realm, the differend is the non-discursive sign of heterogeneity that appears when the absence of a universal rule or set of discourses produces the domination of one entity over another; here, the differend signals that something remains unthought or unexpressed.[72] Without a universal tribunal based on a shared discourse, a differend cannot be heard by those in power, but it can be witnessed by others who attempt to forge translations between discourses.[73] In this way, the sublime offers the possibility of political resistance.

Unlike Burke, but like Kant, Lyotard regards the French Revolution as demonstrating that humanity is both cause and author of its progress. The 'enthusiasm' of the sublime mob manifests the idea of a universal community, and therefore constitutes an 'event' that is a sign of hope that progress is occurring.[74] Lyotard interprets Kant to mean that the spectators' enthusiasm is sublime because it forms a 'passage' or translation between the rational idea of freedom and the non-discursive aesthetic in the form of the mob's emotional outburst that offers indirect evidence of such an idea.[75] A radical politics must allow that there is no predetermined outcome, only an unceasing effort to translate between discourses as differends come into being and are, sometimes, resolved. Inclusive politics are a process, never a final product.

For Lyotard, art is a powerful way to witness differends and foster new idioms. Avant-garde – that is, interrogative – art can trigger feelings not always discursively available or socially acceptable, bridging reason and imagination,[76] including gothic aesthetics. Yet what the audience takes away cannot be entirely predetermined, thereby enabling the opportunity for self-determination. In *Enthusiasm*, Lyotard regards the novel and literature as providing the same potentiality as visual art. Unlike Kant, Burke, and Longinus, who assert that only an educated elite can access a pure sublime, Lyotard implies that Kant's idea of enlightenment, the ability to think for oneself, does not presume an elite education. The novel demands that the reader take on the ethical burden of judgment rather than relying on authorities to tell them how to think, thereby calling into being an ideal reader who is always in a state of awakening. Lyotard thus asseverates that sublime aesthetics can *produce* the desire for moral improvement and education, rather than being the *product* of elite education. The sublime differend is therefore not a permanent condition but a potentiality that may be alleviated by ethical action and the invention of new phrases and languages, even non-discursive ones.[77] While nothing is guaranteed, such a liberated sublime can mobilise our capacity for compassion and political justice.

The implications for the gothic are not dissimilar. As Nick Groom argues, 'If the Gothic is as relevant today as it has been for the past millennium and a half, it is not because the Goths are still at the gate, it is – and always has been – the "normals" who are the real threat'.[78] Jean Rhys, while retaining Antoinette/Bertha's suicide, reclaims her colonial female voice from its silencing by the colonising patriarchy and recasts Rochester as not a Romantic antihero but a villain, putting responsibility where it belongs. Tayo rejects a life of violence and addiction for a healing connection to home and the earth. And Conrad reminds us that the Self was and is the Other. Put another way, the gothic is a mode whose purpose is to *witness* the differend, the power imbalance between the 'normal', who set the terms of any tribunal, and the Other, who is silenced. For although the gothic has been consistently deployed to project modern anxieties into a conveniently vacated present,[79] remembering that the gothic, and the gothic sublime, are fundamentally 'counterfeit'[80] reminds us that they are impermanent, products of specific historical conditions that can, and will, change. Such an understanding of the world-gothic as reflective of systemic power imbalances may enable us to extend beyond a Eurocentric limit and offer a world-gothic sublime as an aesthetic and ethic of translatability.

Notes

1. Joseph Conrad, *Youth, Heart of Darkness, The End of the Tether*, London, Dent, 1946 (1902), 49–50.
2. Chinua Achebe, 'An Image of Africa', *The Massachusetts Review*, 18 (1977), 782–94.
3. Conrad, *Youth, Heart of Darkness, The End of the Tether*, 92–3.
4. Conrad, *Youth, Heart of Darkness, The End of the Tether*, 117.
5. Conrad, *Youth, Heart of Darkness, The End of the Tether*, 45.
6. Conrad, *Youth, Heart of Darkness, The End of the Tether*, 162.
7. Philip Shaw, *The Sublime*, 2nd ed., London, Routledge, 2017, 2.

8. Vijay Mishra, *The Gothic Sublime*, Albany, State University of New York Press, 1994, 37.
9. Mishra, *The Gothic Sublime*, 38.
10. Mishra, *The Gothic Sublime*, 40.
11. Rebecca Duncan, 'Decolonial Gothic: Beyond the Postcolonial in Gothic Studies', *Gothic Studies*, 24 (2022), 304–22.
12. Andrew Smith and William Hughes, 'Introduction', in A. Smith and W. Hughes (eds.), *Empire and the Gothic: The Politics of Genre*, Basingstoke, Palgrave Macmillan, 2003, 1.
13. Mishra, *The Gothic Sublime*, 26.
14. Glennis Byron, 'Introduction', in G. Byron (ed.), *Globalgothic*, Manchester, Manchester University Press, 2016, 3.
15. Byron, 'Introduction', 4.
16. Nick Groom, *The Gothic: A Very Short Introduction*, Oxford, Oxford University Press, 2012, 7.
17. Longinus, *Longinus on the Sublime: The Greek Text Edited After the Paris Manuscript*, 2nd ed., ed. and trans. W. Rhys Roberts, Cambridge, Cambridge University Press, 1907, 1.3–4; all translations are my own.
18. Longinus, *Longinus on the Sublime*, 7.1–2.
19. Longinus, *Longinus on the Sublime*, 9.2.
20. Longinus, *Longinus on the Sublime*, 15.1–2.
21. Jakob Wisse, 'Greeks, Romans, and the Rise of Atticism', in J. G. J. Abbenes, S. R. Slings, and I. Sluiter (eds.), *Greek Literary Theory after Aristotle: A Collection of Papers in Honour of D. M. Schenkeveld*, Amsterdam, VU University Press, 1995, 71–2.
22. Longinus, *Longinus on the Sublime*, 23.4.
23. Groom, *The Gothic*, 1.
24. Groom, *The Gothic*, 12.
25. Groom, *The Gothic*, 38–43.
26. A. O. Scott, 'The Supervillain Is the Hero Now', *The New York Times*, 23 November 2024.
27. Edmund Burke, *A Philosophical Enquiry into the Origin of our Ideas on the Sublime and the Beautiful*, Oxford, Oxford University Press, 1990 (1757), 36.
28. Srinivas Aravamudan, *Tropicopolitans: Colonialism and Agency, 1688–1804*, Raleigh, NC, Duke University Press, 1999, 191.
29. Burke, *A Philosophical Enquiry*, 44, 54–5.
30. Ronald Paulson, *Representations of Revolution (1789–1820)*, New Haven, Yale University Press, 1983, 220–1.
31. Franco Moretti, *Signs Taken for Wonders: Essays in the Sociology of Literary Forms*, London, Verso, 1997 (1983), 83.
32. Simon Gikandi, *Slavery and the Culture of Taste*, Princeton, Princeton University Press, 2011.
33. Heidi Crawford, 'The Cultural-Historical Origins of the Literary Vampire in Germany', *Journal of Dracula Studies*, 7 (2005), DOI: 10.70013/58k4l5m6.
34. Bram Stoker, *Dracula*, Oxford, Oxford University Press, 2011 (1895).

35. Stoker, *Dracula*, 10–11.
36. Lizabeth Paravisini-Gebert, 'Colonial and Postcolonial Gothic: The Caribbean', in J. E. Hogle (ed.), *The Cambridge Companion to Gothic Fiction*, Cambridge: Cambridge University Press, 2002, 230.
37. Paravisini-Gebert, 'Colonial and Postcolonial Gothic', 238.
38. Paravisini-Gebert, 'Colonial and Postcolonial Gothic', 239.
39. Gayatri Spivak, 'Three Women's Tales and a Critique of Imperialism', *Critical Inquiry*, 12, (1985), 243–61, 249.
40. Jean Rhys, *Wide Sargasso Sea*, London, World Books, 1967 (1966), 149.
41. Rhys, *Wide Sargasso Sea*, 69.
42. Rhys, *Wide Sargasso Sea*, 163–4.
43. Elleke Boehmer, 'A Postcolonial Aesthetic: Repeating Upon the Present', in ed. E. Boehmer, J. Wilson, C. Sandru, and S. L. Welch (eds.), *Re-routing the Postcolonial: New Directions for the New Millennium*, London, Routledge, 2010, 178.
44. Terry Eagleton, *The Ideology of the Aesthetic*, London, Blackwell, 1991, 2, 9.
45. Mishra, *The Gothic Sublime*, 21.
46. Mishra, *The Gothic Sublime*, 11.
47. Arthur Schopenhauer, *The World as Will and Representation*, 2 vols., trans. E. F. J. Payne, New York, Dover, 1958 (1844), preface to the first edition, xv, 1:99.
48. Schopenhauer, *The World as Will and Representation*, 1:128–9, 134.
49. Schopenhauer, *The World as Will and Representation*, 1:146–7, 332–3.
50. Schopenhauer, *The World as Will and Representation*, 1:169.
51. Mishra, *The Gothic Sublime*, 36.
52. Schopenhauer, *The World as Will and Representation*, 1:205.
53. Mishra, *The Gothic Sublime*, 37.
54. Arthur Schopenhauer, *The Basis of Morality*, trans. A. B. Bullock, London, Swan Sonnenschein, 1903 (1840).
55. Rudiger Safranski, *Schopenhauer and the Wild Years of Philosophy*, Cambridge, MA, Harvard University Press, 1990, 348.
56. Groom, *The Gothic*, 97.
57. Karl Marx, *Capital*, vol. 1, www.marxists.org/archive/marx/works/1867-c1/ch10.htm, chapter 10.
58. Joseph Conrad, *The Secret Agent*, London, Dent, 1923 (1907), 51.
59. Conrad, *The Secret Agent*, 311.
60. Paravisini-Gebert, 'Colonial and Postcolonial Gothic', 231.
61. Paravisini-Gebert, 'Colonial and Postcolonial Gothic', 233.
62. Jerrold E. Hogle, 'Introduction', in J. E. Hogle (ed.), *The Cambridge Companion to Gothic Fiction*, Cambridge, Cambridge University Press, 2002, 7.
63. Hogle, 'Introduction', 9.
64. Leslie Marmon Silko, *Ceremony*, New York, Viking, 1977.
65. Mishra, *The Gothic Sublime*, 20, 39.

66. Fred Botting, 'Aftergothic: Consumption, Machines, and Black Holes: *Doom with a View*', in J. E. Hogle (ed.), *The Cambridge Companion to Gothic Fiction*, Cambridge, Cambridge University Press, 2002, 281.
67. Botting, 'Aftergothic', 294–5.
68. Paravisini-Gebert, 'Colonial and Postcolonial Gothic', 233.
69. Botting, 'Aftergothic', 281.
70. Jean-François Lyotard, *Lessons on the Analytic of the Sublime: Kant's 'Critique of Judgment', §§ 23–29*, trans. E. Rottenberg, Stanford, Stanford University Press, 1994 (1991), 233–4.
71. Mishra, *The Gothic Sublime*, 39.
72. Jean-François Lyotard, 'After the Sublime: The State of Aesthetics', in *The Inhuman*, trans. G. Bennington and R. Bowlby, Stanford, Stanford University Press, 1988, 13.
73. Jean-François Lyotard, *The Differend*, trans. G. Van Den Abbeele, Minneapolis, MN, University of Minnesota Press, 1988 (1983), 156–7.
74. Immanuel Kant, *Religion and Natural Theology*, Cambridge, Cambridge University Press, 1998, 4:84, 785–6.
75. Jean-François Lyotard, *Enthusiasm: The Kantian Critique of History*, trans. G. Van Den Abbeele, Stanford, CA, Stanford University Press, 2009 (1986), 32–40.
76. Jean-François Lyotard, 'After the Sublime: The State of Aesthetics', 88.
77. Lyotard, *The Differend*, 13, 70.
78. Groom, *The Gothic*, 142.
79. Hogle, 'Introduction', 16.
80. Hogle, 'Introduction', 15.

CHAPTER 9

A Planetary Grotesque

Rune Graulund

In Ari Aster's folk horror film *Midsommar* (2019), a young couple from the United States moves to Sweden for the summer. Christian, the boyfriend, has been invited by Pelle, a Swedish student he has met at graduate school, where they both study anthropology. Dani, Christian's girlfriend, decides to join Christian, Pelle, and two other students in order to put distance between herself and the recent deaths of her sister and parents. In the opening act of the film, we witness Dani in profound grief as she discovers her mentally ill sister has committed suicide after also having gassed their parents. The act ends with a slow pan of rescue workers making the grim discovery of the bodies and a prolonged closeup of falling snow. In act two, as the group of Americans eventually arrives in rural Sweden, the mood and setting shifts radically. The drab grey of American urbanism is replaced with a sun-drenched landscape lush with flowers and verdant fields, just as the dysfunctional relationship between Dani and Christian is momentarily relieved by the warm welcome from the religious commune Pelle belongs to. Dani (along with the viewers) is wary, however. Having just witnessed the gruesome deaths of her entire family, Dani and the viewers both sense that this luminous utopia may not be what it seems. Still, the smiling and generous manners of the locals living a bucolic life put the outsiders, and perhaps also the viewers, somewhat at ease.

In the forty minutes that follow nothing comparable to the horror of the suicide-murders happens. While there are moments of unease, mostly Dani and the other outsiders experience the life in the village as gentle and welcoming. But then the tone shifts once again. The outsiders are invited to witness the ritual of 'ättestuppa', an ancient Norse ceremony, in which the elderly of the tribe are either voluntarily or forcibly cast off from a high cliff because they have reached an age where they are considered to be a burden on their community. Yet the violence of such an arcane and brutal ritual appears incongruent to the mild manners of the locals. At first refusing to believe that what they are witnessing is in fact real, the seriousness of the situation is brought home to the outsiders once an elderly lady throws herself from the top of the cliff, her head smashing into a bloody pulpy mush as it hits the rocks below. This first shot of visceral violence is brief, but shocking. The shattered skull and grisly brains stand out in stark visual contrast to the white background of the cliff and the immaculate white garb of the participants in the ritual. But most of all the shock is perhaps caused by the refined aesthetics of all that has been presented to the viewers up to this point, suddenly displaced by gross and maximalist gore. This jarring contrast is further emphasised by the outside spectators' response to the death. As the visitors cry out in distress and horror, the camera pans to the Swedish cult members (as they will soon turn out to be), all of whom seem genuinely perplexed at the outsiders' emotional outburst. As the camera pans to the dead woman once again, this time lingering on the mangled head for a full seven seconds, we then crosscut to Dani who, like the viewer, is still not quite sure what is going on.

Dani's uncertainty is soon squashed as an elderly man also dives off the cliff. Accentuating the horror, the man jumps feet rather than head first, which results in a damaging but not lethal fall. Again, we get a close-up of gore, this time of the sundered leg of the man, who, still alive, cries out in abject pain. Echoing the man's screams, the outsiders once again wail in unison as a cult member approaches and eventually puts the man out of his misery by smashing his head in with a giant mallet. Here, the camera and the special effects crew pull no punches: the vivid and unsparing details hammer home – so to speak – that this film is different from Aster's acclaimed 'elevated horror' in his critically lauded breakout film *Hereditary* (2018). For while the first hour of the film masterfully telegraphs a refined if also morbid sensibility, we are now suddenly knee-deep in a schlocky and grotesque slasher aesthetic, not far removed from 'a Hammer horror film'.[1] Both violently horrific and exaggeratedly comedic, the beautiful eeriness of flowers and light, of welcoming white smiles and robes, have with little warning been exchanged for caved-in skulls, spatters of blood, mangled limbs, and screams of pain.

As opposed to gothic, which tends to be defined through the uncertainty of the uncanny, of shadows, mystery, and darkness, grotesque is never subtle or undetermined. Gothic is of course *also* characterised by horror, by violence, and by monstrosity, yet ambiguity and opacity remain central to it as a style. Grotesque on the other hand is defined by always being in excess, exaggerated and loudly transgressive. With grotesque, we are never in doubt that one of its defining characteristics is to be in breach, to forcefully disturb and to elicit unambiguous affect whether that is in riotous laughter or in wails of abject horror. Finally, grotesque often contains elements of the comedic, which is rarely present in gothic.

Beginning from the premise that Western or Eurocentric gothic is just one of many kinds of world-gothic, this chapter presents an attempt to unearth the grotesque from its medieval and classical European roots in order to perceive it in the light of a Western modernity that has attempted to regulate and eradicate supposedly premodern (which is to say non-Western) worldviews. First, via a continued reading of *Midsommar*, the chapter will examine the grotesque through a theoretical genealogy of Wolfgang Kayser, John Ruskin, Mikhail Bakhtin, and Michel Foucault. It then engages in a reading of selected texts in the light of their national, regional, and planetary contexts. In this, the chapter examines the role grotesque has played in shaping but also questioning the self-identified 'modernity' of Europe and the West as orderly, rational, and universal. The chapter initially examines the origins of grotesque as an aesthetic concept etymologically and culturally in a European context, but with the explicit aim to expand this into a conversation about what I have here suggested could be termed a planetary grotesque. It does so not in a globalgothic sense of presenting an 'original grotesque' transplanted from a European setting, but of differentiated and situated world-gothic manifestations of grotesque that can all be read as responding to a range of planetary socio-economic and environmental crises facing us in the new millennium.

In addition to *Midsommar*, the chapter reads books by South African J. M. Coetzee's *The Lives of Animals* (1999), American Jonathan Saffran Foer's *Eating Animals* (2009), Dutch Michel Faber's *Under the Skin* (2000), and Argentinian author Agustina Bazterrica's *Tender is the Flesh* (2017). The chapter concludes in a comparative reading of American Chuck Palahniuk's novel *Invisible Monsters* (1999) and the Norwegian film *Sick of Myself* (2022), followed by a consideration of the implications of an environmental, political, and planetary grotesque. Finally, the chapter considers the recent (re)turn towards a female grotesque. The chapter concludes that even as they manifest in multiple grotesque and always amorphous forms, female, political, and planetary grotesque all point to a shared set of social and planetary problems that is at a wider level addressed by contemporary world-gothic in all its forms.

Grotesque in Theory

Midsommar suggests that what one culture deems abnormal, shocking, and transgressive is to the other not only accepted and cherished, but understood as part of the cycle of nature. To the outsiders, and possibly also to many viewers, the film's suicidal jumps and concomitant skull-crushing ballet of mallets constitute acts of grotesquery. The violence is in itself shocking, but so is the cult's perception of the elderly as useless and disposable waste, a burden on the young and on the community. This simply is not done anymore, and perhaps especially not in Sweden, which so often feature in the popular global imaginary as a progressive pinnacle of egalitarianism and 'development'. To the cult, though, the ättestuppa is a noble, honourable, and most of all necessary tradition stretching back a thousand years. 'What you just saw is a long, long, long observed custom!', one of the seemingly well-meaning members explains in a calm and reasonable voice. 'You need to understand that it was a great joy for them', a 'gesture', as she calls it, to the community and the cycle of life.

Midsommar points towards a past and a worldview that is pagan, premodern, and precapitalist. The film flips the linear script of imperial historiography and anthropology. It rewrites the coloniser's journey into supposedly more primitive colonised regions as a journey within Europe itself, while at the same putting paid to any conception of anthropology as an exercise in shedding light on ostensibly strange and mysterious customs. The anthropology students leave the New World of the United States behind and travel back to the Old World, the origin of 'Western civilisation', in order to study a ritual that predates the Columbian exchange. Despite the incessant sunlight, enlightenment is not what the anthropologists find as they continuously fail at reading the true intentions of the cult. As Christian remarks to Dani in a misguided attempt at anthropological relativism: 'That's Cultural, you know? We stick our elders in nursing homes. I'm sure they find that disturbing.' At the end of the film, when Christian is sewn into a bear and set alight (part of a distinctly non-Christian ritual), he seems less sure about the reasonableness of the cult's customs. Dani, on the other hand, whose name, not incidentally, is Hebrew for 'God is my judge', watches first in horror, but then in apparent triumph as she seems to accept a worldview in which human sacrifice is not only normal, but decidedly joyous. As her emotionally unavailable and narcissistic boyfriend literally goes up in smoke, and as the only survivor of the visiting outsiders, she is finally set free from her toxic relationship with Christian, from the traumatic deaths of her family, and from the strictures and 'loneliness of the modern world'.[2] Crowned by the matriarch Liv as May queen, Dani is worshipped by the commune's women, and indeed by the commune in its entirety. She is revered as the female goddess who will renew their bonds with nature and thereby ensure the survival and prospering of their traditional way of life, which, the ending of the film seems to suggest, is altogether more wholesome than the world most of us live in. Once Dani has moved through her shock and horror at the grotesque pageantry she finds herself to be in the centre (and the centre) of, she can emerge on the other side, nominally still in Europe in the twenty-first century, but in spirit somewhere much older than both Europe and modernity.

The etymology of 'grotesque' can be tracked back to ancient Rome, and the concept later came to be viewed as central to Western culture. The perceived, and actual, genesis of the word is worth investigating in some detail. Wolfgang Kayser notes in his germinal book, *The Grotesque in Art and Literature* (1963), that the 'Grotesque (both noun and adjective) and the words which correspond to it in other languages are ultimately derived from the Italian. *La grottesca* and *grottesco* refer to *grotto* (cave) and were coined to designate a certain ornamental style which came to light during late fifteenth-century excavations'.[3] This 'hitherto unknown ancient form of ornamental painting [was] by no means native to the Romans'.[4] Notions of the grotesque have historically been presented, however, as springing from the bosom of the Roman Empire, and in this way have been understood as proto-European. At the same time, it is notable that the grotesque has also been seen as inherently alien to Europe, and more specifically to the modernity which Europe has ascribed to itself. 'By the word *grottesco* the Rennaissance ... understood not only something playfully gay and carelessly fantastic, but also something ominous and sinister in the face of a world totally different from the familiar one – a world in which the realm of inanimate things is no longer separated from those of plants, animals, and human beings, and where the laws of statics, symmetry, and proportion are no longer valid'.[5] The term is thus 'debased' literally as well as figuratively. Both originating in and identified with an underground setting, dug out from dirt and filth only to see daylight after centuries of internment, the grotesque also designates topics that are themselves 'lowly', depicting creatures and acts that are transgressive, vulgar, and impure. Here it is important to distinguish between the fifteenth-century coinage of the grotesque, and the source material referred to by the concept refers, which originates over a millennium earlier, in 'a world totally different from the familiar one' of the Renaissance present. To quote Christian from *Midsommar* once again: 'That's cultural.'

To Roman sensibilities, the depictions of plants, animals, and humans intersecting in hybrid whorls were likely far less transgressive and certainly much more familiar than the fifteenth-century response seems to indicate.

Further, from a contemporary perspective, it seems doubly significant that it was to the lower courts of perhaps the most decadent Roman emperors – Nero – that later centuries would look for a term that would 'inspire ambivalent emotional reactions', indeed 'a civil war of attraction/repulsion' and 'a clash between incompatible reactions'.[6] Nero has traditionally been presented as a symbol of the downfall of the Roman empire, not only literally in terms of monuments toppled, armies defeated, and towns razed to the ground, but also in terms of the empire's moral decay: the lowering of standards and purity of purpose. For Kayser, 'the grotesque spread from Italy to the countries north of the Alps'[7] over the course of the sixteenth century – a perspective that notably envisions Rome as the historical ground zero for the grotesque on a transnational scale. Tellingly, Kayser here positions the Roman empire, on which so many later European empires would model themselves, as both the yardstick and the dark undercurrent of what he and others implicitly frame as the monolithic block of 'Western culture'. As a term, grotesque is thus etymologically, architecturally, historically, and culturally imagined to be acutely European, while also routinely and somewhat confusingly being presented as a central disruptive force undermining, destabilising, and challenging Europe's self-identity. As James Goodwin puts it, 'the grotesque had persisted at least since the Renaissance as a common strain within cultures of the West',[8] where it represents a force of rebellion: a wellspring of vital, unruly and intense emotions that can be employed as a counter to all that is perceived to be proper, ideal, and fixed.

As Alastair Bonnett has pointed out, the idea that 'the West' is a unity and that it offers 'a "perspective", an ethno-cultural repertoire, is a creation of little more than a hundred years'.[9] As such, Kayser's book, written in the midst of the Cold War, offers an interesting perspective on the power of the grotesque to both disturb and affirm the idea of Europe and 'Western' culture, as well as on the resurgent popularity of grotesque in the late-nineteenth and twentieth centuries. The most often-quoted theorists of the grotesque tend to focus on the lack of boundaries designated by the concept, as well as on the challenge of providing a firm definition. Excessive, transgressive, and often violent, the grotesque can provoke strong, or even overwhelming, sensation. It is therefore easy to recognise in the moment, yet to pin it down, to frame, and to define it in theory outside of a specific context is difficult, if not in fact impossible. It is precisely this 'wild' quality that John Ruskin saw as 'evidence of deep insight into nature'[10] in his examination of Venetian art in *The Stones of Venice* (1851–3). Comparing what he terms 'true grotesque' to the mannered and anaemic 'false grotesque', we see with Ruskin a model of history in which a sickly and decadent present is set in contrast to a disturbing yet vitalist construction of nature that predates our (and Ruskin's) world. A similar sentiment can be traced in Michel Foucault's analyses of the birth of the asylum, the hospital, the prison, and sexuality, which although not specifically about the grotesque as a term all share a fascination with – even a valorisation of – the deviant, the transgressive, the mad, and indeed with all things that are considered to be behaviourally and somatically excessive. Even when he does not address it directly, as a loud, raw, and insistent force refusing to be manacled and silenced by modernity, the grotesque flows through all of Foucault's texts as a dissident voice reminding us of all the things modernity has tried (but often failed) to repress. Here, the grotesque is a force of the 'abnormal' that tests and challenges repressive normativity. Most influential of all in the theorisation of the grotesque, and the greatest believer in its restorative power, is however Mikhail Bakhtin. In his reading of François Rabelais's *Gargantua and Pantagruel* (1532–64), Bakhtin connects the grotesque to 'the carnivalesque': a space in which, however briefly, social stratifications and repressive regimes of power are dismantled. As he notes, 'carnival does not know footlights, in the sense that it does not acknowledge any distinction between actors and spectators. . . . Carnival is not a spectacle seen by people; they live in it, and everyone participates because its very idea embraces all the people'.[11] The overall sensation in these theorisations of the grotesque, despite its potentially disturbing and horrific aspects, is clearly one of celebration.

Even as the grotesque has been viewed as a liberating force, something to set us free from and dismantle the repressive modernity of which Europe and 'the West' are supposedly the wellspring, it nonetheless remains a peculiarly Eurocentric phenomenon in all these texts. Perceived as a reaction to a thing that Western modernity has lost, or at the very least repressed, made orderly, hidden away, and bridled, 'the normative' that the grotesque disrupts and pushes back against has been rendered essentially Eurocentric, even as it is paradoxically defined as European modernity's other. As a peripheral if also riotous response to Enlightenment ideas of reason, bourgeois sensibilities of propriety, or capitalist demands on production (e.g., pressure to conform, to be industrious) and policing of consumption (e.g., pressures to conform to a certain body size or type), the grotesque is seen to occupy seemingly paradoxical positions inside and outside the hegemon of Europe. In this way, the grotesque is envisioned as a blunt tool that can shock 'us' into returning to a state of being that is pre-modern, pre-industrialist, pre-capitalist, and pre-European, even as the tool itself is perceived to be the product, or a leftover, of a vitalist proto-Europe.

The celebration of the grotesque presented by Ruskin, Bakhtin, and Foucault all operate on the assumption that something is missing from the respective historical and geographic contexts they are writing from and in. Whether it is a staid Victorian England in which artistic expression cannot run free (Ruskin); a dogmatic post-revolutionary Russia restraining critical thought and free expression (Bakhtin); or a twentieth-century bourgeois France (Foucault) where traditional bonds to the mad, the criminal, and the deviant have been clinically cut, all treat the grotesque as an expression of that which has been repressed, and should be brought back into being. As in *Midsommar*, the modern subject of repression is liberated through acts that are sometimes violent but nevertheless restorative, vibrant, and necessary. We see the point enacted when Dani, bedecked in flowers from top to toe, watches as Christian and all other remnants of the world she has left behind are purified by fire. As human, flower, and flame forge a new Dani, she can at the end of the movie emerge cleansed of modernity, and at one with the cult, their traditions, and their communal bonds with nature. As a hybrid and open entity, Dani is reborn as a Bakhtinian subject outside of modernity: 'Contrary to modern canons, the grotesque body is not separated from the rest of the world. It is not a closed, completed unit; it is unfinished, outgrows itself, transgresses its own limits.'[12]

In *Midsommar*, human bodies are broken, squashed to pulp, cut open, flayed, stuffed with hay or flowers, sown into animal bodies, fused with animal parts and trees, burnt and bedecked in flowers. Cultists as well as outsiders cry and scream, eject semen, tears and blood, all in the name of merging, with each other, with nature and with tradition. This can be construed as horrific and it is certainly violent, but as the ending of the films seems to suggest, to accept such a world rather than run away from it screaming can lead to redemption. Indeed, in an essay on 'the environmental grotesque', literary scholar Phoebe Wagner argues (in the tradition of Bakhtin) for grotesque to be employed as a force of regenerative power, rather than as a source of horror and terror:

> In contemporary literature, the environmental grotesque can be defined as grappling with the current and coming shock of climate change but accepting that struggle as transformative possibility and even cooperative survival with nonhumans. Rather than using fear as a motivator, it rejects fear for transformation ... Through normalizing the disturbing aspects of Anthropogenic climate change, this transformation occurs when we learn

to survive and thrive with the horrors we have created, rather than attempting to return to an imagined pristine landscape.[13]

We may now seem to be living in a world that has become increasingly grotesque, but as Wagner points out, maybe there is transformative potential in this. In the following, I will pursue the path of environmental grotesquery further as I continue to inspect skin, screen, and flesh in a reading of human and animal bodies, and how they intermix in a range of fiction and non-fiction texts.

Skin, Meat, Beauty

The painter Francis Bacon once remarked in an interview that '[w]hen you go into a butcher's shop and see how beautiful meat can be and then you think about it, you can think of the whole horror of life – of one thing living off another'.[14] Known for his depictions of visceral contortions of the human body, Bacon here points to the potential beauty of dissected meat as an isolated aesthetic object, but also to the grotesque nature of meat consumption. In bringing home the bacon, so to speak, one is knowingly complicit in 'the horror of life' not only on an intellectual and existential level, but also in the grisly production and consumption of meat. After all, the meat pondered by Bacon here is presented in a butcher's shop; a small business dependent on the production, butchering, and transportation of animals on an industrial scale.

The display of dissected animal flesh plays a central role in both J. M. Coetzee's *The Lives of Animals* (1999) and Jonathan Saffran Foer's *Eating Animals* (2009). Non-fiction and fiction respectively, Foer's and Coetzee's books nevertheless employ similar strategies to make their readers (re)consider their relationship with meat. Both texts employ a synthesis of philosophical, sociological, historical, and anthropological approaches: *The Lives of Animals* is a hybrid of a fictionalised family narrative and philosophical lecture, while *Eating Animals* straddles polemic and memoir. One is clearly a novel while the other is non-fiction, yet each argues for the abolition of meat-eating, backed up by sober facts on meat production which are interspersed with moments of grotesque horror. In this way, the Coetzee and Foer texts provide tableaus similar to Bacon's butcher shop, seeking both to invite reflection and to shock. Coetzee's central character Elizabeth asserts that contemporary factory-farming 'rivals anything that the Third Reich was capable of', and, quoting Plutarch, declares herself 'astonished that you can put in your mouth the corpse of a dead animal, astonished you do not find it nasty to chew hacked flesh and swallow the juices of death-wounds'.[15] Foer aims for a more measured tone, striving to be 'as objective as any work of journalism can be'; and yet he finds that even in the most '"ideal" slaughterhouse', the core practice remains the same.[16] Offered 'pink petals of ham' by the well-meaning owner of Paradise Locker Meat – an establishment adjacent to a butchery – Foer cannot let go of the fact that delicacy presented to him is the 'end that promises to justify all the bloody means next door'.[17] While less cruel than the practices of factory farms he goes on to describe in gruesome detail over the following pages, even this ethical slaughterhouse deals in death, dissection, and consumption. The factory farms may be places of 'systemic abuse' where grotesque atrocities like 'extinguishing cigarettes on the animals' bodies, beating them with rakes and shovels, strangling them, and throwing them into manure pits to drown'[18] are commonplace, while the supposedly 'ideal' small-scale slaughterhouse he visits deems to do away such excessive cruelty. Yet to be killed with kindness is still, Foer argues, murder.

Michel Faber's *Under the Skin* (2000) and Agustina Bazterrica's *Tender is the Flesh* (2017) share the concerns of Coetzee's and Foer's books, but ask the readers to consider how factory farming might look if the bodies consumed were human and not animal. Clearly works of speculative fiction, Faber's and Bazterrica's books present numerous scenes in which the human body is treated with the same detached indifference humans so often show the animal. At first sight both books seem to revolve around the horrors of cannibalism. Faber's novel depicts the life of Isserley, who drives around Scotland picking up and abducting male hitchhikers in order to take them to an underground facility where they are butchered, rendered, and packaged so that they can be eaten. Although technically not human, Isserley and 'her' fellow extraterrestrials present themselves as such, thus forcing the reader to reflect on the human form both in the state of dismemberment for the consumption of its flesh, and in the human form consuming human flesh. In Bazterrica's novel, humans are butchered on a much larger scale, the slaughtering taking place in the open since the dystopian society depicted can no longer eat animal meat due to a virus. Disregarding veganism as an unacceptable solution to the problem, Bazterrica's social order now deems cannibalism not only acceptable but desirable: human butcher is a reputable occupation; the murder of migrants and institutionalised persons is sanctioned by the state, as is the growth of genetically modified humans without vocal cords, specifically for easy butchering in human abattoirs.

Both books contain numerous and prolonged descriptions of human mutilation, dissection, and consumption, the horror of which is made even more grotesque and absurd by the calm indifference with which such scenes are portrayed:

> A worker picks up her head and takes it to another table where he removes her eyes and puts them on a tray with a label that says 'Eyes'. He opens her mouth, cuts out her tongue and places it on a tray with a label that says 'Tongues'. He cuts off her ears and sets them down on a tray with a label that says 'Ears'. The worker picks up an awl and a hammer and carefully taps the bottom of her head. He continues in this manner until he has cracked a portion of her skull and then he carefully removes her brain and leaves it on a tray with a label that says 'Brains'.[19]

Central to both books, such graphic scenes are clearly intended to make the reader consider what would happen if the tables were turned and humans were treated like cattle: 'As soon as he was satisfied with the state of the animal's mouth, Unser turned his attention to the genitals. Taking up a clean instrument, he sliced open the scrotal sac and, with rapid, delicate, almost trembling incisions of his scalpel, removed the testicles. It was a much more straightforward job than the tongue; it took perhaps thirty seconds.'[20] Where Coetzee and Foer employ sober facts and philosophical reasoning interspersed with the occasional scene of gross butchery, Faber and Bazterrica ratchet up the satirical and the grotesque to an extreme degree. Reminiscent of Jonathan Swift's 'A Modest Proposal' (1729), which employed the horrors of cannibalism and child murder to incite British political action on the Irish famine, Faber and Bazterrica employ a similarly detached style in order to make their readers consider the plight of animals destined for the abattoirs. Swift for instance compares the flesh of pigs unfavourably to the 'a well-grown, fat, yearling child, which roasted whole will make a considerable figure at a lord mayor's feast or any other public entertainment'. In their cool descriptions of human bodies cut and cured so as to end up on the dinner table, Faber and Bazterrica likewise employ the power of the grotesque to shock through the discord of the neutrality of tone with the utter horror of the reality described.

Moving from factory farming and the eating of meat to the beauty industry, Chuck Palahniuk's *Invisible Monsters* (1999) and the film *Sick of Myself* (2022), written and directed by Kristoffer Borgli, present comparable interactions with human flesh in the global beauty industry, where radical transformation is the desired goal. In Palahniuk's novel, we follow Shannon, a former model who has been disfigured beyond all recognition after having had her jaw shot off by a shotgun. Waking up after surgery, Shannon muses that 'sometimes being mutilated can work to your advantage. All those people now with piercings and tattoos and branding and scarification ... What I mean is, attention is attention.'[21] It turns out the damage done is so extensive that what she elicits is attention, but the reactions are of such extreme shock and disgust that no one can look at her. Consequently, as Shannon reflects towards the conclusion, 'If I can't be beautiful, I want to be invisible'.[22]

While also focusing on the damage done to the body in the context of global media industry, *Sick of Myself* revolves around precisely the opposite desire. The film focuses on Signe, a young Norwegian woman living a life of relative affluence, but also a life of emotional insecurity. Like Dani in *Midsommar*, she is caught in an unhealthy relationship; unlike Dani, the emotional damage the couple wreak upon another is evenly distributed. Thomas, Signe's boyfriend, is an incompetent yet successful artist, whereas Signe is stuck in a dead-end job as a barista. Jealous of her boyfriend's success, Signe discovers that she can get the attention that she craves by faking a range of illnesses and mishaps. Initially her quest for attention is steered by a desire for Thomas to see and value her, but it quickly shifts into a competitive relationship in which the two vie for the spotlight. In a series of increasingly grotesque tableaus, Signe goes to extreme lengths to assure this, including ordering illegal drugs online that corrode her skin. 'Narcissists are the ones who make it ... combined with talent, it's a plus', Signe comments, referring to the need for attention that dominates her own life, as well as the society she lives in.

In this context, she determines that the only way she can 'make it' and feel fully seen is by breaking down her exterior completely. In a superb twist on (in)visibility, the film ends with Signe wearing a patient gown and sunglasses, her head swaddled in gauze while she is seated in a wheelchair, smoking a cigarette and absorbed by her mobile phone. Mobile phone aside, the scene is clearly an homage to the original cinematic adaptation of H. G. Wells's *The Invisible Man* (novel 1897, film adaptation 1933), in which the eponymous protagonist of the film is seated in a chair, his head swaddled in gauze and wearing dark glasses. While he looks like an invalid in recovery, he is wearing the gauze and glasses not because he is physically sick but in order to hide his true identity. Confronted by police, he, in the famous reveal of the film, triumphantly shouts that: 'I'll show you who I am! And show *what* I am!' Slowly unwrapping the gauze, he is, of course, like Signe, nothing. Or, in an alternate reading, that the bandages that make the invisible man visible finally make Signe visible, too. Either way, there is no authentic core to either of the two, no real identity, other than what the exterior world perceives them to be (or not to be).

The central axis around which Palahniuk's novel and Borgli's film revolve is the dissonance between inner and outer beauty, and how the former is often ignored in the construction, mediation, and perception of external appearance. Equally important is the fact that Palahniuk's and Borgli's female protagonists are clearly victims of global structures pervaded by patriarchy (the fashion and beauty industry, the art world, social media, the attention economy) beyond their own control or making. Significantly, while both texts are nationally specific, they are nevertheless also clearly part of a global system that shapes the individuals who attempt to navigate it. Here it is however also important to note that in both texts the protagonists actively and brutally ruin their own exterior appearances: Palahniuk's Shannon, it turns out at the conclusion of the novel, was not in fact assaulted, but shot her own face and jaw off. And Signe, as is clear throughout the film, is so sick of herself that she will do literally anything to fuel the pyres of attention. Solely capable of seeing herself through the eyes of others, she ends up invisible, but also monstrous, a piece of gauze wrapped around a hollow core.

Planetary Grotesque

Transgression, it seems, is everywhere. The weather is *wild*, it is *freakish*, and it is *weird*. We are told that we live in a state of *planetary emergency*, a state of abnormality in which the old norms no longer apply. The same can be said of politics. Recent years have seen the surge of the so-called clown kings:[23] political opportunists who are at one and the same time comedic and transgressive, but also ominous and dangerous in their use of exaggeration, freakishness, disruption, violence, the carnivalesque, and the chaotic to further their political goals by any means possible. Such clown kings are distinguishable by their supposedly harmless buffoonery, as in the case of Britain's former prime minister Boris Johnson; but they also engage in terrifying – if ridiculous – strong-man posturing, as demonstrated by the likes of Donald Trump and Jair Bolsonaro. Reminiscent of Achille Mbembe's remarks on the postcolony, a state of affairs is emerging in which 'the official world mimics popular vulgarity, inserting it at the core of the procedures by which it takes on grandeur'. The effect is 'a deliberately cynical operation [that] can only produce "fables" and stupefy its "subjects," bringing on delirium when the discourse of power penetrates its targets and drives them into the realms of fantasy and hallucination'.[24]

Most strikingly grotesque and horror clownish of all have been the antics of Argentinian president Javier Milei, who characteristically wields that most iconic symbol of slasher films, the chainsaw, to symbolise his desire to 'slash' bureaucracy and public spending.

It is important to note that the politics of the grotesque are not limited to the upper echelons of political power, but have increasingly become popular as a strategy employed from the bottom up. In 2021, the Capitol in Washington was invaded by might be seen as precisely a carnivalesque throng, led by the so-called QAanon Shaman, who claimed allegiance to extremist conspiracist theories about cannibalistic child molesting, while dressed in fur, a horned helmet, and body paint. 'Grotesque protest'[25] is also very much part of leftist activism, where members of movements such as Just Stop Oil and Extinction Rebellion have glued their body parts to refineries, landing strips, or famous pieces of art, just as the South African protest Rhodes Must Fall threw a bucket of excrement over a statue of Cecil Rhodes.

Another yet equally important contemporary trend of the grotesque has been renewed focus on the female body. As Mary Russo made it clear in *The Female Grotesque: Risk, Excess and Modernity* (1995) some three decades ago, the links between the grotesque and the female body have always been strong. The secretion of vaginas, lactating mammary glands, the act of giving birth, all have been associated with the fecundity and primal nature of what has tellingly been referred to as 'Mother Earth'. Indeed, as Russo points out, the etymological roots of grotesque connecting it to 'grotto' makes it easy for critics to designate the supposedly cavernous female body as more naturally inclined towards the grotesque than the male. This is reiterated by Maria Barrett in *Grotesque Femininities: Evil, Women and the Feminine* (2010), where she argues that: 'The bodily metaphor that the *grotesque* came to embrace tells us that it can be connected to a vulgar image of the feminine, as associated with all things animal-like, primitive and fallen and which metaphorically casts the feminine down into a dark space, underground into a cave of abjection'.[26] Indeed, speaking of abjection, it is no coincidence that the philosopher Julia Kristeva's classic study of 'the abject', *Powers of Horror: An Essay on Abjection* (1980, translated 1982), defines it as being that which is at one and the same time weirdly ambiguous and out of place, while at the same time continuously referring to the female body as its material and natural site of origin.

As we saw it argued earlier in the chapter with Wagner's concept of an environmental grotesque, and as Ruskin, Foucault, and in particular Bakhtin promote through their celebratory grotesque, to be down in the mud does however not necessarily imply helplessness. There is power, as Kristeva phrases it, in horror and abjection. We see this exemplified with renewed force in novels like Rachel Yoder's *Nightbitch* (2021), Ottessa Moshfegh's *Lapvona* (2022), Ainslee Hogarth's *Motherthing* (2022), Julia Armfield's *Our Wives Under the Sea* (2022), and Ling Ling Huang's *Natural Beauty* (2023), as in short story collections like Mariana Enriquez's *The Dangers of Smoking in Bed* (2009, translated 2021), Samanta Schweblin's *Mouthful of Birds* (2010, translated 2019), Carmen Maria Machado's *Her Body and Other Parties* (2018), Sayaka Murata's *Life Ceremony* (2019, translated 2022), and Eliza Clark's *She's Always Hungry* (2024), where a wild, unruly, and sometimes murderous cast of female characters engage in a range of transgressive and often repulsive acts in which their own and others' bodies are broken, violated, exploding, and brimming over. More often than not, though, the grotesque body presented in these texts is fielded as a strategy for pushing violently and loudly back against oppressive patriarchal systems that have no place for women who do not live up to certain tightly regulated standards of dress, body type, sexuality, and behaviour.

In this chapter, too, the films and texts examined have revolved around the female body. Although many of these have been from the perspective of men insofar as the majority of the examined texts are written and directed by people who identify (and are typically identified) as men, they all in some way or other critically address questions of patriarchy. As such, the texts examined in this chapter all speak to the relationship Duncan and Cumpsty identify in the introduction to this volume between patriarchal global capitalist modernity and the monstrous cultural forms that arise to encode situated and violent encounters with it. The grotesque expressions of corporeal breakdown examined, including ruptures and recombination of singular and plural bodies, can be read along similar lines, as diverse but also connectable responses to a shared body of interconnecting problems – climate change, animal exploitation, gendered inequality – which are inseparable from the daily operation of global capitalism in our present moment, and which now constitute monsters on a planetary scale. Together, the corpus discussed here inexhaustively represents what I am tentatively proposing to call planetary grotesque. Like the world-gothic, the planetary grotesque is plural, hybrid, and always embedded in a specific local context; however, in all its particular, transgressive, and explosive manifestations, it also points to a shared – a planetary – reality that is destabilised, ruptured, and in turmoil. Planetary grotesque is wild and destructive, uncomfortable and over the top, riotously angry and maniacally comedic. Confronted by a world that does not and cannot hold its shape anymore, where indeed the centre itself is collapsing, what else is there left to do.

Acknowledgements

I would like to thank Elliot Berggren for pointing me to Wagner's article as well as Agustina Bazterrica's novel. I would also like to thank Nanna Nerenst for pointing me to Kristoffer Borgli's film.

Notes

1. Cary Elza, '"Do You Feel Held?": Gender, Community, and Affective Design in *Midsommar*', *Journal for Cultural Research*, 27:3 (2023), 272–85, 283.
2. Elza, '"Do You Feel Held?"', 272.
3. Wolfgang Kayser, *The Grotesque in Art and Literature*, trans. U. Weisstein, New York, Columbia University Press, 1981, 19.
4. Kayser, *The Grotesque in Art and Literature*, 19.
5. Kayser, *The Grotesque in Art and Literature*, 21.
6. Geoffrey Galt Harpham, *On the Grotesque: Strategies of Contradiction in Art and Literature*, Princeton, Princeton University Press, 1982, 10–11, and Philip Thomson, *The Grotesque*, London, Methuen, 1972, 2.
7. Kayser, *The Grotesque in Art and Literature*, 22.
8. James Goodwin, *Modern American Grotesque: Literature and Photography*, Columbus, Ohio State University Press, 2015, 2.
9. Alastair Bonnett, *The Idea of the West: Culture, Politics and History*, New York, Palgrave, 2004, 25.
10. John Ruskin, *The Stones of Venice, Volume the Third: The Fall*, Boston, Estes and Lauriat, 1894 (1853), 143.
11. M.M. Bakhtin, *Rabelais and His World*, trans. H. Iswolsky, Bloomington, Indiana University Press, 1984 (1965), 7.
12. Bakhtin, *Rabelais*, 26.
13. Phoebe Wagner, 'Embracing the Environmental Grotesque and Transforming the Climate Crisis', *ISLE: Interdisciplinary Studies in Literature and Environment*, 30:4 (Winter 2023), 911–30, 3.
14. Wilson Yates, 'Francis Bacon: The Iconography of Crucifixion', in J. L. Adams and W. Yates (eds.), *The Grotesque in Arts & Literature: Theological Reflections*, Grand Rapids, W. B. Eerdmans Publishing, 1997, 183.
15. J.M. Coetzee, *The Lives of Animals*, Princeton, Princeton University Press, 2016, 21 and 38.
16. Jonathan Safran Foer, *Eating Animals*, London, Penguin, 2009, 14 and 153.
17. Foer, *Eating Animals*, 163–4.
18. Foer, *Eating Animals*, 182.

19. Agustina Bazterrica, *Tender is the Flesh*, London, Pushkin Press, 2017, 77.
20. Michel Faber, *Under the Skin*, London, Faber, 2017, 214.
21. Chuck Palahniuk, *Invisible Monsters*, London, Vintage, 2000, 53.
22. Palahniuk, *Invisible Monsters*, 214.
23. Edward Docx, 'The Clown King: How Boris Johnson Made It by Playing the Fool', *The Guardians*, 18 March 2021, www.theguardian.com/news/2021/mar/18/all-hail-the-clown-king-how-boris-johnson-made-it-by-playing-the-fool.
24. Achille Mbembe, *On the Postcolony*, Berkeley, University of California Press, 2002, 110 and 118.
25. Kristin Marie Bivens and Kirsti Cole, 'The Grotesque Protest in Social Media as Embodied, Political Rhetoric', *Journal of Communication Inquiry*, 42:1 (2018), 5–25.
26. Maria Barrett, 'Introduction', in M. Barrett (ed.), *Grotesque Femininities: Evil, Women and the Feminine*, Oxford, Interdisciplinary Press, 2010, vii–xix, ix.

CHAPTER 10

Uncanny Animism
Reframing the World-Gothic with Amos Tutuola

Ryan Topper

A necessary step in worlding gothic studies is theorising the underappreciated proximity between the genre's supernatural responses to global capitalist modernity and Indigenous spiritual responses to colonisation in postcolonial literature. To understand the gothic as a world phenomenon requires taking more seriously the non-gothic forms through which postcolonial literature recuperates Indigenous spiritualities to negotiate the alienations and anxieties intrinsic to global capitalism and thus colonial modernity. Such an appreciation of postcolonial forms allows for a critical re-examination of inherited notions of the gothic, a genre which famously negotiates these same affects in response to the same global economy – though often from different historical, geographical, racial, and socioeconomic starting points. In short, taking Indigenous critiques of colonial modernity seriously allows gothic criticism to more clearly situate the genre within a world system that produces a multitude of spiritualised 'folk' critiques of capitalism, many of which are decidedly not gothic, yet perform analogous cultural work.

In this chapter, I exemplify the stakes of such a postcolonial, comparative approach to the world-gothic by considering how Amos Tutuola's use of Yoruba cosmology to narrate modern African subjectivity reframes a concept part and parcel with gothic studies: the uncanny. In the first section I detail Tutuola's blending of modernism and realism through Yoruba cosmology, resulting in his signature style of animist realism. In the second section I delineate the analogous relationship between Tutuola's animist poetics and the gothic, noting their shared spiritual critique of global capitalist modernity. Finally, I use this analogous relationship to place Tutuola's animism in dialogue with the psychoanalytic theory of the uncanny. The animist notion of the uncanny intrinsic to Tutuola's fiction, I argue, provincialises the secularised realism upon which the gothic uncanny depends. Tutuola's animist uncanny thus exemplifies the need for gothic studies to attune itself to the various cosmological starting points undergirding the network of immanent critiques of global capitalism in which the gothic emerges as a distinct cultural form.

Tutuola's Indigenous Modernism

Ever since *The Palm-Wine Drinkard*'s publication in 1952, and its follow-up, *My Life in the Bush of Ghosts* in 1954, Tutuola's reception has been marked by the question of genre. In each of these novels, a protagonist-narrator embarks on an episodic journey in which he uses his wits and his 'native juju' to shape-shift and outsmart various creatures determined to capture, torture, enslave, or kill him. These adventures, often constructed of reformulated folktales, are rendered in a non-standard English prose that has become a signature of Tutuola's style. Although Tutuola wished for corrections to what he viewed as grammatical mistakes due to his lack of expertise in standard British English, Faber and Faber's editors fought to preserve what they perceived as the strange charm of Tutuola's 'African' prose, refusing to standardise many irregularities. As Gail Low documents, this editorial decision was due to the fact that Faber and Faber's investment in Tutuola was motivated by their belief in his fiction's 'anthropological value'.[1] They initially planned to have an anthropologist write the introduction to *Palm-Wine*, and although this plan was dropped, their publicity statements for Tutuola always teetered 'between the anthropological and the literary' – comparing *Palm-Wine*'s plot to Orpheus's search for Eurydice while also promising an exotic romp through the 'spirit-ridden African bush'.[2] Similarly, as Bernth Lindfors details, early British and American reviewers (most famously Dylan Thomas and V. S. Pritchett) were enthralled by the idea of gaining access to an uncorrupted, primitive worldview by way of Tutuola's folk storytelling and his 'young English'.[3] Although these reviews shower Tutuola with praise, they also undeniably demean his fiction as primarily an ethnographic artefact, a folksy form only available to fiction where there is no literary tradition.

Current Tutuola criticism, now versed in postcolonial theory, scoffs at these early reviews, but criticism's common sidestepping of Tutuola's modernism, approaching him instead as a Yoruba traditionalist, is a symptom of similar exotica. For much criticism, there is an often-unacknowledged assumption that Tutuola functions as a traditional Yoruba precursor to a later flourishing of a more globally focused West African magical realism epitomised by Ben Okri's *The Famished Road* (1991). There is a sense in which this historical lineage is correct: Tutuola undeniably influenced Okri, much as Yoruba-language novelist Daniel

Fagunwa undeniably influenced Tutuola. As Brenda Cooper argues in *Magical Realism in West African Fiction*, however, Tutuola's writing lacks the ironic distancing from the spiritual that focalises magical realism as a genre, boasting instead 'mythical, supernatural, allegorical, and epic' dimensions.[4] At the same time, the creatures that make up Tutuola's world of myth, epic, and allegory are often assembled by-products of global capitalist exchange and thus colonial modernity: televisions and telephones, footballs and flashing lights, viruses and bacteria. Perhaps the most famous of these creatures is *Bush of Ghosts*'s 'television-handed ghostess': a bald ghost covered in sores and maggots, with tiny arms and uncountable fingers, whose palm is 'exactly as a television'.[5] Published before Tutuola became a shopkeeper for Nigerian Broadcasting Corporation in 1956 and before Nigeria's first television station opened in 1959, this passage blends horror and humour to depict a creature embodying forms of mass communication emerging in West Africa's late colonial epoch.

Hence Matthew Omelsky's salient intervention in Tutuola criticism. Against Tutuola's early reviewers and postcolonial critics' typical focus on Tutuola's traditionalism, Omelsky highlights the fact that the 'curious and haunting beings' of Tutuola's fiction 'are literally composed of commodities, technologies, and tropes of exchange' all tied to global mid-century capitalism. 'Behind his borrowings from Yoruba oral tradition, Tutuola presents a global constellation of objects and goods', Omelsky writes, 'that rupture the conventional notion of an insular, primitive Africa',[6] depicting instead 'a global system in perpetual motion'.[7] In this sense, despite Faber and Faber's insistence that Tutuola's fiction brought to their list a missing anthropological value, Tutuola fit snugly alongside Eliot, Joyce, Beckett, and the other modernists Faber and Faber famously published throughout the early to mid-twentieth century. Rather than untouched, pre-colonial throwbacks, Tutuola's creatures are folk images undergoing modernist shape-shifting, creatures incarnating their author's intrinsically global form of African modernism.

What Omelsky's analysis underappreciates, however, is the manner in which this modernism operates alongside Tutuola's depiction of the spiritual world, not as differentiated logics, but as a singular aesthetic organism – much like the gothic's supernaturalisation of capitalism. The first critic to take seriously Tutuola's modernism makes precisely this point in a 1963 essay too often ignored in Tutuola criticism. In 'From A Common Backcloth'. Wole Soyinka, then lecturer in English at University of Ife, extolls Tutuola as a writer who 'reject[s] the anthropological novel', embodying instead 'the new Nigerian writer gathering multifarious experiences under, if you like, the two cultures, and exploiting them in one extravagant, confident whole'. As the phrase 'if you like' suggests, for Soyinka the idea of the Indigenous and the modern as 'two cultures' is an incorrect, but at times rhetorically useful binary to conceptualise Tutuola's fictional world, which is actually a vision of tradition and modernity enmeshed as a single world: a world of extravagance, exploitation, and confidence. Anglo-American exotica seekers and African ideologues of the primeval, Soyinka argues, have produced a critical reception for Tutuola in which 'little attention has been paid to his modern experience; after all Tutuola lives *now*, and he responds to change and phenomenon'.[8] At the same time, Tutuola's approach to modern flux is steeped in Yoruba cosmology, Soyinka goes on to argue, casting him not as a primitive, nor as an anti-traditionalist, but as a simultaneously modern novelist and Yoruba storyteller extending his Indigenous tradition. This vision of Tutuola's modernism refuses to separate Indigeneity and modernity, which means the former's spiritual conceptions cannot be relegated to the latter's realm of the non-real – much like the gothic's signature blending of modern and folk logics.

Soyinka's example of this singular Indigenous modernity is a passage in *Palm-Wine* in which the protagonist-narrator, on his way to Heaven's Town, is physically unable to move anywhere but forwards. Tutuola writes,

> But as we were going on and when it was time that we wanted to branch to our left, to continue the journey inside another bush as usual, we were unable to branch or to stop, or to go back, we were only moving on the road towards the town. We tried all our best to stop ourselves but were in vain.[9]

This continuous propelling, Soyinka argues, likely comes from both Yoruba folklore and Christian allegory, despite critics wanting to separate these sources as citizens of different worlds. However, according to Soyinka, the most immediate source material for this passage is the escalator. In Tutuola's world, Yoruba folklore, colonial religion, and capitalist material culture meld into an 'extravagant whole' – a modernism populated by creatures from stories, sermons, and shopping plazas. This syncretism distinguishes Tutuola from lesser African writers, Soyinka claims, who attempt to 'avoid ... foreign bodies in their vision of the traditional backcloth' of African literature. Ironically, though, this acceptance of the 'foreign' into a continuously propelling narrative is, Soyinka claims, traditionally Yoruba. He writes, 'The deistic approach of the Yoruba is to absorb every new experience, departmentalize it and carry on with life. Thus *Sango* (Dispenser of Lightning) now chairmans the Electricity Corporation, *Ogun* (God of Iron) is the primal motor-mechanic'.[10] By incorporating the escalator into his shape-shifting folklore, Tutuola's fiction embodies a form of modernism as an extension of the Yoruba 'deistic approach' in West African popular culture. Just as the new is absorbed into the cosmological imagination of the Yoruba pantheon, so too

> Tutuola involves us in a coordination of the spiritual and the physical, and this is the truth of his people's concept of life. The accessories of day-to-day existence only become drawn into this cosmic embrace; they do not invalidate it. Questioning at the end what Tutuola's reality is, we find only a tight web enmeshing the two levels of perception.[11]

This enmeshment of two levels, the day-to-day and the spiritual, is Tutuola at his most modernist and his most Indigenous. It also reveals his fiction's proximity to the gothic, which similarly enmeshes the day-to-day and the spiritual. Yet, as I will soon argue, Tutuola's modernist use of Yoruba cosmology challenges us to think beyond the latent realism upon which gothic studies depends, a challenge hinging on differing notions of the fantastic.

While Omelsky rightly critiques Tutuola's primitivist reception, Soyinka's similar critique highlights the problem with Omelsky's retention of the rhetoric of the 'fantastic' to articulate Tutuola's idiosyncratic form of modernism, what Omelsky calls 'the singular nonrealism of Tutuola's writing'.[12] This description, much like the body of criticism Omelsky critiques, draws a stark border between the real and the spiritual. If, however, we recognise the secular rationality of the post-Enlightenment European episteme conditioning literary criticism as a provincial logic, rather than an *a priori* of logic as such, we could describe Tutuola's writing as a form of realism. Before rejecting realism, we should ask whose realism we are rejecting. African cosmologies, even amidst a modernity in perpetual flux, depict the real from coordinates that do not always map neatly onto those of Dickens or Tolstoy. This recognition is why Soyinka rejects the urge to uphold a primitive 'backcloth' untouched by modernity for African literature, while at the same time praising Tutuola as a 'storyteller in the best Yoruba tradition, pushing the bounds of credibility higher and higher and sustaining it by sheer adroitness, by a juxtaposition of analogous experience from the familiar'.[13] Yoruba consciousness absorbs the quotidian of the new into a spiritual sensibility constantly in flux, and in doing so

10 Uncanny Animism 191

produces a storytelling tradition in which the Yoruba pantheon navigates and even shapes the world of powerlines and automobiles. Likewise, Tutuola's Indigenous-global-modernism frames capitalism at midcentury within an aesthetic that, despite 'pushing the bounds of credibility', sustains itself as a mode of realism, depicting modernity as peopled by cosmic forces as real as escalators. Positioning Tutuola's modernism as, from the standpoint of Yoruba cosmology, a mode of realism, complicates notions of 'multiple modernities' and 'peripheral realisms'.[14] Yes, modernism has always been more global than critics have recognised; yes, realism is as vital to twentieth-century literature as high modernism; and reading each as intrinsic to the same world-system casts modernism and realism as more variegated than criticism has acknowledged. More fundamentally, though, Tutuola's fiction challenges the provincial borders between these generic categories that such arguments risk perpetuating, and this challenge bears implications for the project of 'worlding' gothic studies.

Consider how Henry John Drewal, John Pemberton III, and Rowland Abiodun explain the relationship between the spiritual and terrestrial realms in Yoruba cosmology. They write,

> The Yoruba conceive of the cosmos as consisting of two distinct yet inseparable realms – *aye* (the visible, tangible world of the living) and *orun* (the invisible, spiritual realm of the ancestors, gods, and spirits) ... Such a cosmic conception is often visualized as either a spherical gourd, whose upper and lower hemispheres fit tightly together, or as a divination tray with a raised figurated border enclosing a flat central surface. The images clustered around the perimeter of the tray refer to mythic events and persons as well as everyday concerns. They depict a universe populated by countless competing forces. The intersecting lines inscribed on the surface by a diviner at the outset of a divination symbolize metaphoric crossroads, *orita meta* (the point of intersection between the cosmic realms).[15]

Since in Yoruba cosmology *aye* (the world of the living) is distinct yet inseparable from *orun* (the world of spirits), 'mythic events' and 'everyday concerns' operate alongside each other. Thus, the parameter of the world as depicted by a divination tray is clustered by the mythic and the mundane, the so-called spiritual and the so-called secular alike. The lines a diviner inscribes on such a tray, then, are not meant to conjure fantastic, non-real images of a spiritual realm, but instead open a 'point of intersection between the cosmic realms' that is already baked into the structure of reality.

The wager of Tutuola's fiction, and its value for a world-gothic perspective, is that global modernity always contains such points of intersection.

The inseparable bond between *aye* and *orun* did not die under colonisation; if anything, these realms' points of intersection have only proliferated in the rapidly shifting, globalised habitus of West Africa at mid-century. In a world where a ghostess' palm has become a television, a new apparatus emerges to function as a gateway between *aye* and *orun*. What Omelsky describes as Tutuola's 'creaturely modernism' can therefore only be recognised by a criticism that also refuses to relegate the spiritual to the world of the fantastic, which is to say a criticism that always provincialises its own inherited form of realism. This task leads us back to Cooper's differentiation between the ironic detachment from the spiritual world central to magical realism and Tutuola's focus on the inseparability of the everyday and the spiritual. Indeed, Tutuola's fiction frames modernity from a far less secularised a priori than magical realism (compare Tutuola to Salman Rushdie, for example), even if his modernity is similarly global and his subject matter similarly supernatural (at least to literary critics taught to believe nature is devoid of spirituality). Tutuola's fiction depicts a world in which creatures of *orun* inhabit the space of the everyday alongside creatures of *aye*; in fact, the intersecting realms of *orun* and *aye* co-constitute such creatures. This circadian cohabitation – the imbrication of the material and spiritual as a structuring principle of reality – marks Tutuola's modernism as harbouring a localised, adaptive mode of realism, a realism anchored to a vision of Yoruba cosmology never inoculated against the forces of global capitalism, but rather part of its singular world. In this sense, another generic analogy is surrealism. As André Breton famously writes, the goal of surrealism is to 'resolve the previously contradictory conditions of dream and reality into an absolute reality, a super-reality'.[16] Although Tutuola's fiction likewise depicts a super-reality, it is not informed by psychic automatism – surrealism's rejection of inherited reason and rationality in hopes of gesturing towards a greater, unconscious reality. Instead, as Soyinka claims, Tutuola extends an inherited form of rationality into the rapidly industrialising habitus of 1950s West Africa.

It is Cooper's differentiation of Tutuola's fiction from magical realism (related to this differentiation from surrealism) that Harry Garuba uses to explain the generic logic of what he terms animist realism, a term I take to be most useful for categorising Tutuola's fiction and appreciating its significance for gothic studies. For Garuba, animist realism is an aesthetic metacategory naming the disparate cultural logics and subgenres that 're-enchant' worlds disenchanted by colonial modernity. By continuously reinscribing the colonised world with Indigenous logics that view all matter as animate, animist realism casts the supernatural as natural (rendering this binary obsolete). It does so not through an aesthetic of Indigenous purity, but by recuperating pre-colonial cultural logics in dialectical response to colonial modernity's 'disenchantment of the world' – a term Garuba borrows from Max Weber's canonical analysis of Western modernity. Magical realism might function as one subgenre of Garuba's umbrella category of animist realism, but, as he argues, across the cultures of African modernity the animistic narrative often operates without the 'urban, cosmopolitan' critical lens or 'ironizing attitude' of magical realism. 'It is in recognition of this limitation that I have ... employed the term *animist realism* to describe this predominant cultural practice of according a physical, often animate material aspect to what others may consider an abstract idea', he writes.[17] This investment of all matter with spirit – not as a separate form, but as the superstructure of historical materialism – is at the core of Garuba's conception of animist realism (which draws on Soyinka's reading of Tutuola to make its case). This conception allows literary criticism to broaden the horizon of literary realism to include the animist cosmology of the Yoruba diviner (which is focussed on the intersectional contacts between *aye* and *orun* present in quotidian reality). Consequently, it recasts Tutuola's modernism as a decidedly animist form of realism: a peripheral aesthetic operating (via Yoruba cosmology) outside the boundary markers criticism uses to separate modernism and realism. *Palm-Wine* and *Bush of Ghosts* each represent the reality of global capitalism in West Africa's late colonial epoch as conditioned by the proliferation and magnification of such cosmic intersections.

The Gothic Analogy

This generic categorisation, in turn, highlights the analogous relationship between Tutuola's fiction and the gothic. Like animist realism, the gothic is an immanent critique of colonial modernity. The origin story through which gothic studies scholars writing in the wake of poststructuralism narrated the genre was primarily philosophical, beginning with the secular rationality of the Enlightenment. The emergence of the gothic in eighteenth-century Europe, this origin story goes, is intrinsic to the rationality of the Enlightenment's secular humanism – not a reaction against its logic. As Terry Castle puts it, the Enlightenment project of obtaining 'objective knowledge of the world' ironically made this world 'more bewildering, inscrutable, and grotesque' to its new reading public.[18] She thus writes, 'The very psychic and cultural transformations that led to the subsequent glorification of the period as an age of reason and enlightenment – the aggressively rationalist imperatives of the epoch – also produced, like a kind of toxic side effect, a new human experience of strangeness, anxiety, bafflement, and intellectual impasse'.[19] In this way the canonical gothic's insistence that the world of European modernity is still subject to magical forces is not antithetical to the Enlightenment project, but rather part of its 'ambivalent secularizing process'.[20] This historical emergence undermines the very idea of a civilised society functioning as the utopian horizon of the Enlightenment project birthing it, and this framing of the genre casts its philosophical claims as a mode of postcolonial critique. The genre is an immanent critique of colonial ideology insofar as it is an immanent critique of the Enlightenment rationality through which European imperial expansion was planned and executed across the eighteenth and nineteenth centuries.

This framing of the gothic as a theoretical critique of its constitutive epoch resonates with the philosophical approach to Tutuola modelled by Francis Nyamnjoh, Caroline Rooney, and myself. For Nyamnjoh, for example, Tutuola's fiction challenges 'a social science founded narrowly on dichotomies, dualisms and bounded identities' by depicting a universe of 'flexibility and fluidity' where 'nimble-footed identities' operate as 'fluid osmotic envelopes for consciousness'. Thinking beyond the narrowly historicist confines of much Tutuola criticism, Nyamnjoh reads Tutuola as an ontologist modelling a metaphysics rooted in the relationship between 'incompleteness' and 'conviviality': since the universe is an open process, subjectivity must include all. Such incomplete conviviality, Nyamnjoh argues, 'could contribute significantly to the reconstruction and recalibration of a decolonised social science in Africa'.[21] Much like the canonical gothic, then, Tutuola's fiction, according to Nyamnjoh, exemplifies a philosophical stance to the world antithetical to a social science founded on rigidly bordered subjects and fixed teleological endpoints.

This recalibration of social theory through African experience is also central to what Rooney defines, somewhat differently than Garuba, as Tutuola's animism.[22] Garuba's animist realism emphasises the genre's dialectical relationship to the post-Enlightenment secular rationality infusing the epoch of Africa's colonial and post-independent stages of capitalism. Rooney's metaphysical approach to animism resonates with Garuba's generic approach, but focusses instead on the ways Africa's Indigenous knowledge systems form a deconstructive gesture to the Western metaphysical tradition. For her, Tutuola is one of many African writers portraying a metaphysics of constant movement and thus a metaphysics of no stable entities, an ontology operating beyond the gridwork of 'being' and 'presence' that Heidegger and Derrida famously critique in the metaphysical ontology of the West. Like Nyamnjoh, then, Rooney approaches Tutuola's fiction as a starting point for a postcolonial philosophy.

In *Animist Poetics: Ancestral Trauma and Regeneration in African Literature*, I build on this trajectory, using Tutuola as one philosophical model for understanding how African literature regenerates Indigenous cosmologies as modern logics.[23] While this project is not in explicit dialogue with gothic studies, this approach to Tutuola as a modernist animist highlights his analogous relationship to the gothic's immanent critique of the secular rationality informing its historical emergence two hundred years before *Palm-Wine*'s publication. What the gothic's epistemically oriented origin story underappreciates, though, is the extent to which the material conditions of colonial subjugation informed the genre's emergence. As Rebecca Duncan and Rebekah Cumpsty explain in this collection's Introduction, the historical materialist interventions in gothic studies exemplified by David Punter and Franco Moretti remind us that the anxieties of modernity to which the gothic gives voice did not emerge solely in Europe, then travel the world. Instead, modernity is what we name the epoch conditioned by the world-system that emerged during the transition from feudalism to merchant and industrial capitalism, which was predicated on plantation and slave trade economies, which have always been global. Likewise, the Enlightenment was at its origin a global phenomenon, an episteme conditioned by rapid industrialisation that, as Sidney Mintz's history of Caribbean sugar plantations suggests, began in the colonies before reaching Europe.[24] The task of 'worlding' gothic studies is thus the task of taking seriously Frantz Fanon's declaration that 'Europe is literally the creation of the Third World'.[25] Simon Gikandi's contextualisation of the gothic's emergence within eighteenth-century Europe's 'culture of taste' is germane to this point. As this culture sought to quarantine the brute realities of the transatlantic slave trade from its development of humane rationality, he argues, it placed slavery in the structural position of 'the great unconscious of modern identity': a repressed horror the gothic invites an emerging European middle class to glimpse.[26] That *Bush of Ghosts*'s protagonist-narrator is lost in a nightmarish bush due to fleeing slave traders suggests Tutuola's fiction circles around the same, albeit unevenly stratifying system.

In this way, pairing the epistemic with a historical materialist framing of the gothic's global emergence – worlding the gothic, as this collection does – deepens the analogous relationship between the gothic and animist realism I have pointed out. This interpretive move also emphasises the analogous relationship between the gothic and the process through which Indigenous knowledge systems writ large have survived and reformulated under the pressures of colonial modernity, the subject of *Animist Poetics*. In this book I draw on Michael Taussig's anthropological studies of South American shamanism as one model for the cultural work that African literary animism, including but extending far beyond Tutuola, performs. Similarly, Stephen Shapiro uses Taussig's study of devil-beliefs among Columbian and Bolivian workers as a model for the canonical gothic. For Taussig, devil-beliefs among this population function as a collective processing of the 'proletarianization of the peasant'.[27] As industrial capitalism supplants Indigenous systems of production and exchange, the new South American proletariat find and barter with devils in the mines and cane fields in which they toil – figures from the canon of colonial religion dwelling in the spaces of industrialisation and embodying the distortion of reciprocity industrial wage labour inaugurates. This immanent critique of capitalism suggests an 'adherence by the workers' culture to the principles that underlie the peasant mode of production, even as these principles are being progressively undermined by the everyday experience of wage labour under capitalist conditions'.[28] Taussig thus frames Indigenous devil-beliefs as 'part of a critique of the modern mode of production' spanning literatures from the seventeenth-century to the present.[29] Taussig's argument can be generalised, Shapiro claims, to conceptualise how the canonical gothic recuperates European folk-belief to 'produce entirely "new" monsters' in response to Europe's historical shift from agrarian to industrial economies (a shift predicated on such shifts already taking place in the colonies). He writes, '"Gothic" is the modern mode for representing the reinstallation of capitalist conditions for an anonymous reading public, which has already been irreversibly separated from the cognitive field of oral, folk customs that might hearken back to primary "devil" fears'. Much like South American peasants reinventing devil-beliefs, then, the canonical English gothic, Shapiro suggests, often appropriates Catholic motifs 'because these act as the next closest bed of prelapsarian associations for (northern) Europeans living within later phases of capitalist development'.[30] Structurally, the gothic's spiritual imaginary is modern in the same way Indigenous knowledge systems are modern: both register colonial modernity's dissolution of sacralised bonds, reading the 'disenchanted' world of the modern in a way that strategically distorts the process of disenchantment into one of re-enchantment.

It would be a mistake, however, to claim this analogous relationship casts Tutuola's fiction as gothic. In terms of content, much of what critics assume to be instances of a proto-magical realism could be interpreted as instances of gothic horror: for example, when *Palm-Wine*'s protagonist is attacked by an army of 400 dead babies – or the more sadistic scenes, such as when unknown creatures bury him jaw-deep in a field and spit, urinate, and 'pas excreta' on his head.[31] Shifting focus from content to cosmology, however, challenges any straightforward 'worlding' of the gothic label. Contextualising animist realism within the gothic ignores Indigenous cosmologies – or, more accurately, refuses to acknowledge them as intellectually cohesive and practically functioning cosmologies, instead misinterpreting them as instantiations of the esoteric and the supernatural – as hauntings. Calling animist realism a mode of the gothic, in other words, filters Indigenous knowledge systems through a post-Enlightenment, Euro-American framework of generic conventions, which hinges on the ways a Euro-American imaginary has historically navigated the divide between the secular and the religious that it invented. Approaching Tutuola's fiction in analogous relation to the gothic highlights the critical function of each in the same world-system, the same modernity; but following Nyamnjoh and Rooney in approaching Tutuola as an ontologist, as I do more extensively in *Animist Poetics*, allows us to differentiate the forms of these critical functions. The gothic points to the supernatural in dialectical response to a modern, secular fixation on the natural; Tutuola's animist realism, on the other hand, reinscribes the allegedly supernatural back into nature, recuperating Indigenous knowledge that secular rationality labels as supernatural.[32] In other words, animist realism operates beyond the binary upon which the gothic depends. Nowhere is this division more apparent than in the role of the uncanny.

Tutuola's Animist Uncanny

In *The Uncanny* (1919), Freud utilises E. T. A. Hoffmann's 'The Sandman' (1815), a canonical example of the nineteenth-century gothic, to theorise a particular form of horror: the horror we experience during moments of strange familiarity – at once 'of the home' and foreign, as the German *unheimlich* ambivalently signifies. While Freud's theory helps illuminate the generic iconography of the gothic and the cultural work it performs, it also helps illuminate the iconography of Tutuola's fiction and the cultural work it performs. At the level of iconography, both use the uncanny to populate their texts with eerie creatures. At the level of cultural work, both use the uncanny to offer an immanent critique of their shared experiences of colonial modernity – albeit from disparate positions. For example, Tutuola's creatures are frequently compared to yet differentiated from humans, thereby incarnating an uncanny reflection of the human form: the creature who walks upright (like a human), yet is the size of a hippopotamus, or the mountain-creatures who are said to resemble humans, or the 'Red-king of the Red-people in the Red-town',[33] who explains that his people 'were once human beings; in the olden days when the eyes of all the human beings were on our knees, when we were bending down from the sky because of its gravitiness and when we were walking backwards and not forwards as nowadays'.[34] Alexander Fyfe interprets these 'between the human and nonhuman'[35] creatures as Tutuola's critique of the 'sovereign human subject'[36] at the core of imperial Europe's humanism. We should note that these examples each challenge imperialism's narrow humanism through uncanny description: these creatures are almost human, but not quite.

This uncanniness is in fact all over Tutuola's fiction. Consider *Palm-Wine*'s most famous narrative sequence: the story of the complete gentleman. A woman sees a beautiful man in the market who appears fully complete. Captivated, she follows him home and witnesses him return all his rented body parts to their various owners until he is reduced to a skull. The skull then captures the woman and drags her into the pit where he lives with his skull family. The skulls strap the woman to a bullfrog and torture her in their pit. In *Animist Poetics*, I interpret this sequence as exemplary of animism's life-death symbiosis, what I call the 'regenerative death drive' intrinsic to African literature's recuperation of Indigenous cosmologies. Considering the world-gothic focus of this chapter, however, I here wish to highlight how this sequence reveals the uncanny nature uniting so many of Tutuola's creatures. The complete gentleman appears to his observers in the market as a Vitruvian totality, but he subverts the familiarity of this European humanist form by steadily losing body parts, becoming an increasingly terrifying creature. Ironically, his final form is a skull: the form most deeply familiar to human consciousness, the psyche's literal home. Given phrenology's role in crafting a racialised science to justify colonial labour practices, the skull is also the form, viewed through a paradigm of colonial realism, determining the boundaries of African subjectivity under capitalism.[37] We could recontextualise this plot within bourgeois courtship economies of eighteenth-century Europe or nineteenth-century America (e.g., a woman duped by a count or estate inheritor who turns out to be a skull), and it could pass for a story by Ann Radcliffe or Edgar Allan Poe – which through a Freudian lens would be an instance of the return of the repressed. But this process of the return of the repressed is where the differentiation between the Tutuolan and Freudian uncanny and thus gothic and animist poetics becomes most apparent.

For Freud, the uncanny can only operate against a backdrop of realism, which he defines through post-Enlightenment, European rationality. As children, he argues, we were all animists clinging to what he calls 'omnipotence of thoughts'.[38] Primitive peoples share this form of magical thinking, he further argues, because it is humanity's original consciousness. Children in civilised societies gradually replace this worldview, as they mature, with modes of logic foundational to their civilisation's advancement, he further reasons. As adults, some slip from their hard-won realism back into the 'omnipotence of thoughts' that governed their young psyches: the 'neurotics' of Freud's case studies. For some societies, this mode of thinking functions as normal logic: the 'primitives' of Freud's anthropologically informed metapsychology. A Freudian reading of Tutuola would categorise Tutuolan animism as an example of this 'omnipotence of thoughts'. The catch, though, is that for Freud, this form of thinking exists in everyone's unconscious, 'ready to seize upon any confirmation'.[39] This seizing of 'civilised' consciousness by a 'primitive' unconscious clandestinely steering its rationality is key to Freud's vision of the uncanny. For him, what separates the animist and the realist is repression. Thus, his uncanny affect requires a backdrop of realism insofar as it elicits horror specifically by threatening, via the return of the repressed, to collapse the precarious boundaries separating the civilised and the savage (i.e., the European and the colonised).

It is easy to recognise why this theory, based in gothic literature, has been used by generations of gothic critics to explain the genre's cultural work. In Tutuola's fiction, however, uncanny affect operates amidst an aesthetic backdrop that would not count as realism in the Freudian paradigm. Still, as I have argued, Tutuola's animism, formulated as a modernist mode of realism, depicting a convivial openness to change and the strange, displays an analogous relationship to the form upon which Freud anchors his theory of the uncanny. As the complete gentleman sequence demonstrates, however, at the level of epistemology the Tutuolan uncanny goes much further than the Freudian uncanny. The complete gentleman is beautiful primarily because of his mythic aura of completeness; his physical form is attractive because it appears total, absolute. A lesson of the sequence is, then, to say *no* to claims of totalisation, sovereign declarations, or acts of enclosure, because nothing in this universe is complete. From this vantage point, Tutuola's post-sovereign ontology – his depiction of existence untethered to illusions of completeness – renders inoperative the binary that the Freudian uncanny critiques. For Freud, European modernity's consciousness must repress its originary animism, which always threatens, via the uncanny, to return (a threat gothic horror aestheticises). For Tutuola, on the other hand, African modernity's consciousness refuses to repress its animism. Instead, it subjects the secular rationality of post-Enlightenment European culture to animistic rationality, exposing the former's mythical thinking. The complete gentleman, for example, appears to his observers as a Vitruvian totality, a European myth he subverts by steadily exposing his form as indebted to others. As he becomes an increasingly terrifying creature, he also increasingly embodies a cosmology in which there is no sovereign subject, in which everything is animated by everything else, in which the secular rationality Freud extolls appears as magical as the animism he hopes to keep at bay. The Freudian uncanny and the Tutuolan uncanny therefore start from opposing sides of an epistemic border separating magic and modernity, and each critique this same border. But while Freud aims to ward off animism (thereby retaining this border), Tutuola shatters it.

Further, moving from the epistemological to the historical-material aspects of this sequence highlights the manner in which the Tutuolan uncanny, similarly to gothic horror, embodies anxieties of industrialisation. For example, Tutuola often utilises symbols that would come to be associated with the oil industry, which would soon radically reshape the landscape of Nigerian literature. Consider this description of the woman attempting to escape the pit of skulls:

> But one day, the lady attempted to escape from the hole, and at the same time that the Skull who was watching her whistle to the rest of the Skulls that were in the back-yard, the whole of them rushed out to the place where the lady sat on the bull-frog, so they caught her, but as all of them were rushing out, they were rolling on the ground as if a thousand petrol drums were pushing along a hard road. After she was caught, then they brought her back to sit on the same frog as usual. If the Skull who was watching her fell asleep, and if the lady wanted to escape, the cowrie that was tied on her neck would raise up the alarm with a terrible noise.[40]

The skulls in this passage roll as if they are a thousand petrol drums while a cowrie, an image of economic exchange, is tied around the woman's neck. We should note that Shell discovered oil deposits in 1956, four years after *Palm-Wine*'s publication. Tutuola's animism thus lays the symbolic groundwork for future writers of the Nigerian oil boom (Okri's magical realism being a prime example). However, Tutuola does so via the region's first extractive economy: palm wine. The titular drinkard is defined by his work (drinking) and his relation to his employee (the tapster). His quest to

Dead's Town, the novel's plot, is spurred by a rupture in an economic relationship: the drinkard's tapster dies. As Jennifer Wenzel thus argues, the novel 'is an economic analysis of resource extraction and labour relations'.[41] The passage quoted above becomes through this lens a striking image of the process through which an economy rooted in extraction interpolates the West African colonial subject within the late colonial polis.

Thus, when the woman strapped to the bullfrog tries to escape her imprisonment and a terrible noise resounds, this noise functions as the sound of capitalist modernity, the noise of mid-century Nigeria's rapid industrialisation. Such an interpretation makes sense of the other sonic components of Tutuola's various creatures. As the king of the field creatures speaks, for example, 'hot steam was rushing out of his nose and mouth as a big boiler and he was breathing at five minutes interval'.[42] Or, happening upon a 'half-bodied baby', the protagonist-narrator hears this baby 'talking with a lower voice like a telephone'.[43] These creatures speak with sounds reminiscent of boilers and phones, symbols of European techno-scientific rationality. Much like gothic monsters, then, Tutuola's creatures incarnate cultural anxieties surrounding the machination of movement, labour, and communication. These anxieties become most uncanny in the aforementioned passage of the television-handed ghostess. When she raises her television-palm to the protagonist-narrator's face, he declares, 'I saw my town, mother, brother and all my playmates'.[44] The global capitalism Tutuola's creatures embody here threatens to capture and irrevocably shift African subjectivity: the drinkard sees his past in the creature's televising hand – a disfiguration of cultural memory I theorise in *Animist Poetics* as the 'ancestral trauma' conditioning African modernity.

As Soyinka's reading of Tutuola emphasises, however, and as Rooney's, Nyamnjoh's, and my readings expand, continuous shape-shifting is baked into the form of the modern African subject Tutuola envisions. Thus, against Freud's and the canonical gothic's assumed bourgeois European subject, whose primitive beliefs (mirroring those of colonised peoples) have been repressed, and must continuously be repressed, Tutuola's subject inhabits a world in which animism and modernity become indistinguishable. Under this world-gothic reading, Tutuolan animism is the horizon to which the gothic points but can never actually enter. To do so would drain the genre of its distinct brand of horror. The Freudian uncanny renders the indistinguishability between animism and realism the fundamental anxiety of modernity, which, for Freud, must be overcome. The Tutuolan uncanny celebrates this indistinguishability, which, for Tutuola, is not possible or even desirable to overcome. This celebration, moreover, disrupts any clean separation between horror and comic affects so that violent and disturbing imagery throughout Tutuola's fiction is rendered undeniably funny (thereby placing his animist realism in proximity to Mikhail Bakhtin's theory of grotesque realism).[45]

This disruption is the endpoint of the analogous relationship I have been tracing between Tutuola's animist realism and the gothic and thus the Tutuolan and the Freudian uncanny. The enmeshment of horror and humour in the Tutuolan uncanny emphasises Tutuola's animist realism as a mode of experimental modernism and highlights its implicit revision of the Freudian coordinates of the uncanny. If the modern subject (European, African, or otherwise) has never been a stable, bordered, secular self, why not laugh at self-preservation's perpetual failures? Ironically, the animist narration of such failure in uncanny form is Tutuola's tactic of Yoruba self-preservation. In Tutuola's world the ipseistic subject fails, yet the shape-shifting subject remains precisely because its co-ordinates are built upon the animist insight that subjectivity is always in a process of rupture and becoming: the regenerative death drive I further theorise in *Animist Poetics*. This insight is why Achille Mbembe interprets Tutuola's fiction as mapping survival strategies for the arbitrary and uncertain nature of life in the postcolony. He writes,

> The act *par excellence* of morphing consists in constantly exiting out of oneself, going beyond oneself in an agonizing, centripetal movement that is all the more terrifying as the possibility of returning to the center is never assured. In this context, where existence is tethered to very few things, identity can only live its life in a fleeting mode. Inhabiting a particular being can only be temporary.[46]

If being is a temporary inhabitation, as Mbembe finds in Tutuola's fiction, then the gothic's threat to ipseistic subjectivity is a statement of realism. Consequently, if the goal of this collection is to 'world' the gothic, the genre must be rethought in analogous relation to postcolonial forms that, like the gothic, offer immanent critiques of the same modernity, yet from disparate cosmological starting points. Such a project must not conflate or divide the postcolonial and canonical, realism and modernism, or gothic and animism. Instead, such a project necessitates a criticism as focused on historical materialism as the cosmological assumptions of generic categories. The horizon of this mode of world-gothic criticism is a comparative analysis of the processes through which disparate-yet-connected literary forms together render colonial modernity uncanny.

Notes

1. Gail Low, 'The Natural Artist: Publishing Amos Tutuola's *The Palm-Wine Drinkard* in Postwar Britain', *Research in African Literatures*, 37:4 (Winter 2006), 15–33.
2. Low, 'The Natural Artist', 72.
3. Bernth Lindfors (ed.), *Critical Perspectives on Amos Tutuola*, Washington D.C., Three Continents Press, 1975, 7.
4. Brenda Cooper, *Magical Realism in West African Fiction: Seeing with a Third Eye*, New York, Routledge, 1998, 44.
5. Amos Tutuola, *The Palm-Wine Drinkard and My Life in the Bush of Ghosts*, New York, Grove Press, 1994, 163.
6. Matthew Omelsky, 'The Creaturely Modernism of Amos Tutuola', *Cultural Critique*, 99 (Spring 2018), 66–96, 66.
7. Omelsky, 'The Creaturely Modernism of Amos Tutuola', 67.
8. Wole Soyinka, *Art, Dialogue, and Outrage: Essays on Literature and Culture*, New York, Pantheon Books, 1988, 9.
9. Tutuola, *The Palm-Wine Drinkard and My Life in the Bush of Ghosts*, 239.
10. Soyinka, *Art, Dialogue, and Outrage*, 9.
11. Soyinka, *Art, Dialogue, and Outrage*, 11.
12. Omelsky, 'The Creaturely Modernism of Amos Tutuola', 91.
13. Soyinka, *Art, Dialogue, and Outrage*, 11.
14. Shmuel N. Eisenstadt (ed.), *Multiple Modernities*, Milton Park, Routledge, 2002; Joe Cleary, Jed Esty, and Colleen Lye, 'Peripheral Realisms Now', *MLQ*, 73:3 (2012), 269–88.
15. Henry John Drewal, John Pemberton III, and Rowland Abiodun, 'The Yoruba World', in A. Wardwell (ed.), *Yoruba: Nine Centuries of African Art and Thought*, New York, Center for African Art, 1989, 14.
16. André Breton, 'Manifesto of Surrealism (1924)', quoted in Ian Chilvers, *The Oxford Dictionary of Art and Artists*, Oxford, Oxford University Press, 2009, 611.
17. Harry Garuba, 'Explorations in Animist Materialism: Notes on Reading/Writing African Literature, Culture, and Society', *Public Culture*, 15:2 (2003), 261–85, 274–5.
18. Terry Castle, *The Female Thermometer: Eighteenth-Century Culture and The Invention of the Uncanny*, Oxford, Oxford University Press, 1995, 16.
19. Castle, *The Female Thermometer*, 8.
20. Diane Long Hoeveler, *Gothic Riffs: Secularizing the Uncanny in the European Imaginary, 1780–1820*, Columbus, Ohio State University Press, 2010, 6.
21. Francis Nyamnjoh, *Drinking from the Cosmic Gourd: How Tutuola Can Change Our Minds*, Mankon, Langaa Research & Publishing, 2017, 21.

22. Caroline Rooney, *African Literature, Animism and Politics*, Abingdon, Routledge, 2000.
23. Ryan Topper, *Animist Poetics: Ancestral Trauma and Regeneration in African Literature*, Albany, SUNY Press, 2025.
24. Sidney Mintz, *Sweetness and Power: The Place of Sugar in Modern History*, New York, Penguin Press, 1985.
25. Frantz Fanon, *The Wretched of the Earth*, New York, Grove Press, 1968, 102.
26. Simon Gikandi, *Slavery and the Culture of Taste*, Princeton, Princeton University Press, 2014, 121.
27. Michael Taussig, *The Devil and Commodity Fetishism in South America*, Chapel Hill, University of North Carolina Press, 1980, 18.
28. Taussig, *The Devil and Commodity Fetishism in South America*, 38.
29. Taussig, *The Devil and Commodity Fetishism in South America*, 10.
30. Stephen Shapiro, 'Transvaal, Transylvania: *Dracula's* World-system and Gothic Periodicity', *Gothic Studies*, 10:1 (May 2008), 29–47, 33.
31. Tutuola, *The Palm-Wine Drinkard and My Life in the Bush of Ghosts*, 243.
32. For a related argument on African horror, see Rebecca Duncan, 'Gothic Supernaturalism in the African Imagination: Locating an Emerging Form', in M. Adejunmobi and C. Coetzee (eds.), *Routledge Handbook of African Literature*, Abingdon, 2019, 154–68.
33. Tutuola, *The Palm-Wine Drinkard and My Life in the Bush of Ghosts*, 254.
34. Tutuola, *The Palm-Wine Drinkard and My Life in the Bush of Ghosts*, 255.
35. Alexander Fyfe, 'Teaching Amos Tutuola's *The Palm-Wine Drinkard* as Part of a Decolonial Literature Syllabus', *Pedagogy*, 23:3 (October 2023), 567–75, 572.
36. Alexander Fyfe, 'Teaching Amos Tutuola's *The Palm-Wine Drinkard*', 571.
37. Andrew Bank, 'Of "Native Skulls" and "Noble Caucasians": Phrenology in Colonial South Africa', *Journal of Southern African Studies*, 22:3 (1996), 387–403.
38. Sigmund Freud, 'The Uncanny', in A. Dickinson (ed.), *The Penguin Freud Library Vol. 14: Art and Literature*, London, Penguin Books, 1985, 362.
39. Freud, 'The Uncanny', 371.
40. Tutuola, *The Palm-Wine Drinkard and My Life in the Bush of Ghosts*, 205–6.
41. Jennifer Wenzel, 'Petro-Magic-Realism: Toward a Political Ecology of Nigerian Literature', *Postcolonial Studies*, 9:4 (2006), 449–64, 456.
42. Tutuola, *The Palm-Wine Drinkard and My Life in the Bush of Ghosts*, 228.
43. Tutuola, *The Palm-Wine Drinkard and My Life in the Bush of Ghosts*, 218.
44. Tutuola, *The Palm-Wine Drinkard and My Life in the Bush of Ghosts*, 163.
45. Steven Tobias, 'Amos Tutuola and the Colonial Carnival', *Research in African Literatures*, 30:2 (Summer 1999), 66–74.
46. Achille Mbembe, 'Life Sovereignty, and Terror in the Fiction of Amos Tutuola', trans. R. Mitsch, *Research in African Literatures*, 34:4 (2003), 1–26, 19.

CHAPTER 11

Abject/Abhuman/Human
Provincialising World-Gothic Monstrosity

Rebekah Cumpsty

In the Introduction to this collection we propose that to think with world-gothic is, in part, to critically provincialise European gothic forms and to demonstrate their regional and cultural specificity. The lexicon of the gothic, including the terms 'abject' and 'abhuman', ought then to be construed as one, overdetermined set of signs for a wider and more plural monstrous and bodily response to socio-ecological transformations under colonialism/capitalism. In this chapter, I contextualise and critique the abject and abhuman, as well as the category 'human' upon which both terms rest. I then demonstrate how Helen Oyeyemi's *The Icarus Girl* (2005) and Akwaeke Emezi's *Freshwater* (2018), clearly conversant with North Atlantic literary and gothic modes, prioritise and centre Yoruba and Igbo onto-epistemologies to unseat secular, colonial, Christian frames. Both texts present a spirit child, an *abiku/ogbanje*, that I construe as a culturally specific iteration of the abhuman monster. I argue that these novels articulate a trajectory away from a simple critique of the abject and abhuman and towards 'other-than-human' modes of embodiment and receptivity, showcasing the possibilities of monstrosity without the Eurocentric straitjacket.

Situating the Abject and Abhuman

Julia Kristeva's influential conception of the abject appears in *Powers of Horror: An Essay on Abjection*. 'What is abject', she explains, 'is radically excluded and draws me toward the place where meaning collapses'.[1] Abjection 'names the expulsion that constitutes both subjectivity and society',[2] it refers to a visceral reaction – horror, nausea, revulsion – to what is disgusting and mortally frightening, and which undermines the distinction between I and not-I, self and other, subject and object. The skin on the surface of warm milk, bleeding or suppurating wounds, menstrual blood, faeces, dead bodies – such things confront the subject with their own proximity to death, meat, objecthood; they demonstrate the porousness or failure of category boundaries. In this sense, they sit at the intersection of the symbolic order (society, law, authority) and the semiotic (bodily drives, instincts); they are that which is 'radically excluded' from the boundaries of self, subject, and society, and yet is constitutive of them. The individual confronted by the abject experiences 'rejection, repulsion, and expulsion'; socially or communally abjection manifests as a rejection or expulsion of 'ideas, people, and practices that threaten the presumed integrity of a society'.[3] As a concept, abjection is influenced by structural anthropology and Lacanian psychoanalysis, to explain how what is excluded or negated actually defines the thing itself – abjection establishes the constitutive boundaries of self and society.

Kristeva's theory of abjection builds on Claude Levi-Strauss's structural anthropology, which she extends from a classification system to a symbolic system and signifying process. Kristeva draws too from Mary Douglas's anthropological study of hygiene and the threat of pollution and impurity. Douglas finds that dirt or 'uncleanness is matter out of place' and must be understood through order, since it 'is that which must not be included if a pattern is to be maintained'.[4] Where Kristeva writes of abjection, Douglas refers to defilement. 'Defilement is never an isolated event', Douglas writes, and 'cannot occur except in view of a systematic ordering of ideas ... For the only way in which pollution ideas make sense is in reference to a total structure of thought whose key-stone, boundaries, margins and internal lines are held in relation by rituals of separation'.[5] In other words, for defilement or the abject to signify, they must operate within a coherent social and/or symbolic order which maintains and establishes cultural and syntactic boundaries. For Kristeva the question which goes unanswered in Douglas's thinking, but is addressed by psychoanalysis, is: 'Why does *corporeal waste*, menstrual blood and excrement, or everything that is assimilated to them, from nail-parings to decay, represent ... the objective frailty of symbolic order?'[6] The answer Kristeva proposes is that defilement or the abject is the 'translinguistic spoor of the most archaic boundaries of the self's clean and proper body'.[7] Put differently: the concept of the abject synthesises anthropological and psychoanalytical thinking to address why, in particular, bodily waste or wasting exposes the vulnerability of the social, linguistic, subjective, and symbolic systems. The socio-cultural fixation on purity and dirt, especially in relation to the body, is explained by Kristeva through the exciting and revolting duality of abject.

11 Abject/Abhuman/Human

Drawing from Douglas's work on defilement and Kristeva's theory of abjection, Kelly Hurley[8] explains that the 'abhuman subject is a not-quite-human subject, characterised by its morphic variability, continually in danger of becoming not-itself, becoming other'. Hurley argues that this figure emerged specifically in fin-de-siècle gothic and primarily functioned to defamiliarise and reconstitute the human subject, which was viewed ambivalently, on the one hand as 'fully human' modern man, and on the other as potentially monstrous – the threat of degeneration being ever present.[9] The 'spectacle of a body metamorphic and undifferentiated' is, Hurley shows, an anxious cultural response to the erosion of a conventional Enlightenment human by 'new' subject forms presented in discourses of 'evolutionism, criminal anthropology, degeneration theory, sexology and pre-Freudian psychology'.[10] The abhuman, therefore, signifies 'the ruination of traditional constructs of human identity'; the liminality and conditionality of the human as a species category and as an embodied experience. This is illustrated in gothic fiction by 'figuring sexuality as horrific, identity as multiple, the boundary between science and supernaturalism to be permeable, and the "normal" human subject as liable to contamination, affective, moral, and physical, by the gothicised subject'.[11] The abhuman and its corollary, the autonomous individual or modern bourgeois subject, are co-implicated, Hurley cautions, in the 'immense cultural labour' of scientific classification that is required to create and maintain these terms.[12] Yet, Hurley does not go far enough to historicise 'human' or the category boundaries viciously policed by racialised, sexualised, and gendered discourses. The abhuman, like the abject and theories of dirt which precede it, are themselves ahistorical and de-territorialised, and are premised upon an ahistorical and de-territorialised construction of the human. For such terms to remain useful in readings of world-literary production they must be provincialised.

The two novels discussed in this chapter, *The Icarus Girl* and *Freshwater*, represent a body of work that draws from African-based cosmologies to model a form of other-than-human receptivity that refuses subordination to the European sovereign subject. Other-than-human is part of a suit of idioms that attempt to reimagine multispecies relations beyond colonial categories: multispecies, more-than-human, other-than-human, and non-human. Other-than-human in particular avoids human exceptionalism and racialised hierarchies that inhere in more-than-human or multispecies, while accommodating a range of actors beyond the biological, that are 'nonetheless animate, agentive' and 'co-shapers of our situated worlds'.[13] Importantly, as Marta Sofia Lopez cautions, this term has also been construed in broadly secular terms, but ought to include sacred and spiritual other-than-human formations, such as those found in Indigenous religions.[14] For the topic at hand, other-than-human sidesteps the human-as-man, racialised, gendered, and speciesist logic of the Linnaean classification system, to which I return below, to foreground a decolonial receptivity drawn from animist epistemologies. As a revision of individual sovereignty and mastery, Zakiyyah Iman Jackson posits the notion of receptivity: an embodied subjectivity that is interdependent, adaptable, permeable, agentive, and context specific. 'Receptivity is the processual experience of embodied humanity – the active, but not always conscious, process of receiving and participating in an encounter'.[15] I consider receptivity to be at the heart of other-than-human embodiment in *The Icarus Girl* and *Freshwater*. Both novels deploy world-gothic aesthetics to articulate the *abiku/ogbanje* and their doppelgänger or abhuman double as 'monstrous agents',[16] while simultaneously situating this figure alongside Yoruba and Igbo onto-epistemologies of other-than-human twins and spirit children. Gothic aesthetics are used differently in these texts: Oyeyemi's novel makes explicit linkages with the gothic, while Emezi's invokes these conventions in a limited way to articulate embodied subjectivity as horrific.

From the Abhuman to the Other-than-Human in *The Icarus Girl*

The Icarus Girl is in dialogue with and exposes the insufficiency of conceptions of the abject and abhuman; instead, it foregrounds other-than-human receptivity drawn from Yoruba views of twins and *abiku* (spirit-children). The novel deploys the gothic tension between madness and the supernatural to juxtapose, and vitally, to contextualise a Yoruba approach to subjectivity against a psychological diagnosis. As Christopher Ouma rightly notes, 'Oyeyemi's novel invites us to consider the tension between the narrative of *abiku* as Yoruba myth/legend with a particular material culture, and its new diasporic double as a subject of psychoanalytic interpretation – specifically, that of Dissociative Identity Disorder (DID)'.[17] Jessamy Harrison, called Jess in the narrative, is an eight-year-old girl residing in London, daughter to a Black Nigerian mother and a white English father. Critics have frequently read *The Icarus Girl* as a postcolonial bildungsroman,[18] understanding Jess's psychological instability as a result of her diasporic and mixed-race parentage, and her struggle to align with continental norms. Attempting to address this fluctuating sense of self, Jess's parents take her to Lagos for the first time, where she encounters TillyTilly, a doppelgänger, 'a veritable Jessamy-echo'.[19] As a ghostly double, TillyTilly reveals Jess as an *abiku* and twin; her sister, Fern, died at birth.

The *abiku* has a long history in African and diasporic literature. The concept is rooted in Yoruba culture and refers to children who die but return to torment their mothers. The *abiku* inhabit and can move between three worlds, the bush, the earth, and the spirit world. Jess's role as an *abiku* is complicated by her status as the living twin. Twins occupy an ambivalent position in Yoruba culture, at once celebrated and feared for their volatility. While all ancestors are to be respected through appropriate rituals, dead twins require *ère ìbejì*, twin sculptures.[20] Fern is not commemorated in this way until the end of the novel, when her statue is brought in by their grandfather to watch over Jess while she recovers from a car accident. The plot of the novel turns on African diasporic notions of doubling and other-than-human relationality, and it is here that ideas of the abhuman and abject are presented and contested. Jess occupies multiple worlds with TillyTilly as her spirit companion, in addition to the (post)colonial entanglements of Nigeria and Britain. This sense of diasporic and cosmological multiplicity is demonstrated by the versions of Jess's name. Gbenga Oyegbebi – Jess's grandfather – addresses her by her Yoruba name Wuraola, which 'sounded like another person. Not her at all. Should she answer to this name, and by doing so steal the identity of someone who belonged here?'.[21] To answer to another name is to take on another self, but we might also read this as already exceeding the classifications of humanist individualism, gesturing to the other-than-human. Jess is also Wuraola, and TillyTilly calls her Jessy: 'She'd always been *Jess* or *Jessamy*, never a halfway thing like Jessy.'[22] Jess similarly renames Titiola TillyTilly because she cannot pronounce the Yoruba name. Naming thus signifies Jess's diasporic *abiku* subjectivity, Wuraola connects her to Nigerian family and tradition, Jessamy to her parents and paternal English family, and Jessy signifies her connection to the spirit world and TillyTilly. Jess struggles with this multiplicity and evidently exceeds Eurocentric constructions of human, even as a diagnosis of DID attempts to define the category limit.

The novel thematises this subjective multiplicity through abjection, while at the same time demonstrating the insufficiency of the concept. Jessamy demonstrates the consequences of being made to inhabit the category of the human, and shows specifically that the only way to relate from within this category is to abject: to be radically excluded and thereafter threaten the symbolic system, reconstituting those boundaries of self and society. Jess's abjection often manifests as a fit or tantrum. On the flight to Nigeria from England 'Jess threw a tantrum.' Caught between two competing registers and regimes Jess decides that Nigeria, 'the leering idea of her mother's country', 'was the problem'.[23] It 'made her begin to struggle and thrash ... Inside her head, she could hear her skin blistering, could almost feel it, and she tried to outscream the sound ... and it felt good to be making this sharp screeching hurting noise. Yet some part of her was sitting hunched up small, far away, thinking scared thoughts'.[24] The intimate point of view depicts Jess's abjection, 'a terror that disassembles'.[25] Outwardly, she is thrashing and screaming; internally, she is blistering and afraid. Jess's feelings of abjection are commonly experienced when her sense of subjective coherence and bodily integrity are metaphorically or materially threatened. It happens frequently at school in London where she is bullied by peers and expected to learn and internalise the conditions and stratifications of 'human'. And while TillyTilly first appears as a friend, many of their interactions leave Jess abjected. Since TillyTilly helps to signify Jess's *abiku* form and seems to feed off of her, it follows that bodily and moral thresholds are threatened by her presence. At the midpoint of the novel, with Tilly and Jess both in London, Tilly is now strong enough to pull Jess with her through the staircase of her home and into the ground beneath. Corpselike and 'claustrophobic', Jess can 'taste blood on her tongue'.[26] Then Tilly pulls her back up and her bodily boundaries are overcome: 'Jess felt earth push into her face and her mouth, and she *drank* it, as a vast amount of air whistled past her ears, and TillyTilly's hand fell away from hers, and she was standing, spitting out the dank taste of the soil, on the staircase, alone.'[27] Tilly initiates Jess into the world-hopping potential of spirit children. Confronted, again, by her multiplicity and other-than-humanness, Jess expels the soil that broke through her corporeal boundary.

TillyTilly invites disgust and revels in flouting standards of cleanliness. She is 'out of proportion', 'trailing, dirty white string', her skin 'ashen' and 'greyish', and towards the end of the novel the 'leafy pomade' smell of Tilly's skin has 'intensified into a wet, rotting vegetation smell'.[28] Tilly's rotten stench increases with her growing 'badness';[29] she becomes more ghoulish and predatory, eventually possessing Jess's body on her ninth birthday. Tilly is Jess's abhuman double and her growing hunger to possess Jess is monstrously figured. Alone in her room Jess realises that '*TillyTilly was no longer safe* ... the very fabric of TillyTilly was stretching, pulling apart, a brown cycle of skin and eyes and voice'.[30] Tilly has 'caught' Jess and while she mockingly chants '"There is no homeland"', there is a grotesque figure hanging from the ceiling, the face centimetres from

Jess's: 'those pupils, dilated until there is no white; those enormous, swollen lips, almost cartoonish except that they were deepest black, encrusted with dead, dry skin, coated here and there with chunks of ... something moist and pinky-white ... Transfixed, she caught a glimpse of them [the lips] as they moved over a small, mauve stump: the remains of a *tongue*'.[31] The threat Tilly poses materialises in her revolting body and the monstrous figures she seems able to conjure. Like a traditional European doppelgänger, Tilly is motivated by a desire to take over Jess's body and her life. '"I want to live, too!"' Tilly yells as she takes Jess over.[32] However, to construe Tilly as only an abhuman doppelgänger is to overlook an entire epistemology, which clearly demonstrates the limits of the abhuman in the world-gothic context.

Jess is an *abiku* and Tilly is her spirit companion, not merely a spectre. And like Jess, Tilly is a twin. Jess calls her double the long-armed woman, and she realises that she and Tilly 'were somehow the same person, like two sides of a thin coin'.[33] When Jess first meets Tilly in the Boys' Quarters she sees a 'charcoal ... sketch of a black woman' as part of a 'display, or maybe a shrine'. Her expression was 'serene' yet her arms were 'grotesque', 'tentaclelike'.[34] Tilly's actions, and indeed Jess's experiences, can only be adequately understood through the Yoruba understanding of twins, which the novel depicts in gothic terms. As Jess's spirit companion, Tilly gives her information she does not know, like that she is a twin: 'there were two of you born, just like there was two of me. The other one of you died'.[35] This also explains Tilly's motivations: 'You have to be so empty, Jessy, without your twin; you have had no one to walk your three worlds with you. I know – I am the same ... But now I am Fern, I am your sister, and you are my twin'.[36] Apparently, Tilly has also been separated from her twin, the long-armed-woman, and so claims Jess as her own. Sarah, Jess's mother, provides additional context after Jess asks if there were '"two of me?"'.[37] Shouting down Daniel's 'rational explanation', Sarah explains: '"THEY ALWAYS KNOW! Twins ... she's like a witch ... Three worlds! Jess lives in three worlds. She lives in this world, and she lives in the spirit world, and she lives in the Bush. She's *abiku*, and she always would have known! The spirits tell her things. Fern tells her things. We should've ... done *ibeji* carving for her!"'.[38] The *ibeji* carving Sarah refers to is a statue created when one or both twins die. This is necessary because twins are divine, and dead or alive can either benefit or harm their parents. To prevent the ire of a twin *ere ibeji* are well cared for and part of rituals designed to appease their desires. No carving was made for Fern. When Daniel, Jess's father, tries to reassure her that Fern is in heaven, Jess 'noted' her mother's 'slight wince'.[39] Sarah doubts Daniel's placating Christian explanation, and Jess feels 'haunted ... scared that Fern might want her to be dead as well'.[40] The novel entangles secular, Christian, and Yoruba onto-epistemologies, while enforcing the Yoruba as phenomenologically real by focalising Jessamy's perspective.

Yoruba cosmology is similarly juxtaposed with continental psychoanalysis. Upon their return from Nigeria Jess's parents send her to see a psychologist, Dr McKenzie, who through talk therapy and free word association tries to unearth Jess's unconscious. Dr McKenzie explains that Tilly is Jess's alter ago. Jess simultaneously rejects his analysis and is fearful that he is right, that she is 'just this mad, mad girl who did things that she couldn't explain'.[41] The novel presents competing explanations for subjectivity and their overarching regimes: the psychoanalytical approach is contrasted with Jess's status as an *abiku* twin. To read Jess as 'mad' or Tilly as an abhuman spectre is to miss the novel's diasporic, world-gothic dimensions. Oyeyemi does not resolve the tension between continental psychoanalysis, Christianity, and Yoruba material culture – it is not a case of one, but all three unevenly entangled. However, because it is focalised through Jess's sometimes stream-of-consciousness narrative, it is her perspective that is 'really really' real.[42]

Gothic aesthetics are evident in *The Icarus Girl*, where, as Rebecca Duncan notes, 'supernatural figures associated with' Yoruba cosmology 'are presented in gothic terms'.[43] The novel is also accurately described, borrowing Nnedi Okorafor's term, as Africanjujuist: 'a subcategory of fantasy that respectfully acknowledges the seamless blend of true existing African spiritualities and cosmologies with the imaginative'.[44] While *The Icarus Girl* deploys and critiques the abject and abhuman, it is Jess's other-than-human receptivity that defines her interdependent relationships with Tilly and Fern. Under this reading, the abject and abhuman are useful but insufficient ideas that cannot be divorced from their colonial genealogy. Yet this is precisely why it is generative to retain them: because of what they expose about Europe's idea of itself, as afraid of African migrants and their religions as they are of the gothic monsters used to depict them.

Decolonial and Black Feminist Critiques of 'Human'

There are longstanding postcolonial and decolonial critiques of anthropology and psychoanalysis, which suggest that these disciplines establish and maintain discourses of 'primitive', racialised, animalised, and gendered others, in order to construct its civilised superior: the white rational

Enlightenment bourgeois male subject. These categories are constitutive of, rather than incidental to the abject and abhuman. As Ashley Bohrer explains, 'all forms of the abject are forms of border confusion, border anxiety, or border ambiguity ... the repressed continually haunts the border as its constitutive outside'.[45] These category borders include race, gender, sexuality, nationality, and reproduction. The abject is 'an eminently feminine figure, as every encounter with the abject forces a confrontation with a denial and derogation of femininity, placed at the heart of both subject and society'.[46] Thus, Bohrer unveils the misogynistic understanding of the feminine, maternal, and natal upon which the abject relies. When the abject and abhuman are de-territorialised, this phallocentrism specific to European abjection is hidden. Bohrer explains:

> Europe's abject [and abhuman] will turn out to be that which troubles the culture and the people of Europe ... The abject is the hallmark of a vision of subjectivity that is individual, that repudiates a primordial connection to the maternal, and that sees ego differentiation, border stability, and a binary conception of me/not-me; each of these elements, while they may characterise a European model of subjectivity, affectivity, and psychic development, can by no means be taken to exist in all cultures or at all times.[47]

In other words, for the abject, abhuman, and indeed human, to signify in world-gothic production they must be situated and historicised, and their literary iterations understood within the combined and uneven system of labour, people, and cultures; they must be read within the specific and intersecting socio-cultural and socio-ecological discourses from which they emerge. Thus, in addition to the critiques of anthropology as Eurocentric and primitivist, which seek to curtail the universalist and transhistorical applications of Douglas's dirt, Kristeva's abject, and, indeed, Hurley's abhuman, it is further necessary to situate the concept of the human within the colonial matrix of power (CMP) or coloniality of power/knowledge.

The coloniality of power, Anibal Quijano explains, is based on two axes of power. 'One was the codification of the differences between conquerors and conquered in the idea of "race", a supposedly different biological structure that placed some in a natural situation of inferiority to the others ... The other process was the constitution of a new structure of control of labour and its resources and products.'[48] Thus, the rise of world capitalism and the racialised hierarchies of people converge to structure asymmetrical relations of power and knowledge. Thinking with Quijano, Walter Mignolo describes coloniality as 'conceptual machinery to regulate all areas of human experience'.[49] It is under this '(epistemic) invention of imperial and colonial difference [that] Western imperial subjects secured themselves and their descendant as the superior subspecies'.⁵⁰ Similarly, the idea of nature is established to distinguish imperial male bodies from all other forms of planetary life. If the apex of human evolution is the civilised European male, then other multispecies bodies rank lower relative to their proximity to nature and the animal, with Black and Indigenous peoples classified closest to nature, resources, and objects of study and extraction. Zakiyyah Iman Jackson further explains that European conceptions of the human are established by negating and denigrating blackness, and particularly female blackness, as the prime 'index of abject human animality'. Blackness, Jackson argues, becomes plastic, endlessly morphable into whatever abject body, shape, or material is required to undergird Eurocentric logics of human, gender, and sex.⁵¹

The description of Bertha Mason in Charlotte Brontë's *Jane Eyre* (1847) is a paradigmatic example of the conflation of abject blackness and animality. Bertha is the beastly abhuman double of Jane's poised, white femininity. Jane describes Bertha as having 'a discoloured ... savage face' with lips 'swelled and dark'.⁵² Jane wishes that she could 'forget the roll of the red eyes and the fearful blackened inflation of the lineaments'. After her wedding to Rochester is interrupted, Jane meets Bertha formally, and the first-person point of view firmly establishes the Creole wife from the colonies as the monstrous, racialised, and animalised other: 'whether beast or human, one could not, at first sight tell: it grovelled, seemingly, on all fours; it snatched and growled like some strange wild animal ... and had a quantity of dark grizzled hair ... the clothed hyena rose up' (125).⁵³ Jane's confrontation with her double is uncanny and tinged with disgust; Jane recognises Bertha as almost, but not quite, human. Her abjection of Bertha turns on the animality and blackening of Bertha's figure. This is precisely the racialised abject animality that Jackson argues is central to how blackness has been violently misconstrued. Jackson's larger point, however, is not to rehearse these antiblack tropes, nor to rescue an impotent liberal humanism, but rather to consider how trans-Atlantic Black cultural production foregrounds dissident ways of being/knowing and relationality drawn from African and African diasporic epistemologies.

The racialised hierarchies of coloniality/modernity are also an imposition of a secular frame under whose logic the sacred and spiritual are read as primitive. Sylvia Wynter points to the 'gradual de-supernaturalization' of ways of being that make possible the human-as-man. She traces a trajectory from the human as construed by and through the religious/spiritual, to the rational/political (Man1) and then to the liberal/economic

(Man2). This disenchanted, materialist conception of the world comes to be the sign of secular modernity and inaugurates the 'human/subhuman distinction', replacing 'the earlier mortal/immortal, natural/supernatural, human/the ancestors, the gods/God distinction as the one on whose basis all human groups had millennially "grounded" their descriptive statement/ prescriptive statements of what it is to be human'.[54] Similarly, Jacqui Alexander argues 'it is not only that (post)modernity's secularism renders the Sacred as tradition, but it is also that tradition, understood as an extreme alterity, is always made to reside elsewhere and denied entry into the modern'.[55] This is precisely the tension upon which the gothic depends: a realistic depiction of a secular world where marvellous, supernatural events sometimes occur. 'In this context', Alexander continues, 'African-based cosmological systems become subordinated to the European cosmos, not usually expected to accord any significance to modernity's itinerary, their provenance of little value in the constitution and formation of the very categories on which we have relied'. The dichotomies of human/abhuman, human/nature, rational/superstitious, secular/religious are constructed by the coloniality of being/knowledge/ power and reinforced by traditional gothic forms. In distinction, world-gothic texts like Oyeyemi's and Emezi's are simultaneously aware of these colonial taxonomies, and reject them in order to depict what Jackson calls 'unruly conceptions of being and materiality'.[56]

Other-than-Human Formations in *Freshwater*

Like *The Icarus Girl*, Emezi's *Freshwater* is self-consciously aware of and refuses Eurocentric conceptions of the abject and abhuman. The novel is easily categorised as Africanjujuist, and, following Jackson,[57] depicts unruly forms of Igbo 'being and materiality that creatively disrupt the human–animal distinction and its persistent raciality'. The narrative is focalised by Ada, an *ogbanje*. *Ogbanje* is the Igbo cognate of an *abiku*: a devious spirit that takes a human form and lives an embodied life, but does not sever ties to the spirit world. Because of this the child-body dies and the spirit is reincarnated again in the same family. Rejecting individual sovereignty, the concept of the *ogbanje* signals the complexity of the subject in Igbo cosmology where physical and spiritual worlds are entwined. While most *ogbanje* die in childhood, Ada survives, constantly tethered to the spirit world. Ada's father, Saul, is a Nigerian doctor; her mother, Saachi, is a Malaysian nurse who leaves to work abroad while Ada is still a child. When Ada is sixteen she too leaves Nigeria for the United States, where she attends college in Virginia. The novel begins with and is partly narrated by 'We', the first-person collective voice of the spirits through whom Ada is introduced. Ada is not singular, not individual; she is a body that contains herself, Vincent, and Asughara – doubles who already share her body. Like Oyeyemi's juxtaposition of *abiku* subjectivity and a DID diagnosis, Ada could be understood through a psycho-social classification as mad, schizoid, but these are not her alter ego's as Jess's Dr McKenzie would have it. Rather they are the spirits contained within her, and she is a bridge that retains her connection to the other 'brothersister' spirits, voiced as 'We'. They explain,

> By the time she (our body) struggled into the world … the gates were left open. We should have been anchored in her by then, asleep inside her membranes and synched with her mind … But since the gates were open, not closed against remembrance, we became confused. We were at once old and newborn. We were her and yet not. We were not conscious but we were alive – in fact, the main problem was that we were a distinct *we* instead of being fully and just her.[58]

The narrative is told primarily from the perspectives of We and Asughara, with three short chapters narrated by Ada. The heterogloss narration formally enacts Igbo cosmology, while the avatars of humanist discourses – Christianity and secularism – are ridiculed. A Christian worldview is mostly clearly demonstrated by Ada's Catholic parents. Saul prays to a Christian God for a daughter and Saachi sings 'Catholic hymns from her family' while Ada is a foetus.[59] When Ada is born the church refuses to baptise her without a second name, because her first was 'unchristian, pagan'.[60] The 'truest' translation of Ada is 'the egg of the python',[61] a name chosen by her uncle, De Obinna, who dies before Ada can remember him. Without her uncle's influence Ada is raised Catholic, in a 'christ-induced amnesia' that is fundamentally at odds with her being in the world. This is because Saul's prayers are not answered by Christ, but by Ala: a female god who is 'the earth itself, the judge and mother, the giver of law' (8), whose messenger and 'flesh form' is the python.[62] Ada is the egg of the python and Ala her mother. Thus, Ada is not merely a sacred bridge, she is divine, animal, and embodied Black subject. 'Ala continued to watch her child. After all, the Ada was her hatchling, her bloodthirsty little sun, covered in translucent scales. We were learning that to be embodied was to be the alter and the flesh and the knife'.[63] The plural narration foregrounds and validates the perspectives of Ada, Asughara, and the brothersisters, depicting an unruly other-than-human subjectivity that overruns the human-animal binary upon which the abhuman rests.

The novel has garnered much scholarly attention for its decolonial expansion of these categories towards a queer other-than-human. Tina Magaqa and Rodwell Makombe argue that 'the *ogbanje* problematises gender by harmonizing the spiritual (genderless) and the embodied (gendered) spheres of being human'.[64] They argue that because the Ada is not 'limited by embodiment' and 'oscillates between desires', Emezi uses the *ogbanje* to 'authorise queer desires in a largely heteronormative Igbo society'. Further, Marta Sofía López insists on the importance of the sacred in reading *Freshwater*'s decolonial revision of the human, which is decidedly postsecular, a sacred spirit embodied in an often profane and violent physical world. Lopez proposes to read Emezi on their own terms through 'border gnoseology', a synthesis of Mignolo's 'border thinking' and VY Mudimbe's 'African Gnosis', as a means of delinking from the coloniality of knowledge/power/modernity to establish relational ontologies. Pulling these arguments together, I will now demonstrate Ada's other-than-human receptivity as a world-gothic counter to the abhuman and abject.

While the familial and cultural threat of an *ogbanje* signifies Ada as monstrous and abhuman, the novel counters this reduction by depicting other-than-human queer subjectivity. Revising colonial separations of humans and non-human nature and related gothic tropes, the novel opens with the first meeting between child and snake. 'The first time our mother came for us, we screamed. We were three and she was a snake, coiled up on the tile in the bathroom, waiting.'[65] 'The python raised its head ... Through its eyes Ala looked at us, and through Ada's eyes we looked at her – all of us looking upon each other for the first time.'[66] Saul kills the python because he 'was a modern Igbo man' who 'spent many years in London', received his medical training in the Soviet Union, and so does not abide by what he calls 'mumbo-jumbo'.[67] Saul's modern, secular education amounts to a rejection of Igbo onto-epistemology, but not of Catholicism, illustrating the untenable and contradictory 'de-supernaturalization' or disenchantment of ways of being, where secular and Catholic modes and colonial hierarchies are upheld, but Igbo mores are denigrated as superstition. The secular, Christian episteme figured by Ada's parents and reinforced in the majority of her social interactions upholds the racialised and gendered taxonomy of the human. Christianity is even personified by Yshwa in the novel, an impotent watchful god 'with a taste for suffering',[68] that We chase away. The polyvocal and first-person narration therefore counters the coloniality of being: the narrative is told by and through the Ada, an *ogbanje*, who is both spirit and embodied being, human and non-human, multiform and polyvocal – other-than-human.

Ada explicitly inhabits a female body that is shared with Asughara, femme, and Vincent, masc and brothersisters. The trouble for this multiform subjectivity is with embodiment: 'this abomination of the fleshly'.[69] 'The first madness was that we were born, that they stuffed a god into a bag of skin'.[70] The only way to relate from within a human body, 'a bag of skin', is through abjection. The price for this imprisonment is a 'sacrifice ... of self worship'. Ada cuts her skin and offers her blood as an offering: 'we battered against the Ada's marble mind until she fed us and that thick red offering sounded almost like our mother ... Blood and belief. This is how the second madness began'.[71] To be in a body is to inhabit the profane, to be physically vulnerable, and to experience madness. The horror in the novel comes from being in material form. When Ada's college boyfriend Soren rapes her, Ada is 'confused' and cannot remember him 'moving unwanted parts of himself in her'.[72] Asughara is birthed from the 'shifting cloud' to protect Ada,[73] entering the 'marble room' of Ada's of mind with Ada 'a shred in the corner, a gibbering baby'.[74] Yet, Asughara 'expanded against the walls, filling it up and blocking her [Ada] out completely. She was gone ... I was powerful and I was mad, and he could not touch me no matter how hard he pushed into her body'.[75] Like Jess, Ada might be diagnosed with dissociative identity disorder. Following the rape and in almost all future sexual encounters Ada retreats and Asughara attacks. She channels her rage and disgust at the violation of Ada's body into a weapon. Asughara 'was the wildness under the skin ... the weapon over the flesh'.[76] She has 'no conscience, no sympathy, no pity'.[77] On the one hand, Asughara is Ada's protector called forth 'in the moment of her devastation, the moment she lost her mind'.[78] On the other hand, Asughara is a greedy doppelgänger that takes control of Ada's body, feeds off of her through her blood sacrifices, sows unrest with family and friends, and reinforces Ada's restrictive eating until 'her shoulders became knives in her back'.[79] Asughara is Ada's protector and abhuman tormentor, asserting a self, an I, a 'beastself';[80] but she only goes so far, because 'Ada was Ala's child ... If you're a python's child, then you are also a python – simple'.[81] The novel simultaneously rejects the binary of human-animal that is central to racialised constructions of gender and sexuality, and deploys gothic aesthetics that cohere around the horror of body, of the category of 'human' as a fleshly cage.

Freshwater contributes to a growing archive of African and Black diasporic cultural production that, on the one hand, critiques the abjection that is inseparable from racialised and animalised discourses, and their Enlightenment taxonomy, and on the other hand, delinks from those iterations of the human to present a sacred, multivoiced other-than-human. The subjective formation of 'the' Ada is echoed in their non-binary embodiment when, following Asughara's failed suicide attempt and having been 'sentenced to meat', they have top surgery to remove their breasts. 'And with Saint Vincent, our little grace, taking the front more than he used to, the body, as it was, was becoming unsatisfactory, too feminine, too reproductive. That form had worked for Asughara . . . but we were more than her . . . . We were a fine balance, bigger than whatever the namings had made'.[82] The *ogbanje*, Ezeiyoke notes, are, by their nature, genderless – signifying a non-conforming gender identity that 'threatens the hegemony of their predominantly heterosexual [and cisgender] cultures'.[83] The abhuman monstrosity of the *ogbanje* and *abiku* looms in their threat to heteronormativity, and their non-binary, polyvocal subjective embodiment celebrates this challenge, articulating a resounding other-than-human receptivity. As Ada says at the close of the novel: 'I am my other; we are one and we are many'.[84] In contrast to the degenerative and racialised teleology of traditional abhuman plotting, the novel demonstrates a subject accepting their multiplicity and becoming other-than-human.

If cultures can be understood by the monsters they create, if the monsters wrought by coloniality/modernity expose more about their makers and their conditions than themselves, then the abhuman in its plastic and mutable forms becomes one catachrestic term for other-than-human subjective embodiment. By exposing the racialised and gendered genealogy of the foundational category 'human', and by provincialising the abject and abhuman, I have sought to centre African literatures that are conversant with gothic aesthetics *and* depict unruly, dissident ways of being/knowing/feeling. I offer other-than-human receptivity as a critical alternative to the abhuman that prioritises local, culturally specific monstrous iteration, such as the *ogbanje* and *abiku*.

Notes

1. Julia Kristeva, *Powers of Horror: An Essay on Abjection*, trans. L. S. Roudiez, New York, Columbia University Press, 1982, 2.
2. Ashley Bohrer, 'The Abject Atlantic: The Coloniality of the Concept of Europe" in Its Maritime Meridian', *philoSOPHIA*, 7: 2 (2017), 215–40, 222.

3. Kristeva, *Powers of Horror*, 222.
4. Mary Douglas, *Purity and Danger: An Analysis of the Concepts of Pollution and Taboo*, London, Routledge, 2002, 41.
5. Douglas, *Purity and Danger*, 42.
6. Kristeva, *Powers of Horror*, 70.
7. Kristeva, *Powers of Horror*, 73.
8. Kelly Hurley, *The Gothic Body: Sexuality, Materialism, and Degeneration at the Fin de Siècle*, Cambridge, Cambridge University Press, 2004, 3–4.
9. Hurley, *The Gothic Body*, 4.
10. Hurley, *The Gothic Body*, 3, 5.
11. Hurley, *The Gothic Body*, 3, 13.
12. Hurley, *The Gothic Body*, 8.
13. Catherine Price and Sophie Chao, 'Multispecies, More-Than-Human, Nonhuman, Other-Than-Human: Reimagining Idioms of Animacy in an Age of Planetary Unmaking', *Exchanges: The Interdisciplinary Research Journal*, 10:2 (28 March 2023), 177–93, 181.
14. Marta Sofia López, 'Border Gnoseology: Akwaeke Emezi and the Decolonial Other-than-Human', E*cozon@: European Journal of Literature, Culture and Environment*, 29 (October 2022), 77–91, 78–9.
15. Zakiyyah Iman Jackson, *Becoming Human: Matter and Meaning in an Antiblack World*, New York, New York University Press, 2020, 150.
16. Chukwunonso Ezeiyoke, 'Beyond Postcolonial Gothic in African Literature', *Journal of the African Literature Association*, 16:3 (2 September 2022), 479–94, 481.
17. Christopher Ouma, 'Reading the Diasporic Abiku in Helen Oyeyemi's The Icarus Girl', *Research in African Literatures*, 45:3 (2014), 188–207, 189.
18. Sarah Ilott and Chloe Buckley, '"Fragmenting and Becoming Double": Supplementary Twins and Abject Bodies in Helen Oyeyemi's *The Icarus Girl*', *The Journal of Commonwealth Literature*, 51 (2016), 402–15.
19. Helen Oyeyemi, *The Icarus Girl*, London: Bloomsbury, 2005, 48.
20. Anthony White, 'The Trouble with Twins: Image and Ritual of the Yoruba Ère Ìbejì', *Electronic Melbourne Art Journal*, 5 (2010), 1–23, 1.
21. Oyeyemi, *The Icarus Girl*, 21.
22. Oyeyemi, *The Icarus Girl*, 44.
23. Oyeyemi, *The Icarus Girl*, 10, 9.
24. Oyeyemi, *The Icarus Girl*, 10.
25. Kristeva, *Powers of Horror*, 4.
26. Oyeyemi, *The Icarus Girl*, 151–2.
27. Oyeyemi, *The Icarus Girl*, 153, emphasis in original.
28. Oyeyemi, *The Icarus Girl*, 258.
29. Oyeyemi, *The Icarus Girl*, 284.
30. Oyeyemi, *The Icarus Girl*, 258.
31. Oyeyemi, *The Icarus Girl*, 260–1.
32. Oyeyemi, *The Icarus Girl*, 316.
33. Oyeyemi, *The Icarus Girl*, 171.

34. Oyeyemi, *The Icarus Girl*, 79.
35. Oyeyemi, *The Icarus Girl*, 174.
36. Oyeyemi, *The Icarus Girl*, 176.
37. Oyeyemi, *The Icarus Girl*, 179.
38. Oyeyemi, *The Icarus Girl*, 180–1.
39. Oyeyemi, *The Icarus Girl*, 182.
40. Oyeyemi, *The Icarus Girl*, 182.
41. Oyeyemi, *The Icarus Girl*, 290.
42. Oyeyemi, *The Icarus Girl*, 171.
43. Rebecca Duncan, 'Gothic Supernaturalism in the "African Imagination": Locating an Emerging Form', in M. Adejunmobi and C. Coetzee (eds.), *Routledge Handbook of African Literature*, New York, Routledge, 2019, 158.
44. Nnedi Okorafor, 'Africanfuturism Defined' in *Nnedi's Wahala Zone Blog*, 19 October 2019, https://nnedi.blogspot.com/2019/10/africanfuturism-defined.html.
45. Bohrer, 'The Abject Atlantic', 224.
46. Bohrer, 'The Abject Atlantic', 223–4.
47. Bohrer, 'The Abject Atlantic', 224–5.
48. Anibal Quijano, 'Coloniality of Power, Eurocentrism, and Latin America', *Nepantla: Views from South*, 1:3 (2000), 533–79, 533–4.
49. Walter D. Mignolo, 'Coloniality and Globalization: A Decolonial Take', *Globalizations*, 18:5 (4 July 2021), 720–37, 724–5.
50. Walter D. Mignolo and Catherine Walsh, *On Decoloniality: Concepts, Analytics, Praxis*, Durham, Duke University Press, 2018, 154.
51. Zakiyyah Iman Jackson, *Becoming Human*, 4, 9.
52. Charlotte Brontë, *Jane Eyre: A Norton Critical Edition*, ed. D. Lutz, New York, W. W. Norton & Company, 2022, 254.
53. Brontë, *Jane Eyre*, 263.
54. Sylvia Wynter, 'Unsettling the Coloniality of Being/Power/Truth/Freedom: Towards the Human, After Man, Its Overrepresentation – An Argument', *CR*, 3:3 (2003), 257–337, 263, 264.
55. M. Jacqui Alexander, *Pedagogies of Crossing: Meditations on Feminism, Sexual Politics, Memory, and the Sacred*, Durham, Duke University Press Books, 2006, 296.
56. Zakiyyah Iman Jackson, *Becoming Human*, 3.
57. Jackson, *Becoming Human*, 1.
58. Emezi, *Freshwater*, New York, Grove Press, 2018, 5. Excerpt from *Freshwater* copyright © 2018 by Akwaeke Emezir. Used by permission of Grove/Atlantic, Inc.
59. Emezi, *Freshwater*, 1.
60. Emezi, *Freshwater*, 8.
61. Emezi, *Freshwater*, 9.
62. Uchechukwu Ajuzieogu, '13 Popular Gods of Igbo Culture', *Medium*, 15 March 2021, https://uchechukwuajuzieogu.medium.com/13-popular-gods-of-igbo-culture-366630ac4752.

63. Emezi, *Freshwater*, 38–9.
64. Tina Magaqa and Rodwell Makombe, 'Decolonising Queer Sexualities: A Critical Reading of the Ogbanje Concept in Akwaeke Emezi's *Freshwater*', *African Studies Quarterly*, 20:3 (2021), 24–39, 25.
65. Emezi, *Freshwater*, 1.
66. Emezi, *Freshwater*, 11.
67. Emezi, *Freshwater*, 13.
68. Emezi, *Freshwater*, 36.
69. Emezi, *Freshwater*, 4.
70. Emezi, *Freshwater*, 20.
71. Emezi, *Freshwater*, 42.
72. Emezi, *Freshwater*, 58.
73. Emezi, *Freshwater*, 61.
74. Emezi, *Freshwater*, 61.
75. Emezi, *Freshwater*, 64.
76. Emezi, *Freshwater*, 66.
77. Emezi, *Freshwater*, 70.
78. Emezi, *Freshwater*, 71.
79. Emezi, *Freshwater*, 68.
80. Emezi, *Freshwater*, 187.
81. Emezi, *Freshwater*, 70.
82. Emezi, *Freshwater*, 187.
83. Ezeiyoke, 'Beyond Postcolonial Gothic in African Literature', 489.
84. Emezi, *Freshwater*, 226.

PART IV

World-Gothic: Transregional Comparisons

CHAPTER 12

Gothic Inheritances in Oceania
Problems of Origins and Ownership
Caitlin Vandertop

Introduction: Who Owns the Gothic?

In Oceania, or the island nations of the Pacific Ocean, the gothic has been widely understood as a 'European' or 'Western' genre that fits uneasily with Indigenous experiences and worldviews. Critics have described it as 'a product of the Western mind' and an 'imaginative export' to the region; a style 'imported' and 'transplanted' to Pacific shores; and a category reflective of the 'consciousness of Europe' rather than of Indigenous aesthetics and concerns.[1] Across these critiques, there is a shared assumption that the gothic is inherently foreign to Oceanic writers: whether they 'write back' to or reject its conventions, the genre is ultimately *not theirs*.

Yet this characterisation of the gothic as a genre that originates in Europe before it is exported to the Pacific presents several problems when approached from the perspective of textual genetics. Consider the example of the 'South Seas Gothic' stories compiled in Grove Day and Kirtley's *Horror in Paradise: Grim and Uncanny Tales from Hawaii and the South Seas* (1986), which brings together 'tales of the kahuna cult of Hawaii and the witch doctors of New Guinea, ghosts on high isles and reef-decked atolls, diabolism and fatal tabus'.[2] Although the acknowledged authors of the stories are of European and European-derived descent – including popular 'South Seas' writers R. L. Stevenson, Louis Becke, Pierre Loti, Somerset Maugham, and Jack London, as well as various foreign missionaries, traders, and visitors to the region – the narratives themselves and the ghosts, spirits, demons, taboos, cults, and curses that drive them are in every instance taken from the storehouse of Oceanic orature and folklore. Given these creative origins, a description of the stories as strictly 'European' attributes too much to Europe.

The same applies to many of the now 'classic' works of South Seas Gothic. The source for Pierre Loti's gothic episode in *The Marriage of Loti*

(1880), for example, 'lies in indigenous Tahitian culture, not in the European archive of travel writing and exotic literature', its tupapa'u (devil-spirits) arising from the 'horrified nocturnal imagination' of the Polynesian storyteller, as Roslyn Jolly shows.[3] Likewise, the 'father' of South Seas Gothic, R. L. Stevenson, borrowed extensively from the 'graveyard stories' gleaned during his travels through Hawai'i and Tahiti, as well as from the rumours overheard on his estate during four years spent living in Sāmoa. While Stevenson saw the gothic arising in different regions at the same time – describing the Polynesian *aitu* as 'the near kinsman of the Transylvanian vampire' and remarking that 'we have in Europe stories of a similar complexion' – he played an active role in transforming the diversities of world folklore into a single, recognisable genre.[4] What his example makes clear is that it was never simply the creativity of individual writers that led to the consolidation of the gothic as a 'European' genre but rather their access to resources. For it was only with the assistance of missionary printers, translators, and legal teams that such authors were able to transcribe, publish, and copyright world folklore in a way that essentially converted it into individual property and profit. These writers may not have formally acknowledged the local sources upon whom they relied, but their stories were rarely the singular products of 'the European mind'.

Given that this Oceanic source material existed in oral traditions before its appropriation by European writers and the consolidation of the 'gothic' as a literary category, the narrative of the gothic as a European genre substitutes a vague idea of cultural *origins* for what is in fact a complex matter of cultural *ownership*. Yet even with the European ownership of South Seas Gothic under dispute, it would still be justified to claim that the genre, through its historic appropriation of folkloric forms, centres perspectives that fail to account for the internal complexities of island life. Nevertheless, to argue that the creative materials deriving from storytellers in nineteenth-century Tahiti or Sāmoa were purely local forms, arising endogenously to register exclusively local realities, would fail to account for the global sources of horror to which both original and transcribed materials respond. Consider, again, Stevenson's sources: the graveyard stories heard in and around his plantation. Were these local forms? As scholars have shown, the stories discussed in his letters and incorporated into his fiction – stories of spirits preying on the living, of bush-demons, and devil-women – circulated among Sāmoan communities and appeared in articles in the Sāmoan press in the 1890s.[5] Yet even here, in their local articulations and registers, these stories addressed horrors that extended well beyond village life: they incorporated rumours of violence on Sāmoa's British and German-owned plantations, the 'blackbirding' (kidnapping) of Melanesian labourers forced to work in the plantations and mines, and the runaways fearfully imagined as 'bushmen', 'savages', and 'cannibals' by Europeans and Sāmoans themselves. Situated in this context, both local stories and the European texts that incorporated them can be read as responses to the same – albeit differently experienced – world-historical situation, as waves of colonisation, enslavement, and resistance swept Sāmoa and the wider Pacific World in this period.

While scholars have acknowledged the transatlantic relations that inform the gothic's emergence in the eighteenth century, a closer account of the transpacific relations shaping its development in the nineteenth century is necessary if we wish to provincialise the genre more fully. In the case of the Atlantic World, Simon Gikandi has viewed enslavement in the Americas as a factor crucial to the genre's formation in Europe, showing how the African cosmologies transported during the Middle Passage; the occult forms such as Obeah kept alive by enslaved peoples on the plantations; and the cultures of resistance in Haiti all found their way into the 'ghost stories' of eighteenth- and nineteenth-century literature.[6] Inspired by this method, we can trace the narratives of enslavement, indenture, and resistance circling the nineteenth-century Pacific as they find their way into island folklore, village stories, and shipboard tales, before following them as they enter, from there, the gothic imaginaries of published texts such as Edgar Allan Poe's *The Narrative of Arthur Gordon Pym* (1838), Herman Melville's *Benito Cereno* (1855), R. L. Stevenson's 'The Beach of Falesá' (1892), Joseph Conrad's *Lord Jim* (1900), or Jack London's 'Mauki' (1909). Similarly, historical traces of kidnapping, trafficking, forced labour, plantation violence, and rebellion emerge in later texts such as Totaram Sanadhya's 'The Haunted Line' (1922), Vincent Eri's *The Crocodile* (1970), Albert Wendt's *Leaves of the Banyan Tree* (1979), or Subramani's *The Fantasy Eaters* (1988), where ghosts and evil spirits haunt plantations, ancestral curses shatter family lines, and predatory vampires and sorcerers deplete local foodways and island ecologies. The supernatural and monstrous figures that appear in these texts are, just as in earlier waves of Pacific culture, inspired by the terrors of colonial capitalism, the scale and violence of its transformations, and the unsettling effects of its afterlives.

Taken together, these examples complicate a European genealogy of the gothic, showing how the genre evolved in response to the horrors witnessed and experienced across the Pacific Ocean in and after the nineteenth century. Rather than separating European gothic texts from their Oceanic and folkloric intertexts, then, they can be read together as distinct but dialogic responses to the *world-historical* transformations that swept Oceania in the modern period. Situated in this context, a diversity of cultural forms can be viewed as instances of what Duncan and Cumpsty term *world-gothic*. The genre, approached in this way, becomes less a 'European' mode of classification than a critical invitation to read world folklores and their textual derivations in relation to world-historical experiences of extractivism, enclosure, dispossession, and resistance, whose effects generate distinct but connected world-gothic forms across the globe, from the Scottish Highlands to the Pacific Islands.

Taking up Duncan and Cumpsty's provocation, this chapter identifies instances of world-gothic in Oceania as they respond to these connected histories. Specifically, it interrogates the idea of the gothic as an 'inheritance' from Europe by considering how the trope of inheritance itself appears as a world-gothic theme in Oceanic writing. As critics have pointed out, inheritance has been a central motif in gothic literature from its earliest beginnings. This is evidenced by the genre's obsession with secret bloodlines, unreliable parentage, and unknown genealogies; its preoccupation with the trauma inherited by children and with violence that persists across generations; and its interest in the transmission of property, wealth, and landed titles. Jessica Cox suggests that the various 'concealed marriages, forged documents, secret wills, and hereditary maladies' populating Victorian gothic, like the sensational novel with which it overlaps, reveal 'a concern with the inheritance of wealth, property, title, and names, as well as physical and mental health and characteristics'.[7] Similarly, Kohlke and Gutleben note the 'typical Gothic intergenerational plot[s] surrounding genealogy, inheritance, contested legacies and family secrets', while Andeweg and Zlosnik argue that 'Gothic is always in some way a family matter', drawing on Anne Williams's discussion of the haunted 'house' as it refers to both 'structure' and 'family line'.[8] Likewise, Christine Berthin, borrowing from Abraham and Torok's psychoanalytic study of the 'secrets' transmitted from parents to children, asserts that 'the Gothic enacts the idea of transgenerational haunting'.[9] Each of these critics, in showing how the 'sins of the father' are visited on their direct and distant descendants in gothic literature, places anxieties of inheritance at the centre of the genre.

Similar anxieties of inheritance are visible in Oceania, where narratives of familial hauntings, paternal betrayals, and ancestral curses appear across different regions, from Sāmoa to the Marshall Islands. These narratives, this chapter will argue, can be read as examples of world-gothic insofar as they speak to the way histories of colonial-capitalist violence are 'inherited' – that is, embodied and transmitted across generations. Turning first to the contested gothic of Albert Wendt's 'Inside Us the Dead', I highlight the text's engagement with the corporeal legacies of colonial extractivism as they persist across multiple generations of the same family. In the second section, I identify a similarly world-gothic vision in Robert Barclay's *Meḷaḷ* (2002), a multigenerational novel that dramatises the enduring violence of nuclear radiation, toxicity, and the transformation of the Pacific Ocean into a deathscape by the US military. While both texts reflect on the colonial damage done to lineages, their world-gothic anxieties speak also to literature's own status: Wendt acknowledges the imposition of print itself as a technology that shapes structures of literary succession, while Barclay incorporates Oceanic mythology in a way that troubles European literary genealogies. Through their formal innovations, the texts throw into confusion literature's status as an 'inheritance' from Europe and allow for a critical reflection on the assumptions of European origins at work in gothic studies more broadly. While this chapter works against these assumptions at a methodological level by identifying connected articulations of world-gothic across regions, it also makes a case for centring the island cultures of Oceania, and the wider relations of the Pacific World, as constitutive parts of world-gothic's story.

'Inside Us the Dead': Colonial Inheritance in Wendt's World-Gothic

In his 1976 essay 'Towards a New Oceania', Albert Wendt draws on a diversity of supernatural figures to imagine predatory forces that threaten Oceania in the decades following postcolonial independence. Invoking 'the *aitu* that will continue to destroy us ... as individuals, cultures, nations', he asserts that '[w]e [Pacific Islanders] must try to exorcise these *aitu* both old and modern' as, without a process of exorcism, 'we will continue to be exploited by vampires of all colours. creeds. fangs', the most 'rapacious' of which is a homegrown species of 'elite vampires' and comprador 'revenants'.[10] The hybrid lexicon of world-gothic here, which combines *aitu,* spirits, and ancestors with revenants and vampires, mirrors a broader tendency within Wendt's work to show how different cultural and folkloric forms intersect and intermingle. By connecting Polynesian *aitu* to colonial racism and European vampires to local 'elites', he draws on this composite archive of world folklore to imagine exploitative forces that operate in and on Oceania, taking aim at both international and local 'inheritors' of the former regime.

If Wendt's world-gothic language articulates anxieties about colonial-capitalist inheritances in the decade following Sāmoan independence, these anxieties also colour the gothic features of his fiction from this period. Wendt's novel, *Leaves of the Banyan Tree* (1979), centres on a copra trader from Sāmoa who, in seeking to expand his plantation and accumulate wealth for his future heirs, inherits a colonial property regime and internalises a colonial mindset; yet, following the untimely deaths and disappearances of his children and his own subsequent infertility, he finds his lineage 'cursed' and his plantation haunted by the *aitu* he had attempted to banish to the forest. Anticipating this novel's theme of cursed genealogies, Wendt's short story collection, *Flying-Fox in a Freedom Tree* (1974), dramatises a series of inheritance crises by telling the stories of sons who are betrayed by their fathers. As in *Leaves*, these stories take aim not only at European colonisers but also at the local patriarchs with whom they collaborated by selling off inherited land. Across the texts, the plantation and the colonial house appear as gothic spaces that haunt these patriarchs with their past betrayals; much like the castle of European gothic, they embody legacies of power, property, and paternal lineage. Read in the context of land dispossession and the wider effects of the plantation system in Sāmoa, the gothic character of these spaces, with their ability to harbour vengeful *aitu* and to curse descendants, dramatises the real forms of intergenerational violence – economic, physical, environmental – that colonial property regimes inflict on future generations.

The same world-gothic preoccupation with colonial inheritances can be observed in what is perhaps Wendt's best-known work from this period, even if its gothic status has been contested: the long poem, 'Inside Us the Dead' (1976). Here Wendt imagines the spirits of the ancestors who live 'inside' him ('woven into my flesh'), beginning with the stories of Polynesian voyagers, European missionaries, and copra traders, and ending with the untimely loss of his mother, who died of cancer when he was twelve, and that of his brother in a car accident.[11] As Alice Te Punga Somerville notes, 'the collective "us" only appears once, and after that, history – genealogy – is individualized ("inside me") and personalized ("my mother, dead since I was twelve")'.[12] Asking what it means 'to say our dead are inside us', Somerville shows how the body in Wendt's poem 'becomes a site and record of inheritance'.[13] Yet while she rightly argues that there is nothing inherently 'morbid' about locating the dead 'inside' the living and goes on to emphasise the future of Indigenous bloodlines, it is worth engaging with the world-gothic aspects of the poem for what they tell us about the context of colonial capitalism evoked in the poem and in contemporaneous works including 'Towards a New Oceania' and *Leaves*. This context can be seen to inform the conspicuous centring of the body across 'Inside Us the Dead', whose images of interconnected bodies and islands anticipate what Verónica Gago has recently termed the 'body-territory', to show how colonialism, capitalism, and heteropatriarchy exploit both the land and body simultaneously.[14] The world-gothic crisis of inheritance staged in 'Inside Us the Dead' anticipates this emphasis on the body in contemporary critiques of extractivism. Going further, it dramatises the forms of intergenerational violence that are unleashed on the 'body-island' as they disrupt the formerly nourishing, reciprocal relations between the living and the dead.

The first part of 'Inside Us the Dead', titled 'Polynesians', tells the story of the poet's Polynesian forefathers (using the plural 'fathers') as they voyaged across vast regions of the Pacific Ocean. Described as 'plankton fossils in coral' and 'turtles / scuttling to beach their eggs / in fecund sand', smelling of 'dead / anemone and starfish', these ancestors are imaginatively connected to the islands they settle in a way that resists a strict separation of the living from the dead.[15] The island is likewise visualised as a living body, inseparable from the bodies of the Polynesian voyagers who have 'pierced the muscle / of the hurricane into reef's retina', travelling beyond 'the sky's impregnable shell', their 'blisters / bursting blood hibiscus / to gangrened wounds salt-stung'.[16] As blood mixes with seawater and bloody blisters merge with the land's red flora, the poem evokes the kind of physical sacrifice involved in navigating and populating new islands, doing so in a way that visually fuses the genealogy of a people with that of an island. Through these techniques, 'Polynesians' gives a literal quality to the poem's theme of 'the dead' existing 'inside' the living: like the decaying marine life that fertilises the land, the bones of the dead provide the essential nutrients, minerals, and energy needed to reproduce the life of the island and the lives of those migrating to it. Just as the ancestors tend to the earth when living, their bodies nourish the soil and, in turn, allow it to nourish future generations. There is, emphatically, nothing gothic in this section of the poem, because there is nothing to fear from the dead – they are a source of life rather than a threat to it.

Viewed in isolation, the first part of 'Inside Us the Dead' resists a gothic reading of death and the dead: rather than imagining the dead 'living on' as ghosts, vampires or zombies, it emphasises their nourishing presence in harmony with the living and, in this way, it works against the kind of anthropocentric or monotheistic separation of the living and non-living upon which gothic fears are often predicated. Yet, while 'Polynesians' condenses over ten thousand years of inter-island travel and settlement, the poem's next section, 'Missionaries', gives comparatively more attention to the European contact period that intensified in the nineteenth century, and it is here that the language of world-gothic begins to invade and colour the poem's representation of death and the dead. Towards the beginning of this section, the poet's Polynesian ancestors 'sleep waking to nightmare / ... of children unborn, sacrificed'; subsequently, the poet imagines the arrival of his European ancestors ('Inside me / the Sky-Piercers terrible as moonlight / in black and winged ships breaking') as they outlaw Polynesian gods ('into sanctuary of bleeding coral') and introduce Christianity (forcing the poet's forefathers to 'bow in the pulpit's shadow', 'waking to men / of steel hide exuding / a phosphorescent fear').[17] Just as missionaries banish the ancestral dead in the form of the 'heathen' gods who must hide away in 'bleeding coral', so the 'steel hide' of their armour, weapons, and ships forms an imaginative barrier to the porosity and reciprocity between body and island imagined earlier. The 'phosphorescent fear' evokes a force that, in glowing without heat and absorbing energy only to emit it in the form of light, disrupts the metabolic interaction between the living and non-living: instead of providing a source of nourishment, death becomes associated with the 'terror', 'fear', and 'nightmare' of a violent and premature end to life, and it is this disruption which underlies the poem's progressively gothic tone. Likewise, the early reference to the 'unborn, sacrificed' suggests a future that does not materialise and, by evoking a rupture with the previously reciprocal relationship between generations, it signals the beginning of the genealogical crisis that the rest of the poem will enact.

This narrative of genealogical decline appears more fully in the third section, 'Traders', which situates the failed fortunes of the poet's European ancestors amid the series of resource rushes that swept Sāmoa from the 1860s. Despite the ambitions of the poet's great grandfather, a German copra trader, his insatiable 'lust' for coconut oil leads to an early death: 'Too late / for a fortune, reaped a brood / of "half-castes" and then fled / for the last atoll and a whisky death. / His crew tossed him to the sharks'.[18] A similar sense of failed ambition characterises the story of his son: 'hollywood trader marooned. / Arrogant gleam in his eyes / with nowhere to sail / ... inhaling / the bitter serenity / of failure'.[19] As family fortunes are lost and inheritances squandered, the narrative echoes historical accounts of European prospectors pursuing copra fortunes only to arrive late or to lose their investments during the busts that inevitably followed commodity booms. In this way the poet's family story is coloured by the historical temporality of the resource rush: the copra fortunes of his ancestors are lost as quickly as they are made, just as the depletion of the island's resources generates an inevitable decline in fortunes as extraction leads to exhaustion, rush leads to crash. This temporality of the crash is then symbolically enacted at the end of the poem, when, after mythologising his deceased mother as a source of creativity, the poet recalls the violent death of his brother in a car accident. Having wished to become an engineer and to travel on an aeroplane, this final descendant '[slips] off / an ordinary / highway / . . . / car buckling in, like / a cannibal flower, to womb / him in / death'.[20] As ambitions to defy the laws of gravity through the combustion of fossil fuels go up in smoke, dreams of modernity and development become a nightmare, and the poem's final line dwells on the scene of the crash and the destruction of the genealogy it represents, visualising 'petrol fumes rising . . . the ball / coming down / to stone, / (breaking)'.[21]

Read in its entirety, 'Inside Us the Dead' articulates a critical perspective on European colonialism and its missionary practices, resource rushes, plantation system, and petroculture, dramatising a relatively short colonial history as a gothic incursion that threatens to derail Indigenous genealogies. From 'Missionaries' to its final line, the poem shows how the futures imagined by early Polynesian settlers, and the material practices that sustained their descendants over thousands of years of island history, are reversed over the course of a single century. As the final representative of the poet's lineage is swallowed up by a vengeful 'cannibal flower' that 'womb[s] him in death', the effects of this reversal are imagined as a gothic inversion of reproductive order, mirroring the poem's images of damaged relations between dead and living, ancestors and descendants, past and future generations. Yet even as Wendt dramatises the damage caused by colonial inheritances, he enacts a 'break' with them at an epistemic level. Specifically, the poem's final image of a ball shattering as it hits the ground mirrors an earlier image of the glass eye inherited by the poet's grandfather: 'blue glass / eye – crystal ball of Europe . . . buried under / a palm, a fitting monument / to his father's copra lust'.[22] This glass eye – a 'crystal ball' that projects Europe's visions of future prosperity onto the islands – is quite literally a mode of seeing that enables the copra trader to scan the horizon for coconuts, viewing each passing island as nothing but a locus of extractable resources. The inherited glass eye here becomes a metonym for the inheritance of a colonial property regime, whose extractivist mode of seeing requires the separation of living bodies from the 'dead' islands and ancestors that nourish them. 'Inside Us the Dead', which insists that the dead are alive 'within us', works against these divisions and breaks with the modes of seeing that are – like the glass eye itself – the poet's colonial inheritance.

Gothic Lineages in the Post-Nuclear Pacific

A similarly world-gothic vision can be found in Robert Barclay's *Meḷaḷ* (2002), a novel preoccupied with the legacies of nuclear radiation, toxicity, and the militarisation of the Pacific. *Meḷaḷ* tells the story of three generations of the same family in the Marshall Islands. Set during the independence period, its events take place on Good Friday 1981, yet it also weaves together a parallel narrative gleaned from ancient Oceanic mythology, which sketches a genealogy of the islands and dramatises their imminent threat from a set of demonic, cannibalistic forces. The name 'Meḷaḷ', as the epigraph explains, derives from an archaic Marshallese word for 'playground of demons and place uninhabitable by people'.[23] The title evokes the novel's depiction of Kwajalein Atoll – the site of over sixty nuclear weapons tested by the US military from 1946–58, which included the first hydrogen bomb – and more specifically its setting on the island of Ebeye. Here, the novel draws out the vast, visible differences between the US army base at Kwajalein, which provides a habitable, modern, and sanitary place of work and residence for those Americans permitted to remain, and neighbouring Ebeye, an impoverished, overpopulated, and ecologically devastated urban centre that was largely the creation of the US military, established to house Marshallese day labourers following the evacuation of their contaminated homelands.

Critics have commented on the novel's use of the gothic to register the violence of colonisation, noting how the successive waves of Spanish, British, German, Japanese, and American colonisers who targeted the islands from the sixteenth century onwards brought foreign pathogens, viruses, and toxins that had a devastating effect on Marshallese populations. The novel's gothic figures – a group of archaic, grotesque demons who appear periodically throughout the text – are described as 'hateful curses' that 'seep' into the island surface to turn everything into poison, sickness, and waste: 'Staining the water as if from a thin green gruel leaking out from under a bloated corpse on the beach', they spread the 'curse' of 'infection, pollution, perversions'.[24] Compared frequently to sea-slugs sucking the reef, these demons are parasitic forces intent on 'wringing death from life' and producing 'stinking rot and ruin, a living death, life inside-out'.[25] Hannah Straß, who views *Meḷaḷ* as a work of 'postcolonial toxic Gothic', reads the demons as symbols of toxicity which attest to the 'persistent, contaminating and corroding effects of the environmental degradation that is part and parcel of colonialism'.[26] Placing a similar emphasis on environmental damage, Sharae Deckard reads the novel as an 'Ecogothic' engagement with 'the unravelling of the whole web of life as a result of nuclear colonialism'.[27] For Deckard, 'one of the most powerful aesthetic effects of Ecogothic' is its ability 'to offer a portal into the contemporary imagination of compound ecological crises with complex temporal antecedents, to materialise with an uncanny immediacy those revenants of "undead" processes in the past that continue to shape contemporary environments'.[28] Although *Melal*'s demonic spirits are invisible to its characters, they steadily encroach on the world of the living and threaten to consume it. Much like the legacies of nuclear colonialism, they haunt those places rendered 'uninhabitable' with violent pasts that refuse to go away.

While then *Melal* has been described as a work of 'postcolonial gothic', 'toxic gothic', and 'Ecogothic', it can also be read as an example of *world-gothic* insofar as it draws on representations of mythic monstrosity from Oceanic culture to explore the world-historical effects of nuclear colonialism. Specifically, it draws on world-gothic to highlight a form of intergenerational violence that, as in Wendt's 'Inside Us the Dead', disrupts the formerly reciprocal interactions between living and dead, or future and past generations, in Oceania. The novel's demons, which resemble 'bloated corpse[s]', refuse to depart the world of the living and threaten to 'pollute' and 'corrupt' it; similarly, they are described as a 'curse' throughout the novel, which suggests that, like radiation as it arrests biological lifecycles and causes chromosomal damage, they interrupt the lifecycles of existing generations and inhibit the possibilities of future ones. These disruptions also threaten the unborn, as we see in the novel's depiction of 'jellyfish babies' or 'what some Marshallese women called monster babies because they looked inside-out'.[29] The mother of the protagonist, Jebro, is taken to a US military ship with other 'radiated people' for testing before she suffers numerous miscarriages, the final one killing her three years after the conception of Jebro's younger brother, Nuke.[30] Just as toxicity here claims the life of Jebro's mother, so it leads to the dispossession of his matrilineal land: Jebro notes that he can never return to the island of his mother's birth, Rongelap, due to the fact that it has been poisoned.[31] He also reveals that he is unable to visit Tar-Woj – 'island of my birth, where coconuts, pandanus, and breadfruits fall to the ground and rot because that is the Americans' law'[32]– due to its use as a missile testing site. Describing 'the bomb' as an 'inheritance' that destroys both the land and the lives of those inhabiting it,³³ he imagines colonialism as a form of genealogical violence that disinherits living generations of their ancestral land and deprives them of its sources of nourishment. In this way, it is both a 'cursed inheritance' that unleashes violence on future generations and a form of collective matricide that deprives existing generations of sustenance from the natal body and the natal land.

Through this emphasis on intergenerational violence, *Meḷaḷ* shows how future generations are separated from their ancestors, not only in the form of land dispossession and contamination but also insofar as they are unable to inherit the knowledges previously preserved through oral transmission and cultural practices such as tattooing and weaving. Jebro mentions the secret fishing techniques known to his grandfather – the whereabouts of octopus holes, how to swim with sharks – but laments that his own father failed to transmit these knowledges due to his missionary indoctrination. This erasure is further alluded to when one of the novel's mythical beings, the dwarf Noniep, embeds his ancestral knowledge in the land by chanting into a breadfruit tree, doing so on an island targeted for missile testing. Noniep chants the region's history, from ancient stories of creation to the dragging of 'basalt stones ... into the ocean by angry missionaries', and from the arrival of the Spanish ('who claimed the island and promised life through Christ and gave death by syphilis') to that of the Germans (who brought 'mumps and measles and TB') and the Americans ('who brought the bomb and jellyfish babies and Happy Days on TV').³⁴ Showing how each of these encounters promises life but brings early death, Noniep reflects on the fact that the ancestral healing and medicinal practices abolished by missionaries could have provided a salve for burns. This idea that the dead could have aided the living becomes critical to the plot when a group of American teenagers sink the boat carrying Jebro and Nuke: as the latter attempt unsuccessfully to paddle to safety, it occurs to Jebro that his grandfather would have known which tidal currents to swim against, but that there is no way of acquiring that knowledge now.

Across these examples, the incursion of world-gothic can be seen to register the violence that separates future generations from their ancestors, presenting nuclear colonialism as a dark inheritance that bestows toxicity instead of nourishment, infertility instead of reproductive futurity, extinction instead of genealogical continuity, death instead of life. This threat grows towards the end of *Meḷaḷ* as the demons arrive on canoes to consume the lives of all the inhabitants of Ebeye. While some scholars have criticised the way that mythological forces intervene at the end of the novel – when, at the last minute, the trickster figure Etao diverts an American missile to kill the demons – others have understood the novel's mythological interventions as a mode of valorising Indigenous accounts of the region. Anthony Carrigan, for example, argues that '*Meḷaḷ* indigenizes this assault on local sovereignty through a process of mythopoiesis which reconfigures nuclearization as part of the historical battles staged in the richly textured spirit-world'.[35] Equally, the novel's incorporation of the spirits of the dead as narrative agents can be read historically as an attempt to work against colonialism's intergenerational violence. *Meḷaḷ* notably concludes with the fate not of Ebeye's living inhabitants but of its dead: in the final paragraph, a flotilla of 'sunken spirit canoes' surfaces to release the dead among the living and to restore them to the islands from which they were banished, and in the final sentence Noniep brings the souls of the 'jellyfish babies' into his canoe.[36] By concluding in this way, the novel recognises those future generations that never materialised, or those genealogies that were never permitted to flourish, and it attempts to restore both the ancestors and the unborn to the living environments of which they are a part. In a strong echo of Wendt's 'Inside Us the Dead', it shows how colonialism entails a gothic derailing of the reciprocal relations between living and dead; yet it also insists, against this, on the latter's living presence.

Conclusion: Oceania Under the Sign of World-Gothic

This chapter has associated world-gothic in Oceania with the problem of colonial inheritance, identifying genealogical disturbances, temporal disruptions, archaic demons, violent ancestors, and inverted relations between living and dead as they mediate the effects of colonial-capitalist violence across the connected scales of islands, bodies, and generations. Through their world-gothic interventions, 'Inside Us the Dead' and *Meḷaḷ* show how the inheritances of the colonial era unleash lasting forms of toxicity and damage; yet by incorporating the voices of the dead into the narrative present, they also work against the ways of seeing and knowing 'inherited' from the colonial past.

In reading texts from Oceania as instances of world-gothic, this chapter does not suggest that they borrow from a 'European' literary tradition. Rather, it argues that to read the gothic as a European import is to overlook the histories of cultural encounter and exchange that brought world folklores into contact, as 'ghost stories' and 'uncanny tales' made their way from island to island and ship to ship, travelling from the Black Forest and the Scottish Highlands to Sāmoan villages and back again. To describe the gothic as European, in this context, would be to minimise the extent to which those texts 'officially' associated with the genre borrow from a wealth of folkloric and pre-copyrighted materials (as the example of South Seas Gothic, with its liberal use of Pacific plantation stories and village tales, suggests). By reading a diversity of texts under the sign of world-gothic, this chapter works against the narrative of the gothic's emergence in Europe 'first' to instead prioritise the world-historical relations that shape texts published in Europe *and* the world-cultural forms from which they frequently borrow.

In fact, when read closely, world-gothic texts direct our attention to the specific textual mechanisms by which Europe claims its originary status in the genealogical hierarchy. Wendt, for example, is highly attentive to the historic imposition of colonial publishing, print, and the cultural property regimes that allow writers to convert Polynesian orature into genres such as South Seas Gothic. While 'Inside Us the Dead' reclaims island genealogies against the extractive forces that threaten to erase them, the poem is also keenly aware of its own status as a text written and published in English, and in this way it gestures to the problem of its own colonial 'inheritance' in textual terms. Just as elements of world-gothic first appear in 'Missionaries', it is in this section that the establishment of an attendant regime of colonial textuality becomes visible: 'Calico. Axe. Words / captured in print / like bird footprints / on the white sand / of my breath ... Beads. Tobacco. Knives. / Nails for each palm cross'.[37] Words here mingle with commodities and weapons, prints become footprints, and language is transformed into something capable of leaving an imprint on both the island and the body of the poet, whose 'breath' is 'captured in print'. This vision of the 'nailing' down of orature into writing reveals how literature and the larger cultural property regime of which it is a part enshrine a genealogy according to which certain genres can claim to emerge in Europe 'first'. The 'capture' of breath by print, in other words, gestures to the material processes – textualisation, adaptation, the legal acquisition of authorship – by which genres such as the gothic become European in the first place. In evoking the violence of writing as it 'captures' breath in print, Wendt acknowledges literature's own status as a colonial institution of which the text is inheritor.

While *Melal* is less overtly attentive to the colonial politics of textuality, the novel's attempt to narrate the history of the region through Indigenous mythopoesis allows for a similar challenge to European literary genealogies. Amid the various episodes of Oceanic history orated by Noniep, the entry of the first European ships in the Marshall Islands is described by the trickster figure, Etao, as an arrival of 'demons'. He observes that these demons 'didn't know how to speak'; they had skin red 'like the skin of a cooked pig', and they looked hungry, unclean, and thin, their eyes betraying 'a hungry fear' – the hunger of the 'runt too often denied its turn at the teat'.[38] Through this description of European contact, the narrative inverts early gothic narratives of the Pacific which, as Smith-Browne shows, represented Pacific Islanders as fearsome, hungry 'cannibals' and 'wild' Goths (themselves described as 'hard, ferocious' barbarians whose 'poor soil' made them accustomed to hunger).[39] In *Meḷaḷ*, it is not the Islanders but the colonisers who fit this description, their demonic appearance arising from an insatiable hunger itself driven by a deprivation from natal sustenance following the enclosures and extractions visited on their own lands. In shifting the perspective from the ship to the island, the text does not appropriate a 'European' gothic for a postcolonial project so much as articulate corresponding visions, rooted in Oceanic folklore, of world-historical contact driven by a rapaciousness that threatens, cannibalistically, the integrity of the body and land.

By way of conclusion, it is worth pointing out that to argue against the narrative of the gothic's emergence in Europe is not simply to make a case for alternative claims to property rights and cultural ownership. Rather, it is to highlight the world-historical transformations and global social relations that have produced 'European' culture and from which it cannot be separated. And while this chapter has worked against narratives of European origins by identifying connected expressions of world-gothic across regions, it has also made a case for centring the islands of Oceania, and the wider relations of the Pacific World, as constitutive parts of world-gothic's story.

Notes

1. Stephanie Smith-Browne, *Gothic and the Pacific Voyage: Patriotism, Romance, and Savagery in South Seas Travels and the Utopia of the Terra Australis*, PhD diss., Princeton University, 2007, iii; Gerry Turcotte, 'Postcolonial Gothic: Australia, Canada, New Zealand, South Pacific', in C. A. Howells, P. Sharrad, and G. Turcotte (eds.), *The Oxford History of the Novel in English, volume 12: The Novel in Australia, Canada, New Zealand, and the South Pacific Since 1950*, Oxford, Oxford University Press, 2017, 206; Mudrooroo (Colin Johnson), cited in Turcotte, 'Postcolonial Gothic', 217; Alice Te Punga Somerville, 'Inside Us the Unborn: Genealogies, Futures, Metaphors, and the Opposite of Zombies', in W. Anderson, M. Johnson, and B. Brookes (eds.), *Pacific Futures*, Honolulu, University of Hawai'i Press, 2018.

2. A Grove Day and Bacil F. Kirtley, *Horror in Paradise: Grim and Uncanny Tales from Hawaii and the South Seas*, Honolulu, Mutual Publishing, 1986.
3. Roslyn Jolly, 'South Seas Gothic: Pierre Loti and Robert Louis Stevenson', *English Literature in Transition, 1880–1920*, 47:1 (2004), 28–49, 31.
4. Robert Louis Stevenson, *In the South Seas*, London, Chatto & Windus, 1900, 196.
5. Carla Manfredi, 'R. L. Stevenson's Samoan Gothic: Representing Late Nineteenth-Century Plantations', *Pacific Studies* 39:3 (2016), 343–69.
6. Simon Gikandi, *Slavery and the Culture of Taste*, Princeton, Princeton University Press, 2011.
7. Cited in Emily Horton, *21st-Century British Gothic: The Monstrous, Spectral, and Uncanny in Contemporary Fiction*, London, Bloomsbury Academic, 2024, 70–1.
8. Cited in Horton, *21st-Century British Gothic*, 73; Agnes Andeweg and Sue Zlosnik, 'Introduction', in A. Andeweg and S. Zlosnik (eds.), *Gothic Kinship*, Manchester, Manchester University Press, 2013, 1.
9. Christine Berthin, *Gothic Hauntings: Melancholy Crypts and Textual Ghosts*, London, Palgrave 2010, 9.
10. Albert Wendt, 'Towards a New Oceania', *Mana Review*, 1:1 (1976), 49–60, 51–3.
11. Albert Wendt, 'Inside Us the Dead', in Robert Borofsky (ed.), *Remembrance of Pacific Pasts: An Invitation to Remake History*, Honolulu, University of Hawai'i Press, 2000, 35. Hereafter references to this text are given in parentheses.
12. Somerville, 'Inside Us the Unborn', 71.
13. Somerville, 'Inside Us the Unborn, 71–7.
14. Verónica Gago, *Feminist International: How to Change Everything*, trans. L. Mason-Deese, London, Verso, 2020.
15. Wendt, 'Inside Us the Dead', 35–6.
16. Wendt, 'Inside Us the Dead', 36.
17. Wendt, 'Inside Us the Dead', 36–7.
18. Wendt, 'Inside Us the Dead', 38–9.
19. Wendt, 'Inside Us the Dead', 39.
20. Wendt, 'Inside Us the Dead', 41–2.
21. Wendt, 'Inside Us the Dead', 42.
22. Wendt, 'Inside Us the Dead', 39.
23. Robert Barclay, *Meļaļ: A Novel of the Pacific*, Honolulu, University of Hawai'i Press, 2002.
24. Barclay, *Meļaļ*, 14.
25. Barclay, *Meļaļ*, 14.
26. Hannah Straß, '"A Living Death, Life Inside-Out": The Postcolonial Toxic Gothic in Robert Barclay's *Meļaļ: A Novel of the Pacific*', in J. Habjan and F. Imlinger (eds.), *Globalizing Literary Genres*, London, Routledge, 2016, 228.
27. Sharae Deckard, 'EcoGothic', in M. Wester and X. A. Reyes (eds.), *Twenty-First-Century Gothic: An Edinburgh Companion*, Edinburgh, Edinburgh University Press, 2019, 186.
28. Deckard, 'EcoGothic', 186.

29. Barclay, *Meḷaḷ*, 82.
30. Barclay, *Meḷaḷ*, 21.
31. Barclay, *Meḷaḷ*, 78–9.
32. Barclay, *Meḷaḷ*, 10.
33. Barclay, *Meḷaḷ*, 80.
34. Barclay, *Meḷaḷ*, 84–6.
35. Anthony Carrigan, 'Postcolonial Disaster, Pacific Nuclearization, and Disabling Environments', *Journal of Literary & Cultural Disability Studies*, 4:3 (2010), 261.
36. Barclay, *Meḷaḷ*, 296.
37. Wendt, 'Inside Us the Dead', 38.
38. Barclay, *Meḷaḷ*, 65–6.
39. Smith-Browne cites Anders Sparrman, the botanist aboard Cook's H. M. S. Resolution during his 1772–5 voyage, and Tacitus on Germanic Goths, in *Gothic and the Pacific Voyage* (52; 3–4).

CHAPTER 13

Tough Oil Gothic
Contemporary Petrofiction across the North–South Divide

Karl Emil Rosenbæk Reetz

This chapter explores world-gothic forms and figurations relating to the enclosure, extraction, and global distribution of oil in contemporary literary fiction from Denmark and Nigeria. Touching on key issues of visibility, vulnerability, and world-systemic interrelation, the chapter argues that gothic as a form of irrealism excels in revealing the bewildering experience of a lifeworld remade around fossil fuels. As fossil extraction is undeniably experienced in hugely unequal ways across the world-system, this chapter highlights the need for cross-hemispheric readings of contemporary petrofiction to identify and relate these differences. Sharae Deckard writes, with reference to Jason W. Moore's 'synthesis of Marxist ecology and world-systems theories', that 'late capitalism is mired in a crisis of "cheap nature"'.[1] With this in mind, I argue that comparative readings across the Global North–Global South divide provide insights into shifting world-systemic dynamics. In our particular age of declining cheap natures – of exhausted commodity frontiers and tougher measures to procure previously unavailable (and/or profitable) resources – these oil texts reveal how the longstanding socially exploitative and ecologically eroded conditions in the Niger Delta are slowly seeping from peripheral oil sites to core regions. As such, these world-gothic petrofictions anticipate a Global North future that resembles the present-day realities of the Global South.

The Nordics and West Africa

Geographically, Null Island – the cartographical point where the prime meridian and the equator intersect – is located in the Gulf of Guinea off the West African coast. This island and its surroundings constitute the centre of the globe: 0°N 0°E. During the long centuries of colonialism, the centrality of the West African region was chiefly expressed by its function as a provider of resources to European powers. By way of the Danish West

India-Guinea Company, the North Sea marine state of Denmark (of which Norway was a part until 1814) exploited the so-called 'Gold Coast' of West Africa for transatlantic trade. At the zenith of colonialism in the eighteenth and nineteenth centuries, gold, spices, and enslaved people linked the North Sea to the Gulf of Guinea as a consequence of the expansion of the capitalist 'modern world-system' of trade, commerce, and unequal wealth accumulation from its European and American cradle.[2] Like the Caribbean, the Gulf of Guinea has therefore long signified 'a space of trauma, a "living graveyard" choked with the debris of history'.[3] And now, despite the putative hemispheric line that divides them, modernity's commodity par excellence – fossil fuel – once again aligns these two regions within the much larger net of the contemporary petrocapitalist world-system.

The Gulf of Guinea, seat of numerous multinational oil conglomerates, holds as much as a tenth of the world's oil reserves. Similarly, the North Sea is one of the most industrialised seas in the world, with fossil extraction as a main enterprise.[4] The material, social, cultural, environmental, and economic experience of the petroeconomy is, however, markedly different across the two regions. As these figures illustrate, the colonial relations of power live on today, since the Nordics are relatively insulated from human exploitation and ecological corrosion, as well as from the climatic and ecosystemic shifts arising from carbon emissions that stem from the burning of fossil fuels. This is crucially not the case in West Africa. According to the 2022 Sixth Assessment from the IPCC, the two main nations at question here, Denmark and Nigeria, sit at opposite ends of the chart depicting the 'human vulnerability to climate change'. Denmark's 'relative vulnerability' sits in the 'very low' range, while Nigeria's is in the 'very high'.[5] Equally, in relation to social and material conditions, the global measurement for the distribution of wealth within an economy – the Gini-index – also indicates a higher degree of inequality in Nigeria (35.1) contra Denmark (28.3).[6] So, while both nations are producers of fossil fuels – that is, oil nations – the social and ecological effects of the oil system are experienced very differently in each place. In general, the Nordic oil enterprise which began in the late 1960s is closely related to the nation-building origin-story of Nordic post-war social welfare states securing a high degree of social equality, safety, and governmental trust. In West Africa, on the contrary, oil exploration began under British rule and has continued in the postcolonial present, with extremely deleterious socio-ecological consequences. Indeed, West Africa continues to function as a site of colonial conquest and resource extraction, as the petroeconomy has done little to ameliorate inequalities established during this earlier period of plunder. Even though the Nordics and West Africa share a direct economic dependency on oil, it is therefore obvious that these two regions also demonstrate the vastly unequal ways in which the social and ecological reality of oil and its consequences are lived.

In this context, where experiences of oil are highly uneven but interconnected, the challenge is to make the global petroeconomy visible, by foregrounding, as Judith Butler does in *Frames of War* (2009), the question of whose lives are grievable. The relevance of this question of framing becomes obvious when considering the media attention allocated to events in the Global North, as opposed to similar events in the Global South. As argued by Rob Nixon in his formative *Slow Violence* (2011), the disclosure of inevitable environmental damages associated with the extraction and processing of fossil fuels, for instance, varies immensely.[7] Consider the due attention given to the oil leak from Exxon Valdez in 1989 or the Deepwater Horizon blowout in 2010 compared to the infinitesimal media coverage of the Niger Delta, where leaks of oil the size of the Exxon Valdez spill (approximately 37,000 tonnes) have occurred annually over the past fifty years. As a government official from Eket, Nigeria says: 'We don't have an international media to cover us, so nobody cares about it . . . Whatever cry we cry is not heard outside of here.'[8] This hierarchical division of lives, of value, and worth, this basic epistemological question of whether one's life is considered 'lose-able and injurable', keeps returning as colonial debris washes up on the beaches of an allegedly postcolonial world.[9] Thus, the overall tenor of cultural and economic geopolitics regarding fossil-fuel extraction clearly debunk a neoliberal, flat-earth notion of a globalised 'level playing field', as they emphasise the intersection of global inequality and oil extraction.[10] Examining the position of Nigeria within this late globalised world of alleged free trade and fair competition, Michael Watts explores 'the violence that surrounds oil' and its uneven distribution. Watts underscores the issue of framing in the global context and stipulates that 'petro-violence is in fact rarely off the front pages of the press' precisely *because* petro-violence predominantly takes place at peripheral sites within the capitalist world-system.[11]

When it comes to literary fiction, I argue, the grand socio-economic, geoenvironmental, and geopolitical spectra of global oil are closely connected to both form and content. As such, contemporary literary fiction is best understood – implicitly or explicitly – as a registration of the last decades' neoliberal order and its claimed, but crucially undelivered commitment to ensure fairness across the board. Understanding the production of a specific work of fiction as intricately related to the world-systemic position of the author of said work helps to shed light on the differences in literary style spanning the globe. More remarkable still is the way in which aesthetics seem to recur across differently located texts in an uneven yet combined relation. And this, I argue, is increasingly the case when the obscure, gothic matter of fossil enters the works of fiction.

Tough Oil and the World-Ecology

To conceptualise how oil extraction and climate change shape the Nordic region and West Africa in unequal but connected ways, the chapter draws on environmental historian Jason W. Moore's concept of the 'world-ecology'.[12] This notion refers to a set of transregional relationships, in which certain (peripheralised) parts of the world provide the cheap labour and resources from which other (core) regions benefit, and to which they have historically gained access through colonial rule. David Orr provides a vivid depiction of this continued colonial relation as he writes: 'Show me the hamburger stands, neon ticky-tacky strips leading toward every city in America, and the shopping malls, and I'll show you devastated rain forests, a decaying countryside, a politically dependent population, and toxic waste dumps. It is all of a fabric.'[13] In other words, the effects of climate change are felt most intensely across the postcolonial Global South precisely because the long history of social and environmental plunder has rendered these regions more vulnerable to environmental and economic crises.

The world-ecology concept helps to clarify how a history of colonisation underpins the different experiences of oil across the Nordics and West Africa, but it also provides insight into the geopolitically tense and environmentally harmful expansionist efforts currently underway in the North Sea and further north into Arctic waters. Now that the relatively easily accessible sites of 'cheap natures' from which oil and other commodities have so far been extracted are increasingly depleted, new extraction sites are needed. Paralleling the intensified effort to extract every last drop from the peripheries regardless of the nations' peoples and environments, a heightened 'post-oil anxiety' of the late twentieth century onwards has also led to a more risk-averse approach to oil extraction at the cores.[14] Alongside the historic and nostalgic (and environmentally devastating) sight of pumpjacks on American soil, new techniques have ensured the extraction of oil at core sites by way of hydraulic fracturing along with tar sands mining (with the largest tar sand deposit being located in Alberta, Canada) and developments within Arctic- and ultra-deepwater drilling.

Combined, these methods are critically referred to as 'Tough Oil', emphasising both their ability to reach deposits hitherto rendered inaccessible *and* their increased harmfulness to the environment as a consequence. As Jennifer Wenzel says: 'The oil era isn't over, but the era of easy oil is likely gone forever.'[15] But as Sharae Deckard reminds us, Tough Oil is by no measure limited to the core. On the contrary, Deckard writes that 'extreme extractivism' seems to reinforce 'core–periphery relations across the world-ecology'. Even so, Deckard also explains that Tough Oil in the Global North *has* brought forth environmental destruction that used to be confined to the Global South.[16] In other words, cheap raw materials are now being harvested from the economic centres themselves, meaning that these regions are beginning to encounter experiences that the colonised societies have lived through for decades. In this context, a cross-hemispheric world-gothic reading of Nigerian and Danish petrofiction becomes urgent.

Experiences of oil are reported in journalism and non-fiction accounts, but they are also narrated through literary texts that provide a different and complementary perspective on how oil, oil extraction, and the climate emergency are lived in different parts of the world. Yet so far, despite the transnational character of energy production and trade, both Nordic and West African petroculture studies have maintained a largely regional focus, meaning that the productive possibilities of addressing fiction from these areas together have so far been overlooked.[17] This chapter is therefore an attempt to read across the Global North–Global South divide and carve out a common approach to the matter of oil from two utterly disparate regions of the petrocapitalist world-system.

Gothic Irrealism

Building on the world-literary method developed by the Warwick Research Collective (WReC), Michael Niblett, Graeme Macdonald, Treasa de Loughry, Sharae Deckard, Stephen Shapiro, Jennifer Wenzel, and others, this chapter reads a small sample of literary texts as part of a larger discussion concerning the combined and uneven distribution and exchange of natural resources and aesthetic forms. As such, the argument I propose follows the trajectory of gothic irrealism: a formal response to processes of socio-ecological extraction and exploitation under capitalism. According to the WReC, formal deviations from realism can often be understood as encoding the experience of socio-ecological inequality from the vantage of the world's peripheralised regions. What the WReC call 'irrealism' is exemplified by 'anti-linear plot lines, meta-narratorial devices, un-rounded characters, unreliable narrators, [and] contradictory points of view' – characteristics that tend to appear 'wherever literary works are composed that mediate the lived experience of capitalism's bewildering creative destruction (or destructive creation)'.[18]

The fossil capitalist world-system and its reliance on colonial relations of exploitation and ecological desecration undergirds the thematisation and registration of oil from the Global South. As such, it is perhaps not surprising that a violent and dark tone of gothic horror is often present in oil texts from this region. However, what seems more striking and telling regarding our contemporary state of ongoing and escalating ecocide is the fact that literary production from core regions appears increasingly to be addressing oil via the same uneasy techniques: an irrealist gothic residue has travelled in Tough Oil's wake. What we are beginning to see are oil narratives from the core registering and commenting on their own societies' unfolding peripheralisation. The pertinent question examined in this chapter is therefore: Do the experiences and literary registrations of the periphery reveal the future of the core?

To explore this possibility, I focus on a short story by the Nigerian-American author Nnedi Okorafor – 'Spider the Artist' – along with two recent texts from Denmark that touch on offshore oil, namely, Jesper Brygger's collection of poems *Transporterne* (2017; *The Transporters*) and Gitte Broeng and Lasse Krog Møller's very short monologue *Mare* (2023). Other Nigerian texts of relevance could be Helen Habila's *Oil on Water* (2010), Imbolo Mbue's *How Beautiful We Were* (2021), or Ben Okri's 'What the Tapster Saw' (1986). Just as the work of the Danish author Ursula Scavenius (2015, 2020) would benefit from a world-gothic reading. But for this article, the focus is on Okorafor, Brygger, and Broeng and Møller.

As Hugh Charles O'Connell writes, Okorafor excels in 'African SF' that '[challenges] the hegemony of SF as a purely Western, metropolitan genre'.[19] Formally, I argue that she does this by introducing gothic elements to her SF tales. Specifically, this means that her stories often linger on the *visceral* and *monstrous* effects of local incorporation into the capitalist world-system. This is especially evident when her narratives turn to oil – a substance that in the context of Nigeria is inextricably connected to the wetlands of the Niger Delta. Similarly, I argue that recent texts from Denmark touching upon offshore oil enterprise likewise express a tendency towards the gothic register, however here there is a focus on the eerie, the obscure, and the uncanny.

Niger Delta Gothic

'My mother's grandmother was known for lying on the pipeline running through her village. She'd stay like that for hours, listening and wondering what magical fluids were running through the large never-ending steel tubes. This was before the Zombies, of course. I laughed. If she tried to lie on a pipeline now she'd be brutally killed.'[20] These lines are from Okorafor's short story 'Spider the Artist' (2014). The story tells of a woman living in a small village in the Niger Delta. She is violently abused by her husband, who is a member of the 'Niger Delta People's Movement', which is concerned with the illegal bunkering of crude oil and other activities aimed at resisting and countering the infringement by foreign oil companies in the Niger Delta. In that sense, Okorafor's story echoes Philip Aghoghovwia's declaration that: 'To write about Nigeria in relation to energy and culture is to write about the Niger Delta.'[21]

Interconnecting the larger story of foreign abuse of local natural resources to the detriment of the local communities with abuse of women in the impoverished rural Niger Delta, the protagonist of the story hides out from her husband in front of the pipelines that run through the bushes behind their house. In this way, the text points to the interrelationship between (neo)colonial extractivism and patriarchy – as both nature and women are treated as exploitable and expendable in ways that corrode them – a point made by Esthie Hugo's reading of Mies in Chapter 3 in this collection.[22] But what begins as a rather grim social realist text about the connections between domestic abuse, social and environmental degradation, and the extraction of natural resources (explicitly identified by Okorafor as exclusively benefiting the United States), quickly shifts into a more speculative – and specifically a gothic – register when the so-called Zombies enter the scene. The reader discovers that rather than the undead brain-eaters of blockbuster zombie horror, these creatures are eight-legged robot soldiers who patrol the pipeline, programmed to sense its every vibration and designed to annihilate the intruder: 'It is said that Zombies can think. Artificial Intelligence, this is called ... Zombies kill anyone who touches the pipelines'.[23] The figure of the zombie is first and foremost a reference to the local vernacular term for the Nigerian military's methods and overreach.[24] Yet, it also signals Okorafor's conscious investment in discourses of the gothic, while suggesting a broader connection to the African occult, where the zombie frequently appears as an undead labouring body. As David McNally has influentially argued, the plenitude of such zombies in recurring folktales and urban legend across the continent should be understood as an effort to give perceptible shape to experiences of neoliberal capitalism, which subject humans (in Africa and elsewhere) to bewildering conditions of extreme exploitation and precarity.[25]

Published in 2014, Okorafor's text stands out as an eerie foreshadowing of subsequent developments in Nigeria. In 2022, the Vice President Yemi Osinbajo presented the official launch of the first humanoid robot using ominously extractivist language. Osinbajo references 'intensify[ing] efforts at harnessing talents among Nigerian youths in the area of Artificial Intelligence (AI), for national development', as well as a 'need to encourage our indigenous African technology by encouraging our people to be digitally visible and get the data available for the artificial intelligence' – the latter, poorly disguising a desire to extend the reach of government surveillance. Viewed in this light, the future potentials of the humanoid robot may make one wary. In Osinbajo's presentation, the applicability of AI robots ranged from being able to 'farm [and] teach in classes', to 'the construction of road and cities' and all the way to more militaristic purposes such as 'intelligence gathering, detection of bombs and in fighting insecurity'.[26]

With this example of gothic foreshadowing in mind, Okorafor's description in her short story of the creation of the spider robots sits even more uneasily for the reader: 'The government came up with the idea. To create Zombies, and Shell, Chevron, and a few other oil companies (who were just as desperate) supplied the money to pay for it all'. Okorafor's narrator continues: 'The Zombies were made to combat pipeline bunkering and terrorism. It makes me laugh. The government and the oil people destroyed our land and dug up our oil, then they created robots to keep us from taking it back'.[27] In 2015, Okorafor reintroduces the robots in her sci-fi novel *The Book of Phoenix*: 'the Nigerian government's engineers created the prototype. Can you imagine? We came up with these things ourselves FOR ourselves. We're so colonized that we build our own shackles.' The narrative continues, with tongue firmly in cheek: 'Some young engineer ... came up with the idea after reading a science fiction story about robot spiders guarding the pipelines in Niger Delta. Life imitating art, except this particular story was actually *critiquing* the government, not giving them a blueprint. The author must be rolling in her grave.'[28]

As for the nickname 'Zombie', we learn that this is indebted precisely to the local folklore. 'They were originally called Anansi Droids 419 but we call them "*oyibo* contraption" and, most often, Zombie, the same name we call those "kill-and-go" soldiers who come in here harassing us every time something bites their brains'.[29] Likewise, in her depiction of the question of multinational oil extraction and local resistance, Okorafor mobilises the gothic vocabulary of urban legend, which resonates with McNally's analysis: 'When the Zombies were first released, no one knew about them. All people would hear were rumors about people getting torn apart near pipelines or sightings of giant white spiders in the night. Or you'd hear about huge pipeline explosions, charred bodies everywhere. But the pipeline where the bodies lay would be perfectly intact'.[30] The spectacle of arachnid monstrosity – with the added component of extra-human intelligence granted by the artificial intelligence – also draws clearly on ecohorror tales of beasts and a human fear for the natural (and the technological) world.

Yet, as the story progresses, the protagonist befriends one of these spiders, meeting up with it in secret at the pipelines where they play guitar together. As their friendship develops, we learn that 'a group of Zombies' also begins to turn against the oil workers and soldiers by attacking them deep in the Delta: 'Ten of the men were torn limb from limb, their bloody remains scattered all over the swampy land. Those who escaped told the reporters that nothing would stop the Zombies'.[31] Amidst these incidents of robot killings, the friendship between the woman and the spider evolves further. The spider even teaches her to play such 'beautiful music' that the woman notes that her husband has not 'laid a heavy hand on [her] in weeks'. Furthermore, before she met the spider, she had been trying to conceive a baby for three years without success, but now she again begins 'to hope. To hope for a baby'.[32] Here again, one cannot miss the story's alignment of the woman's difficulty in conceiving with the plunder of the land by the foreign oil conglomerates. For this very reason, in fact, her restored appetite for life does not come without a haunted sense of uncertainty: 'My mind told me to move away. Move away fast. I'd befriended this artificial creature. I knew it. Or I thought I knew it. But what did I *really* know about why it did what it did? Or why it came to me?.'[33]

As the story comes to its conclusion, the protagonist's inability to really know the zombies' intentions turns out to be merited. One day, her husband rushes into the bushes: 'there's a break in the pipeline near the school! Not a goddamn Zombie in sight yet! Throw down that guitar, woman! Let's go and get . . . '.[34] But before he finishes the line, he sees the spider next to her and abandons the scene in a mixture of contempt and fear. At the school, 'people came in cars, motorcycles, buses, on foot' to gather fuel for themselves wondering why the spiders have not reacted to the clear violation of the oil firms' property. However, back alongside the woman, the spider friend suddenly clicks its 'legs together so hard that it produced a large red spark and an ear splitting *ting!*' Quickly, 'a great mob' of spiders is conjured and runs off 'with amazing speed, to the east' in the direction of the school'.[35] It seems that the human-made machine-beasts, as already hinted in the story, have grown tired of their subservient and confined role as pipeline guards and are preparing to revolt. The woman thinks to herself, 'the Zombies weren't "zombies" at all. They were thinking creatures. Smart beasts. They had a method to their madness. And most of them did *not* like human beings'.[36] And why should they? Their masters did not regard them as anything but mindless killer tools that could keep the villagers in a constant state of fear, and the deprived local residents similarly disdained the spiders for their actions against them when they tried to uphold some sort of livelihood.

The scenario at the school offers a new perspective on the spiders as themselves colonised beings, confined and constricted to help secure the orderly extraction of natural resources, for the sole benefit of their masters. They are isolated and turned against their closest co-inhabitants – the villagers – and forced to travel up and down the pipelines in a hostile environment. Equally, the woman in the story is constricted to a life in misery, by a combination of the oil firms that have turned her local soil sour, prevented her body from conceiving new life, and, as a result of both, also turned her husband abusive. It is fair to say, the story does not end on a straightforwardly happy note. At the school, the locals stand in large pools of oil trying to fill buckets with fuel, only to stop when the zombie spiders arrive. As they quickly scope the scene, two of the spiders resolve to clicking 'their legs together, producing two large sparks'. The scene ends with the horrid onomatopoetic words: '*Ting! WHOOOOOOOOSH!*'.[37]

Still, a small glimmer of revolutionary liberation can be discerned. The spiders are now free to roam as they please, and the woman turns out to be pregnant at last. These two liberated beings, the woman and her spider-friend, are all that stands in the way of 'a flat out war between the Zombies and the human beings who created them' – 'otherwise', the woman thinks with clear reference to the violent structure of Niger Delta oil extraction, 'the delta will keep rolling in blood, metal, and flames', only with robot zombies added to the mix.[38] Thus, with the use of highly visceral and corporal gothic irrealism, the short story is able to register the ingrained patriarchal and ecocidal violence of a postcolonial lifeworld organised around oil-extraction. And moreover, the imaginative possibilities of irrealism – exemplified through the odd relationship that transpires between the protagonist and the confined robot spider – is also what makes visible the need to unravel and remake the objectification of women and nature under this extractivist regime.

A Sense of a Larger World

There are no spider-robots or oil bunkering in Danish oil fiction. Yet, oil nonetheless makes its presence felt in recent texts through a gloomy and gothic atmosphere. That is not to say that oil has hitherto been presented in an overtly positive manner. Earlier critical representations of oil have tended, however, to focus on local, environmental impacts, while newer texts seem much more attentive to the world-system of fossil capitalism. As a result of this recent turn, I argue that the sentiment of the texts has also shifted towards a somewhat bleak and defeatist stance. Here, the North Sea often plays a crucial part in telling this more gothic story of oil. As I have argued elsewhere, Peter Høeg's bestseller *Miss Smilla's Feeling for Snow* (1992) already hints at this emphasis on the structure of global oil with its offshore reorientation of the otherwise locally embedded genre of Nordic Noir. In its effort to depict an obscure and uncanny 'Arctic petroleumscape', Høeg's novel prefigures a gothic mixture of site (the petroleum waterway) and sight (the obscure reality of global oil) that has gained traction in Danish fiction of late.[39] I will provide two examples of this strategy here.

Jesper Brygger's poems in *Transporterne* are about infrastructure, distribution, and containerisation. But most of all, they are about the human and ecological costs of the capitalist world-system's constant desire for frontier expansion: '*it is about the fence, the transformer: and who we become on the other side*'.[40] Here are just two examples to illustrate the book's constant oscillation between the massive-scale global organisation of commodity transport, and the local in/visibility of this world-system from the local vantage of Denmark:

> on the golden strait the dredgers, oil tankers, and containerships sail
> by the isthmus in a more and more mystical company
> and only the unfolded has a visible shape, into the panorama
> out again[41]

These verses at the beginning of a poem depict the massive vessels used to transport different materials such as sand, oil, and other commodities. But the lines also hint at the mystic, obscure systems which underpin these transporters' free passage. These structures are only visible in some instances, at an isthmus, for instance, before they venture out at the open sea again. They pass in and out of the represented panorama, indicating a fundamental act of concealment. The language used to describe this offshore practice of resource movement is opaque as well, stressing the darker atmosphere of the entire process.

This next poem further accentuates the sense of world-systemic obscurity with its use of bleak and gothic aesthetics:

> out of the haze cranes appear
> And 200,000-tonnage transport capital to
> Copenhagen, Stockholm, Petersburg, and Helsinki
> to stand here at the coast in February's ice rain
> and mud with a starved mass of mercenaries
>
> do you feel manipulated
> too poor to cry in therapy
> ask for a glass of water
> from your leg lock?
>
> to stand here at the coast in February's ice rain
> and mud with a starved mass of mercenaries
> opposite a bastion rotten to the core
>
> crappy skullcans, heavy moments,
> lungs of princes, caustic tongues of fog
>
> far away millions of fires burn in the sun
> train station lit and the arm of the gangway
> suck the weary commuters onboard[42]

The setting is hazy, the weather is cold and muddy, the mercenaries (a precarious reserve army of labourers waiting to be temporary hired) are starving. The commuters are weary, the masters of the containerised world are rotten to the core, and caustic tongues of fog surround the speaker. It is hard not to read this poem as a tale of the horror of the shipping industry: precarious working conditions, environmental ruin, poverty, consumption, and addiction. Yet, compared to Okorafor's tale, written from the vantage of the Niger Delta, the physical proximity of the petro-materiality is remarkably distant and opaque.

Broeng and Møller's *Mare* touches on some of the same issues. Their book is a small hybrid book of pictures and twelve pages presented as a 'monologue with interruptions' starring eight characters: the Sea, the Kelp Forest, the Wind, the Rocks, the Sand, the Microplastic, the Fish, and the colourless bacterial filament called *beggiatoa* (in Danish nicknamed 'the Corpse Sheet' due to its visual resemblance to a dead body on the seabed).[43] The story begins with the Sea bragging about its size and its elevated rank as 'the lungs of the Earth' before the Kelp Forest interrupts, saying that 'you are beginning to lose breath'. Throughout the book, the Sea keeps on being interrupted as it tries to describe its own wondrous status: 'Life on this planet originated in me, and my nature makes the land pale in comparison. I am biodiversity itself and hold millions of species! Not just one or two as on land, but in the mil-li-on.' Another interruption comes, this time from the Microplastics and the Corpse Sheet, who both interject that the Sea is home to them as well – along with 'five enormous plastic gyres floating around'. Slowly, the Sea diverts from its elevated position as the bringer of life on Earth to a much darker stance as the devourer of the same. 'I eat summer houses in Northern Jutland and villages in Fiji, paddy fields in Vietnam' and 'I am especially looking forward to the historical palaces in Venice, and Copacabana'. Eventually, the Wind explains to the Sea that *mare* is not only a classical Greek term for 'sea', but also an Old English term for a folkloric entity that haunts people in their dreams. In other words, the Sea is increasingly depicted as a prime-carrier of the nightmare of climate change, of planetary erosion – just as it used to be the carrier of dangerous sailor mythos like the Kraken or the elusive sirens – and every aspect of ecological destruction is yet another haunting realisation that the tranquil waterways are giving way to something dark and eerie. As the destructive effects of growing greenhouse gas emissions wash ashore – 'the Sea: The ice is melting as the poles. How lucky can you be? I will only continue to grow as long as humans' – the text, then, succeeds in flipping the human indifference towards the environment, and lets us experience how it feels to be regarded as a resource for use.

The capitalist world-system's exploitation of peripheralised places and lives (colonised people, women, and natural resources) without any regard for the repercussions has eventually turned the Sea into an ecocidal being that increasingly haunts us all. Thus, Denmark's insulated position is, like the colonial waterways, increasingly becoming 'choked with the debris of history'. Floodings, plastic gyres, and seabed desolation are no longer only examples of what Hannah Freed-Thall terms 'cracks in a containerized world'.[44] Juxtaposing the erosion of summer houses in Jutland with the depletion of Vietnamese paddy fields illustrates how these cracks are growing wider, and the world is taking on water at an enormous speed, meaning that Denmark, the Nordics, and the Global North more widely now have to reckon with the arrival of conditions already long experienced in regions like the Niger Delta.

Conclusion

The author and critic Amitav Ghosh has influentially argued that oil is generally absent from literary fiction, an oversight he understands as requiring urgent remedy, since global realities are shaped by fossil capitalism. Oddly, though, Ghosh makes this assessment within a study limited to canonical works of realism, and even within this corpus, ignores the irrealist strategies that characterise the so-called realism of – for example – Upton Sinclair's *Oil* (1926) or Emile Zola's *Germinal* (1885). Fossil extraction, a process that profoundly remakes socio-ecological relations in the site where it takes place, would in fact appear to demand that the author veers away from a strictly realistic register. In *Germinal*, the sheer scale of the coal mine emerges via a discourse of monstrosity; its darkness and obscurity and its grand, labyrinthic design invoke fear and awe in the protagonist, as well as the reader. Likewise, the black substance in *Oil* appears as a beastlike entity, one which demands domestication in order for extraction to proceed. As these realist works demonstrate, realism must give way to other discourses when the matter of fossil fuel comes into play. Notably, these discourses – invoking threat, monstrosity, and anxiety – sit in close proximity to the gothic mode. Since the extraction, processing, trading, and transporting of oil takes place on a transregional scale, and since oil itself fuels the operation of the capitalist world-system, gothic figurations of oil encounters need to be understood as instances of what contributors to this volume understand as *world*-gothic: they represent anxious, irrealist registrations of the local experience of global socio-ecological processes and histories.

In this chapter, I have examined examples of this oil-centred world-gothic from Denmark and Nigeria, two littoral nations with industrialised oil seas, but very different histories and experiences of oil-extraction. In Okorafor's 'Spider the Artist', oil is bound up with colonial history and patriarchal domination, which are together represented in a grim and specifically visceral gothic register: Zombie robots patrol the Niger Delta pipelines and graphically obliterate any intruder. In the Danish oil texts *Transporterne* and *Mare*, gothic features are equally present, though the tendency here is to focus on oil's obscure, uncanny, subliminal features. Read together, these texts demonstrate how world-gothic affords insight into shifting world-systemic dynamics in the age of Tough Oil, when modes of aggressive extraction previously associated chiefly with postcolonial oil regions are increasingly characteristic of the fossil industry everywhere, and the climate effects of such processes are equally globally threatening. As the temperatures keep on surging, as the sea levels carry on rising, and as the firestorms continue to sweep the landscapes of the Global North, we will surely see more explicit and visceral literary registrations of the fossil-fuelled planetary havoc. And so, a more radically horrifying world-gothic – a world-gothic in the vein of Okorafor's text – may, before long, come to displace the vocabulary of obscure and shadowy threats that currently characterises Nordic writing around the oil encounter.

Notes

1. ´Sharae Deckard. 'Water Shocks: Neoliberal Hydrofiction and the Crisis of "Cheap Water"', *Atlantic Studies*, 16:1 (January 2019), 108–25, 111, 108, https://doi.org/10.1080/14788810.2017.1412181.
2. Immanuel Wallerstein, *World-Systems Analysis: An Introductory*, Durham, Duke University Press, 2004, 23.
3. Sharae Deckard and Kerstin Oloff, "The One Who Comes from the Sea": Marine Crisis and the New Oceanic Weird in Rita Indiana's *La mucama de Omicunlé* (2015)', *Humanities*, 9:3 (2020), 1–14, 1, https://doi.org/10.3390/h9030086.
4. Ricardo Soares de Oliveira, *Oil and Politics in the Gulf of Guinea*, London, Hurst, 2007; Nancy Couling and Carola Hein, 'Blankness: The Architectural Void of North Sea Energy Logistics', *Footprint*, 12:23 (Autumn/Winter 2018), 87–104, 90, https://doi.org/10.7480/footprint.12.2.2038.
5. IPCC, *Climate Change 2022: Impacts, Adaptation, and Vulnerability*, 'Contribution of Working Group II to the Sixth Assessment Report of the Intergovernmental Panel on Climate Change', Figure 8.6: 'Global Map of Vulnerability', 2022, www.ipcc.ch/report/ar6/wg2/figures/chapter-8/figure-8-006.
6. World Bank Group, 'Gini index – Nigeria, Denmark', 2021, https://data.worldbank.org/indicator/SI.POV.GINI?end=2018&locations=NG-DK&start=2018&view=map&year=2021.
7. Rob Nixon, *Slow Violence and the Environmentalism of the Poor*, Cambridge, Havard University Press, 2011.
8. Adam Nossiter, 'Far From Gulf, a Spill Scourge 5 Decades Old', *The New York Times*, 16 June 2010, www.nytimes.com/2010/06/17/world/africa/17nigeria.html
9. Judith Butler, *Frames of War: When is Life Grievable?* London, Verso Books, 2009, 1.
10. WReC (Warwick Research Collective), *Combined and Uneven Development: Towards a New Theory of World-Literature*, Liverpool, Liverpool University Press, 2015, 22.

13 Tough Oil Gothic

11. Michael Watts, 'Petro-Violence: Community, Extraction, and Political Ecology of a Mythic Commodity', in N. L. Peluso and M. Watts (eds.), *Violent Environments*, New York, Cornell University Press, 2011, 192, 190.
12. Jason W. Moore, 'The Modern World-System as Environmental History? Ecology and the Rise of Capitalism', *Theory and Society*, 32:3 (June 2003), 307–77; Jason W. Moore, *Capitalism in the Web of Life*, London, Verso, 2015.
13. David W. Orr, *Ecological Literacy: Education and the Transition to a Postmodern World*, Albany, State University of New York Press, 1992, 88.
14. Graeme Macdonald, 'Containing Oil: The Pipeline in Petroculture', in S. Wilson, A. Carlson and I. Szeman (eds.), *Petrocultures: Oil, Politics, Culture*, Montreal: McGill-Queen's University Press, 2017, 55; Michael T. Klare, 'The Third Carbon Age', *The Nation*, 8 August 2013, www.thenation.com/article/archive/third-carbon-age/.
15. Jennifer Wenzel, 'How to Read for Oil', *Resilience*, 1:3 (Fall 2014), 156–61, 157.
16. Sharae Deckard, 'Extractive Gothic', in R. Duncan (ed.), *The Edinburgh Companion to Globalgothic*, Edinburgh, Edinburgh University Press, 137. Deckard here refers to Ashley Dawson's 'Extreme Extraction', *Counterpunch*, 9 September 2011, www.counterpunch.org/2011/09/09/extreme-extraction/.
17. E.g., Jennifer Wenzel, 'Petro-Magic-Realism', *Postcolonial Studies*, 9:4 (December 2006), 449–64, https://doi.org/10.1080/13688790600993263; Katie Ritson, *The Shifting Sands of the North Sea Lowlands*, London, Routledge, 2018; Fiona Polack and Danine Farquharson (eds.), *Cold Water Oil*, London, Routledge, 2022; Philip Aghoghovwia, *Violent Ecotropes: Petroculture in the Niger Delta*, Cape Town, HSRC Press, 2022; Karl Emil Rosenbæk, 'Oceanic Irrealism: Danish Petrofiction Below the Surface', *The Journal of Energy History*, 10 (August 2023), 1–19, https://energyhistory.eu/en/node/357.
18. WReC, *Combined and Uneven Development*, 51.
19. Hugh Charles O'Connell, '"We are Change": The Novum as Event in Nnedi Okorafor's *Lagoon*', *Cambridge Journal of Postcolonial Literary Inquiry*, 3:3 (September 2016), 291–312, 291, https://doi.org/10.1017/pli.2016.24.
20. Nnedi Okorafor, 'Spider the Artist', in *Kabu Kabu*, Maryland, Prime Books, 2013, 101–15, 103.
21. Philip Aghoghovwia, 'Nigeria', in I. Szeman, J. Wenzel, and P. Yaeger (eds.), *Fueling Culture: 101 Words for Energy and Environment*, New York, Fordham University Press, 2017, 238–41, 238.
22. Maria Mies, 'Colonization and Housewifization', in M. Mies (ed.), *Patriarchy and Accumulation on a World Scale*, London, Zed Books, 2014.
23. Okorafor, 'Spider the Artist', 105.
24. This metaphor was populated with the release of Nigerian afrobeat-artist Fela Kuti's album *Zombie* in 1977.
25. David McNally, *Monsters of the Market: Zombies, Vampires, and Global Capitalism*, Leiden, Brill, 2011, 193–201.

26. Tina Abeku, 'Osinbajo launches Africa's first humanoid robot, Omeife', *The Guardian*, 4 December 2022, https://guardian.ng/news/osinbajo-launches-africas-first-humanoid-robot-omeife/.
27. Okorafor, 'Spider the Artist', 104.
28. Nnedi Okorafor, *The Book of Phoenix*, New York, DAW Books, 2015, chapter 10: Wazobia, original uppercasing and italics.
29. Okorafor, 'Spider the Artist', 104, original italics.
30. Okorafor, 'Spider the Artist', 106.
31. Okorafor, 'Spider the Artist', 109.
32. Okorafor, 'Spider the Artist', 110.
33. Okorafor, 'Spider the Artist', 108, original italics
34. Okorafor, 'Spider the Artist', 111.
35. Okorafor, 'Spider the Artist', 112, original italics.
36. Okorafor, 'Spider the Artist', 113, original italics.
37. Okorafor, 'Spider the Artist', 114.
38. Okorafor, 'Spider the Artist', 114–15.
39. Rosenbæk, Karl Emil. *Nordic Literature and the Oil Impasse: Contemporary Petrofiction from Denmark and Norway*, PhD. diss, University of Southern Denmark, Faculty of Humanities, 2023, https://doi.org/10.21996/r3g0-xq42.
40. Jesper Brygger, *Transporterne*, Copenhagen, Forlaget Kronstork, 2017, 10. My translation.
41. Brygger, *Transporterne*, 24.
42. Brygger, *Transporterne*, 77.
43. Gitte Broeng and Lasse Møller, *Mare*, Aarhus, Forlaget *[asterisk], 2023. No pagination, my translation.
44. Hannah Freed-Thall, 'Beaches and Ports', *Comparative Literature*, 73:2 (June 2021), 131–49, 141, https://doi.org/10.1215/00104124-8874051.

CHAPTER 14

Scheherazade and Bluebeard
The World-Gothic and Bloody Chambers in Arab Women's Writing

Roxanne Douglas

The printing press has, historically, done a number on women. According to Silvia Federici, disseminating propaganda against witches was 'one of the first tasks of the printing press'.[1] Federici's claim comes from her seminal work on the European witch hunts, which were part of how early world-capitalism enclosed women's labour and reproductive capacities. It is thanks to engraved images that could be easily reproduced that an entire iconology developed surrounding witchcraft, which directly affected cultural attitudes and laws about women's sexual and economic autonomy. The combination of cheap literary products and a strong, grisly, eventually gothicised, aesthetic was part of the popularity of these cultural objects. This developed into the easily pirated woodcut images of cheap nineteenth-century chapbooks. How do you imagine Bluebeard, the tyrannical fairy tale husband, for example? Perhaps he is leering, beturbaned, and wielding a scimitar? 'Bluebeard' is a French import to the Anglophone world, so how did he turn into this Orientalist vision? The answer is in print production itself: the rough production of (often pirated) cheap chapbooks in the nineteenth century meant that illustrations for the *Arabian Nights* and 'Bluebeard' were used interchangeably.[2] As this chapter will discuss, the mimetic aspects of 'Bluebeard'/*Nights* as an artefact of world-folklore sublimate anxieties about women's enclosure within the patriarchal marriage system, including the dangers of childbirth, and thus by turns sex and desire.

'Bluebeard' was first printed by Charles Perrault in France in 1697, but it existed as an oral story in Europe long before. It follows a young woman who marries a fearsome man who forbids her from entering one room in his castle. Due to the young woman's curiosity – a moral failure in conservative iterations – she discovers a 'bloody chamber' bedecked with the corpses of Bluebeard's former wives, who all also ostensibly betrayed him in this way. In some versions of the story, such as 'Fitcher's Bird', the young woman discovers and saves her dead sisters by putting their bodies back together, and makes her own escape disguised as a bird. We see similar themes about male violence and controlling women in the frame narrative of the *Thousand and One Nights* [*Alf Layla wa Layla*], where Scheherazade is married off to King Shahrayar who is so afraid of being cheated on that he has taken to marrying and beheading a new wife every night. Scheherazade gets around this by telling him interwoven stories for a thousand and one nights, by which time she wins his trust, apparently healing his murderous streak. The *Nights*, like 'Bluebeard', emerged from oral traditions. They represent a condensation of folklore from across the near and far East, but have come to be characterised as distinctly 'Arabian' following a long publication history.

Scholars like Casie E. Hermansson and Jack Zipes concur that the *Nights* frame story is a variation of 'Bluebeard', making the mythos a good example of world-folklore. Notably, scenes of women's incarceration and transgression within the edifice of patriarchy – the scenes which structure the 'Bluebeard'/*Nights* mythos – are also foundational to the Western gothic canon. They recur in such key examples of the female gothic mode as Charlotte Brontë's *Jane Eyre* (1847), Daphne Du Maurier's *Rebecca* (1938), and Angela Carter's *The Bloody Chamber* (1979), while also manifesting in horror film offerings from *The Silence of the Lambs* (1991), to *Crimson Peak* (2015), and the serial television series *You* (2018 – 25), based on the 2014 novel series of the same name by Caroline Kepnes. Though critics have frequently identified appropriations – direct and indirect – of the Bluebeard scenario in gothic fiction, they have less often made the link to *Nights*, despite the two narratives' mutual history as print artefacts within patriarchal capitalism, and their shared investment in tensions between potential danger and pleasure in sexuality. Grasping this interrelationship is generative because it helps to bring into view connections and resonances between the western (female) gothic tradition, and a wider body of writing which may not ordinarily be understood as gothic, but which – taking Scheherazade's tale as an organising matrix – features scenarios, concerns, and aesthetics analogous to those of the western corpus informed by the plight of Bluebeard's wives. This chapter explores how the 'Bluebeard'/*Nights* mythos reverberates as a highly complex world-gothic aesthetic though Arab women's writing.

Arab Women Writers and Scheherazade

Translation and mistranslation heavily influenced how we now imagine these proto-gothic tales: as Hermansson points out that one translator,

Guy Miège, changes Bluebeard's cutlass into a scimitar in the late eighteenth century, for example. 'Bluebeard' and the *Nights* evidence, separately and together, the mutation of the gothic genre from folklore to a form that is sensitive to the economy and exchanges of the world-literary system. However, Arab women writers are still perceived today as Scheherazade figures due to the early Orientalist reception of both texts. This is a problematic characterisation, but one which has nevertheless seen Arab women writers reactivate and mobilise the 'Bluebeard'/*Nights* mythos, not as predictable testimonies to violence, but as a sardonic strategy which engages with the ambiguities of the relationship between violence and pleasure with women's agency, as it is shaped by the global market. In this chapter, I show that the technology of the world-gothic is idiosyncratically complicated in Arab women's writings in a double register: in its content about patriarchal violence, and in its self-consciousness as a world-market object. The availability of information media, namely the printing press, finds an uncanny double in the availability of global texts in a digitised and translation-rich contemporary market. The ongoing Orientalist approach to Arab women writers persistently evidences entanglements of economics and class, as well as race and gender, which characterise the world-gothic. As Duncan and Cumpsty explain in the Introduction to this volume, gothic emerges not just as a response to the alienating effects of capitalism, but to the forms of appropriation that made global capitalism possible. We will see that the move from folklore to print, which corresponds to the encounter with capitalist modernity, has impacted how we tell stories about Arab women who tell stories.

Scholarship about Arab women's writings regularly turns to Scheherazade. Her survival through storytelling is invoked as metaphor for Arab women's testimony in the face of supposedly inevitable peril. Al-Samman identifies her as a 'poignant' and unthreatening 'cultural icon' whose voice can 'heal the nation',[3] which is rather a lot of responsibility for someone trying to avoid being murdered. Fedwa Malti-Douglas suggests that Scheherazade is 'queen of narrators' who has 'provoked the envy of male writers from Edgar Allan Poe to John Barth'.[4] Malti-Douglas frames Scheherazade as a sister-peer, an exceptional addition to a typically masculine literary tradition. Joumana Haddad criticises how Scheherazade has to 'save herself from death by bribing "the man"'.[5] The exceptionalism in Scheherazade's cunning ability to navigate male violence has impacted how Arab women's writings are perceived on the Anglophone market, even today; Michelle Hartman argues that 'Arab women's literature is still most frequently read and "appreciated" for its sociological value … the exemplary woman who works on behalf of her oppressed sisters'.[6] This is a direct consequence of the Orientalism that saw the co-development of the *Nights* and 'Bluebeard' in the eighteenth- and nineteenth-century Anglophone market, where the *Nights* were seen as a valuable window into the 'Orient'. We still see the Arab female storyteller as a cunning figure, frozen in a tableau of survival, rather than an artist in her own right.

One idiosyncrasy of the 'Bluebeard'/*Nights* mythos is that it simultaneously draws our attention to authorship – Scheherazade is the 'ultimate' Arab female author; the 'original' 'Bluebeard' story is Perrault's – and to erasure of the author – Scheherazade is a frame narrator who we forget during the stories; the 'real' 'Bluebeard' story is actually an assemblage of oral folklore, not Perrault's at all. Zipes points out how Perrault assembled a tale 'that was to eliminate his own name, for "Bluebeard," a tale that still breathes, has become more important than Perrault's name and his life'.[7] Ironically, Zipes casts Perrault as a kind of Scheherazade figure, where Scheherazade 'warns . . . against the dangers of male appropriation of . . . [Arab women's] literature'.[8] Yet we might think of the myriad famous feminist 'Bluebeard' retellings, by literary giants such as Angela Carter and Margaret Atwood, which have 'appropriated' Perrault's tale as an inversion of this threat. The feminist reappraisal of fairy tales exemplifies the gothic's facility for inversion and the reversal of social roles, and the potential for such revolt specifically in 'Bluebeard'/*Nights*. Exchange and inversion are crucial to this discussion: the exchange of literary goods in a global market, the pouring back and forth of cultural influences, translation and mistranslation, and perhaps the sensual and sexual exchanges of power such as we might see in fantasies of domination and submission, especially in their reversal along gendered lines. Moreover, these tales allow us – in some iterations – to hold both violence and sensuality together as seemingly disparate realities in women's complex experiences of patriarchy.

In what follows, I will sketch the technology of this mythos as it moves from an oral tale to a printed one, which erased the sensuality of women's storytelling. I will then examine how Arab feminists are engaging with the central themes of knowledge and sensuality, before reading Nawal El Saadawi's *The Fall of the Imam* [*suqut al'iimam*] (2009 [1988]) through the 'Bluebeard'/*Nights* mythos.

From the Mouth to the Press

As we have seen, the story of the *Nights* and 'Bluebeard' is one of mimesis, translation, mistranslation, piracy, and the Orientalist Anglo-imagination.

Hermansson explains that Bluebeard existed in oral forms long before Charles Perrault captured it in ink. The 'Bluebeard'/*Nights* formations emerge from an oral tradition from which we can easily assume women have been erased. Zipes points out that Perrault was highly influenced by 'deep oral currents of the literary myths that ... were disseminated over hundreds of years in ... public places', which he broke with by 'using a male Cartesian rational style'.[9] Zipes points out the masculinised aspects of Perrault's retelling (no doubt influenced by Enlightenment philosophies), yet omits that the most common types of fairy tale were probably told by women at home. To roll out an old chestnut, as Virginia Woolf taught us, 'Anon' 'was a woman ... who made the ballads and the folksongs, crooning them to her children, beguiling her spinning with them'.[10] The contemporary postcolonial theorist Trinh Minh-ha also teaches us that 'the world's earliest archives or libraries were the memories of women. Patiently transmitted from mouth to ear, body to body, hand to hand'.[11] Minh-ha and Woolf together remind us of the sensory and sensual aspects of the history of women's oral storytelling, which find their way into the sumptuousness of the gothic as we now know it.

The oral story has an undeniable relationship to gendered work; whether that is storytelling while performing domestic or manual work, or the work of childrearing where storytelling becomes a way of supplying pedagogic information; or, indeed, female authorship as work. In the Arab world, the *hakawâtî*, usually a male storyteller in the public coffeehouse, is seen as responsible for preserving cultural heritage. This is a position not usually attributed to a woman, unless that woman is Scheherazade who 'at the end of [*Nights*], is relegated to the traditional role of wife and mother. In essence, she is doomed to reside eternally within the walls of orality'.[12] In other words, feminised authorship was erased by the gendered capitalist system, where women become confined to the home, and work within the home was recategorised as 'non-work' which 'was worthless even when done for the market',[13] including the creative arts. Esthie Hugo's chapter in this volume engages with social reproduction in relation to the domestic gothic. For this discussion, it is important to note that practices done in the home – like oral storytelling or spinning – are often assumed not to be art, and thus by extension also not to be work. This leads into wider problems, where women are not only 'trapped in the walls of orality' without written records of their lives, but are left economically vulnerable in 'the traditional role of wife and mother'. Yet, in the world-gothic mode, pleasure and power are woven together in women's hands. Husain Haddawy describes being told *Alf Layla wa Layla* by an old woman when he was a child, relating how 'her pauses were just as delicious as her words, as we waited, anticipating a pleasure certain to come'.[14] Here we do not see an imposed silence through suppression or violence, but rather a woman's chosen silence, a rhythmic pause which, if anything, enriches the moments of speech to solicit yet more pleasure.

Assemblage is a key aspect of the 'Bluebeard'/*Nights* mythos. Bluebeard himself assembles a scene of carnage for each new wife, Scheherazade assembles stories each night. Mark Allen Peterson argues that the *Nights* take bits and pieces from Indian folklore, Arab and Asian oral tales, and religious stories. This makes the mythos a great example of world-literary systems in action. Zipes argues similarly that Perrault wove aspects of 'Adam and Eve', 'Pandora's Box', and even the *Nights* into 'Bluebeard'. All this is to say that neither text is a pure invention. Both elude discrete ownership and control, principles upon which capitalist patriarchy relies, and themes which manifest in the 'Bluebeard'/*Nights* mythos. Peterson points out that two of the tales in the *Nights* were inserted by Antoine Galland in the early 1700s, and 'have strong parallels with some European folktales' which were then translated back into 'Arabic and incorporated from the nineteenth-century on into the most popular versions of *Alf Layla wa Layla*'.[15] This re-adoption of the new version is an example of how the capitalist world-market invented traditions. So strong was this invented tradition that there were efforts to reclaim the *Nights* from Europe as part of Middle Eastern literary heritage. At the same time, the first Calcutta edition of '*Alf Laylah wa Laylah* (1814–18) was heavily edited to teach British army officers Arabic.[16] The *Nights* have therefore travelled far and wide, changing in the hands of translators and nationalists, becoming an object that is ambiguously non-Western whilst serving British colonialism, coming to represent both colonial domination and resistance to it.

In this collection's Introduction, Duncan and Cumpsty observe how Caribbean rituals belonging to Obeah or Vodou became vilified and exoticised in British and North American gothic literature. A similar process of 'gothicisation' characterises how folkloric practices and stories from 'the Orient' have been represented in the Western imagination at large. Indeed, traces of this development might be found in gothic classics like *Jane Eyre* and *Rebecca*, since these text draw directly on the Bluebeard mythos, which was itself influenced by Orientalisations of *Nights*. In some iterations of the 'Bluebeard' story, Bluebeard himself is described as a 'Turkish tyrant'. Warner discusses how one illustrated retelling places Bluebeard's castle in Baghdad. According to Maria Tatar some versions of the story call Bluebeard's wife Fatima, so it is she who is the exotic and mysterious Other, taking on the visage of resourceful Scheherazade. In the case of the 'Bluebeard'/*Nights* mythos, it is notable that Hermansson calls her study of 'Bluebeard' a guide to an '*English Tradition*'. As the 'Bluebeard'/*Nights* gothic formation homogenised Arab, Middle East, and Far Eastern cultures into a broad, decadent Orient, it therefore simultaneously invented 'Bluebeard' as a local commodity for English readers. Indeed ownership, legitimacy (in many senses) and copyright haunt these tales in ways that Arab women writers then upend in their reactivation of these formulations, as we will see in the following sections.

The *Nights* emerge as an important market object in 'the development of a new economy of mass-produced books in Western Europe, Iran, and the Arab world' through the eighteenth and nineteenth centuries, with translations from Arabic, through French, to English. They were popular both in chapbooks and in official copies, which meant that cheap and expensive versions circulated simultaneously via formal and informal (read: pirated) economies, with the illustrations of the cheaper or copied texts being recycled between different stories. Genres are perpetuated by aesthetic cues, which in the case of 'Bluebeard's 'strain of Orientalism ... took permanent root in the chapbook tradition'.[17] In other words, this mythos has moved from the mouth to the page as an object which registered the turbulence of colonialism for literary markets who wanted to (re)claim *Alf Layla* as a part of their cultural heritage, whether it was actually so or not, as well as anxieties about the Oriental Other whose decadence and enclosure of women in harems are still imagined to be corrupting forces in the Western imagination.

The nineteenth century saw wider literacy among women, the working classes, and children across Europe and the Middle East, which caused a great deal of moral panic. For example, a 1901 edition of the *Nights* 'promises a careful abridgement, suitable for "the modest woman", a matter of new concern for the new definition of reading as a social activity for both sexes'.[18] The gothic, which found its way into cheap editions, was seen as a morally questionable genre. This is because the gothic for women writers became a language, a generic technology, to explore secrets, hidden by patriarchy, their the reasons to be scared. Diana Wallace argues that 'the Gothic works as a "mode of history" ... Women writers have used Gothic historical fiction with its obsession with inheritance, lost heirs and illegitimate offspring, to explore the way in which the "female line" has been erased in "History"'.[19] Given the lost authors and workers in fairy tales' earliest oral forms, and their appropriation by a male-dominated literary world, we can easily read Arab women's reactivation of the 'Bluebeard'/*Nights* mythos as contending with lost 'herstories' alongside contemporary encounters with violence. Indeed, Peterson writes, 'in spite of its polyglot nature, the work has a number of themes ... Primary among these is the inability of men to control women'.[20] Hermansson also notes 'the dangerous husband, the unknown secrets of the spouse, the retribution for transgressive female curiosity'.[21] Though it is not immediately obvious, these critics are discussing *Nights* and 'Bluebeard'(respectively) as two distinct texts. The world-gothic's earliest intertextual themes attend quite distinctly to fortunes and secrets, particularly secrets about women's peril and sexuality due to the enclosure of women's labour and the dangers around their reproductive capacities. According to Federici, following capitalist enclosure 'women lost the control they had exercised over procreation, and were reduced to a passive role in child delivery' where male doctors 'prioritized the life of the foetus over that of the mother'.[22] Sophie Lewis writes about the 'carnage' ongoing today 'in the United States, [where] almost 1,000 people die while doing childbirth'; things 'are like this for political and economic reasons', she concludes, 'we made them this way'.[23] As Walker puts it 'for the wife, we might say, the locked room contains History, the history of violence against women and the complicity of culture in that violence'.[24] What could be more gothic than discovering the bodies of women who have come before?

Knowing and Telling

Bluebeard and the *Nights* are about knowledge and power in marriage. In the patriarchal world-system women's bodies are resources, yet Scheherazade/Fatima are resourceful in ways that do not involve their reproductive or sexual capacities. As Zipes points out, 'it is not inconceivable that people told numerous tales ... to alert others about these murderers ... what is distinctive about the Bluebeard discourse is that it stemmed from a misogynist strain of storytelling within patriarchal cultures'.[25] Zipes draws our attention to the power of oral tales, and perhaps to gossip, which Federici also suggests was vital to women's culture, which was then criminalised during the witch trials in Europe. As we saw in the preceding section, the essentialist categorisation of the female body as a producer of children was designed to shut down women's relationship to knowledge about her own body. The classic readings of the 'bloody chamber' as a fearsome womb space that represents women's initiation into sex and childbirth – the potentially fatal work of the body – is easily evoked here. Patriarchy does not only operate at the moment of violence, at the moment that Bluebeard raises his sword to kill his next wife; it is in the psychological mazes that are constructed by patriarchy to keep women trapped.

Knowledge dissemination remains an issue for contemporary Arab feminism. For instance, there is an Arabic equivalent to the Anglophone #MeToo social media movement, #AnaKaman. One Twitter user, @mjberr, wrote: 'That sickening moment you realize not a single woman/mother/daughter/girl you personally know has been spared. #MeToo #UsToo'. Akin to the moment of horror in the bloody chamber, this twitter user identifies with the women who have not 'been spared', by not only identifying with the 'me' but also with the network of 'us'. While the knowledge is 'sickening', there are mechanisms available to alert others to the unpleasant truth. Al-Samman argues that 'diaspora [Arab] women writers draw a picture of a female body that is often mutilated, violated, restricted, reconstructed, symbolically consumed, suffocated, and buried. It is a terrifying portrait – one that is meant to trigger individual memories and ... to protest the history of women's erasure'.[26] One such mechanism which inverts and operationalises the mutilated female body is gothicised activism which recalls 'Bluebeard'/*Nights*. In 2016 an NGO called ABAAD MENA campaigned to revoke the Lebanese Penal Code Article 522, which stated that if a man rapes a woman he can avoid criminal prosecution by marrying her. As part of this campaign, Mirelle Honein erected a public installation on the Beirut corniche, which depicted thirty-one wedding dresses made from paper that hung like ghosts, or, indeed, like Bluebeard's dead wives in the bloody chamber. Except, these dead wives were not hidden away; they were in a busy public walkway, where pedestrians would have struggled to avoid bumping into them, and certainly could not avoid seeing them. The ABAAD campaign raised awareness of this rapacious Penal Code. Only one per cent of the Lebanese population knew that Article 522 existed before the campaign started.

This installation reverses Bluebeard's tyranny, not only by dragging corpses into the light, but also because Bluebeard himself is a figure who, as Hermansson points out, 'has always been an "artist" ... Bluebeard crafted the tableau of dead wives in the "forbidden" chamber presupposing a specific spectator: his transgressing wife'.[27] The inversions here are many. The bodies are to be seen not as a warning, but as a call for the cessation of suffering and 'to protest the history of women's erasure' as Samman put it. The brides are not made of flesh, the material which marks the female body as an essentialised resource, but of paper: the stuff of knowledge, of the printed story. The artistic arrangement by Bluebeard is indeed intended as an intimidation technique, but the hanging paper brides invert this as a call to action. The campaign also involved activists donning bloodied white wedding dresses during a protest, animating the dead wives – in some ways, these activists re-membered, reconstituted, the dead women like in the 'Fitcher's Bird' variation of 'Bluebeard', where a young wife revives her dead sisters and rescues them. Arab women writers use fiction to re-assemble partial knowledge, and invert patriarchal threat.

An analogously subversive effect is discernible in what Ghenwa Hayek calls the 'Sensation Story' of the nineteenth-century *Nahḍa*, or 'Arab Awakening', though the overt politics of these tales tends to be conservative. Like the gothics in Europe at the same time, sensation stories excited the body and emotions, thus allowing space for the sensuality of women's oral storytelling within the printed medium. As Hayek explains, the sensation story responded to changing discourses about women's bodies and social roles in conversation with colonial modernity. Taking *Henry wa Amelia* as an example, she writes that this *Nahḍa* narrative 'reaches its befuddled climax by troubling gender and sexual norms and rules of behaviour ... disciplining the transgressive female body, but also producing an assertive masculine one'.[28] Hayek's term 'befuddled climax' highlights what Arab women writers have reactivated using the technology of the 'Bluebeard'/*Nights* formation: these tales contend with the blurring of violence and pleasure which women negotiate in capitalist patriarchy. Walker writes that Angela Carter's 'Bluebeard' retelling, 'The Bloody Chamber', 'is wonderful because it doesn't simply give us a plot where feminine good meets masculine evil ... but his repulsiveness is also part of his sexual attraction to this young innocent who finds in her relations with him a horrifying capacity to enjoy her own dissolution and reconfiguration'.[29] The difference between nineteenth-century mobilisations of the 'Bluebeard'/*Nights* mythos and contemporary ones is that where the *Nahḍa* sensation writers reproduced a good/evil moralistic dichotomy, contemporary Arab women writers dispute prescriptive colonial modernity which casts them as 'the exemplary woman who works on behalf of her oppressed sisters'.[30] The colonial project of modernity was one which labelled, weighed, measured, and categorised all things, including women as sexual resources. In the contemporary mobilisation of the 'Bluebeard'/*Nights* mythos Arab feminists are making use of its potential for inversion and pleasure, despite being cast as victims in the global publishing market.

Bloody Bed Chambers

There are well-worn arguments that the 'bloody chamber', the fatal secret, is an allegory for the loss of virginity, which, in the time of Perrault's version, may very well have meant death by childbirth. Of course, the room also stands in for the virgin's fear of sex and sexuality, of which she has no knowledge until her husband initiates her, placing power firmly in his hands. We see echoes of this in Al-Samman's reading of the *Nights*, where '*sarir* (bed) and *sirr* (secret) are also linked by virtue of alliteration and assonance to *sard* (narration)'. For Al-Samman, this means that Scheherazade's '*sard* and *sarir* activities are strongly determined by the nexus of sex and death'.[31] To be sure, we can discern such connections between sex and death in the (female) gothic canon, and across Arab women's writings more widely, particularly around childbirth and marital violence.

For instance, in Miral Al-Tahawy's *The Tent* [*al-khibaa*] (1998 [1996]), Fatim discovers that her mother suffers sexual and physical abuse at the hands of her father. He 'used to lie on top of her and put his hands round her neck. . . . my mother would make those sighs I had heard last night'.[32] The 'sighs' speak to the double-edge of violence and sensuality, where terror and sexual arousal might produce similar vocal responses. In the mornings, her sisters 'would find on her neck dark lines that were blue like the thin shadowy veins on her swollen eyelids. They might also see on her dress or on her bed a patch of dried blood'.[33] It is no mistake that the markers of the fearsome bed chamber are the neck, which aligns with Shahrayar's beheadings, and the vaginal blood of sexual violence. The attention to her eyes also alerts us to the questions of witnessing and knowledge that 'Bluebeard' thematically activates. The ambiguities and clashes between sex and violence colour Fatim's journey from childhood to maturation, where the mother's body becomes a page upon which the dangers of patriarchy are printed, and thus also a place where knowledge about the female body's place in a global patriarchy becomes legible. Walker suggests that 'perhaps Bluebeard's closet, then, is the scene of writing, a chamber littered with corpses, bathed in a reddish light, and who knows what will emerge'.[34]

Al-Tahawy is a Bedouin writer. Anthony Calderbank describes in a 'Translator's Note' how Bedouin women are kept out of sight because they are seen to have the potential to bring dishonour on family and social groups. This is potentially referring to how, when women exercise sexual agency, the legitimacy of children becomes muddied. There are clear links between the translator's interpretation of Bedouin sexual propriety and Orientalist ideas of the enclosed Arab woman – and yet, Al-Tahawy went to university in Egypt and worked as a teacher before becoming an academic in the United States: she is a public-facing knowledge worker. At the same time, the sexual violence in the text reminds us that these are real, potentially fatal problems that some Arab women face. The tension between these realities culminates in an artistic depiction of entrapment that mobilises the ambiguities in the 'Bluebeard'/*Nights* frame to express the double jeopardy of sexual violence and Orientalism.

But are women's rewritings of this frame just 'about the carnage of patriarchy'? Walker theorises that some women writers' use of the 'Bluebeard' mythos 'play with the sensuality of violence',[35] to turn pain into pleasure. We now test this theory by turning to Nawal El Saadawi's highly surreal *The Fall of the Imam*, which brings together uncanniness, carnage, and the sensual possibilities of inversion. The novel follows the young, orphaned Bint Allah's attempt to assassinate her father, the Imam; at the same time, the Iman's guards pursue Bint Allah and her mother interchangeably, and all three figures regularly die in variations of repeated scenes, calling to mind the assemblage and reproduction in chapbooks in the early 'Bluebeard'/*Nights* canon. Although the Imam quite literally compares himself to King Shahrayar at one point (151),[36] the repeated assassinations align him with Bint Allah and her mother, as well, of course, as Bluebeard's and Shahrayar's dead wives. El Saadawi has Bint Allah narrate her incestuous wedding to the Imam like a funeral, where 'they wed me. I had no choice. They wrapped me up in a pure white robe like the ... shroud surrounding a dead body ... I found myself naked in a bed of rich marble with gilt decorations like the graves of queens' (160). Wallace explains how, in the Anglophone women's gothic tradition, the marital bed is likened to a grave. The decorous bed in *Fall of the Imam* highlights material wealth as well as cultural heritage, thematically engaging with the sumptuous temptations of Bluebeard's wealth in many (re)tellings, but also with the imagined cultural heritage that the *Nights* represented to male elites in the nineteenth century. The bed here becomes a symbol of legitimacy, which pertains, on the one hand, to sexual practices and thus to lineage and the inheritance of the Imam's wealth and class, and, on the other, to an historicised cultural heritage which grants the Imam status.

This wedding night demonstrates the potential for inversion, using the technology of the 'Bluebeard'/*Nights* stories, where it is retold in three variations. The Imam plays out a fantasy of Shahrayar, where sexuality and murderousness become entangled when he holds Bint Allah 'in a close embrace, leaving her with one remaining night in which to live' (159). Bint Allah, on the other hand, 'whispered to herself, "I must either save my life or I must die for my sisters. I must deliver them from the tyrant for all time"' (159). Her self-declaration sets her up to be like the final sister in the 'Fitcher's Bird' variant, where she may be able to save her sisters. Equally, it casts her as the brave Scheherazade who volunteers to try and appease King Shahrayar in some versions of *Nights*. However, Bint Allah is also speaking to El Saadawi's Western readership, a readership who might imagine that the author and character are both 'the exemplary woman who works on behalf of her oppressed sisters'.[37] El Saadawi uses irony to criticise the west's tendency to characterise all Arab women as belonging to a sisterhood that is connected through violent oppression. This irony is foregrounded by Bint Allah's ostensible responsibility to tell stories about this sorority of suffering – a feature which is stretched to its ironic and metatextual limits as the narrative is translated for Anglophone audiences. Translation for this readership also transforms questions of looking and observation into questions of voyeurism, which thematically adjoins this text to 'Bluebeard'. The connection becomes clear when we move from Bint Allah's declaration to the perspective of the Imam's Chief of Security, who watches this wedding night 'through the keyhole of the door' (159). However, the rape that he presumably hopes to see is waylaid. Bint Allah uses magic to turn the Imam into a sheep – an animal regularly used for religious feasts in the novel – and then, when dawn returns, she turns him back into a human (159). There is something to be said here about the animal husband tradition across a variety of global folklores. The Imam at one point refers to his being able to 'rape her [his daughter] like a wolf' (57), but in respect to Bint Allah his animality is equivalent to vulnerability. He becomes a slaughter animal that can be eaten; his flesh thus becomes like the feminised flesh that he also rapaciously (and later, literally) consumes. This scene therefore inverts the gendered power and vulnerability paradigms that we might otherwise expect from it, especially given that the Imam is later restored to human form, and so the tale is not about lasting revenge, only temporary vulnerability.

This ambivalence is taken further in *The Fall of the Imam*, when El Saadawi provides another version of the same scene. This time, the Imam's rape of Bint Allah is described through him literally consuming her flesh. The author describes the grisly aspects of his 'cracking' her bones and 'sucking' on them, using the trope of cannibalism as an allegory for sexual violence (164). The sequences is written as a violent realisation of 'his desire' for 'a woman who refuses to be possessed' (164), an assertion which echoes Peterson's proposal that, among other things, the *Nights* are about 'the inability of men to control women'.[38] Notably, however, the Imam experiences eroticisation within his *lack* of control, which aligns him more fully with Walker's reading of Bluebeard's virgin wife who seemingly revels in her own undoing, and who possesses 'a horrifying capacity to enjoy her own dissolution and reconfiguration'.[39] In a later iteration of the scene the Imam describes how 'my whole body melted into thin air, taking with it all my desires, so that nothing was left of me' (167). Perhaps this melting away imposes on the Imam the fate of the oral authoresses who have faded to obscurity; or that of the brides of the ABAAD campaign who have been forgotten by society and the law. In this iteration, however, Bint Allah is being consumed, but through the surreal magic of the text she is seemingly unaffected, she can look on, now the voyeur, and observe that 'there was nothing but fear, a terrible fear' (164) in his eyes. The line likens the Imam again to the sacrificial sheep, and to the virgin of the Bluebeard mythos who both wants and fears in equal measure. Bint Allah then hands him 'bone after bone' herself because he 'was never satisfied', which causes the Imam's belly, in a further absurd turn, to swell and explode, inverting the fatal dangers of the belly that the bloody chamber signifies for women onto the body of the patriarch (164–5).

El Saadawi revisits this scene of rape, with its ambiguous, ambivalent power dynamics, once more in the novel, positioning Bint Allah herself as the animalistic eater. Unlike the Imam's consumption of Bint Allah's flesh where he felt fear, the Imam now feels pleasure while being eaten by her, again presenting the sexual and sensual power dynamics in the scene in an ambiguous light. El Saadawi writes, 'she bit so hard on my hand that she cut it off from the arm, and as her teeth went through it I felt pleasure with the pain, so I gave her my other hand and again she sank her teeth into it' (166). The Imam mirrors Bint Allah's previous actions, but whereas her feeding the Imam is penetrative and agential, here the Imam sensually revels in his own undoing. His body and voice begin to disappear into thin air, but before disappearing he makes a patriarchal declaration par excellence: 'the only thing I long for now is to open the skull of this woman and crush her brain so that, like all the ideal women, she will become an invisible body possessing nothing else except a womb' (168). This declaration at the end of a series of allegorical rape scenes of course recalls the fleshly foundations of capitalist patriarchy. The bloody chamber represents the restrictions placed upon the essentialised female flesh for sex and childbirth during the throes of early enclosure.

In all three versions of the rape, Bint Allah always escapes relatively unscathed. This suggests Bint Allah is neither good nor bad, neither wholly victim nor wholly aggressor, meaning that, from a narrative perspective, she is free to leave the would-be bloody chamber, because she has not, strictly speaking, transgressed. Yet, we should not forget the very real stakes of death and violence that are highlighted by #AnaKaman and the ABAAD 'Undress 522' campaign. Indeed, while *The Fall of the Imam* is highly surreal, El Saadawi's preface and dedication to the text recounts her meeting several women who have survived rape and mutilation. Bint Allah's ambivalence and escapes, then, offer a counter-imaginary to the image of the Arab woman who only suffers. Following this ambivalence, Arab women writers, like Bluebeard himself, are artists who (re)arrange the 'picture of a female body that is often mutilated ... [and] symbolically consumed'. Anglophone readers thus must be sensitive to the ambiguities entailed by writing towards such an uneven global audience, while, at the same time, bearing witness to these writers' 'protest [of] the history of women's erasure' as Samman said. These writers cannot only be characterised through victimhood, but they are also not simply pandering to Western audiences' perceptions of themselves and their so-called sisters. The inversion, revolt, and multiplicity that inhere within the 'Bluebeard'/*Nights* frame alert us to the ambiguities and tensions in women's experiences, and these complexities are engaged also by the world-gothic fiction in which this mythos is taken up.

Escape – 'Fitcher's Bird'

From dis-assembly and loss of self, we now return to the foundations of (re)assembly in the 'Bluebeard'/*Nights* formula, primarily through the 'Fitcher's Bird' variant of the 'Bluebeard' tale. In this version, the third sister not only reassembles her sisters and brings them back to life, but she is also able to escape by disguising her body as a bird. In a felicitous coincidence, this motif echoes Hélène Cixous's call for women to 'fly/steal' through the phallocentric orders of signification. Translators Keith Cohen and Paula Cohen footnote that the original French term '*voler*' means to both 'fly' and 'steal'.[40] She writes that 'women take after birds and robbers ... They ... fly the coop, take pleasure in jumbling the order of space, ... dislocating things and values, ... and turning propriety upside down'.[41] In 'Fitcher's Bird' the third sister also puts her sisters in a basket with gold to send them home, thus becoming a bird while stealing, and so fulfilling the disruptive interventions of flight and robbery. Arab women's reconfiguration of the 'Bluebeard'/*Nights* mythos flies in the face of, whilst stealing from, a genre which Othered and victimised them. The technology of the story, of the word whether oral or printed, can be reclaimed from its history of misogyny through re-assembly. Such a process entails a playful theft and re-membering of meaning, in order to create stories about escaping colonialist patriarchal modernity. The world-gothic form for Arab women writers is one in which it is possible to subvert the strict categories of aggressor/victim and of sensuality/violence.

Notes

1. Silvia Federici, *Caliban and the Witch: Women, the Body and Primitive Accumulation*, New York, Autonomedia, 2004, 180.
2. Casie E. Hermansson, *Bluebeard: A Reader's Guide to the English Tradition*, Jackson, University Press of Mississippi, 2009, 53.
3. Hanadi Al-Samman, *Anxiety of Erasure: Trauma, Authorship, and the Diaspora in Arab Women's Writings*, Syracuse, Syracuse University Press, 2015, 3.
4. Fedwa Malti-Douglas, *Woman's Body, Woman's Word: Gender and Discourse in Arabo-Islamic Writing*, Princeton, Princeton University Press, 1991, 11.
5. Joumana Haddad, *I Killed Scheherazade: Confessions of an Angry Arab Woman*, London, Saqi, 2010, 141.
6. Michelle Hartman, 'Gender, Genre, and the (Missing) Gazelle: Arab Women Writers and the Politics of Translation', *Feminist Studies*, 38:1 (2012), 17–49, 20.
7. Jack Zipes, *The Irresistible Fairy Tale: The Cultural and Social History of a Genre*, Princeton, Princeton University Press, 2012, 54.
8. Al-Samman, *Anxiety of Erasure*, 11.
9. Zipes, *The Irresistible Fairy Tale*, 48.
10. Virginia Woolf, *A Room of One's Own*, London, Flamingo, 1994, 55.
11. Trinh T. Minh-ha, *Woman, Native, Other: Writing Postcoloniality and Feminism*, Bloomington, Indiana University Press, 1989, 121.
12. Al-Samman, *Anxiety of Erasure*, 11.
13. Federici, *Caliban and the Witch*, 92.
14. Husain Haddawy, 'Introduction', in M. Mahdi (ed.), *The Arabian Nights*, New York, Norton, 1990, xii.
15. Peterson, 'From Jinn to Genies', 99.
16. Kamran Rastegar, 'The Changing Value of "Alf Laylah Wa Laylah" for Nineteenth-Century Arabic, Persian, and English Readerships', *Journal of Arabic Literature*, 36:3 (2005), 269–87, 278.
17. Hermansson, *Bluebeard*, 70.
18. Rastegar, 'The Changing Value of "Alf Laylah Wa Laylah"', 281.
19. Diana Wallace, *Female Gothic Histories: Gender, History and the Gothic*, Cardiff, University of Wales Press, 2013, 5.

20. Peterson, "From Jinn to Genies", 97.
21. Hermansson, *Bluebeard*, x.
22. Federici, *Caliban and the Witch*, 98.
23. Sophie Lewis, *Full Surrogacy Now: Feminism Against Family*, London: Verso, 2019, 9.
24. Cheryl Walker, 'In Bluebeard's Closet: Women Who Write with the Wolves', *Literature Interpretation Theory*, 7:1 (January 1996), 13–26, 23.
25. Zipes, *The Irresistible Fairy Tale*, 53–4.
26. Al-Samman, *Anxiety of Erasure*, 60.
27. Hermansson, *Bluebeard*, 161.
28. Hayek, 'Experimental Female Fictions', 255–6.
29. Walker, 'In Bluebeard's Closet', 17.
30. Hartman, 'Gender, Genre, and the (Missing) Gazelle', 20.
31. Al-Samman, *Anxiety of Erasure*, 236.
32. Miral Al-Tahawy, *The Tent*, trans. A. Calderbank, Cairo, The American University in Cairo Press, 1998, 24.
33. Al-Tahawy, *The Tent*, 24.
34. Walker, 'In Bluebeard's Closet', 24.
35. Walker, 'In Bluebeard's Closet', 15.
36. Nawal El Saadawi, *The Fall of the Imam*, trans. S. Hetata, London, Telegram, 2009, 151.
37. Hartman, 'Gender, Genre, and the (Missing) Gazelle', 20.
38. Peterson, 'From Jinn to Genies', 97.
39. Walker, 'In Bluebeard's Closet', 17.
40. Hélène Cixous, 'The Laugh of the Medusa', trans. Keith Cohen and Paula Cohen, *Signs*, 1:4 (1976), 875–93, 887, n. 6.
41. Cixous, 'The Laugh of the Medusa', 887.

Coda
Catachresis and the Politics of Gothic Naming
Rebekah Cumpsty and Rebecca Duncan

The authors in this collection have identified a range of monstrous cultural forms: precolonial supernatural regimes; eruptions of terror and dread during periods of socio-economic/socio-ecological crisis; and locally specific occult registrations of the world-system that do not have a precolonial antecedent. The gothic is one name for this cultural production of terror, anxiety, and excess, but, because of the European literary historiography within which it has been conceptualised, it is also frustratingly insufficient. Gothic studies is now transregional, and gothic figures (vampire, zombie, ghost) and concepts (abject, uncanny, sublime) have come to symbolise the crises of the present. Though at times generative, the notions of hybridisation, deterritorialisation, and globalisation with which these developments and associations have been scaffolded also – as we suggested in this volume's Introduction – reaffirm a narrative in which gothic appears in late-eighteenth-century Britain, and is subsequently taken up and appropriated by postcolonial writers and those beyond the so-called West. This 'empire writes back' conception has led to a proliferation of region-specific iterations – Pan-Asian gothic, African gothic, South African gothic – that overstretch the meaning of the gothic, expanding the initially British version to global proportions, and in this way occluding local aesthetics and cultural forms. In this critical context, gothic scholars are increasingly questioning how a gothic corpus is formed and how it is named.

With respect to Indigenous gothic for example, Ian Conrich,[1] on the one hand, has cautioned that it would be inappropriate to freely conflate autochthonous Māori beliefs and practices with the gothic. On the other hand, as Krista Collier-Jarvis notes in this collection, there is a sense in which this situation leaves authors and scholars with a 'non-choice', where 'Indigenous storytellers cannot contribute to the gothic, and yet those gothic writers and filmmakers who engage Indigenous culture in their works are potentially doing so problematically'. All the while authors such as Silvia Moreno-Garcia (*Mexican Gothic*) make self-conscious appeals to the gothic's generic label, its conventions and consumers, and scholars continue to use the concept as a way to group, differentiate, and analyse texts. Is there a way out of this 'non-choice'? Can the gothic remain critically useful?

In this Coda, we address the loaded question of gothic naming, considering how and why it remains valuable to understand fiction with diverse regional and cultural roots within a (world-)gothic horizon. Our discussion unfolds in two parts. First, we will briefly rehearse the argument that underpins one of this volume's central claims: namely, that to extricate gothic studies from the taxonomic bind in which it is placed concerning fiction from beyond the so-called West, the origin story of the gothic needs to be reconceived. Specifically, the Eurocentric picture of modernity within which gothic has been understood – one that begins with bourgeois and industrial revolutions at the end of the eighteenth century – should be broadened to account for the preceding history of colonial and capitalist extraction and exploitation in the Americas, which facilitates the rise of Europe – and Britain – to global hegemony. In the Introduction, we have outlined this longer and wider view of modernity, drawing on Immanuel Wallerstein's world-systems theory, which locates the rise of the capitalist world-economy in the 'long' sixteenth century. Thinkers such as C. L. R. James, Eric Williams, Sylvia Wynter, Sidney Mintz, and Enrique Dussel affirm this historical picture, allowing us to understand industrialisation and modernity as processes that happen first in the plantation economies of the 'New World'. Similarly enabling is Simon Gikandi's extensive analysis of the central shaping force exerted on the culture of Europe's age of reason and taste by the global trade in enslaved African people.[2] In the light of these and related perspectives, it becomes clear that the Enlightenment, industrialisation, and modernity have always been global processes, and that the 'proper' gothic which responds to them from the vantage of Britain is in fact a provincial example of world-cultural production: one that conjoins 'oral cultures, folkloric materials, and Indigenous knowledge-systems from the periphery, with the printed traditions, behavioural performances, and institutionally consecrated notations of the core'.[3] In other words, all gothic – including the canonical, 'original' version – is in fact world-gothic: a situated cultural response that encodes, from the located vantage of its production, encounters with global capitalist modernity. How do we begin to account for world-gothic cultural production that is at once cognisant of the systemic global processes of colonialism and capitalism, and attentive to local, culturally specific forms of literary production?

The second part of our answer builds on and draws together world-cultural and postcolonial theorisations of catachresis – outlined more fully below – to conceptualise the categorisation and linking of discrete world-cultural forms as world-gothic. For 'the gothic' to remain useful as a way of designating fiction, we suggest that the term should be understood as just one possible name, which *catachrestically* – imperfectly and partially – describes heterogeneous and always situated cultural, folk, and spiritual responses to the socio-ecological changes wrought unevenly by the capitalist world-system. To the end of elaborating this thesis, this collection has assembled a range of world-gothic perspectives, which together offer a 'critical invitation' (to borrow phrasing from Caitlin Vandertop's contribution): 'Rather than separating "European" gothic texts from their "Postcolonial" inheritors', world-gothic allows us to 'read them all together as distinct but dialogic responses to ... world-historical transformations'. For a clarifying example of what is at stake in this project, we can turn to the concept of haunting – a universalised and overdetermined sign of the gothic. Gothic haunting is an illustrative representation of 'proper' gothic's Eurocentric, monotheistic, and specifically Christian assumptions. In order to avoid collapsing this mode of haunting into other forms of spirit-relation, it is necessary to situate religion and the secular in the developmental narrative of modernity as the Age of Reason, that was facilitated by 'its defeat of "superstition"' and irrational religion.[4] 'The concept of religion' was created and 'enshrined in Western epistemology',[5] helping to secure Enlightenment Europe's self-identified supremacy, as well as providing the 'religious origins of secular modernity'.[6] Thinking with Talal Asad, Sîan Melvill Hawthorne emphasises the overdetermined and ethnocentric sense of religion as a universal category that 'obscures the history of its production and its subsequent violent inscription'.[7] The point here is that to apply 'religion' to 'non-western traditions is to subject them to a conceptual regime that always already implies their inferiority whilst at the same time mistakenly assuming a shared referentiality'.[8] If religion, like the gothic, is an unavoidable but insufficient term, then, like Hawthorne, we find profit in catachresis as a tool to conceptualise the heterogloss and asymmetrical enunciations of gothic and cosmological world-culture.

Prosaically, catachresis refers to the misuse of words. It can include formulations that replace an intended or expected word with another of a different, or more ambiguous meaning; or those that transgress lexical boundaries when no adequate word exists or when the meaning is already strained.[9] In his formative theorisation of catachresis, Jacques Derrida reflects on the concept as a way to figure the discursive plurality that undergirds the production of cohesive philosophical discourse, with a view to making a deeper point about the always-partial nature of signification itself. Addressing the assumption that instances of catachresis occur when theoreticians encounter 'a meaning which did not yet have its own proper sign in language',[10] Derrida argues that this unsignified meaning does not exist in the world, but is in fact itself only made possible through pre-existing systems of (philosophical) signification. Moments of catachresis, when meaning appears markedly in excess of the sign that tries to capture it, therefore actually dramatise something essential to philosophical language, and by extension to language generally: meaning *always* partially escapes the sign, because all signs only gain their meaning in the context, and through the interplay, of differences within much wider networks of signification.

Extending Derrida's analysis in the domain of postcolonial theory, Spivak calls attention to the irruptive potential that arises when the apparent coherence of established signs – like religion, gothic, modernity – begins to falter in the face of referents that exceed them. Spivak understands these moments of catachresis as opportunities for 'reversing, displacing, and seizing the apparatus of value-coding';[11] they enable an intentional and disruptive critique, which 'signals a necessary category *crisis* because of the sign's inadequacy'.[12] This inadequacy arises from the erroneous universal application of a master term 'without literal referents' – a line that certainly describes the situation gothic studies currently finds itself in.[13] Transregional and culturally plural inscriptions of gothic figures and tropes, as well as the multivocal criticism that is currently addressing these, have together unveiled a category crisis at the heart of the field: the signifying capacity of the gothic is straining, as the term is being considered in relation to cultural production for which – at least in its established formulations – it was not coined to describe.

Thinking with Derrida and (more fully) with Spivak, it becomes clear that the way beyond this bind is not to double down on the parameters and characteristics that adhere to the gothic of an inherited critical tradition, but instead to consider the ways in which this initial, master act of naming may itself have been a misnaming. Indeed, as Jaqueline Howards warns, attempts to read the gothic as 'a system of certain unifying stylistic and structural features are bound to see them as flawed'. For Howard, gothic has always been legible through Mikhail Bakhtin's concept of 'heteroglossia', which provides a view of the genre – even in its canonical iterations – as a 'plural form', that 'draws on and recontextualises or transforms prior discursive structures, fragments of "the already said", both literary and non-literary'.[14] Under Bakhtin's reading, the novel form in which gothic is articulated is dialogic: heteroglossia enters it through 'the totality of the world of objects and ideas depicted and expressed in it [and] by means of the social diversity of speech types and by the differing individual voices that flourish under such conditions'.[15]

Howard's Bakhtinian analysis in fact helps us to see that gothic form can itself be understood as a kind of catachresis: a response to the disruptive encounter with capitalist modernity, which synthesises new figures and narratives from existing cultural materials, in an effort to find the terms in which an unfamiliar reality can be grasped. This point has been made influentially by Stephen Shapiro and thinkers associated with the Warwick School. In an analysis on which many contributors to this collection draw, Shapiro observes that 'terrific representations' reappear cyclically alongside phases of capitalist accumulation: 'forms of catachrestic narrative emerge as a structure of feeling that attempts to make sense of this strongly felt but inchoately understood phagocytosis'.[16] Relatedly, the Warwick Research Collective argues that 'irrealist or catachrestic features' register the spatio-temporal disjuncture and compression of competing realities caused by the combined and uneven development of the world-system. Viewed with Howard, these insights help to underscore the linkages between all the forms of world-gothic tracked and analysed across this collection. In the Introduction, we drew attention to the much-discussed contemporary proliferation of gothic fictions on a global scale – narratives which characteristically integrate canonical gothic conventions with figures and forms in local circulation in the text's regional context of production. What is interesting about these fictions, we proposed, is precisely their (re)activation of diverse cultural responses to (prior) encounters with capitalist modernity, in order to forge what Shapiro names catachrestic lexica, capable of giving shape to socio-ecological shifts underway unevenly across the world-system. Howard's reading thus helps us to discern the symmetry between these present works and the heteroglossic narrative form that came to be called 'the gothic' after the late eighteenth century: itself an assemblage of existing cultural materials, produced in response – as we have shown – to the new, located reality ushered in by shifts in world-systemic relations.

Following Spivak, we can therefore understand the congealed conception of 'gothic' – a set of conventions inaugurated with Walpole, Radcliffe, and others and then disseminated around the world – as a catachrestic category, which specifically mistakes for the definitive instance an aesthetic mode that was (and is) in fact a rooted and provincial example of a much more heterogeneous cultural form. Rephrased in the particular terms of the arguments we and the contributors to this volume have made, this insight requires us to move away from an approach that lays stress on the identification of modulations to an initial gothic form, or that entombs gothic within a hermetically sealed 'Western' culture, operating on a parallel track with other cultures that may or may not possess coincidentally analogous figures. Rather, world-gothic asks us to consider how discrete cultures of the monstrous respond in irreducibly specific ways to linked shifts within the same world-historical horizon. World-gothic methodology thus needs to be as attuned to the multiscale and polyglot as it is to connectivity. Or put differently: to revive the critical use of the gothic in the transregional context, we ought to consider it as a catachrestic term that imperfectly and insufficiently brings heterogeneous registers, discourses, and texts into a nonetheless generative *strategic formation*.

Edward Said explains that a strategic formation 'is a way of analysing the relationship between texts and the way in which groups of texts, types of texts, even textual genres, acquire mass, density, and referential power among themselves and thereafter in the culture at large'.[17] The now-globalised critical category of the gothic has certainly organised fiction in this way, chiefly – as demonstrated in the Introduction and across this volume – by addressing how texts rooted in a range of cosmological formations dialogue with, or deviate from, an inaugural 'Western' gothic form. Other strategic formations are possible, however. In an instructive example, Ato Quayson extends Said's methodology to African writing, in order to affirm that fiction should not be taken as a transcription of Indigenous cosmology.[18] Rather, Quayson reminds us that these cosmologies exist 'interdiscursively' with the hegemonic culture and materiality of capitalist modernity. Fiction, he writes, is not a 'mirror of discrete cultural elements but rather a prismatic field of interaction between cultural and literary discourses'. Further, the particular structure of this interaction in a given text is shaped by the material conditions under which that text is written, and to which it responds. Taking this point up in the context of gothic studies, it becomes possible to see how reading gothic forms across regions and cultures need not collapse fictional genre and spiritual/cultural resources. Gothic literary production instead can be understood as prismatically mediating folk narrative, performance, rumours, and spirituality, which are brought into specific interdiscursive relations to register processes unevenly unfolding within the same world-historical horizon. In place of a gothic studies organised around an 'original' gothic form,

Quayson and Said thus help us to posit a different strategic formation, in which cultural production is assembled into relationships through a world-gothic principle.

The strategic formation of world-gothic brings into dialogue the full scope of monstrous cultural forms that follow in the wake of alienating encounters with capitalist modernity. The hyphenated 'world' component of the term is vital. It signals an acknowledgement of the interlinked but unequal context of the world-system and its world-cultures, providing the foundation on which differentially situated texts can be considered together, while at the same time affirming their irreducible specificity. That the gothic is an inexhaustive, catachrestic signifier is therefore built into the world-gothic approach, which sets out from the premise that gothic is only one name among many possible ways of conceptualising cultural responses to the located effects of world-systemic shifts. As a means of shaping a new strategic formation, the term gothic, modified by a 'world-' prefix, becomes generative because of this plurality: moving beyond a criticism that has mistaken the 'original' European gothic for a normative standard, world-gothic relocates this form as a single, situated expression within a wider world-historical cultural field. 'World-*gothic*' is thus necessary to restore the hegemonised category of the gothic to its actual position of provinciality; part of its critical power lies precisely in dethroning gothic's hegemony. Rendered provincial and catachrestic by the modifier 'world', gothic is then able to do the significant work of connecting apparently disparate cultural encodings of alienation and anxiety – imperfectly, partially, but also productively. As we have seen across this collection, the archive of world-gothic production attests to the violence through which our unequal planetary present has been wrought. World-gothic witnesses this history from vantages across a range of regions, subject positions, and cultural locations, illustrating the effects of power that fractures human lives and extra-human nature into strange and terrible hierarchies. At the same time, it allows us to discern the symmetries that connect these scalar experiences of harm, in turn helping us to grasp how the relationships that contour the world in jagged and violent ways also create the conditions of their own demise through collective and creative response.

Notes

1. Ian Conrich, 'Maori Tales of the Unexpected: The New Zealand Television Series Mataku as Indigenous Gothic', in G. Byron (ed.), *Globalgothic*, Manchester, Manchester University Press, 2013, 41.

2. Simon Gikandi, *Slavery and the Culture of Taste*, Princeton, Princeton University Press, 2011; Eric Williams, *Capitalism and Slavery*, Chapel Hill, The University of North Carolina Press, 2021; Sidney W. Mintz, *Sweetness and Power: The Place of Sugar in Modern History*, New York, Penguin, 1986.
3. Sharae Deckard and Stephen Shapiro (eds.), *World Literature, Neoliberalism, and the Culture of Discontent*, 1st ed., New York, Palgrave Macmillan, 2019, 11.
4. Sîan Melvill Hawthorne, 'Displacements: Religion, Gender, and the Catachrestic Demands of Postcoloniality', *Religion and Gender*, 3:2 (2013), 168–87, 172.
5. Daniel Dubuisson, *The Western Construction of Religion: Myths, Knowledge, and Ideology* Baltimore, MD, Johns Hopkins University Press, 2007, 94.
6. Hawthorne, 'Displacements', 172.
7. Hawthorne, 'Displacements', 174.
8. Hawthorne, 'Displacements', 174.
9. 'Catachresis', *Wikipedia*, 8 February 2024, https://en.wikipedia.org/w/index.php?title=Catachresis&oldid=1205050220.
10. Jacques Derrida, *Margins of Philosophy*, trans. A. Bass, Chicago, University of Chicago Press, 1982, 255.
11. Gayatri Chakravorty Spivak, 'Poststructuralism, Marginality, Postcoloniality and Value', in H. Geyer-Ryan and P. Collier (eds.), *Literary Theory Today*, 1st ed., Ithaca, NY, Cornell University Press, 1990, 228.
12. Hawthorne, 'Displacements', 183.
13. Hawthorne, 'Displacements', 183.
14. Jacqueline Howard, *Reading Gothic Fiction: A Bakhtinian Approach*, New York, Clarendon Press, 1994, 15–16, https://doi.org/10.1093/acprof:oso/9780198119920.001.0001.
15. Mikhail M. Bakhtin, *The Dialogic Imagination: Four Essays*, ed. M. Holquist, trans. M. Holquist and C. Emerson, Austin, University of Texas Press, 2010, 264.
16. Stephen Shapiro, 'Transvaal, Transylvania: Dracula's World-System and Gothic Periodicity', *Gothic Studies* 10:1 (May 2008), 29–47, 31, https://doi.org/10.7227/GS.10.1.5.
17. Edward W. Said, *Orientalism: Western Conceptions of the Orient*, London, Penguin, 2003, 20.
18. Ato Quayson, *Strategic Transformations in Nigerian Writing: Orality & History in the Work of Rev. Samuel Johnson, Amos Tutuola, Wole Soyinka & Ben Okri*, Oxford, J. Currey, 1997, 16–17.

Further Reading

Bakhtin, M. *Rabelais and his World*, trans. H. Iswolsky, Bloomington, Indiana University Press, 1984 (1965).
Deckard, S., N. Lawrence, N. Lazarus, et al. (Warwick Research Collective). *Combined and Uneven Development: Towards a New Theory of World Literature*, Liverpool, Liverpool University Press, 2015.
Deckard, S., M. Niblett, and S. Shapiro. *Tracking Capital: World-Systems, World-Ecology, World-Culture*, New York, SUNY Press, 2024.
Duncan, R. (ed.). *The Edinburgh Companion to Globalgothic*, Edinburgh, Edinburgh University Press, 2023.
Duncan, R. (ed). 'Decolonising Gothic', special issue, *Gothic Studies*, 24 (2022), 219–332.
Dussel, E. 'Europe, Modernity and Eurocentrism', *Nepantla: Views from the South*, 1 (2000), 465–78.
Federici, S. *Caliban and the Witch: Women, the Body and Primitive Accumulation*, London, Penguin Books 2021 (2004).
Garuba, H. 'Explorations in Animist Materialism: Notes on Reading/Writing African Literature, Culture, and Society', *Public Culture*, 15 (2003), 261–85.
Marx, K. *Capital: Volume 1*, trans. B. Fowkes, London, Penguin, 1976.
McNally, D. *Monsters of the Market: Zombies, Vampires and Global Capitalism*. Leiden, Brill, 2011.
Moore, J. W. *Capitalism in the Web of Life: Ecology and the Accumulation of Capital*, London, Verso, 2015.
Moretti, F. *Signs Taken for Wonders: Essays on the Sociology of Literary Form*, trans. S. Fischer, D. Forgacs, and D. Miller, London, Verso, 1983.
Niblett, M. *World Literature and Ecology: The Aesthetics of Commodity Frontiers, 1890–1950*, London, Palgrave Macmillan, 2020.
Oloff, K. *Ecology of the Zombie: World-Culture and the Monstrous*, Liverpool, Liverpool University Press, 2023.
Punter, D. *The Literature of Terror: The Gothic Tradition*, vol. 1, 2nd ed., London, Routledge, 1996.
Quijano, A. 'Coloniality of Power, Eurocentrism, and Latin America', *Nepantla: Views from the South*, 1 (2000), 533–80.
Shapiro, S. 'Transvaal, Transylvania: *Dracula*'s World-System and Gothic Periodicity', *Gothic Studies*, 10 (2008), 29–47.

Wallerstein, I. *World-Systems Analysis: An Introduction*, Durham, Duke University Press, 2004.
Williams, E. *Capitalism and Slavery*, Richmond, University of North Carolina Press, 1944.
Wynter, S. 'Jonkonnu in Jamaica: Towards the Interpretation of Folk Dance as a Cultural Process', *Jamaica Journal*, 4:3 (1970), 34–48.

Introduction: Five Hundred Years of World-Gothic

Chakrabarty, D. *Provincializing Europe: Postcolonial Thought and Historical Difference*, Princeton, Princeton University Press, 2000.
Comaroff J. and J. L. Comaroff. 'Occult Economies and the Violence of Abstraction: Notes from the South African Postcolony', *American Ethnologist*, 26 (1999), 279–303.
Geschiere, P. *The Modernity of Witchcraft: Politics and the Occult in Postcolonial Africa*, Charlottesville, University of Virginia Press, 1997.
James, C. L. R. *The Black Jacobins: Toussaint L'Ouverture and the San Domingo Revolution*, New York, Vintage, [1938] 1989.
Mintz, S. *Sweetness and Power: The Place of Sugar in Modern History*, New York, Penguin, 1985.
Ong, A. *Spirits of Resistance and Capitalist Discipline: Factory Women in Malaysia*, New York, SUNY Press, [1987] 2010.
Paravisini-Gebert, L. 'Colonial and Postcolonial Gothic: The Caribbean', in J. E. Hogle (ed.), *The Cambridge Companion to Gothic Fiction*, Cambridge, Cambridge University Press, 229–58.
Taussig, M. T. *The Devil and Commodity Fetishism in South America*, Chapel Hill, University of North Carolina Press, 2010(1980).
White, L. *Speaking with Vampires: Rumor and History in Colonial Africa*, Berkeley, University of California Press, 2000.

1 The Undead's Capitalist World-System

Anderson, B. *Imagined Communities: Reflections on the Origin and Spread of Nationalism*, London, Verso, 1983.
Lukács, G. *The Theory of the Novel: A Historico-Philosophical Essay on the Forms of Great Epic Literature*, trans. A. Bostock, Cambridge, The MIT Press, 1971.
Memmi, A. *Decolonization and the Decolonized*, trans. R. Bononno, Minneapolis, University of Minnesota Press, 2006.
Moreno-García, S. *Mexican Gothic*, New York, Del Ray, 2021.
Shaviro, S. 'Introduction', in M. Bould and S. Shaviro (eds.), *This Is Not a Science Fiction Textbook*, London, Goldsmiths Press, 2024, 8–10.
Wallerstein, I. *Historical Capitalism: With Capitalist Civilization London*, New York, Verso, 1983.

Wallerstein, I. *The Modern World-System IV: Centrist Liberalism Triumphant, 1789–1914*, Berkeley, University of California Press, 2011.
Weinstock, J. A. 'The Anthropocene', in J. D. Edwards, R. Graulund, and J. Höglund (eds.), *Dark Scenes from Damaged Earth: The Gothic Anthropocene*, Minneapolis, University of Minnesota Press, 2022, 7–25.
Zombi Child, dir. B. Bonello, Paris, Ad Vitam, 2019.

2 Whiteness and the 'Western' Gothic Tradition

Arendt, H. 'Imperialism, Nationalism, Chauvinism', *The Review of Politics*, 7 (1945), 441–63.
Bonnet, A. 'How the British Working Class Became White: The Symbolic (Re)formation of Racialized Capitalism', *Journal of Historical Sociology*, 11 (1998), 316–40.
Brantlinger, P. *Rule of Darkness: British Literature and Imperialism, 1830–1914*, Ithaca, Cornell University Press, 1988.
Dyer, R. *White*, London, Routledge, 1997.
Gikandi, S. *Slavery and the Culture of Taste*, New Jersey, Princeton University Press, 2011.
Ledger, S. 'In Darkest England: The Terror of Degeneration in Fin-de-Siecle Britain', in P. Childs (ed.), *Post-Colonial Theory and English Literature: A Reader*, Edinburgh, Edinburgh University Press, 1999, 216–26.
Malchow, H. L. *Gothic Images of Race in Nineteenth-Century England*, Stanford, Stanford University Press, 1996.
Wester, M. 'The Gothic Origins of Anti-Blackness: Genre Tropes in Nineteenth-Century Moral Panics and (Abject) Folk Devils', *Gothic Studies*, 24 (2022), 228–45.

3 Gothic and Labour: Metabolic, Reproductive, International

Bhattacharya, T. (ed.). *Social Reproduction Theory: Remapping Class, Recentering Oppression*, London, Pluto Press, 2017.
Duncan, R. *South African Gothic: Anxiety and Creative Dissent in the Post-Apartheid Imagination and Beyond*, Cardiff, University of Wales Press, 2018.
Fraser, N. *Cannibal Capitalism: How Our System is Devouring Democracy, Care, and the Planet and What We Can Do About It*, London, Verso, 2022.
Segato, R. *The War Against Women*, trans. R. McGlazer, London, John Wiley & Sons, 2024.

4 Pre-colonial Gothic and the Windigo

Borwein, N. S. (ed.). *Global Indigenous Horror*, Jackson, University Press of Mississippi, 2025.

Crow, C. L. (ed.). *A Companion to the Gothic: American Gothic and Race*, Hoboken, John Wiley & Sons, 2014.
Faflak, J. and J. Haslam (eds.). *American Gothic Culture: An Edinburgh Companion*, Edinburgh, Edinburgh University Press, 2016.
Gore, A. 'Gothic Silence: S. Alice Callahan's Wynema, the Battle of the Little Bighorn, and the Indigenous Unspeakable', *Studies in American Indian Literatures*, 30 (2018), 24–49.
Simmons, K. '"It Has to Stop": Refusing Colonial Narratives in The Only Good Indians', *American Indian Quarterly*, 47 (2023), 70–85.
Starrs, B. 'Writing Indigenous Vampires: Aboriginal Gothic or Aboriginal Fantastic?', *M/C: A Journal of Media and Culture*, 17 (2014), n.p.
Velie, A. R. 'Vizenor's Indian Gothic', *MELUS*, 17 (1991–2), 75–85.

5 Hauntings: African-Based Spirituality in World Gothic Literature

Anderson, J. *Conjure in African American Society*, Baton Rouge, Louisiana State University Press, 2005.
Chireau, Y. *Black Magic: Religion and the African American Conjuring Tradition*, Berkeley, The University of California Press, 2006.
Cumpsty, R. *Postsecular Poetics: Negotiating the Sacred and Secular in Contemporary African Fiction*, New York, Routledge, 2023.
Hogle, J. E. (ed.). *The Cambridge Companion to Gothic Fiction*, Cambridge, Cambridge University Press, 2002.
Redding, A. *Haints: American Ghosts, Millennial Passions, and Contemporary Gothic Fictions*, Tuscaloosa, University of Alabama Press, 2011.
Weinstock, J. (ed.), *The Cambridge Companion to American Gothic*, New York, Cambridge University Press, 2017.
Wester, M. *African American Gothic: Screams from Shadowed Places*, New York, Palgrave MacMillian, 2012.
Wester, M. and X. Aldana Reyes (eds.). *Twenty-First Century Gothic: An Edinburgh Companion*, Edinburgh, Edinburgh University Press, 2021.

6 Vampiric Exhaustion and Extractive Form: The Mozambican Miner

Deckard, S. 'Extractive Gothic', in R. Duncan (ed.), *The Edinburgh Companion to Globalgothic*, Edinburgh, Edinburgh University Press, 2023, 131–47.
First, R. *Black Gold: The Mozambican Miner, Proletarian and Peasant*, Brighton, Harvester Press, 1983.
Mendes, O. *Portagem*, Maputo, Instituto Nacional do Livro e do Disco, 1981 (1965).
Okoth, C. 'The Extractive Form of Contemporary Black Writing: Dionne Brand and Yaa Gyasi', *Textual Practice*, 35 (2021), 379–94.

Sousa, N. 'Magaíça', in *Sangue Negro*, Maputo, Associação de Escritores Moçambicanos, 2001 (1950), 84–5.

Waller, T. *Genres of Transition: Literature and Economy in Portuguese-Speaking Southern Africa*, Liverpool, Liverpool University Press, 2024.

7 Subversive Sorcery and Reparative Witchcraft: *Huesera*'s Challenges to Coloniality

Federici, S. *Beyond the Periphery of the Skin: Rethinking, Remaking and Reclaiming the Body in Contemporary Capitalism*, Oakland, PM Press, 2020.

Hutton, R. *The Witch: A History of Fear, from Ancient Times to Present*, New Haven, Yale University Press, 2017.

Krzywinska, T. *A Skin for Dancing In: Possession, Witchcraft and Voodoo in Film*, Trowbridge, Flicks Books, 2000.

Lander, E. *La Colonialidad Del Saber: Eurocentrismo y Ciencias Sociales. Perspectivas Latinoamericanas*, Buenos Aires, Consejo Latinoamericano de Ciencas Sociales (CLACSO). 1993.

Taylor, L. *Darkly: Black History and America's Gothic Soul*, London, Repeater, 2020.

Tuck, E. E., and C. Ree. 'A Glossary of Haunting', in Stacey Holman Jones, Tony E. Adams, and Carolyn Ellis (eds.), *Handbook of Autoethnography*, Walnut Creek, Left Coast Press, 2013, 639–58.

Wynter, S. 'Beyond Miranda's Meanings: Un/Silencing the "Demonic Ground" of Caliban's "Woman"', in Joy James and T. Denean Sharpley-Whiting (eds.), *The Black Feminist Reader*, Malden, Blackwell Publishers, 2000, 109–27.

8 World-Gothic and the Sublime

Bourdieu, P. *Distinction: A Social Critique of the Judgment of Taste*, trans. R. Nice, London, Routledge, 1984.

Eagleton, T. *The Ideology of the Aesthetic*, London, Blackwell, 1991.

Giles, J. M. 'Can the Sublime Be Postcolonial? Aesthetics, Politics, and Environment in Amitav Ghosh's *The Hungry Tide*', *Cambridge Journal of Postcolonial Literary Inquiry*, 1 (2014), 223–42.

Groom, N. *The Gothic: A Very Short Introduction*, Oxford, Oxford University Press, 2012.

Mishra, V. *The Gothic Sublime*, Albany, State University of New York Press, 1994.

Nayar, P. K. *English Writing and India, 1600–1920: Colonizing Aesthetics*, London, Routledge, 2008.

Paravisini-Gebert, L. 'Colonial and Postcolonial Gothic: The Caribbean', in J. E. Hogle (ed.), *The Cambridge Companion to Gothic Fiction*, Cambridge, Cambridge University Press, 2002, 229–58.

Shaw, P. *The Sublime*, London, Routledge, 2017.

9   A Planetary Grotesque

Arens, S. 'Killer Stories: "Globalizing" the Grotesque in Alain Mabanckou's *African Psycho* and Leïla Slimani's *Chanson douce*', *Irish Journal of French Studies*, 20 (2020), 143–72.
Cruickshank, D. *The Grotesque Modernist Body: Gothic Horror and Carnival Satire in Art and Writing*, London, Palgrave Macmillan, 2024.
Edwards, J. D. and R. Graulund. *Grotesque*, 2nd ed., Abingdon, Routledge, 2025.
Graulund, R. 'Grotesque', in J. Frow (ed.), *The Oxford Encyclopedia of Literary Theory*, Oxford, Oxford University Press, 2022.
Siddique, S. and R. Raphael. *Transnational Horror Cinema: Bodies of Excess and the Global Grotesque*, London, Palgrave Macmillan, 2016.

10   Uncanny Animism: Reframing the World-Gothic with Amos Tutuola

Durrant S. and P. Dickinson (eds.). 'Animism in a Planetary Frame', special issue, *New Formations*, 104–5 (2021), 4–251.
Garuba, H. 'On Animism, Modernity/Colonialism, and the African Order of Knowledge: Provisional Reflections', *e-flux*, 36 (2012), n. p.
Kumavie, D. 'The Para-Worlds of Lesley Nneka Arimah's *What It Means When a Man Falls from the Sky*', *Qui Parle*, 31 (2022), 37–65.
Nyamnjoh, F. B. *Drinking from the Cosmic Gourd: How Tutuola Can Change Our Minds*, Mankon, Langaa, 2017.
Phalafala, U. P. 'Time Is Always NOW: Animist Materialism in Keorapetse Kgositsile's Temporal Order', *Scrutiny2*, 22, (2017), 33–48.
Rooney, C. *African Literature, Animism and Politics*, Abingdon, Routledge, 2000.
Soyinka, W. *Myth, Literature and the African World*, Cambridge, Cambridge University Press, 1976
Topper, R. *Animist Poetics: Ancestral Trauma and Regeneration in African Literature*, Albany, SUNY Press, 2025.

11   Abject/Abhuman/Human: Provincialising World-Gothic Monstrosity

Condren, M. 'Women, Shame and Abjection: Reflections in the Light of Julia Kristeva', *Contact*, 130 (1999), 10–19.
Duncan, R. 'Gothic Supernaturalism in the "African Imagination": Locating an Emerging Form', in M. Adejunmobi and C. Coetzee (eds.), *Routledge Handbook of African Literature*, Abingdon, Routledge, 2019.
Khanna, R. *Dark Continents: Psychoanalysis and Colonialism*, Durham, Duke University Press, 2003.

Lugones, M. 'Heterosexualism and the Colonial / Modern Gender System', *Hypatia*, 22 (2007), 186–209.
Ouma, C. 'Reading the Diasporic Abiku in Helen Oyeyemi's *The Icarus Girl*', *Research in African Literatures*, 45 (2014), 188–205.
Rudge, T. 'Julia Kristeva: Abjection, Embodiment and Boundaries', in F. Collyer (ed.), *The Palgrave Handbook of Social Theory in Health, Illness and Medicine*, London, Palgrave Macmillan, 2015, 504–19.
Williams, S. 'Abjection and Anthropological Praxis', *Anthropological Quarterly*, 66 (1993), 67–75.

12 Gothic Inheritances in Oceania: Problems of Origins and Ownership

Deckard, S. 'EcoGothic', in M. Wester and X. A. Reyes (eds.), *Twenty-First-Century Gothic: An Edinburgh Companion*, Edinburgh, Edinburgh University Press, 2019.
Jolly, R. 'South Seas Gothic: Pierre Loti and Robert Louis Stevenson', *English Literature in Transition, 1880–1920*, 47 (2004), 28–49.
Long, M. and M. Hayward. 'Subramani's Sugarcane Gothic', in *The Rise of Pacific Literature: Decolonization, Radical Campuses, And Modernism*, New York, Columbia University Press, 2024, 189–211.
Manfredi, C. 'R. L. Stevenson's Samoan Gothic: Representing Late Nineteenth-Century Plantations', *Pacific Studies*, 39 (2016), 343–69.
Straß, H. '"A Living Death, Life Inside-Out": The Postcolonial Toxic Gothic in Robert Barclay's *Meḷaḷ: A Novel of the Pacific*', in J. Habjan and F. Imlinger (eds.), *Globalizing Literary Genres*, London, Routledge, 2016, 228–40.
Vandertop, C. 'Ghosts of the Plantation: Sugar, Narrative Energetics and Gothic Ecologies in Fiji', *Green Letters: Studies in Ecocriticism*, 24 (2020), 155–68.
Vandertop, C. '(Dis)inheriting Stevenson: Inheritance Crisis, Postcolonial Periodization, and Literary Property in the Pacific', in S. Ponzanesi and P. de Medeiros (eds.), *Postcolonial Theory in Crisis*, Berlin, De Gruyter, 2024, 173–88.
Vandertop, C. '"The Land Has Eyes and Teeth": Copra, Gothic Fertility and Literary Genealogies in Oceania', in M. Niblett, C. Campbell, E. Hugo, and C. Okoth (eds.), special issue 'World Literature and Commodity Frontiers', *Interventions*, in press.

13 Tough Oil Gothic: Contemporary Petrofiction across the North–South Divide

Adunbi, O. *Oil Wealth and Insurgency in Nigeria*, Bloomington, Indiana University Press, 2015.

Aghoghovwia, P. *Violent Ecotropes: Petroculture in the Niger Delta*, Cape Town, HSRC Press, 2022.
Deckard, S. and S. Shapiro (eds.). *World Literature, Neoliberalism, and the Culture of Discontent*, Cham, Palgrave, 2019.
Niblett, M. *World Literature and Ecology: The Aesthetics of Commodity Frontiers, 1890–1950*, Cham, Palgrave, 2020.
Parsons, L. *Carbon Colonialism: How the Rich Countries Export Climate Breakdown*, Manchester, Manchester University Press, 2023.
Sæther, A. K. *De beste intensjoner: Oljelandet i klimakampen*, 2nd ed., Oslo, Cappelen Damm, 2019.
Tidwell, C. and C. Soles (eds.). *Fear and Nature: Ecohorror Studies in the Anthropocene*, University Park, The Pennsylvania State University Press, 2021.
Wenzel, J. *The Disposition of Nature: Environmental Crisis and World Literature*, New York, Fordham University Press, 2020.

14 Scheherazade and Bluebeard: The World-Gothic and Bloody Chambers in Arab Women's Writing

Douglas, R. *Feminist Gothic, Critical Irrealism and Arab Women's World-Literature: 'Living with Ghosts'*, London, Palgrave Macmillan Springer, 2025.
Haddad, J. *I Killed Scheherazade: Confessions of an Angry Arab Woman*, London, Saqi, 2010.
Said, E. W. *Culture and Imperialism*, London, Vintage, 1994.
Seigneurie, K. 'Arabic Literature and World Literature', in *Teaching Modern Arabic Literature in Translation*, M. Hartman (ed.), New York, The Modern Language Association of America, 2018, 21–40.
Shapiro, S. 'The World-System of Global Gothic, Horror and Weird', in R Duncan (ed.), *The Edinburgh Companion to Globalgothic*, Edinburgh, Edinburgh University Press, 2023, 38–52.
Tatar, M. *Secrets Beyond the Door: The Story of Bluebeard and His Wives*, Princeton, Princeton University Press, 2004.
Walker, C. 'In Bluebeard's Closet: Women Who Write with the Wolves', *LIT: Literature Interpretation Theory*, 7 (1996), 13–25.

Coda: Catachresis and the Politics of Gothic Naming

Jacques Derrida, *Margins of Philosophy*, trans. A. Bass, Chicago, University of Chicago Press, 1982.
Howard, J. *Reading Gothic Fiction: A Bakhtinian Approach*. New York, Clarendon Press, 1994.
Hawthorne, S. M. and A. S. Van Klinken. 'Catachresis: Religion, Gender, and Postcoloniality', *Religion and Gender*, 3:2 (2013), 159–67.

Quayson, A. *Strategic Transformations in Nigerian Writing: Orality and History in the Work of Rev. Samuel Johnson, Amos Tutuola, Wole Soyinka and Ben Okri*, Oxford, James Currey, 1997.

Spivak, G. C. 'Poststructuralism, Marginality, Postcoloniality and Value', in H. Geyer-Ryan and P. Collier *ed.*, *Literary Theory Today*, Ithaca, Cornell University Press, 1990.

Index

abhuman, 205, 207, 217, *see also* abjection
   double, 208, 211
   historicised, 213
abjection, 31, 182, 206, 209
   European, 213
abolition, 7, 52
Achebe, Chinua, 108, 109–11, 151
alienation, 6, 8, 18, 50, 186, *see also* Marx, Karl; Wynter, Sylvia
   culture of, 13
   literature of, 5, 52
animality, 135, 214, *see also* abjection
animism, 192, 208, *see also* realism
apartheid, 72, 74, 120
   post, 74, 75
apocalypse, 31, 41, 91, 92
appropriation, 83, 226, 262, 265
   cultural, 36
   ecological, 63
   historic, 226
Artificial Intelligence (AI), 249
Atlantique (film), 38

Bakhtin, Mikhail, 7, 175, 182
   heteroglossia, 280
Barclay, Robert, *see Meļaļ*
Beloved (novel), 61, 103–4
Black Metamorphosis (book), 7–8, 35
Blackwood, Algernon, 88, 90
Blood Quantum (film), 92–5
Brontë, Charlotte, 159, *see also Jane Eyre*
bruja, 141, *see also* witch; witchcraft
Brygger, Jesper, *see Transporterne*
Burke, Edmund, 153, 157, *see also* sublime
Byron, Glennis, 1, *see also* globalgothic; Globalgothic

cannibalism, 81, 87, 152, 162, 178, 179
capitalism, 48, 52, 54, 57, *see also* colonialism; extractivism; enslavement; consumerism; coloniality

colonial, 126, 205
   global, 63, 65, 114, 183
   gothic, 64
   historical, 28–30, 62
   industrial, 53, 121
   late, 242
   neoliberal, 249
   patriarchal, 62, 260
   racial, 47, 72, 123, *see also* apartheid
   transition to, 29
cash crop, 119, *see also* commodity
catachresis, 278–9
Chakrabarty, Dipesh, 13
class, *see also* capitalism
   bourgeois, 201
   insurgent bourgeoisie, 33
   middle, 49, 71, 146, 195
   peasant, 29
   settler, 117
   tension, 53, 121
   working, 54, 56, 125, 128, 196, 265
climate
   catastrophe, 27
   change, 243, 245
   emergency, 246
colonialism, 55, 57, 70, 108
   European, 233
   nuclear, 237
   settler, 58, 82, 85, 91, 119
coloniality, 111, 135, 138, 143, 194, 214
   embodied, 88
   erasure, 86
   gendered, 142
   history, 86
   negotiated, 136
   power, 84, 87, 89, 93
   resistance to, 85, 134
commodity, 188
   agricultural, 67–9
   coal, 126
   exchange, 122

commodity (cont.)
  fetish, 6, 48, 126, see also Marx, Karl
  frontier, 242
  ivory, 70, 152
  oil, see resource; extraction
  sugar, 8, 36, 127
Conrad, Joseph, 152, 153, see also Heart of Darkness
consumerism, 51, 93
consumption
  meat, 177
core, 26, 35, 245, 247
cosmology, 100, 112–13, 207, 281
  Caribbean, 8
  Catholic, 113, 216
  Igbo, 215, 216
  Indigenous, 195
  Judeo-Christian, 99, 103, 105, 108–9, 144
  Yoruba, 186, 189–91, 211–12
crisis, 58, 245
  agricultural, 119

Deckard, Sharae, 65, 118, 235, 242, 246
decolonial, 217
  aesthetic, 137
  critiques, 212
  studies, 11, 36, 154, 160
decoloniality, 37, 154
decolonisation, 38, 94
Derrida, Jacques, 194, 278, 279
diaspora, 100–1, 209, 267
  cultural production, 219
domestic
  gothic, 61, 67, 75, 228, see also inheritance
  labour, 62, 71
  production, 119
  violence, 62, 269
Dracula (novel), 47, 55, 156, 158, 161
dystopia, 158, 163, 178

ecology, 3, 15, 123, see also world-ecology; climate
  corrosion, 243
  devastated, 234
  Marxist, 242
  socio-, 3
Emezi, Akwaeke, see *Freshwater* (novel)
Enlightenment, 99, 263
  humanist, 154
  intellectual tradition, 16
  reason, 175
enslavement, 35, 47, 49, 70, 103
estrangement, 8
ethno-gothic, 86
Eurocentrism, 4, 11, 34, 103, 135, 146
  gothic, 171
  resistance to, 136

exorcism, 104, 229
exploitation, 13, 64, 71, 75, 135
  capitalist, 254
  colonial, 134
extraction, 121, 127, see also mining; resource
  capitalist, 3
  fossil fuel, 243, 244
  oil, 251
extractivism, 41, 48, 201, 228
  capitalist, 118
  colonial, 121, 129, 229, 248
  critique of, 231
  resource, 233, see also commodity, modernity

Fanon, Frantz, 127, 138, 195
Federici, Silvia, 139, 259, 266
feminism, 62, 268
fin de siècle, 47, 56, 151
folklore, 104, 261
  Caribbean, 112
  global, 272
  Indian, 264
  island, 227
  oceanic, 226, 239
  oral, 262
  practice, 264
  world, 226, 229
  Yoruba, 189, see also cosmology
Frankenstein (novel), 9, 25, 47, 52, 53, 158
Freshwater (novel), 215
Freud, Sigmund, 125, 199–200

gender, 14, 73, 143, 145, 207
  inequality, 183
genocide, 85, 138
ghost, 103, 111, 114, 188, see also haunting
  spirit, 12
Ghostkeeper (film), 88–9
Gikandi, Simon, 7, 46, 195, 227, 277, see also *Slavery and the Culture of Taste*
globalgothic, 10, 63, 83, 87
  definition, 1
  scholarship, 96
Globalgothic (book), 63, 154
grotesque, 170–1, 210
  body, 183
  etymology, 173
  horror, 177
  pageantry, 173
  planetary, 183
  politics, 182
  protest, 182

haunting, 61, 99, 100, 102, 105, 112, 254
  colonial history, 109, 229

cycle of, 125
Eurocentric, 102
Euro-Christian, 105
familial, 156, 228
landscape, 117
mode, 278
narratives of, 3, 114
overdetermined, 278
plantation, 230
Heart of Darkness (novella), 151, 152, 161, 162
hegemony, 11, 138
heteronormative, 17, 65, 135, 141, 145, 219, 231
horror, 26, 33, 38
   body, 158, 176, 177, 218
   eco-, 250
   film, 140
   folk, 169
   global, 105
   imaginaries, 139
   new, 39
   systemic, 65
   visual culture, 146
Hurley, Kelly, *see* abhuman

immigration, 68, 212
imperialism, 29, 54, 152, 155
   capitalist, 36
   critical, 11
   cultural, 111, 114
industrialisation, 4, 52, 54, 195, 277, *see also* capitalism; modernity; revolution
   anxiety of, 200
   Britain, 6, 9, 45, 47, 54
   European, 3
   Nigerian, 201
   South Africa, 72
industry
   beauty, 180
   fossil, 256
   publishing, 265
inheritance, 66, 228
   colonial, 230, 234
   cursed, 236
irrealism, 242, 246, 280, *see also* Warwick Research Collective (WReC)

Jane Eyre (novel), 40, 159, 214, 264

Kant, Immanuel, 153, 160–1
Kristeva, Julia, 206, *see also* abjection

labour, 73, 139, 213
   alienated, 12
   capital, 9
   division of, 118, 123
   immigrant, 68
   industrial, 53
   market, 119
   migrant, 117, 120, 127
   slave, 73
   wage, 65, 196
liberalism, 31, 41
Lugones, María, 136
Lyotard, Jean-François, 152, 160, 163, 164–5

Marx, Karl, 5–6, 8, 28, 117, 122
Marxism, 35, 48, 63
materialism, 64, 75
   historical, 195
Meḻaḻ (novel), 229, 234, 236, 238
Mendes, Orlando, *see Portagem*
Mexican Gothic (novel), 40–1
Midsommar (film), 169–70, 171, 180
Mies, Maria, 62, 72, 139
mining, 40, 117, 120, 124, 127, *see also* extraction
   capital, 128
   coal, 126, 127, *see also* commodity
   colonial, 118, 124
   complex, 121, 123
   gold, 117, 119
   silver, 41
Mishra, Vijay, *see* sublime
Mlungu Wam (film), 71
modernism, 189
   African, 188
modernity, 45, 50, 99, 115, 171
   African, 201
   capitalist, 10, 13, 153, 186, 277
   colonial, 136, 186, 214, *see* capitalism
   Indigenous, 189
monsters, 90, *see also* abhuman
   feminine, 66
   mythic, 235
   supernatural, 227
   undead, 25–6, 34–5
   werewolf, 117
monstrosity, 6, 31, 170, 205, 250
   discourse of, 255
   extractive, 255
Moore, Jason W., 3, 64, 242, *see also* world-ecology
Moreno-Garcia, Silvia, 14, 276, *see also Mexican Gothic*
Morrison, Toni, 61, *see also Beloved*
mythology, 37
   oceanic, 229, 234

nahual, *see* witch
neoliberalisation, 14, 41, 244
Nixon, Rob, *see Slow Violence*

Okorafor, Nnedi, 247, 248
Oloff, Kerstin, 9, 64, 134
Oyeyemi, Helen, *see The Icarus Girl*

pagan, 110, 172, 216
pathogen, 68, 92, 234
patriarchy, 62, 119, 135, 144, 259, 260
   capitalist, 268, 272
   cultural, 266
   femicide, 62
   violence, 260, 262
periodisation, 28
periphery, 26, 128, 247, 277
   semi-periphery, 117
phantasia, 155
plantation, 7–8, 35–6, 195, 226–7
   Caribbean, 7
   Haiti, 90
   industrialised, 15
   system, 230
pollution, 68, 206
Portagem (novel), 123, 125, 127
psychoanalysis, 206, 212

queer, 95, 133, 142–3, 217
   coded, 145
Quijano, Aníbal, 46, 84, 135, 213–14,
    see also coloniality; race

race, 46, 124
   blackness, 214
   hierarchies, 207
   Orientalism, 50, 261, 270
   racism, 53, 108
   whiteness, 45, 46, 47, 134
radicalism, 30
realism, 137, 190
   animist, 193, 194, 202
   magical, 105
Reformation, 156
Renaissance, 156
resource
   body as, 266
   coal, 126
   extraction, 243
   natural, 248, 251
   oil, 243, 247, 250, 255
revolution
   Haitian, 7, 36, 52
   industrial, 5, 158, *see also* industrialisation
   proletarian, 53
Rhys, Jean, *see Wide Sargasso Sea*
Ruskin, John, 174–5

Saloum (film), 38
Schopenhauer, Arthur, 160–1

Shapiro, Stephen, 3, 6, 45, 56, 64, 196
Sharp Objects (series), 65, 66–8
Shelley, Mary, 14, 53, *see also Frankenstein*
Sing, Unburied, Sing (novel), 14, 102
slaughterhouse, 68, 69, 178
Slavery and the Culture of Taste (book),
   48–9, 51
Slow Violence (book), 244
spectrality, 120, 127, 129, *see also* haunting; ghost
Spivak, Gayatri, 279, 280
Stevenson, Robert Louis, 161, 225, 226
Stoker, Bram, 57, 153, *see also Dracula*
sublime, 152, 153, 160
   death of, 155
   differend, 152, 164–5, *see also* Lyotard, Jean-François
   gothic, 162

The Castle of Otranto (novel), 44, 49–51, 83–4
The Icarus Girl (novel), 209
The Wretched of the Earth (book), *see* Fanon, Frantz
Transporterne (book), 252–3
Tutuola, Amos, 186, 187, 188

uncanny, 162, 247, 270
   affect, 199
   animist, 186, *see also* animism

vampire, 12, 14, 25, 85, 120, 163, 231
   slayer, 40
   Transylvania, *see also Dracula*
Vodou, 7, 9, 14, 101, 102, 264

Wallerstein, Immanuel, 2, 28, 29, 117, 119,
   see also world-system
Walpole, Horace, 47, 57, 280, *see The Castle of Otranto*
Ward, Jesmyn, 14, 101, *see also Sing, Unburied, Sing* (novel)
Warwick Research Collective (WReC), 120, 246–7, 280
Wide Sargasso Sea (novel), 159
Windigo, 81, 87, 89, *see also* monsters; zombies
witch, 134, 137–8, 140
   gothic, 136, 141, 146
witchcraft, 137, 139, 146, 259
   ritual, 133
world-culture, 25
world-ecology, 2, 9, 14, 245–6
world-folklore, 259
world-gothic, 25, 27, 58, 64, 277
   approach, 282
   cross-hemispheric, 246
   definition, 4, 19
   double register, 261

lexicon, 229
methodology, 76, 281
perspective, 14
planetary, 171
pre-colonial, 82, 86
sublime, 152, 163
world-history, 227
world-market, 264
world-order
   neoliberal, 12
world-system, 26, 139, 261
   capitalist, 65, 118, 244, 247
modern, 243
neoliberal, 130
petrocapitalist, 243, 246
uneven, 12
Wynter, Sylvia, 12, 35, 215, 277, *see also* Black
   Metamorphosis

zemiperipheries, 27, 33
zombies, 36, 93, 95, 163, 248–9
   Caribbean, 10, *see also* Oloff, Kerstin;
   monsters; undead
Zombies and Indians (film), 91–2

Cambridge Companions To …

AUTHORS

Edward Albee edited by Stephen J. Bottoms

Margaret Atwood edited by Coral Ann Howells (second edition)

W. H. Auden edited by Stan Smith

Jane Austen edited by Edward Copeland and Juliet McMaster (second edition)

James Baldwin edited by Michele Elam

Balzac edited by Owen Heathcote and Andrew Watts

Beckett edited by John Pilling

Bede edited by Scott DeGregorio

Aphra Behn edited by Derek Hughes and Janet Todd

Saul Bellow edited by Victoria Aarons

Walter Benjamin edited by David S. Ferris

William Blake edited by Morris Eaves

Boccaccio edited by Guyda Armstrong, Rhiannon Daniels, and Stephen J. Milner

Jorge Luis Borges edited by Edwin Williamson

Brecht edited by Peter Thomson and Glendyr Sacks (second edition)

The Brontës edited by Heather Glen

Bunyan edited by Anne Dunan-Page

Frances Burney edited by Peter Sabor

Byron edited by Drummond Bone (second edition)

Albert Camus edited by Edward J. Hughes

Willa Cather edited by Marilee Lindemann

Catullus edited by Ian Du Quesnay and Tony Woodman

Cervantes edited by Anthony J. Cascardi

Chaucer edited by Piero Boitani and Jill Mann (second edition)

Chekhov edited by Vera Gottlieb and Paul Allain

Kate Chopin edited by Janet Beer

Caryl Churchill edited by Elaine Aston and Elin Diamond

Cicero edited by Catherine Steel

John Clare edited by Sarah Houghton-Walker

J. M. Coetzee edited by Jarad Zimbler

Coleridge edited by Lucy Newlyn

Coleridge edited by Tim Fulford (new edition)

Wilkie Collins edited by Jenny Bourne Taylor

Joseph Conrad edited by J. H. Stape

H. D. edited by Nephie J. Christodoulides and Polina Mackay

Dante edited by Rachel Jacoff (second edition)

Daniel Defoe edited by John Richetti

Don DeLillo edited by John N. Duvall

Charles Dickens edited by John O. Jordan

Emily Dickinson edited by Wendy Martin

John Donne edited by Achsah Guibbory

Dostoevskii edited by W. J. Leatherbarrow

Theodore Dreiser edited by Leonard Cassuto and Claire Virginia Eby

John Dryden edited by Steven N. Zwicker

W. E. B. Du Bois edited by Shamoon Zamir

George Eliot edited by George Levine and Nancy Henry (second edition)

T. S. Eliot edited by A. David Moody

Ralph Ellison edited by Ross Posnock

Ralph Waldo Emerson edited by Joel Porte and Saundra Morris

William Faulkner edited by Philip M. Weinstein

Henry Fielding edited by Claude Rawson

F. Scott Fitzgerald edited by Ruth Prigozy

F. Scott Fitzgerald edited by Michael Nowlin (second edition)

Flaubert edited by Timothy Unwin

E. M. Forster edited by David Bradshaw

Benjamin Franklin edited by Carla Mulford

Brian Friel edited by Anthony Roche

Robert Frost edited by Robert Faggen

Gabriel García Márquez edited by Philip Swanson

Elizabeth Gaskell edited by Jill L. Matus

Edward Gibbon edited by Karen O'Brien and Brian Young

Goethe edited by Lesley Sharpe

Günter Grass edited by Stuart Taberner

Thomas Hardy edited by Dale Kramer

David Hare edited by Richard Boon

Nathaniel Hawthorne edited by Richard Millington

Seamus Heaney edited by Bernard O'Donoghue

Ernest Hemingway edited by Scott Donaldson

Hildegard of Bingen edited by Jennifer Bain

Homer edited by Robert Fowler

Horace edited by Stephen Harrison
Ted Hughes edited by Terry Gifford
Ibsen edited by James McFarlane
Kazuo Ishiguro edited by Andrew Bennett
Henry James edited by Jonathan Freedman
Samuel Johnson edited by Greg Clingham
Ben Jonson edited by Richard Harp and Stanley Stewart
James Joyce edited by John Nash (third edition)
Kafka edited by Julian Preece
Keats edited by Susan J. Wolfson
Rudyard Kipling edited by Howard J. Booth
Lacan edited by Jean-Michel Rabaté
D. H. Lawrence edited by Anne Fernihough
Primo Levi edited by Robert Gordon
Lucian edited by Simon Goldhill
Lucretius edited by Stuart Gillespie and Philip Hardie
Machiavelli edited by John M. Najemy
David Mamet edited by Christopher Bigsby
Thomas Mann edited by Ritchie Robertson
Christopher Marlowe edited by Patrick Cheney
Andrew Marvell edited by Derek Hirst and Steven N. Zwicker
Ian McEwan edited by Dominic Head
Herman Melville edited by Robert S. Levine
Arthur Miller edited by Christopher Bigsby (second edition)
Milton edited by Dennis Danielson (second edition)
Molière edited by David Bradby and Andrew Calder
William Morris edited by Marcus Waithe
Toni Morrison edited by Justine Tally
Alice Munro edited by David Staines
Nabokov edited by Julian W. Connolly
Eugene O'Neill edited by Michael Manheim
George Orwell edited by John Rodden
Ovid edited by Philip Hardie
Petrarch edited by Albert Russell Ascoli and Unn Falkeid
Harold Pinter edited by Peter Raby (second edition)
Sylvia Plath edited by Jo Gill
Plutarch edited by Frances B. Titchener and Alexei Zadorojnyi

Edgar Allan Poe edited by Kevin J. Hayes
Alexander Pope edited by Pat Rogers
Ezra Pound edited by Ira B. Nadel
Mary Prince edited by Nicole N. Aljoe
Proust edited by Richard Bales
Pushkin edited by Andrew Kahn
Thomas Pynchon edited by Inger H. Dalsgaard, Luc Herman and Brian McHale
Rabelais edited by John O'Brien
Rilke edited by Karen Leeder and Robert Vilain
Philip Roth edited by Timothy Parrish
Salman Rushdie edited by Abdulrazak Gurnah
John Ruskin edited by Francis O'Gorman
Sappho edited by P. J. Finglass and Adrian Kelly
Seneca edited by Shadi Bartsch and Alessandro Schiesaro
Shakespeare edited by Margareta de Grazia and Stanley Wells (second edition)
George Bernard Shaw edited by Christopher Innes
Shelley edited by Timothy Morton
Mary Shelley edited by Esther Schor
Sam Shepard edited by Matthew C. Roudané
Spenser edited by Andrew Hadfield
Laurence Sterne edited by Thomas Keymer
Wallace Stevens edited by John N. Serio
Tom Stoppard edited by Katherine E. Kelly
Harriet Beecher Stowe edited by Cindy Weinstein
August Strindberg edited by Michael Robinson
Jonathan Swift edited by Christopher Fox
J. M. Synge edited by P. J. Mathews
Tacitus edited by A. J. Woodman
Henry David Thoreau edited by Joel Myerson
Thucydides edited by Polly Low
Tolstoy edited by Donna Tussing Orwin
Anthony Trollope edited by Carolyn Dever and Lisa Niles
Mark Twain edited by Forrest G. Robinson
John Updike edited by Stacey Olster
Mario Vargas Llosa edited by Efrain Kristal and John King
Virgil edited by Fiachra Mac Góráin and Charles Martindale (second edition)
Voltaire edited by Nicholas Cronk
David Foster Wallace edited by Ralph Clare

Edith Wharton edited by Millicent Bell
Walt Whitman edited by Ezra Greenspan
Oscar Wilde edited by Peter Raby
Tennessee Williams edited by Matthew C. Roudané
William Carlos Williams edited by Christopher MacGowan
August Wilson edited by Christopher Bigsby
Mary Wollstonecraft edited by Claudia L. Johnson
Virginia Woolf edited by Susan Sellers (second edition)
Wordsworth edited by Stephen Gill
Richard Wright edited by Glenda R. Carpio
W. B. Yeats edited by Marjorie Howes and John Kelly
Xenophon edited by Michael A. Flower
Zola edited by Brian Nelson

TOPICS

The Actress edited by Maggie B. Gale and John Stokes
The African American Novel edited by Maryemma Graham
The African American Slave Narrative edited by Audrey A. Fisch
African American Theatre edited by Harvey Young
Allegory edited by Rita Copeland and Peter Struck
American Crime Fiction edited by Catherine Ross Nickerson
American Gothic edited by Jeffrey Andrew Weinstock
The American Graphic Novel edited by Jan Baetens, Hugo Frey and Fabrice Leroy
American Horror edited by Stephen Shapiro and Mark Storey
American Literature and the Body edited by Travis M. Foster
American Literature and the Environment edited by Sarah Ensor and Susan Scott Parrish
American Literature of the 1930s edited by William Solomon
American Modernism edited by Walter Kalaidjian
American Poetry since 1945 edited by Jennifer Ashton
American Prison Literature and Mass Incarceration edited by David Coogan
American Realism and Naturalism edited by Donald Pizer
American Short Story edited by Michael J. Collins and Gavin Jones
American Travel Writing edited by Alfred Bendixen and Judith Hamera
American Utopian Literature and Culture since 1945 edited by Sherryl Vint
American Women Playwrights edited by Brenda Murphy
Ancient Rhetoric edited by Erik Gunderson
Arthurian Legend edited by Elizabeth Archibald and Ad Putter
Australian Literature edited by Elizabeth Webby
The Australian Novel edited by Nicholas Birns and Louis Klee
The Beats edited by Stephen Belletto
The Black Body in American Literature edited by Cherene Sherrard-Johnson
Boxing edited by Gerald Early
British Black and Asian Literature (1945–2010) edited by Deirdre Osborne
British Fiction: 1980–2018 edited by Peter Boxall
British Fiction since 1945 edited by David James
British Literature of the 1930s edited by James Smith
British Literature of the French Revolution edited by Pamela Clemit
British Postmodern Fiction edited by Bran Nicol
British Romantic Poetry edited by James Chandler and Maureen N. McLane
British Romanticism edited by Stuart Curran (second edition)
British Romanticism and Religion edited by Jeffrey Barbeau
British Theatre, 1730–1830 edited by Jane Moody and Daniel O'Quinn
British Utopian Literature and Culture since 1945 edited by Caroline Edwards
Canadian Literature edited by Eva-Marie Kröller (second edition)

The Canterbury Tales edited by Frank Grady

Children's Literature edited by M. O. Grenby and Andrea Immel

The City in World Literature edited by Ato Quayson and Jini Kim Watson

The Classic Russian Novel edited by Malcolm V. Jones and Robin Feuer Miller

Comics edited by Maaheen Ahmed

Contemporary African American Literature edited by Yogita Goyal

Contemporary Irish Poetry edited by Matthew Campbell

Creative Writing edited by David Morley and Philip Neilsen

Crime Fiction edited by Martin Priestman

Dante's 'Commedia' edited by Zygmunt G. Barański and Simon Gilson

Dracula edited by Roger Luckhurst

Early American Literature edited by Bryce Traister

Early Modern Women's Writing edited by Laura Lunger Knoppers

The Eighteenth-Century Novel edited by John Richetti

Eighteenth-Century Poetry edited by John Sitter

Eighteenth-Century Thought edited by Frans De Bruyn

Emma edited by Peter Sabor

English Dictionaries edited by Sarah Ogilvie

English Literature, 1500–1600 edited by Arthur F. Kinney

English Literature, 1650–1740 edited by Steven N. Zwicker

English Literature, 1740–1830 edited by Thomas Keymer and Jon Mee

English Literature, 1830–1914 edited by Joanne Shattock

English Melodrama edited by Carolyn Williams

English Novelists edited by Adrian Poole

English Poetry, Donne to Marvell edited by Thomas N. Corns

English Poets edited by Claude Rawson

English Renaissance Drama edited by A. R. Braunmuller and Michael Hattaway (second edition)

English Renaissance Tragedy edited by Emma Smith and Garrett A. Sullivan Jr.

English Restoration Theatre edited by Deborah C. Payne Fisk

Environmental Humanities edited by Jeffrey Cohen and Stephanie Foote

The Epic edited by Catherine Bates

Erotic Literature edited by Bradford Mudge

The Essay edited by Kara Wittman and Evan Kindley

European Modernism edited by Pericles Lewis

European Novelists edited by Michael Bell

Fairy Tales edited by Maria Tatar

Fantasy Literature edited by Edward James and Farah Mendlesohn

Feminist Literary Theory edited by Ellen Rooney

Fiction in the Romantic Period edited by Richard Maxwell and Katie Trumpener

The Fin de Siècle edited by Gail Marshall

Frankenstein edited by Andrew Smith

The French Enlightenment edited by Daniel Brewer

French Literature edited by John D. Lyons

The French Novel: from 1800 to the Present edited by Timothy Unwin

Gay and Lesbian Writing edited by Hugh Stevens

German Romanticism edited by Nicholas Saul

Global Literature and Slavery edited by Laura T. Murphy

Gothic Fiction edited by Jerrold E. Hogle

The Graphic Novel edited by Stephen Tabachnick

The Greek and Roman Novel edited by Tim Whitmarsh

Greek and Roman Theatre edited by Marianne McDonald and J. Michael Walton

Greek Comedy edited by Martin Revermann

Greek Lyric edited by Felix Budelmann

Greek Mythology edited by Roger D. Woodard

Greek Tragedy edited by P. E. Easterling

The Harlem Renaissance edited by George Hutchinson

The History of the Book edited by Leslie Howsam

Human Rights and Literature edited by Crystal Parikh

The Irish Novel edited by John Wilson Foster

Irish Poets edited by Gerald Dawe

The Italian Novel edited by Peter Bondanella and Andrea Ciccarelli

The Italian Renaissance edited by Michael Wyatt

Jewish American Literature edited by Hana Wirth-Nesher and Michael P. Kramer

The Latin American Novel edited by Efraín Kristal

Latin American Poetry edited by Stephen Hart

Latina/o American Literature edited by John Morán González

Latin Love Elegy edited by Thea S. Thorsen

Literature and Animals edited by Derek Ryan

Literature and the Anthropocene edited by John Parham

Literature and Climate edited by Adeline Johns-Putra and Kelly Sultzbach

Literature and Disability edited by Clare Barker and Stuart Murray

Literature and Food edited by J. Michelle Coghlan

Literature and the Posthuman edited by Bruce Clarke and Manuela Rossini

Literature and Religion edited by Susan M. Felch

Literature and Science edited by Steven Meyer

The Literature of the American Civil War and Reconstruction edited by Kathleen Diffley and Coleman Hutchison

The Literature of the American Renaissance edited by Christopher N. Phillips

The Literature of Berlin edited by Andrew J. Webber

The Literature of the Crusades edited by Anthony Bale

The Literature of the First World War edited by Vincent Sherry

The Literature of London edited by Lawrence Manley

The Literature of Los Angeles edited by Kevin R. McNamara

The Literature of New York edited by Cyrus Patell and Bryan Waterman

The Literature of Paris edited by Anna-Louise Milne

The Literature of World War II edited by Marina MacKay

Literature on Screen edited by Deborah Cartmell and Imelda Whelehan

Lyrical Ballads edited by Sally Bushell

Manga and Anime edited by Jaqueline Berndt

Medieval British Manuscripts edited by Orietta Da Rold and Elaine Treharne

Medieval English Culture edited by Andrew Galloway

Medieval English Law and Literature edited by Candace Barrington and Sebastian Sobecki

Medieval English Literature edited by Larry Scanlon

Medieval English Mysticism edited by Samuel Fanous and Vincent Gillespie

Medieval English Theatre edited by Richard Beadle and Alan J. Fletcher (second edition)

Medieval French Literature edited by Simon Gaunt and Sarah Kay

Medieval Romance edited by Roberta L. Krueger

Medieval Romance edited by Roberta L. Krueger (new edition)

Medieval Women's Writing edited by Carolyn Dinshaw and David Wallace

Modern American Culture edited by Christopher Bigsby

Modern British Women Playwrights edited by Elaine Aston and Janelle Reinelt

Modern French Culture edited by Nicholas Hewitt

Modern German Culture edited by Eva Kolinsky and Wilfried van der Will

The Modern German Novel edited by Graham Bartram

The Modern Gothic edited by Jerrold E. Hogle

Modern Irish Culture edited by Joe Cleary and Claire Connolly

Modern Italian Culture edited by Zygmunt G. Baranski and Rebecca J. West

Modern Latin American Culture edited by John King

Modern Russian Culture edited by Nicholas Rzhevsky

Modern Spanish Culture edited by David T. Gies

Modernism edited by Michael Levenson (second edition)

The Modernist Novel edited by Morag Shiach

Modernist Poetry edited by Alex Davis and Lee M. Jenkins

Modernist Women Writers edited by Maren Tova Linett

Narrative edited by David Herman

Narrative Theory edited by Matthew Garrett

Native American Literature edited by Joy Porter and Kenneth M. Roemer

Nineteen Eighty-Four edited by Nathan Waddell

Nineteenth-Century American Literature and Politics edited by John Kerkering

Nineteenth-Century American Poetry edited by Kerry Larson

Nineteenth-Century American Women's Writing edited by Dale M. Bauer and Philip Gould

Nineteenth-Century Thought edited by Gregory Claeys

The Novel edited by Eric Bulson

Old English Literature edited by Malcolm Godden and Michael Lapidge (second edition)

Performance Studies edited by Tracy C. Davis

Piers Plowman edited by Andrew Cole and Andrew Galloway

The Poetry of the First World War edited by Santanu Das

Popular Fiction edited by David Glover and Scott McCracken

Postcolonial Literary Studies edited by Neil Lazarus

Postcolonial Poetry edited by Jahan Ramazani

Postcolonial Travel Writing edited by Robert Clarke

Postmodern American Fiction edited by Paula Geyh

Postmodernism edited by Steven Connor

Prose edited by Daniel Tyler

The Pre-Raphaelites edited by Elizabeth Prettejohn

Pride and Prejudice edited by Janet Todd

Queer Studies edited by Siobhan B. Somerville

Renaissance Humanism edited by Jill Kraye

Robinson Crusoe edited by John Richetti

Roman Comedy edited by Martin T. Dinter

The Roman Historians edited by Andrew Feldherr

Roman Satire edited by Kirk Freudenburg

The Romantic Sublime edited by Cian Duffy

Romanticism and Race edited by Manu Samriti Chander

Science Fiction edited by Edward James and Farah Mendlesohn

Scottish Literature edited by Gerald Carruthers and Liam McIlvanney

Sensation Fiction edited by Andrew Mangham

Shakespeare and Contemporary Dramatists edited by Ton Hoenselaars

Shakespeare and Popular Culture edited by Robert Shaughnessy

Shakespeare and Race edited by Ayanna Thompson

Shakespeare and Religion edited by Hannibal Hamlin

Shakespeare and War edited by David Loewenstein and Paul Stevens

Shakespeare on Film edited by Russell Jackson (second edition)

Shakespeare on Screen edited by Russell Jackson

Shakespeare on Stage edited by Stanley Wells and Sarah Stanton

Shakespearean Comedy edited by Alexander Leggatt

Shakespearean Tragedy edited by Claire McEachern (second edition)

Shakespeare's First Folio edited by Emma Smith

Shakespeare's History Plays edited by Michael Hattaway

Shakespeare's Language edited by Lynne Magnusson with David Schalkwyk

Shakespeare's Last Plays edited by Catherine M. S. Alexander

Shakespeare's Poetry edited by Patrick Cheney

Sherlock Holmes edited by Janice M. Allan and Christopher Pittard

The Sonnet edited by A. D. Cousins and Peter Howarth

The Spanish Novel: From 1600 to the Present edited by Harriet Turner and Adelaida López de Martínez

Textual Scholarship edited by Neil Fraistat and Julia Flanders

Theatre and Science edited by Kristen E. Shepherd-Barr

Theatre History edited by David Wiles and Christine Dymkowski

Transnational American Literature edited by Yogita Goyal

Travel Writing edited by Peter Hulme and Tim Youngs

The Twentieth-Century American Novel and Politics edited by Bryan Santin

Twentieth-Century American Poetry and Politics edited by Daniel Morris

Twentieth-Century British and Irish Women's Poetry edited by Jane Dowson

The Twentieth-Century English Novel edited by Robert L. Caserio

Twentieth-Century English Poetry edited by Neil Corcoran

Twentieth-Century Irish Drama edited by Shaun Richards

Twentieth-Century Literature and Politics edited by Christos Hadjiyiannis and Rachel Potter

Twentieth-Century Russian Literature edited by Marina Balina and Evgeny Dobrenko

Utopian Literature edited by Gregory Claeys

Victorian and Edwardian Theatre edited by Kerry Powell

The Victorian Novel edited by Deirdre David (second edition)

Victorian Poetry edited by Joseph Bristow

Victorian Women's Poetry edited by Linda K. Hughes

Victorian Women's Writing edited by Linda H. Peterson

War Writing edited by Kate McLoughlin

Women's Writing in Britain, 1660–1789 edited by Catherine Ingrassia

Women's Writing in the Romantic Period edited by Devoney Looser

World Literature edited by Ben Etherington and Jarad Zimbler

World Crime Fiction edited by Jesper Gulddal, Stewart King and Alistair Rolls

World-Gothic Literature edited by Rebecca Duncan and Rebekah Cumpsty

Writing of the English Revolution edited by N. H. Keeble

The Writings of Julius Caesar edited by Christopher Krebs and Luca Grillo

For EU product safety concerns, contact us at Calle de José Abascal, 56–1°,
28003 Madrid, Spain or eugpsr@cambridge.org.

www.ingramcontent.com/pod-product-compliance
Ingram Content Group UK Ltd.
Pitfield, Milton Keynes, MK11 3LW, UK
UKHW022141180326
469138UK00017B/2397